Measuring
Profitability
and
Capital Costs

Books from
The Lincoln Institute of Land Policy

The Lincoln Institute of Land Policy is a school that offers intensive courses of instruction in the field of land economics and property taxation. The Institute provides a stimulating learning environment for students, policy-makers, and administrators with challenging opportunities for research and publication. The goal of the Institute is to improve theory and practice in those fundamental areas of land policy that have significant impact on the lives and livelihood of all people.

Constitutions, Taxation, and Land Policy   Michael M. Bernard

Constitutions, Taxation, and Land Policy—Volume II
   Michael M. Bernard

Federal Tax Aspects of Open-Space Preservation   Kingsbury Browne

Taxation of Nonrenewable Resources   Albert M. Church

Conflicts over Resource Ownership   Albert M. Church

Taxation of Mineral Resources   Robert F. Conrad and R. Bryce Hool

World Congress on Land Policy, 1980   Edited by Matthew Cullen and
   Sharon Woolery

Land Readjustment   William A. Doebele

Measuring Profitability and Capital Costs   Edited by Daniel M. Holland

Incentive Zoning   Jerold S. Kayden

Building for Women   Edited by Suzanne Keller

Urban Land Policy for the 1980s   Edited by George Lefcoe

Fiscal Federalism and the Taxation of Natural Resources   Edited by
   Charles E. McLure, Jr., and Peter Mieszkowski

State Land-Use Planning and Regulation   Thomas G. Pelham

The Role of the State in Property Taxation   Edited by H. Clyde Reeves

Funding Clean Water   Edited by H. Clyde Reeves

Land-Office Business   Gary Sands

The Art of Valuation   Edited by Arlo Woolery

Measuring Profitability and Capital Costs

An International Study

Edited by
Daniel M. Holland
Alfred P. Sloan School of
Management, Massachusetts
Institute of Technology

LexingtonBooks
D.C. Heath and Company
Lexington, Massachusetts
Toronto

Library of Congress Cataloging in Publication Data
Main entry under title:

Measuring profitability and capital costs.

   Includes bibliographical references and index.
   1. Profit—Statistical methods.   2. Corporate profits
—Statistical methods.   I. Holland, Daniel Mark.
HB601.M387 1984   658.1′5   82–48491
ISBN 0–669–06159–X (alk. paper)

Published simultaneously in Canada

Printed in the United States of America

International Standard Book Number: 0–669–06159–X

Library of Congress Catalog Card Number: 82–48491

Contents

Preface

This book publishes the final product of a research project in which scholars from ten countries have participated over the last eight years.

It was not a formal, centrally run, efficiently organized and managed project. Rather, we were a loosely affiliated group of scholars who shared a common objective and started work on it with some "seed" support from the Massachusetts Institute of Technology. But most of the research was carried out under the individual auspices described in each chapter. For each country we wanted to develop a set of estimates of rates of return on capital (and a few related measures) that would be comparable over time.

Never easy to define analytically and derive empirically, measures of profitability had been rendered more difficult to derive and interpret by the brisk inflation of the 1970s. In fact one could say about rates of return what Arthur F. Burns said about production indexes. "Strict logic is a stern master and if one respected it, one would never construct or use any production index" (Arthur F. Burns, *Production Trends in the United States Since 1870*. New York: National Bureau of Economic Research, 1934, p. 262).

Nonetheless measures of rates of return are constructed, used, and serve as the basis of policy recommendations. Estimates of rates of return that are comparable within each country over time were sorely needed. It was reasonable to believe that a group of scholars with the same objective could enrich their understanding by meeting a number of times over the course of their research to share their problems and methodologies.

In addition we hoped that from these meetings we could develop a set of definitions and methods of estimation that would permit comparisons of rates of return across countries. As the reader will note, however, when she/he studies the chapters in our book (which give the sources and methodological notes for each country's estimates) the basic data, required adjustments, tax and other institutional factors, methods of estimation, and definitions of profitability all differ strongly among countries. Therefore our ability to make comparisons across them is limited.

In the summary chapter, we do make some comparisons, but for the most part we deal with changes in level over time, that is, "In Country A, the rate of return declined over the period, while in Country B it appeared to remain about the same." We think that this kind of comparison can be made with greater validity than by saying that "In

Country A businesses earned higher rates of return than in Country B."

The project was initially suggested by Professor Franco Modigliani. It started with a grant from MIT's Project in International Business (a joint effort of the Center for International Studies and the Sloan School of Management, both at MIT). Professor Everett Hagen, then director of the center, identified a number of possible country teams. I visited with some of them and set up a meeting in London in 1974. For this and the succeeding three London meetings I served as organizer and MIT as host. I am grateful to my colleague Stewart Myers, who played a major role in these meetings and in the evolving design of the project.

At the last of the London conferences we felt that we had made sufficient progress on our research to warrant preparation of reports for each country involved, which, assembled together with a summary chapter, would constitute a useful publication. But we had run out of funds to complete the last stage of our project. At this juncture it was our good fortune to elicit the interest and support of Arlo Woolery, executive director of the Lincoln Institute of Land Policy. Mr. Woolery arranged to bring the group together once more, this time at the Lincoln Institute in Cambridge, Massachusetts. Meeting in that stimulating environment in June 1981, we discussed and worked over drafts of the country reports, revised versions of which make up this volume.

This volume, then, is the final accomplishment of a project that has been jointly supported by MIT and the Lincoln Institute of Land Policy. We are grateful to these two institutions and to the men behind them: Professors Everett Hagen and Eugene Skolnikoff (the Center for International Studies), Dr. Geoffrey Clarkson (MIT's Project in International Business), Dean William Pounds, Dean Abraham Siegel, Professor Franco Modigliani, and Professor Richard Robinson (the Sloan School of Management), and Arlo Woolery (Lincoln Institute of Land Policy). We thank them all for their interest in our work and the support that lent additional substance to that interest.

Daniel M. Holland

1 Introduction and Summary

Daniel M. Holland

All of the studies in this volume have as their common purpose the measurement of the rate of return to capital and a number of related variables. Whenever possible, two sets of rates of return were derived— returns on capital employed by business firms and returns on the debt and equity portfolios of investors in these firms. All of the symbols used in this chapter are defined in the common glossary in Appendix 1A. While all the chapters in this book share a common purpose, each embodies also different uses to which the estimates are put, as well as individual analyses and interpretations of their findings.

In this introductory chapter we summarize and compare briefly some of the estimates of rates of return and related measures.

Company-Based Rates of Return

Return on Capital Employed—ROC[1]

For purposes of measuring the rate of return on corporate assets, a conventional definition of the denominator, that is, capital employed, is the current value of plant, equipment, and inventories. And a conventional definition of the numerator is inflation-adjusted profits plus net interest paid. The rate of return measured this way we designate ROC_A, and it or something close to it is found in every chapter in the volume. King and Mairesse in their chapter note that in the long run changes in the ROC can be taken to be indicative of changes in the social productivity of capital. For most countries another rate of return (ROC_W) was computed. It has the same numerator but an augmented capital base that includes net non–interest-bearing monetary assets and land as well as plant, equipment, and inventories $(ROC_W$ in the common glossary).

There is no reason in principle to stop with this latter definition of capital employed. More broadly conceived the capital stock could also include human capital, property rights (particularly patents and copyrights), the results of research and development (R&D) and advertising, and special earnings opportunities open to the firm. But extended definitions of the capital stock were not used in the studies in this volume.

In many of the studies, however, the numerator was more broadly defined to include (in addition to inflation-adjusted profits and net interest paid) holding gains (and losses), that is, increases (or decreases) in the value of company assets over and above the change in a standard (generally consumption-based) deflator. The reader will find wide variations in the treatment of holding gains, ranging from the U.S. paper, in which no holding gains are estimated, to the Japanese paper, which adjusts rates of return for holding gains on all assets.[2]

Finally, we note that various *ROC*s have been measured both before and after tax. The difference between the *ROC(BT)* and the *ROC(AT)* is simply that the corporate tax, that is, government's share, has been subtracted from the numerator in computing the latter. The *ROC(AT)* is the company analog of the rate of return to suppliers of debt and equity capital (see below).

The tax, in this case, has generally been taken to be the levy on corporate profits (in some countries ameliorated to some extent by credits at the personal level), but in some countries it is defined to include property and franchise taxes as well. There are variations among countries, too, in the way company tax is accounted for. In some cases taxes are taken to be current payments. In others an attempt is made to recognize deferred taxes. The research team in each country has measured an "effective rate" of tax (t_y) defined as the ratio of tax to operating income (that is, inflation-adjusted profits plus net interest). It is, therefore, *not* an "effective" tax rate measured on nominal profits as the tax base. Rather it is measured on an inflation-adjusted profits plus net interest payments base.

Return on Net Worth

For most countries, in addition to *ROC*s, a complementary set of measures usually designated as returns to equity, returns to net worth, or returns to own capital have been presented. Their intent is to measure the returns to capital owned by stockholders. Thus in measuring the return to net worth, net interest payments are not included in the numerator and, in principle, the market value of debt is subtracted from the denominator. But in practice, book value of debt was frequently substituted. The simplest measure of return to equity, *REQ*, had inflation-adjusted profits in the numerator and assets minus debt in the denominator. But, for most countries in which equity returns were estimated, another measure, *REG*, was presented. For this measure a "gearing adjustment," which recognized the annual gain (loss) accruing to stockholders from the decline (rise) in the real value of company debt, was added to the numerator.

Capital Market-Based Rates of Return

Claims on corporate assets—equity and debt (bonds, mortgages, and bank loans)—sum to the market value of the company. Holders of these claims earn a rate of return defined as the ratio of (a) dividends, interest, and capital gains (or losses) on equity and debt holdings over a period to (b) the market value of equity plus debt at the start of the period.[3] This ratio is converted to a real (that is, inflation-adjusted) return R, by subtraction of the annual change in a current price index.

In an important sense R is a more clear-cut measure than $ROC;$ it is observed unambiguously in the market. The ROC on the other hand is based on data from which it is impossible to expunge completely the effect of accounting conventions and arbitrary rules. Whenever possible, researchers in each country have tried to devise a measure of R. But it has proved difficult for a number of them and impossible for some. In a number of countries the equity markets are not broad enough to value a meaningful segment of nonfinancial or manufacturing companies. Only a few companies are traded in public markets, so the price of equities cannot be observed, and much debt is privately placed (and the interest paid on it not publicly known), preventing market valuation of debt. Therefore for a number of countries we do not have a measure of R that we can compare with ROC.

R, as defined, is the return to all private claimants to corporate earnings. A prior claim to those earnings stands in the form of government taxes. Therefore R, the rate of return to private investors, is properly to be compared with $ROC(AT)$, the rate of return to corporate assets *after tax*.

Links between Company-Based and Capital Markets-Based Rates of Return

Where we have a measure of the market value of equities and debt instruments and the current replacement cost of corporate assets, we can also derive q, a ratio originally developed by James Tobin. And we can also develop a rough measure of the cost of capital, ρ, by relating operating income to corporate market value. This provides a series of measures that constitute a bridge between markets for real assets and markets for financial assets as follows:[4]

$$\frac{Y}{MV} = \rho; \; MV = \frac{Y}{\rho} \tag{1.1}$$

where Y = operating income, MV = market value of equities and debt.

$$Y = ROC(CS) \tag{1.2}$$

where Y = operating income, $ROC = \dfrac{Y}{CS}$, and CS = current replacement cost of capital stock, which corresponds to A, W, or some other total as the case may be in the common glossary.

$$MV = CS\left(\frac{ROC}{\rho}\right) \tag{1.3}$$

$$q = \frac{MV}{CS} = \frac{ROC}{\rho} \tag{1.4}$$

The measures briefly described here are more formally defined in the common glossary. Their derivation for each country is explained in the chapters in this volume. As the reader works through these chapters he will see numerous details in which countries' measure of ROC, R, ρ, and so on, vary from each other. In this summary chapter, however, we will nonetheless attempt some comparisons across countries. The comparisons we make will be limited to those that can be made with a broad brush.

While the definitions discussed up to this point sketch out the framework of our measures, it cannot be stressed too strongly that, for a variety of reasons, related both to data availability and methodological and analytical preferences, most of the measures for each country vary in one way or another from their description here and in the common glossary.

In a Utopian moment, the editor prepared the set of definitions that he hoped would serve as a common glossary. But it proved to be less helpful than intended and, in the preparation of the final version of the chapters, was perhaps "More honour'd in the breach than the observance." In a number of the chapters, however, some or all of the symbols of the common glossary are used. Further, where the notations are particular to a chapter, their correspondence to or difference from a particular item in the common glossary is frequently noted.

Rates of Return on Capital (Plant, Equipment, and Inventories) Employed in Manufacturing—ROC_A

The data of table 1–1 are the closest we can come to a collection of time series of rates of return for the countries in our study that purport to measure the same thing, namely, the ROC_A, that is, the rate of return on corporate capital defined as plant, equipment, and inventories in manufacturing industries. While a closer examination of the country reports will indicate that they differ in details of definition and industry coverage (and, of course, they cover different periods for each country), nonetheless, we consider them sufficiently similar to present broad-brush comparisons.

1. Averaged over a common period—1961–81 (or as close an approximation thereto as the data permit) the nine countries show very large differences in ROC_As, ranging from Germany's 14 percent to Sweden's 5.8 percent on a before-tax basis, and Finland's 9.2 percent to Austria's 4.0 percent on an after-tax basis. While duly aware of the ambiguity in comparing absolute levels of rates of return, one can conclude, it appears, that rates of return differ importantly among countries. On a before-tax basis we can identify three groups of countries.

1. Germany and the United States, for whom the $ROC_A(BT)$ for manufacturing firms averaged about 13 to 14 percent.
2. Canada, Finland, France, and Japan, characterized by rates of return between 9 and 11 percent.
3. The United Kingdom, Austria, and Sweden, for whom the $ROC_A(BT)$ averaged 6 to 8 percent.

On an after-tax basis, we find a somewhat different ranking.

1. Finland with an average $ROC(AT)$ greater than 9 percent.
2. United States, Canada, France, and Japan with after-tax rates of return from 6 to 7.5 percent.
3. Germany, the United Kingdom, Sweden, and Austria, for whom after-tax rates of return averaged 4 to 5 percent.

As the summary in table 1–2 indicates, with the exception of the clear reversals in ranking for Germany and Finland, the countries fall in about the same ranking on both a before- and after-tax basis. Effective tax rates in Germany, the highest in our ten countries (see table 1–6 below), account for the pronounced difference between that coun-

Table 1-1
Rates of Return in Manufacturing—ROC_A before (BT) and after (AT) Tax
(Rate of Return on Plant, Equipment, and Inventories)
(in percent)

Year	Austria BT	Austria AT[a]	Finland BT	Finland AT	Germany BT	Sweden BT	Sweden AT	Japan[b] BT	Japan AT	United States BT	United States AT	United Kingdom BT	United Kingdom AT	France[c] BT	France AT	Canada BT	Canada AT
1947										18.5	9.2					15.4	8.9
1948										19.4	11.3					13.1	7.0
1949										16.7	10.5					15.2	9.5
1950										21.3	9.7					18.1	11.0
51						6.8	3.2			21.8	8.5					15.7	6.3
52						5.0	2.9			17.0	7.6					17.5	9.6
53						6.2	3.5			16.6	6.8					15.7	8.8
54						6.6	3.7			13.8	6.3					13.1	7.5
55						6.6	3.5			18.6	9.0					15.2	8.8
56	10.4	6.2				6.0	3.4			15.4	7.3	8.7	5.1			13.7	7.6
57	11.0	7.4				6.5	3.8			13.8	6.7	8.6	5.1			11.2	6.6
58	9.3	6.4				7.4	5.1			10.6	5.3	8.5	5.8			10.5	6.6
59	11.0	7.6				8.3	6.0			15.5	7.9	8.6	5.6			11.9	7.0
1960	14.0	9.5	13.9	11.3	19.5	7.7	5.6			13.6	7.0	9.2	6.0	10.4	7.6	9.6	5.3
61	8.7	5.9	11.1	8.5	17.0	7.4	5.2			13.3	6.9	7.7	5.3	10.1	7.3	8.4	4.3
62	7.9	4.6	11.3	9.1	15.8	5.8	4.0			15.5	8.6	7.3	5.1	9.6	7.2	9.5	5.1
63	7.8	4.6	11.1	9.0	16.5	6.1	4.2			17.5	9.8	8.0	5.8	9.7	7.4	10.8	6.3
64	8.8	5.0	9.7	7.7	16.0	7.2	5.2			18.6	10.9	8.7	6.2	10.3	7.8	11.0	6.6
65	6.6	3.9	8.4	6.4	14.3	7.3	5.4			21.6	13.0	7.8	6.4	9.8	7.4	15.4	8.0
66	5.9	3.3	8.3	6.6	14.8	6.1	4.4	15.2	11.5	21.0	12.3	6.5	5.4	9.5	7.5	13.9	7.3
67	4.1	2.2	10.9	9.3	17.4	5.6	4.0	16.8	12.6	17.4	10.6	6.6	5.7	9.7	7.6	11.6	6.2
68	3.2	1.3	15.0	13.4	16.9	5.9	4.0	16.5	12.3	17.2	9.6	6.4	5.0	10.6	8.5	13.6	7.5
69	6.7	4.2				7.2	5.5	17.0	12.3	14.2	7.7	5.5	4.2	12.3	9.7	13.8	7.5

Year																	
1970	8.3	5.2	14.8	13.5	14.8	5.9	4.6	15.4	11.1	9.7	5.5	4.2	3.3	11.3	8.6	9.7	5.0
71	6.0	3.9	10.0	8.9	13.6	4.5	3.6	13.0	9.8	11.3	6.6	4.6	3.3	11.5	9.1	10.1	5.9
72	7.1	5.3	10.8	9.4	12.9	5.2	4.0	12.3	8.4	12.8	7.5	4.9	3.4	12.0	9.3	11.0	6.5
73	4.7	3.5	11.6	10.6	12.9	7.7	6.5	5.6	0.8	12.9	7.2	3.5	3.8	11.0	8.3	13.4	8.1
74	5.4	3.6	14.8	13.9	11.4	9.6	8.7	0.3	−3.5	8.7	4.1	−0.6	1.5	9.7	6.6	12.4	6.7
75	3.1	2.0	8.0	7.0	9.9	5.8	4.7	4.9	2.3	8.8	5.1	−0.6	1.3	5.8	3.9	8.9	4.6
76	5.2	4.0	6.4	5.4	11.4	4.2	3.3	5.5	2.0	10.9	6.0			4.7	3.2	9.1	5.3
77	2.3	1.5	5.8	4.9	11.2	1.4	0.8	5.6	2.3	11.9	6.6			6.8	4.3		
78	4.0	2.8	8.4	7.6	11.5	0.9	0.2	7.1	3.5	11.5	6.4			6.7	4.6		
79	7.0	5.2	11.7	10.8	11.7			5.8	1.4	9.4	5.1			7.5	5.1		
1980	10.9	7.7	11.1	10.2	9.4			8.0	2.6	6.2	3.2						
81								11.0	6.1	6.2	3.7						
Series average	7.2	4.7	10.6	9.2	14.0	6.1	4.3	10.0	6.0	14.6	7.7	6.2	4.7	11.0	7.1	12.6	7.1

Source: Papers in this volume. The United Kingdom series is from chapter 6.

aEstimated by the editor from the data in chapter 11.

bNonfinancial corporations.

cEstimated using 1971 base year National Accounts.

Table 1–2

Countries Ranked by Average ROC(A)s in Manufacturing before and after Tax 1961–81

	ROC$_A$(BT)			ROC$_A$(AT)	
Rank	Country	ROC$_A$		Country	ROC$_A$
1	Germany	14.0		Finland	9.2
2	United States	12.8		United States	7.5
3	Canada	11.3		France	6.9
4	Finland	10.6		Canada	6.3
5	Japan[a]	10.0		Japan	6.0
6	France	9.4		Germany	5.2[b]
7	United Kingdom	6.2		United Kingdom	4.7
8	Austria	6.2		Sweden	4.4
9	Sweden	5.8		Austria	4.0

[a]Nonfinancial corporations.
[b]Estimated roughly by assuming same ratio of ROC$_A$(AT) to ROC$_A$(BT) as found in table 7–3 for the weighted ROCs for manufacturing.

try's pre- and post-tax ranking, while the extremely low effective tax rates in Finland account for that country's higher rank on an after-tax basis.

2. While their ROC$_A$s run at very different characteristic levels, visual inspection of table 1–1 suggests a common experience in the time pattern of rates of return over the last twenty years. ROC$_A$s appear to have declined over that period. Table 1–3 summarizes this change. For every country before-tax rates of return were lower in the period 1970–81 (or closest approximation) than in the period 1961–69 (or closest approximation). This, of course, is no surprise. But it is interesting to observe the differential degree of this common experience. On a before-tax basis, the decline in profitability was most pronounced for the United States, the United Kingdom, and Japan—on the order of 40 to 70 percent. Austria, Finland, and France experienced modest declines, around 10 to 15 percent. Whether Canada should be included in this group is questionable, since the time series ends in 1976 and it is quite likely that including the years that followed would have indicated a sharper decline in the average ROC$_A$(BT).

But the results are somewhat different and more disparate for after-tax rates of return. In some countries, compensating adjustments in taxes tend to cushion the fall; indeed in Finland and Austria the ROC(AT) averaged slightly higher in the 1970s than in the 1960s. But in Germany, Japan, the United States, and the United Kingdom the ROC$_A$(AT) was between 40 to 70 percent less, on average, in the most recent decade than in the 1960s. (For the United States this decline was less pronounced for all nonfinancial corporations than the manu-

Table 1–3
Average ROC_A

Country	Average $ROC_A(BT)$		Percentage Change 1961–69 to 1970–81
	1961–69	1970–81	
A.			
Austria	6.6	5.8	− 12%
Finland	11.1	10.3	− 7
Germany	16.5	11.9	− 28
Sweden	6.5	5.0	− 23
Japan	16.4	7.9	− 52
United States	16.6	10.0	− 40
United Kingdom	7.2	2.7	− 63
France	10.2	8.7	− 15
Canada	12.0	10.7	− 11
	Average $ROC_A(AT)$		Percentage Change 1961–69 to 1970–81
	1961–69	1970–81	
B.			
Austria	3.9	4.1	+ 5%
Finland	9.0	9.3	+ 3
Germany[a]	7.7	4.5	− 42
Sweden	4.7	4.0	− 15
Japan	12.2	3.9	− 68
United States	10.0	5.6	− 44
United Kingdom	5.5	2.8	− 49
France	7.8	6.3	− 19
Canada	6.5	6.0	− 8

[a]Estimated roughly by assuming same ratio of $ROC_A(AT)$ to $ROC_A(BT)$ as found from data in table 7–3 for the weighted ROCs in manufacturing.

facturing sector that is the subject of this section.) For the United Kingdom, where company tax structure was recently modified in the direction of lower rates, it is likely that we would have seen a more moderate decline in after-tax rates of return had the data in table 1–3 covered the years after 1975.

Rates of Return on Total Capital (Plant, Equipment, Inventories, Land, and Net Monetary Assets) Employed in Manufacturing—ROC_W

The results reported to this point cover rates of return based on the plant, equipment, and inventories employed in manufacturing. But in generating returns business firms also employ other assets. While we cannot measure all of them, we can in some cases get estimates of the current value of land and net monetary assets.

How do rates of return on a base that (in most cases) includes land

and monetary assets compare with the ROC_A of table 1–1? We know that the ROC_W or the ROC_F proxy (that includes land but not monetary assets in the capital base) will be lower, since the denominator of the fraction is higher. How much lower can be seen from table 1–4, which tabulates rates of return for countries for which data on the augmented capital base were available.

The results differ considerably from those in table 1–1. It is not merely that measured profitability runs at lower levels, but the ranking of countries with respect to rates of return is very different. On the basis of averages over the years 1961–81 (or closest approximation that the data permit) as summarized in table 1–5, when profitability is measured on the augmented capital base, on a before-tax basis, the United States, Canada, and Finland rank highest at 9 percent; Germany and the United Kingdom in the middle, about 7 percent; with Japan (4.2 percent) and Sweden (4.3 percent) having the lowest averages. On an after-tax basis, Finland stands alone, with an average of almost 8 percent; the United States and Canada are in the 5 percent range; and Japan and Germany are at the bottom of the ranking, with average after-tax rates of return of 2.5 percent for both countries. Since the Japanese ROC_F excludes net monetary assets from the capital base, the average rate of return for Japan compared with the others in the table could be more like 3.5 percent before tax and under 2 percent after tax.

The changed position of Japan from the middle of the array of average rates of return—defined as the ratio of inflation-adjusted profits plus net interest to plant, equipment, and inventories, that is, ROC_A (in table 1–2)—to the country with the lowest rates of return in a ranking based on a definition of capital employed that is extended to include land and monetary assets emphasizes the difficulties in interpreting rate of return data. Depending on which measure we use, Japan has either enjoyed a middling rate of return (ROC_A) or has one of the lowest rates of return $(ROC_F$ or $ROC_W)$ of the countries covered in our book.

The proximate numerical explanation for this difference is the apparently much heavier weight of land in the value of corporate capital stock in Japan than in other countries. In 1981 in the United States, for example, the value of land came to about 12 percent of the value of plant, equipment, and inventory for non-financial corporations. In Japan the comparable figure was 167 percent. Why this is the case may be explained both by the greater "scarcity" of land in Japan, that is, its higher value relative to other capital inputs, and by the zealousness of our Japanese colleagues in estimating the market value of land. In most other countries, while attempts are made to estimate the market

Table 1–4
Rate of Return on Total Capital Employed in Manufacturing, ROC_w
(in percent)

Year	Finland BT	Finland AT	Germany[a] BT	Germany[a] AT	Sweden BT	United Kingdom BT	Japan[cd] BT	Japan[cd] AT	Canada BT	Canada AT	United States[c] BT	United States[c] AT
1946											8.6	3.5
47									12.5	7.1	10.1	4.8
48									10.3	5.1	11.4	6.3
49									12.4	8.0	9.7	5.9
1950									14.9	9.1	11.6	5.2
51									12.9	4.9	11.7	4.5
52									15.3	8.3	9.8	4.2
53									13.7	7.6	9.4	3.8
54									11.1	6.2	8.7	4.2
55									12.7	7.2	10.9	5.4
56									11.4	6.0	9.4	4.4
57									9.4	5.4	8.6	4.2
58									8.6	5.1	7.3	3.7
59									9.7	5.6	9.2	4.8
1960									7.7	4.1	8.4	4.5
61	13.1	10.6	9.8	3.9		10.1			6.6	3.2	8.4	4.5
62	10.4	8.0	9.4	3.7		8.3			7.3	3.7	9.6	5.6
63	10.6	8.5	9.7	4.2		8.7			8.3	4.7	10.3	6.1
64	10.0	8.1	10.2	4.0		11.6			8.5	4.9	11.2	6.9
65	8.6	6.8	8.8	3.9		10.8			10.8	6.2	12.4	7.8
66	7.6	5.8	8.1	3.8	6.3	9.4	6.7	5.1	10.1	5.9	12.3	7.7
67	7.4	5.9	8.3	4.8	6.2	9.9	7.3	5.5	8.2	4.7	11.0	7.1
68	9.4	8.1	10.1	5.4	6.1	9.7	7.1	5.2	9.9	5.9	11.0	6.6
69	12.9	11.6	8.8	4.2	7.8	8.7	7.0	5.0	10.1	5.8	9.8	5.7

Table 1-4 (continued)

Year	Finland BT	Finland AT	Germany[a] BT	Germany[a] AT	Sweden BT	United Kingdom BT	Japan[cd] BT	Japan[cd] AT	Canada BT	Canada AT	United States[c] BT	United States[c] AT
1970	12.2	11.1	6.1	3.2	3.1	6.6	6.2	4.5	6.8	3.4	7.7	4.7
71	8.2	7.3	4.3	1.8	3.9	5.8	5.4	4.0	8.4	4.5	8.3	5.2
72	8.4	7.6	5.5	2.2	5.4	4.2	4.8	3.3	9.4	5.2	8.9	5.7
73	9.4	8.6	5.1	1.6	8.6	5.8	2.0	0.3	11.6	6.6	8.9	5.4
74	11.4	10.7	1.7	−1.6	8.8	4.8	0.1	−1.3	11.5	6.0	6.7	3.7
75	6.4	5.6	4.1	1.1	3.8	−0.3	2.2	1.0	8.3	4.0	7.4	4.8
76	5.4	4.5	6.2	2.3	2.1	−1.0	2.5	0.9	8.1	4.4	8.0	4.9
77	4.8	4.1	6.4	1.8	−4.2	2.9	2.6	1.1			8.6	5.4
78	7.0	6.4	6.6	1.9	0.8		3.3	1.6			8.5	5.3
79	9.4	8.6	5.8	0.6	2.1		2.6	0.6			7.5	4.6
1980	8.8	8.0	3.5	−0.3			3.3	1.1			6.5	4.1
81			4.1	0.5			4.3	2.4			6.9	4.8
Average 1961–81[b]	9.1	7.8	6.8	2.5	4.3	6.8	4.2	2.5	9.0	4.9	9.0	5.6

Source: Chapters in this volume. UK estimates are from chapter 5.

[a]Weighted.

[b]Or closest available dates to this point.

[c]Nonfinancial corporations.

[d]ROC_F: the denominator of which is plant, equipment, inventories, and land.

Table 1–5
Average ROC_W 1961–81 for Finland, Germany, Sweden, Japan, Canada, the United Kingdom, and the United States

Country	$ROC_W(BT)$	$ROC_W(AT)$
Finland	9.1	7.8
United States	9.0	5.6
Canada	9.0	4.9
Germany	6.8	2.5
United Kingdom	6.8	—
Japan[a]	4.2	2.5
Sweden	4.3	—

[a]ROC_F; Nonfinancial corporations.

value of land, it is generally not a figure the estimator is particularly proud of or a figure that comes close to the current market value of land.

If we look at patterns of rates of return across countries with the ROC_A as the relevant evidence, Japan's position in the middle of the ranking would be somewhat surprising given that country's remarkable economic performance in the last twenty years. But if the ROC_W is taken as the appropriate measure we have not a mild surprise but a real puzzle. How are we to explain Japan's position as the country with the lowest rates of return?

The underlying explanation of low rates of return may lie in aspects of Japanese culture and institutions. Reischauer,[5] for example, notes several factors that would lead to a "greater drive for growth rather than simply profits" in Japan. He points to the higher proportion of debt to total capital, which would tend to make Japanese businessmen more interested in growth than in high profits as a basis for issuing equity capital. Another is that Japanese businessmen seem to esteem the size of their enterprise, its growth and its importance "in the life of the nation," more highly than profits per se. While profits and growth are linked, "still there does seem a basic difference in emphasis on growth and profits between Japanese and Western businessmen."

In this same vein Jeremy Hardie has asserted that "it remains one of the oddities of modern Japan that profit-making is neither in fact nor in ideology a critical part of what business and commerce are for."[6]

Some of the other estimates in the Japanese paper are consistent with that country's low rates of return measured on this basis, reinforcing our belief in their validity. Specifically the return to investors over the period 1966–81 averaged 3.6 percent, much closer to the after-tax return on corporate assets under the more inclusive (ROC_F) definition than the average return in table 1–2.

The case of Japan, then, is particularly interesting. That Japan is in the middle range of $ROC_A(AT)$ over the last twenty years of all the countries covered is mildly surprising given that country's economic performance relative to the others: its economic record in other respects suggests that Japan has made productive use of its industrial plant, equipment, and inventory in this period.

But Japan also has the lowest rate of return on total capital employed. When we take account of the value of land employed in Japanese manufacturing, that country's industrial capital appears to have yielded the lowest rate of return. Land, it appears, is a much higher fraction of total capital in Japan than in other countries and is probably more costly relative to other factors of production. This suggests that industry in Japan should be viewed not simply as benefiting from relatively low cost, highly productive labor, but as having also to suffer the disability of extremely costly land.

Some might counter that for an ongoing firm high-cost land is a fiction. The cost is an opportunity cost, not a cash outlay. And measuring the value of land in its highest and best use even as an opportunity cost is debatable, since, given the specific aggregation of plant and equipment that constitute the firm, the land cannot be put to its highest and best use without very heavy transaction costs. But to a firm just starting up, which has to buy land as well as plant, equipment, and inventories, the high cost of land in Japan is a meaningful and real item, as real as labor or other capital costs.

Effective Tax Rates

For all countries except Italy an effective rate of tax, t_y, on operating income was computed as the ratio of tax payments (generally company income tax, but for Germany and Austria including property and franchise taxes as well) to operating income, that is, inflation-adjusted profits plus net interest payments. Note that the base of t_y is not nominal profits, the legislated base of the corporation income tax, but rather inflation-adjusted profits plus net interest, which latter is not included in the corporation income tax base. This definition of effective rate of tax, t_y, reflects our concern with the returns to corporate investment no matter how financed.

The effective rate as we have defined it will be affected both by changes in tax rules and in economic conditions. Raising (or lowering) legislated rates will raise or lower effective rates. Acceleration of depreciation, shortening of depreciable lives, provision of investment tax credits, allowances or grants, stock relief, and so on, are all changes in the tax rules that will lower effective rates.

An increase in the rate of inflation will raise the effective rate since the nominal capital gains on inventory and depreciable assets included in the unindexed tax base will increase. But higher nominal interest payments, another consequence of inflation, will tend to lower the effective rate, as we measure it, by increasing the base of tax with no effect on the tax liability.

What happens to effective rates on balance, is the result of a weighting of a set of factors that would vary in relative importance from country to country. And this shows up in the disparate results of table 1–6.

In general, however, the net result in most countries has been a decline in effective rates. In fact only in Germany and Japan has there been an increase in effective rates of company tax over time. In Canada they appear to have run at about the same level over the whole of the postwar period.[7] In the United States, for the manufacturing sector there is a slight downward drift, but for all nonfinancial corporations (not shown in table 1–6, but discussed in the Holland-Myers chapter) the declining tendency is more pronounced. The United Kingdom currently appears to have a tax subsidy on average; Finland, very low rates of effective tax; and Sweden, ostensibly the prototypical income taxing country, shows a substantial decline (with the exception of the several most recent years) in the rate of taxation of corporate operating income. The general experience, then, is that in most countries the tax system has acted to cushion decline in rates of return. *ROC*s before tax show more substantial declines than their after-tax counterpart because the tax itself has become less severe.

It is interesting to note that the ranking of countries by effective rate as we define it is similar to the ranking obtained recently in a very careful study of effective rates, more analytically precise in design than our procedures and with a different definition of effective rate. King and Fullerton have studied extensively the marginal tax rates on investment in four countries—Germany, the United States, Sweden, and the United Kingdom.[8] In their summary of "The Overall Effective Tax Rate as Inflation Varies" in each country, the United Kingdom has the lowest schedule over all rates of inflation (the tabulation covers rates of inflation from 0 to 16 percent), Germany has the highest for rates of inflation under 12 percent, the United States lies below Germany and above the United Kingdom at rates of inflation up to 14 percent, while Sweden is below the United States for rates of inflation up to 11 percent.

Table 1–6
Effective Tax Rates in Manufacturing
(percent)

Year	Austria	Finland	Germany	Sweden	Japan[a]	United States	United Kingdom (1)	United Kingdom (2)	France	Canada[b]
1946						50				44
1947						42				48
1948						37				38
1949						55				40
1950						61				60
1951				53		56				46
1952				42		59				46
1953				44		54				45
1954				44		52				45
1955				47		53				47
1956	40			43		51		41	33	44
1957	33			42		50		41	31	41
1958	31			31		49		32	39	44
1959	31			28		49		35	42	50
1960	32	19		27		48		35	34	56
1961	47	19	60	30		44		31	35	52
1962	42	23	61	31		44		30	33	46
1963	42	20	58	31		41	35	27	31	43
1964	43	19	60	28		40	34	29	30	52
1965	45	21	56	26		42	35	17	30	52
1966	44	24	52	28	20	39	40	16	26	53
1967	47	20	42	29	20	44	42	14	27	51
1968	60	14	47	32	21	44	44	22	23	53
1969	38	10	52	24	22	46	39	24	21	59
1970	37	9	47	22	21	44	40	22	25	49
1971	35	12	58	20	18	42	43	29	22	46
1972	26	10	61	23	23	42	30	30	21	43
1973	25	9	70	16	46	45	11	-9	25	

Year										
1974	33	6	193	9	76	52	−10	343c	32	47
1975	37	12	73	19	29	42	25	321c	42	52
1976	23	16	62	21	36	46	—			47
1977	33	15	73	43	34	45	−4			
1978	29	10	71	78	35	44	1			
1979	26	8	90		47	46	−20			
1980	29	8	108		43	48	−17			
1981			87		32	41	−41			

Sources: all data are from chapters in this volume. Austria: table 11–9; Finland: table 10–3; Germany: table 7–3 (weighted); Sweden: computed from $ROC_A(BT)$ and $ROC_A(AT)$, no holding gains by use of the formula

$$Effective\ Rate = \frac{ROC(BT) - ROC(AT)}{ROC(BT)};$$

Japan: chapter 9, from appendix, table 9A3, column 5; United States: chapter 2, table 2–3; United Kingdom (1): based on chapter 4, table 4–3. (posttax real, backward looking) and computed by the formula:

$$Effective\ Rate = \frac{ROC(BT) - ROC(AT)}{ROC(BT)};$$

United Kingdom (2) and France: chapter 6; Canada: computed from chapter 8, appendix 8B1, by the formula

$$Effective\ Rate = \frac{ROC(BT) - ROC(AT)}{ROC(BT)}.$$

[a] Nonfinancial corporations.

[b] Effective rates for Canada are considered to be subject to wide margins of error because of data deficiencies.

[c] These numbers are misleading. In the King-Mairesse estimates the UK posttax profit rates for the UK were positive in 1974 and 1975 even though their pretax counterparts were negative. And King-Mairesse note that since the early 1970s the UK tax rate "becomes virtually undefined because both taxes and profits fall to very low levels. Subsequent to 1975, it is possible to show that although profits recovered, tax payments have virtually disappeared. For the average industrial company in Britain, corporation tax has virtually been abolished."

Rates of inflation of 11 percent or more have been the exception rather than the rule even in the last twenty years. So from their findings the usual ranking for the marginal investment, reading from low to high marginal rates, would be the United Kingdom, Sweden, the United States, and Germany. And that is the same ranking of these four countries as in our table 1–6.

Has the Rate of Return Declined?

The answer appears in each country's chapter, where the question is usually studied in some detail. The answers will differ for a number of reasons. Different results could be found simply because one country's run of data covers a different period than another's. As appendix 2D of the Holland-Myers chapter illustrates, there might well be a difference in trends depending on the time span covered by a country's data. The answer might also be different for rates of return measured on different capital bases, or measured for different sectors (nonfinancial or the manufacturing subsector). Different trends could be found for before and after tax rates of return.

All these matters and more are discussed generally at length in each of the chapters that follows. The discussions illustrate that trend analysis is an exercise in judgment rather than precision. Thus, in essence, whether there is a trend lies in the eye of the beholder.

So in this section, rather than seek to interpret each country's data as I might see it, I reproduce the author's summary judgment for each country with the warning that in their chapters numerous caveats and qualifications attach to the bare bones summary. In a word, the findings are mixed. For some countries, a declining trend is reported; for others, time per se plays no role in explaining the behavior of profitability; and in some a declining trend is found for certain measures of the rate of return but not for others. What follows is, insofar as possible, a succinct verbatim summary of conclusions on the trend in rates of return taken from the chapters in this book. The conclusions are those for the nonfinancial sector as a whole or a major subsector such as manufacturing.

Italy—1951–81

"In the thirty years [1951–81] under investigation the rate of return to capital does not show any detectable decreasing trend."

Finland—1960–80

"Over the period as a whole [1960–80] there appears to have been no clear declining trend in profitability."

Sweden—1951–78

"The conclusion closest at hand is, then, that return on capital has varied with the level of economic activity (but not with the rate of inflation) and *not* with time per se."

United States—1948–81

"We have not found a declining trend in profitability for either MCs [manufacturing corporations] or NFCs [nonfinancial corporations]."

Japan—1965–81

The authors conclude that the "ROC_W has no trend . . . but a falling trend can be clearly seen" in the ROC_A.

Britain and France—Compared (King-Mairesse)—
1956–75

Pre-Tax Profitability: "For the United Kingdom, a time trend or a dummy variable is essential in order to explain the behavior of pre-tax profitability, whereas in France a reasonably good explanation can be obtained by assuming that the profit rate was equal to a constant plus a term measuring the degree of capacity utilization."

Post-Tax Profitability: ". . . As far as the United Kingdom is concerned a time trend is insignificant and provides no explanatory power at all for total manufacturing. Instead, there was a discrete fall in the post-tax rate of profit at the end of the 1960s from which there is little evidence of a recovery.

"The behavior of post-tax profitability in France has been very different. Again, the time trend and dummy variables seem to be significant but in this case they have a positive sign reflecting the quite sharp increase in post-tax profitability experienced in the period since the mid-1950s." (In their chapter King and Mairesse note variations in these conclusions for total manufacturing for the three subsectors by which they disaggregate manufacturing.)

United Kingdom (Williams) 1961–77

In explaining pre-tax rates of return, ". . . the time trends are negative and significant in all of the equations, except for electrical engineering." (The negative trend characterized manufacturing as a whole and eight of nine sub-industries.)

Austria—1956–80

"The trend term is always negative . . . [and] stronger for before- than for after-tax rates of return. . . ."

Canada—1947–76

". . . One of the most unambiguous findings is a significant downward trend in the inflation-adjusted rate of return on capital employed in manufacturing. . . . No such trend is present in the inflation-adjusted rate of return on the capital employed in nonfinancial firms, of which manufacturing accounts for a substantial share. This indicates that a rising trend occurred in the inflation-adjusted rates of return on capital employed of nonmanufacturing firms."

Germany—1961–81

"There is a significant negative trend in the time series of rates of return on capital invested."

To repeat, these succinct conclusions are excerpted from discussions that emphasize the limitations on the analysis from which they were derived, and the caveats that attach to the interpretation of their findings. Recognizing all this, it seems fair to conclude:

1. No consensus characterizes our authors' evaluation of trends in

profitability. The countries are evenly divided between those that find a declining trend and those that do not.

2. Countries for which there is a long run of rate of return estimates are less likely to report a declining trend than countries for which shorter time series, for example, going back no further than 1961, are available.

Return on Net Worth (REG)

For a number of countries, estimates were prepared of returns to net worth or stockholders' equity. Return on Capital *(ROC)*, in essence, measures the rate of return on total capital employed by the company while the Return on Net Worth *(REG)* measures the rate of return to the assets owned by stockholders. The numerator of the *REG* is the sum of inflation-adjusted profits (before or after tax) plus the decrease (or minus the increase) in the value of debt outstanding, that is, the gains or losses made by stockholders at the expense of holders of company debt. The denominator is the value of assets residually owned by stockholders, that is, total assets minus the sum of debtholder claims against them.

In principle, the change in the value of debtors' claims component of the numerator of the *REG* should be measured by changes in the market value of debt while the net value of equity claims should be measured after the subtraction of the market value of debt from the current value of assets. In practice, however, for a number of countries included in this volume, only the book value of debt was available.

This is one factor that makes the estimates in table 1–7, somewhat ambiguous data for comparisons of return on net worth across countries. Another is that, in estimating *REG*, for some countries the data are aggregated from individual company accounts, while for others they are assembled from national income estimates of corporate assets.

While the *REG* has been estimated both before and after company tax, it is the latter that takes account of government's prior claim, which is more relevant for evaluating what has happened to the return to "own" capital. Changes in tax liability whether legislated or due to changing price levels will affect the *REG*, as will changes in interest rates that are inflation-induced or otherwise caused. Specifically, in a period of inflation, (1) the numerator of the *REG(AT)* will be lowered by higher income tax liabilities, (2) but it will be enhanced by the decline in the market value of the company's debt, (3) and the denominator will be enlarged by the subtraction of debt of smaller market value. Therefore, the net change in the *REG* is not predictable a priori, al-

Table 1–7
Real Return on Net Worth (Equity) with "Gearing Adjustment"
(Manufacturing)

Year	Austria[a] BT	AT	Finland AT	Sweden AT	United States (nonfinancial Companies) BT	AT	Canada BT	AT
1947							15.0	8.4
48					19.1	11.1	13.4	6.8
49					16.5	10.5	15.6	9.7
1950					20.7	9.4	18.6	11.2
51					20.8	8.0	17.2	6.9
52					16.8	7.4	20.0	10.8
53					16.6	6.8	17.8	9.6
54				2.7	13.9	6.3	14.7	8.0
55				0.6	18.7	9.0	16.7	9.2
56	12.2	7.0		5.3	15.4	7.2	15.5	8.2
57	13.8	9.4		1.5	13.9	6.8	12.7	7.1
58	11.9	8.3		2.6	10.8	5.3	11.6	6.8
59	11.5	7.2		5.3	16.1	8.2	13.4	7.6
1960	14.3	9.2	15.1	6.7	14.1	7.1	10.7	5.4
61	9.2	4.8	14.6	5.7	13.8	7.0	9.1	4.0
62	8.9	4.8	12.7	5.6	16.3	9.0	10.5	5.1
63	8.4	4.3	14.0	2.7	18.4	10.3	12.2	6.6
64	9.0	4.4	18.2	5.5	19.7	11.4	12.7	7.2
65	7.8	3.9	11.8	4.3	23.2	13.8	17.3	8.3
66	6.7	3.3	9.7	2.9	23.1	13.4	15.1	7.3
67	5.1	2.1	11.1	5.8	19.5	11.7	12.7	6.0
68	4.5	1.5	19.3	4.4	19.7	10.8	15.7	7.7
69	6.2	3.0	18.7	0.6	16.2	8.5	15.4	7.0
1970	8.3	4.3	19.3	4.6	10.9	5.7	10.4	4.3
71	7.1	4.1	17.8	1.9	13.4	7.4	11.1	5.6
72	8.8	6.3	19.2	4.1	15.2	8.4	12.7	6.8
73	7.1	5.3	26.6	7.4	15.8	8.4	16.0	9.2
74	3.6	0.9	38.5	13.2	11.0	5.4	15.9	8.5
75	4.0	1.8	31.7	5.5	10.3	5.9	11.0	5.3
76	5.8	3.8	25.4	3.4	12.3	6.4	10.7	5.7
77	4.7	2.9	21.5	−3.1	13.5	7.2		
78	3.8	1.3	19.1	3.0	13.4	7.3		
79	6.5	4.1	22.6		10.8	5.9		
1980	6.7	3.9	27.4		7.3	3.9		
81					6.6	3.8		
Series average	7.8	4.5	19.7	4.1	15.4	8.1	14.1	7.3

[a]"Equity II" from chapter 11.

though there is the presumption that the higher debt in total capitalization, the smaller the decline in the *REG(AT)* that would otherwise occur because of higher taxes.

The estimates in table 1–8, for two periods with distinctly different rates of inflation,[9] however, do not provide unambiguous comparable

Table 1–8
Comparison of Percentage Change in ROC(AT) and REG(AT)

	ROC(AT)			REG(AT)		
			Percentage Change 1961–69 to			Percentage Change 1961–69 to
	1961–69	1970–81	1970–81	1961–69	1970–81	1970–81
Austria[a]	3.9	4.1	+5	3.6	3.5	−3
Finland[b]	9.0	9.3	+3	14.5	25.0	+72
Sweden[a]	4.7	4.0	−15	4.2	4.4	+5
United States[a]	8.5	6.0	−21	10.7	6.3	−41
Canada[b]	5.0	4.9	−2	6.6	6.5	−2

Note: For all countries except the United States the ROC_A is for the manufacturing sector. For the United States it is for all nonfinancial corporations.
[a]ROC_A.
[b]ROC_W.

evidence on the *REG*, since for most of the countries tabulated therein, book value of debt rather than market value has been used in estimating "owned" assets and in the "gearing adjustment." Recognizing these limitations, what can we say about the return to equity? More specifically, has the rate of return to net worth *(REG)* declined more or less severely than the rate of return on all assets *(ROC)*?

For one reason or another (no after-tax estimates for the United Kingdom, no "gearing" adjustment for Germany, and so on) we were able to examine this point for only five countries. What we found is summarized in table 1–8, where we compare the percentage decline (or rise) in *ROC(AT)* averaged over 1961–69 and 1970–81 (or as far as the data go) with the percentage change in *REG(AT)*. In only two countries—Finland and Sweden—was the percentage change in the average return to equity between these two periods more favorable than the rate of return to all capital. In two countries—Austria and the United States—the percentage changes were less favorable for return on owners' equity than on all capital. And in one—Canada—percentage changes of the same magnitude characterized both measures.

Profitability in Manufacturing versus Other Industries

Some years back in commenting on a paper by Feldstein and Summers on trends in the rate of return, Michael Wachter noted that it would be interesting to break out the manufacturing sector and nonmanufacturing sector separately because "He suspected that such a disaggregation might show a significant decline, for manufacturing in the seventies."[10]

With the estimates in several of the papers in this volume we can explore Wachter's conjecture, to some degree at least.

For both the United States and Canada estimates were made directly for all nonfinancial corporations and the manufacturing subsector thereof. Then by simple subtraction estimates for the nonmanufacturing sector were obtained. For Germany we have rates of return estimates for a sample of nonfinancial corporations and a sample of manufacturing corporations. And for the United Kingdom, we can compare manufacturing corporations' rates of return with rates of return for a larger aggregate made up of manufacturing, distribution, and service companies. The relevant data are summarized in the following tables in the country chapters: (1) United States—Table 2–5; (2) Canada—table 8B–1; (3) Germany—table 7–3; (4) United Kingdom—table 5D–1.

Inspection of the U.S. data suggests that while the manufacturing sector has tended to have higher rates of return than all nonfinancial corporations, the gap between the two has narrowed over time, particularly for the $ROC(AT)$. Manufacturing has suffered a stronger relative decline in profitability than all nonfinancial corporations. In fact, if the nonmanufacturing sector is broken out (a procedure subject to substantial statistical error as noted in the U.S. chapter), the disparate experience under the nonfinancial corporation aggregate is emphasized. Manufacturing corporations suffered a sharply lower level of profitability in the last decade, and nonmanufacturing corporations experienced a rising trend in rates of return over the postwar period.

While Holland and Myers do not find a declining trend in manufacturing rates of return (that is, they are able to explain the low levels of ROC in manufacturing by factors other than time), they do find a rising trend in the $ROC(AT)$ for nonmanufacturing.

In Canada, too, rates of return in manufacturing declined more severely than for nonfinancial corporations as a whole. Tarasofsky finds a significant downward trend for manufacturing corporations' ROC, but not for the nonfinancial sector as a whole. And he infers a rising trend in rates of return for the nonmanufacturing sector.

In Germany, while profitability was higher in manufacturing than in all nonfinancial corporations in the 1960s, in the 1970s the profitability gap was definitely smaller. Manufacturing suffered a sharper decline in rates of return.

In the United Kingdom, manufacturing rates of return were lower than for distribution, services, and manufacturing combined for the whole period covered by Williams's study—1961–77. From 1961 through 1969, the former averaged 88 percent of the latter. For the most recent years 1970–77, manufacturing rates of return declined relatively, that is, 82 percent of the rate of return for total distribution, services, and manufacturing.

So in all the countries for which we have the evidence it seems fair to conclude that the recent decline in profitability has been particularly severe in manufacturing. Holland and Myers (United States) conjecture that a major explanatory factor may be the growing international competition in manufacturing in the postwar period. A much higher proportion of the nonmanufacturing sector's output is sold domestically. Albach (Germany) notes additionally the increase in oil prices and "the end of the Bretton Woods system" as factors responsible for the more severe recent decline in manufacturing profitability.

Investors' Returns versus Company Returns

The last fifteen to twenty years have not been kind to investors, nor have they been good years for the corporations in which they invest. For the five countries for which we have estimates of returns to investors, we have calculated both sets of returns, R and ROC_W (AT), and compare them in table 1–9.

In the long run we would expect returns to investors and returns on company assets to be equal since, in essence, what companies are expected to earn determines the returns experienced by investors in their equity and debt. Over shorter periods observed results may not

Table 1–9
Rates of Return to Investors Compared with $ROC_W(AT)$, Japan, Sweden, United States, and Germany
(percent)

Country	Period	Return to Investors	$ROC_W(AT)$
Japan (nonfinancial corporations)	1965–81	3.6	2.5[a]
Sweden (business groups)	1967–80	−0.8	2.6
United States (nonfinancial corporations)	1963–81	1.3	5.6
Germany (manufacturing)	1963–81	1.7	2.4
Germany (nonfinancial corporations)	1963–79	1.7	2.6
Italy	1963–81	−3.0	9.8[b]

[a]$ROC_F(AT)$.

[b]$ROC_A(BT)$. Corporate taxes are not very high in Italy. $ROC_A(AT)$ would not be much lower.

be as likely to reflect expectations; company and investor rates of return could well be different.

In fact, in the last fifteen to twenty years in four of the five (Japan is the only exception) countries, companies appear to have enjoyed higher rates of return on their invested capital than earned by investors in corporate equity and debt. Given the margins of error associated with these estimates, however, the two rates of return for Japan and Germany can be considered substantially the same. But for Sweden, the United States, and Italy it is more likely that there has been a real disparity between individual investors' rates of return and company rates of return.

For two countries—the United States and Italy—we have a long run of R and ROC data, covering almost the whole postwar period. In the United States, for nonfinancial companies R and ROC average to just about the same number, and for the manufacturing sector they are fairly close. For Italian industry, however, R and ROC are quite different over the long run, averaging 4.1 and 10.6 percent, respectively. How much of this difference in findings is to be explained by the different methodologies employed in the estimates for the two countries is impossible to ascertain.

Comparisons of q

In those countries where the data permitted estimates were made of q—the ratio of the market value of debt and equity to the current value of corporate assets—a measure originally developed by James Tobin.

In a general sense q tells us something about the relative worth of acquiring a "stake" in existing assets as against constructing new assets. In equilibrium, if we correctly measured all assets and fully evaluated all debt and equity claims, we would expect q to equal 1. In fact, it is impossible to measure the value of the full array of corporate assets—especially the value of human capital, property rights, "good will," or special market positions established by advertising or research and development outlays, patents, copyrights, and so on. But they should, in principle, be reflected in the market value of equity and debt claims. Therefore the q we are able to measure should be greater than 1.

It is surprising, therefore, to find in table 1—10 that q has averaged less than 1 in three of the six countries in which it could be estimated. And for the United Kingdom the value of q is estimated on a corporate asset base of plant, equipment, and inventories. With land and net monetary assets added, q for the United Kingdom could well have averaged under 1 also. Only for Finland and Germany has the value

Table 1–10
A Comparison of Tobin's q: United Kingdom, United States, Sweden, Finland, Japan, and Germany

Year	United Kingdom NFCs q_A	United States NFCs q_A	United States NFCs q_W	United States MCs q_A	Sweden[b] Business Groups q_F	Sweden[b] Business Groups q_W	Finland MCs q_W	Japan NFCs q_F	Japan NFCs q_A	Germany MCs q_W	Germany NFCs q_W
1946											
47		0.9	0.6	0.6							
48		0.8	0.6	0.6							
49		0.7	0.5	0.6							
1950		0.8	0.8	0.6							
51		0.7	0.5	0.6							
52		0.8	0.6	0.6							
53		0.7	0.5	0.7							
54		0.8	0.6	0.8							
55		1.0	0.8	0.9							
56		1.0	0.7	0.8							
57		0.9	0.7	0.8							
58		0.9	0.7	0.8							
59		1.1	0.8	1.1							
1960		1.1	0.8	1.1							
61		1.2	0.9	1.1			1.3			1.2	1.7
62		1.1	0.8	1.1			1.4			1.6	1.4
63	1.6	1.3	0.9	1.2			1.4			1.6	1.4
64	1.6	1.4	1.0	1.4			1.3			1.6	1.4
65	1.3	1.4	1.0	1.6			1.3			1.4	1.2
66	1.2	1.3	1.0	1.5	0.6	0.5	1.2	0.7	1.7	1.2	1.1
67	1.2	1.4	1.1	1.4	0.6	0.5	1.3	0.7	0.6	1.4	1.4
68	1.5	1.3	1.0	1.6	0.8	0.6	1.3	0.7	1.7	1.4	1.4
69	1.3	1.1	0.9	1.4	0.8	0.6		0.7	1.8	1.4	1.4

Table 1–10 (continued)

Year	United Kingdom[a] NFCs q_A	United States NFCs q_A	United States NFCs q_W	United States MCs q_A	Sweden[b] Business Groups q_F	Sweden[b] Business Groups q_W	Finland MCs q_W	Japan NFCs q_F	Japan NFCs q_A	Germany MCs q_W	Germany NFCs q_W
1970	1.0	0.9	0.7	1.2	0.6	0.5	1.3	0.7	1.6	1.2	1.2
71	1.1	1.0	0.8	1.1	0.6	0.5	1.3	0.7	1.9	1.2	1.2
72	1.2	1.1	0.9	1.2	0.7	0.5	1.4	0.8	2.3	1.2	1.3
73	1.2	1.0	0.8	1.0	0.7	0.5	1.5	0.6	1.7	1.1	1.1
74	0.7	0.8	0.6	0.5	0.6	0.5	1.3	0.7	1.5	1.0	1.1
75	0.8	0.7	0.6	0.5	0.6	0.5	1.3	0.7	1.6	1.2	1.1
76	0.7	0.8	0.6	0.7	0.6	0.5	1.2	0.8	1.6	1.1	1.2
77	0.9	0.7	0.6	0.6	0.6	0.5	1.2	0.8	1.7	1.1	1.1
78	0.9	0.6	0.5	0.6	0.6	0.4	1.2	0.8	1.8	1.1	1.1
79	0.7	0.6	0.5	0.5	0.5	0.4	1.2	0.7	1.9	1.1	1.2
1980	0.7	0.5	0.5	0.5	0.6	0.5	1.2	0.8	1.9	1.0	1.1
81		0.5	0.5	0.5				0.7	1.9	1.0	—
Series average	.1	0.9	0.7	0.9	0.6	0.5	1.3	0.7	1.7	1.2	1.3
Average 1961–81	1.1	1.0	0.8	1.0	0.6	0.5	1.3	0.7	1.7	1.2	1.3

[a]Estimated from figure 4–2 in chapter 4.

[b]For Swedish business groups, that is, Swedish-owned companies and their foreign subsidiaries.

of equity and debt tended to reflect, on average, the value of corporate assets. (The q_F of 1.0 for Japan would be < 1 if net monetary assets were added to the capital base.)

What we have just written is asserted more positively than the underlying data can support. Comparing q across countries is a treacherous exercise. Both numerators and denominators will differ from country to country for many reasons both with respect to what is included and how it is valued. For some countries, Japan and Germany in particular, debt is valued at book, but, as noted, the market value of debt is the correct value in principle for measuring q. In both Germany and Japan, compared with most other countries included in this volume, debt is a high proportion of total capitalization. Given the sharp rise in interest rates in recent years, market valuations could well have meant q's well below 1 for Germany and considerably lower than those in table 1–9 for Japan.

Of course, whatever its average value we should expect variations over time in q because, as we have seen q can also be defined as ROC/ρ, and both the rate of return and the "cost of capital" have fluctuated over time. Again it is somewhat surprising, therefore, to find substantial annual variations in q only for the United Kingdon, the United States, and Germany. The time series of q for Finland, Japan (both definitions), and Sweden are remarkably stable.

Variations in q reflect changes in the return on capital relative to changes in the cost of capital, or alternatively changes in the value investors put on corporate assets relative to the cost of constructing these assets. A rising q therefore should signal an increase in the incentive to invest, and a declining q portends a decrease in the desire to invest.

It would appear, therefore, that in the United Kingdom, the United States, and Germany in the last decade there has been a pronounced decline in the inducement to invest. In Sweden, Finland, and Japan there has not been. But it must be emphasized that, because Finland, Japan, and Sweden have much higher ratios of debt to total capitalization, and the value of debt (especially at book) tends to be more stable than the value of equity, the numerator of q in these three countries would tend to vary over time less strongly than in the United Kingdom or the United States.

The Cost of Capital and the Rate of Return

Over the long pull we would expect that the rate of return investors require, that is, the cost of capital measured (roughly) as ρ, the ratio of operating income to the market value of debt plus equity, would tend to equal the rate of return earned by companies on their invested capital. And as we noted earlier, under simplifying assumptions, this is equivalent to the expectation that in the long run q would average out to 1.

But q has not, in general averaged 1 for the countries in our project. For most countries the time series probably cover too short a span for a long-run expectation to eventuate, and there are serious questions as to whether all the components of corporate capital are brought into our estimates of the capital stock. But even for the country with the longest run of data, the United States over the period 1948–81, ρ and ROC_W averaged 7.7 and 6.8 percent, respectively. And comparisons among countries are possible only for the shorter period 1961–81 or something close to it that they have in common.

In table 1–11 we present ρs and ROCs for six countries averaged over the years 1961–81 (or the closest approximation thereto that each country's data permitted).

1. Clearly costs of capital differed widely among countries, ranging from just over 2 percent for Germany to 7.5 percent for the United States.
2. Countries with low (high) rates of return tended to have low (high) costs of capital.
3. In three countries—Finland, Germany, and the United Kingdom— the cost of capital averaged out lower than the rate of return. In

Table 1–11
Comparison of ρ and $ROC_W(AT)$ for Selected Countries
1961–81 (or Closest Approximations)

	Average	
Country	ρ	$ROC_W(AT)$
Finland[a]	5.7	7.8
Germany[b]	2.1	2.7
Japan[bc]	6.0	2.5[d]
United Kingdom[a]	5.4[g]	6.1[f]
Sweden[e]	4.0	2.6
United States[b]	7.5	6.9

[a]Manufacturing.
[b]Nonfinancial.
[c]"Nominal" cost of capital.
[d]$ROC_F(AT)$.
[e]Business groups.
[f]From chapter 4, $ROC_A(AT)$.
[g]Estimated from figure 4–2 in chapter 4.

the three others—Sweden, Japan, and the United States—the average cost of capital exceeded the average rate of return.

4. But given the margins of error attached to these estimates, these disparities between ROC and ρ might be significant only for Sweden, Japan, and Finland.

Debt Ratios

For six of the ten countries covered in this volume we have estimates of the value of debt and equity, which have been summarized in table 1–12 by K_M, the ratio of debt to total capitalization. In principle, K_M should be a ratio of market values, but, as explained earlier, for some countries debt was valued at book.

Over the last twenty years or so, with all countries experiencing inflation and languishing markets for equities, debt could be expected to become an increasing fraction of total capital. For five of the six countries this expectation was borne out, but for Japan the debt ratio fell slightly. King and Mairesse report that two measures other than K_M in their chapter suggest the "growing importance of debt finance" in France and the United Kingdom. A common experience, then, has been an increase in the ratio of debt to total capitalization accompanying declining profitability and rising inflation.

Comparisons of the absolute level of K_M across countries are subject even more strongly than other measures to reservations already noted. But the differences if very pronounced are probably real.

The United States stands out as having a low debt ratio despite a substantial increase in K_M over the postwar period. For the manufacturing sector in the United States the debt ratio is currently between 20 and 25 percent; for Austria and Sweden K_M in manufacturing runs at about 45 percent; in Japan and Finland debt is about 60 percent of total capitalization; in Germany the debt ratio is about 70 percent.

A Few Technical Comments

We close this introductory chapter with a few observations on our measures—cautions on their interpretations and deficiencies in scope or method.

First, to emphasize the limitations on comparing absolute levels of rates of return, consider the intra-country comparisons in table 1–13. These are estimates of rates of return for the same (or a similar) sector in a given country derived from different bodies of data or by different investigators from the same underlying data.

Table 1–12
Ratio of Debt to Total Capitalization: United States, Sweden, Germany, Finland, Austria, and Japan

Year	United States NFCs	United States MCs	Sweden MCs	Sweden Business Groups	Germany MCs	Finland MCs	Austria MCs	Japan NFCs
1946								
47	17							
48	19	−2						
49	24	−2						
1950	19	−6						
51	18	−7	37					
52	19	−2	35					
53	18	0	34					
54	22	1	33					
55	17	−1	35					
56	16	−1	35					
57	16	1	35				33[a]	
58	19	4	34					
59	16	4	35					
1960	17	4	37			41		
61	17	4	37		61	42	31[b]	
62	22	5	36		61	44		
63	19	5	36		61	45		
64	19	5	37		62	45		
65	20	5	40		62	47		60
66	20	7	42	39	62	48	31[c]	59
67	19	10	41	45	61	52		63
68	18	10	42	41	62	50		59
69	22	12	46	41	64	52		57

Year								
1970	29	16	48	51	68	54		64
71	25	18	46	48	66	57		62
72	24	18	46	50	67	57		52
73	29	21	46	56	68	53		60
74	36	38	44	61	68	57		64
75	31	35	46	56	68	59	36[d]	64
76	27	23	44	62	68	61		62
77	35	25	47	70	68	61		60
78	37	27	47	67	68	62		58
79	38	28		66	67	59		59
1980	35	26		68	69	60	44[e]	57
81	30	20		68	69			56

[a] Average 1956–58.
[b] Average 1959–63.
[c] Average 1964–68.
[d] Average 1969–75.
[e] Average 1976–80.

Table 1-13
Intracountry Comparisons of Selected Rates of Return—Germany, Japan, and the United Kingdom

	Germany		Japan		United Kingdom		
Year	Manufacturing Corporations $ROC_A(BT)$ National Income Accounts	Manufacturing Corporations $ROC_W(BT)$ Company Accounts	Nonfinancial Corporations $ROC_W(BT)$ National Accounts	Nonfinancial Corporations $ROC_F(BT)$ Company Accounts	Nonfinancial Corporations $ROC_A(BT)$	Manufacturing Corporations Williams $ROC_W(BT)$	Manufacturing Corporations King-Mairesse $ROC_A(BT)$
1955							8.7
56							8.6
57							8.5
58							8.6
59							9.2
1960							7.7
61	19.5	9.8				10.1	7.3
62	17.0	9.4				8.3	8.0
63	15.8	9.7			11.4	8.7	8.7
64	16.5	10.2			11.9	11.6	7.8
65	16.0	8.8			11.2	10.8	6.5
66	14.3	8.1		6.7	9.9	9.4	6.6
67	14.8	8.3		7.3	10.0	9.9	6.4
68	17.4	10.1		7.1	10.1	9.7	5.5
69	16.9	8.8		7.0	9.9	8.7	4.2
1970	14.8	6.1	12.9	6.2	8.6	6.6	4.6
71	13.6	4.3	10.2	5.4	8.9	5.8	4.9
72	12.9	5.5	9.6	4.8	9.3	4.2	3.5
73	12.9	5.1	8.7	2.0	9.1	5.8	-0.6
74	11.4	1.7	6.9	0.1	6.0	4.8	-0.6
75	9.9	4.1	6.2	2.2	-5.2	-0.3	
76	11.4	6.2	7.0	2.5	5.5	-1.0	
77	11.2	6.4	6.9	2.6	6.9	2.9	
78	11.5	6.6	7.6	3.3	7.2		
79	11.7	5.8	7.0	2.6	5.2		
1980	9.4	3.5	7.0	3.3	3.6		
81		4.1		4.3	2.7		
Series average	14.0	6.8	8.2	4.2	8.0	6.8	6.2

The disparities are substantial, suggesting that the variance of within-country rate of return estimates could be as great as the variance of rates of return between countries.

The German figures both purport to measure the rates of return in manufacturing but are derived from two different sources—national income account aggregates in one case and company accounts in the other—and two different definitions of the capital stock. For the national income data, corporate capital includes fixed assets plus inventory, for the company account data capital includes "total assets employed in business operations."

The more inclusive capital stock concept of the corporate accounts data would explain a consistent shortfall between ROCs based on them and on the narrower definition of the capital base. But it could hardly explain a discrepancy of the magnitude indicated by a comparison of columns 1 and 2 of table 1–13, for the other assets additional to plant, equipment, and inventory, that is, net monetary assets and land, are not likely to be of the same magnitude or greater than fixed capital assets, which is what they would have to be to explain the differences between the two columns.

But the pattern over time of rates of return is substantially the same. From each we would conclude that over the decade of the 1960s rates of return in German manufacturing industry clustered fairly tightly around a characteristic value (averaging 16.5 for the ROC_A measured from national income data and 9.2 for the ROC_W measured from company accounts) and in the 1970s were at a noticeably lower level (averaging 11.9 and 5.0, respectively).

The same point can be illustrated with data for Japan. Here the sectors and ROCs being compared are substantially similarly defined (the time series, however, do not cover the same time span). But the differences between them are very substantial. And while both of the series drift down over time, rates of return derived from national accounts are less volatile than those derived from company accounts.

For the United Kingdom Williams presents ROC_As derived from national account data essentially for nonfinancial corporations with the exception of North Sea petroleum and natural gas extraction companies. He presents another measure akin to the ROC_W for manufacturing companies, derived from company data. Also for the United Kingdom King and Mairesse have provided measures of the ROC_A for manufacturing derived from national accounts.

As far as averages go, the NFC estimates Williams presents from national accounts do not seem to be too far out of line with the MC estimates derived from company accounts, particularly since manufacturing seems to have experienced lower rates of return than have other industries in the United Kingdom over this period at least. But the Williams manufacturing estimates derived from company data and the

King-Mairesse estimates for manufacturing derived from national accounts differ substantially. For the period they cover in common, one averages out to 7.4 percent, the other to 5.0 percent. The difference is greater than it seems, since the King-Mairesse measure is the ROC_A, which would, other things equal, be higher than an equivalent ROC_W.

Yet from all three U.K. series the decline in profitability starting in the middle 1960s is quite apparent.

All this goes to reinforce an earlier judgment. Comparisons of *levels* of rates of return are ambiguous at best, and not likely to mean too much unless the differences are very pronounced. But patterns of behavior of rates of return over time are more trustworthy evidence.

Second, it should be remembered that in all countries the analysis has covered company taxes only. The full story on rates of return should include taxes levied on corporate earnings received by individuals and intermediaries (personal income taxes) or "belonging to" them (capital gains taxes). Moreover, in taxes at the company level in most countries only income taxes were included. But property, franchise, and net wealth taxes should also be taken into account where applicable.

Third, the structure of claims against corporate assets is more subtle and diverse than our simple methodology recognizes. With respect to equity, for example, we do not as a rule distinguish between common and preferred shares. A considerably greater complication is the structure of claims to corporate earnings and assets that in all countries, to a varying degree, have been built up in the form of what Bayer (Austria) calls "social capital"—reserves for pension benefits, severance pay, and so on. In some cases these are "claims," with ill-defined property rights. In other countries a pension reserve is simply an accounting notation. But in still others it represents a well-defined and funded company obligation. In the United States, the legal standing of pension claims was dramatically strengthened with the Employee Retirement Income Security Act of 1974.

Finally, it is comforting to be able to report that there is a degree of robustness in rate of return estimates. King and Mairesse (Britain and France) provide two pieces of relevant evidence. First, their primary estimates for France are based on the "1962 base year national accounts." But a major change was introduced in the methodology, data, and nomenclature of the national accounts in "1971 base year national accounts." Yet rates of return that were estimated alternatively from each base turned out to be very similar in absolute magnitude and behavior over time. They note that this was due to offsetting discrepancies in numerator and denominator, Second, they obtained a similar result when they made alternative capital stock estimates, assuming very different service lives for Britain than they did in their primary estimates. They did get substantially different values for the aggregate capital stock, but in calculating rates of return these were offset in good part by correspondingly different estimates of capital consumption.

A similar finding is reported by Holland and Myers (United States) with respect to different assumptions both as to length of asset lives and the time pattern of depreciation. Substantial variations in estimates of capital stock were compensated for by variations in estimated depreciation. While these results suggest an element of robustness in rate of return estimates, they also imply, of course, wide variation ("non-robustness") in estimates of q.

The reader will note in the chapters in this book references to "nominal" and "real" measures. "Nominal" refers to measures derived from data not standardized with respect to time, while the data for "real" measures are all as of the same time. The choice between these two terms, however, is sometimes a matter of taste, not principle. In the Japanese chapter what are referred to as "nominal" rates of return without holding gains approximate the *ROC* without holding gains that would be designated as "real" in most of the other chapters. Therefore in the rate of return comparisons in this chapter I have used the "nominal" rates of return without holding gains from the Japanese chapter.

Notes

1. For a succinct definition of this term and all other symbols in this chapter, see the common glossary at the end of the chapter.

2. This treatment reflects preference of the researchers as well as what it was feasible to estimate. Stewart Myers and I felt that holding gains were not important for the long-run behavior of rates of return because, over the long pull, they would tend to cancel out. This view is borne out by results reported for Sweden and Finland, which show sharp annual variations because of holding gains but similar long-run averages for *ROC*s with or without holding gains. For Japan, however, with land an unusually high proportion of capital employed and experiencing a rather steady rate of price advance in excess of the consumer price index, holding gains result in a different story. But since land does not turn over in the ordinary course of business activity, some researchers felt that holding gains on land should not be included in the numerator, while others disagreed.

3. As explained earlier, for some countries book value of debt had to be used as a proxy for market value.

4. See more formal development in Holland-Myers chapter in this volume.

5. Edwin O. Reischauer, *The Japanese* (Cambridge, Mass.: Harvard University Press, 1977), p. 190.

6. Jeremy Hardie, "A Confucian Kind of Capitalism," review of Michio Morishima, *Why Has Japan "Succeeded?"*, *Times Literary Supplement,* July 19, 1982, p. 475.

7. Effective rates are "inferred" from rates of return before and after tax. Data on effective rates per se are not provided in the Canadian chapter because of the wide margins of error to which estimates of tax were subject.

8. Mervyn A. King and Don Fullerton, "Taxation of Income from Capital: A Comparative Study of the U.S., U.K., Sweden and West Germany—Comparisons of Effective Tax Rates," National Bureau of Economic Research, Working Paper No. 1073, February 1983, figure 7–1.

9. For example:

	Compound Rate of Changes in CPI	
	1963–69	1970–81
United States	3.0%	8.0%
Sweden	3.9%	9.5%
Canada	3.4%	8.4%

Source: Federal Reserve Bank of St. Louis, *International Economic Conditions,* Annual Edition: June 1983.

10. Arthur M. Okun and George L. Perry (Editors), *Brookings Papers on Economic Activity, 1977–1* (Washington, D.C.: Brookings Institution, 1977), p. 228.

Appendix 1A
A Common Glossary

In an attempt to be helpful, the editor prepared a "common" glossary, which, in practice, turned out to be too inflexible to be used consistently. But it does indicate generally what we set out to measure and provides a set of symbols fairly widely used in the chapters in this volume. Moreover, where authors have developed their own measures, they frequently explain how they are related to the common glossary's definitions.

Basic Variables

A. *"Business Entity" Variables*
1. *Income Variables*
   P = Inflation-Adjusted Profits
   I = Net Interest Payments
   Y = Income from Operations = $P + I$
   T = Income Taxes on the Business Entity
2. *Capital Stock Variables* (All at Current Cost)
   G = Inventories or Stocks
   E = Equipment
   B = Plant
   M = Net Monetary Assets = Cash + Accounts Receivable − Accounts Payable
   L = Land
   A = Inventories + Plant and Equipment = $G + E + B$
   O = Inventories + Plant and Equipment + Net Monetary Assets = $G + E + B + M$
   W = Total Assets Employed in Business Operations = $G + E + B + M + L$
   F = Total Fixed Assets Employed in Business Operations = $G + E + B + L$
B. *Investors' and Capital Market Variables*
   ω = Dividends Received by Stockholders
   I = Net Interest Received by Lenders (= Net Interest Payments Section A)
   S_1 = Market Value of Stock at end of Period 1 (or Start of Period 2)

39

D_{MI} = Market Value of Debt at End of Period 1 (or Start of Period 2)

D_{BI} = Book Value of Debt at End of Period 1 (or Start of Period 2)

MV_I = Market Value of Investors' Holdings at End of Period 1 (or Start of Period 2) = $S_I + D_{MI}$

CP = Consumer Price Index

Derived Measures

A. *"Business Entity" Measures*

$ROC(BT)$ = Rate of Return on Business Assets, Before Tax

$ROC_A(BT) = Y / A$

$ROC_O(BT) = Y / O$

$ROC_W(BT) = Y / W$

$ROC_F(BT) = Y / F$

$ROC(AT)$ = Rate of Return on Business Assets, After Tax

$ROC_A(AT) = Y - T / A$

$ROC_O(AT) = Y - T / O$

$ROC_W(AT) = Y - T / W$

$ROC_F(AT) = Y - T / F$

$REQ(BT)$ = Rate of Return on Equity, Before Tax

$REQ_A(BT) = P / A - D_M$

$REQ_O(BT) = P / O - D_M$

$REQ_W(BT) = P / W - D_M$

$REQ_F(BT) = P / F - D_M$

Note: In this and all other measures of rates of return on equity where D_M is not available D_B is used.

$REQ(AT)$ = Rate of Return on Equity, After Tax

$REQ_A(AT) = P - T / A - D_M$

$REQ_O(AT) = P - T / O - D_M$

$REQ_W(AT) = P - T / W - D_M$

$REQ_F(AT) = P - T / F - D_M$

$REG(BT)$ = Rate of Return on Equity with Gearing Adjustment, Before Tax: where "gearing adjustment," g, is equal to percentage change in $CP \cdot$ Market Value of Debt, that is, $g = DM_I \cdot [(CP_I - CP_O) / CP_O]$

$$REG_A(BT) = P + g / A - D_M$$
$$REG_O(BT) = P + g / O - D_M$$
$$REG_W(BT) = P + g / W - D_M$$
$$REG_F(BT) = P + g / F - D_M$$

$REG(AT)$ = Rate of Return on Equity with Gearing Adjustment, After Tax

$$REG_A(AT) = P + g - T / A - D_M$$
$$REG_O(AT) = P + g - T / O - D_M$$
$$REG_W(AT) = P + g - T / W - D_M$$
$$REG_F(AT) = P + g - T / F - D_M$$

REGM(BT) = Rate of Return on Equity with Gearing Adjustment and Adjustment for Change in Value of Net Monetary Assets, Before Tax: where m, change in the value of monetary assets, is equal to percentage change in $CP \cdot$ Nominal Value of Net Monetary Assets, that is, $m = M_1 \cdot [(CP_1 - CP_O) / CP_O]$

$$REGM_A(BT) = P + g - m / A - D_M$$
$$REGM_O(BT) = P + g - m / O - D_M$$
$$REGM_W(BT) = P + g - m / W - D_M$$
$$REGM_F(BT) = P + g - m / F - D_M$$

REGM(AT) = Rate of Return on Equity with Gearing Adjustment and Adjustment for the Change in Value of Monetary Assets, After Tax

$$REGM_A(AT) = P + g - m - T / A - D_M$$
$$REGM_O(AT) = P + g - m - T / O - D_M$$
$$REGM_W(AT) = P + g - m - T / W - D_M$$
$$REGM_F(AT) = P + g - m - T / F - D_M$$

$t_y = T / Y$ = Effective Rate of Tax on Income from Operations
$t_p = T / P$ = Effective Rate of Tax on Inflation-Adjusted Profits

B. *Investors' and Capital Market Measures*
$R_N = \omega + I + (S_1 - S_O) + (D_{MI} - D_{MO})/S_O + D_{MO}$ = Nominal Return to Investors
$R_R = R_N - (CP_I - CP_O)/CP_O$ = Real Return to Investors

q = Valuation Ratio = Ratio of Market Value of Firms' Securities to the Market Value of Their Assets

$q_A = MV / A$

$q_O = MV / O$

$q_W = MV / W$

$q_F = MV / F$

$\rho = Y - T/MV$ = Cost of Capital

$K_M = D_M / D_M + S$ = Ratio of Market Value of Debt to Total Market Value

$K_B = D_B / D_B + S$ = Ratio of Book Value of Debt to Total Book Value of Debt + Market Value of Stock

K_K = Ratio of Debt to Total Capitalization as Derived from Corporate Records

2

Trends in Corporate Profitability and Capital Costs in the United States[1]

Daniel M. Holland and
Stewart C. Myers

Objectives and Major Conclusions

One striking aspect of the performance of the U.S. economy during the last ten to fifteen years is the decline in the rate of return on corporate capital. This rate of return is frequently taken as an index of economic efficiency and as a proxy for expected returns to corporate investment; its decline is therefore viewed as bad news.

The potential significance of this profitability decline is clear, but its actual significance is not. It may or may not indicate a basic structural shift in the U.S. economy. It may reflect a serious weakness, a natural and benign result of market forces, or something in between. For example: (1) Whether the decline is serious depends on the level from which it starts. Since the mid-1960s was a period of unusually high profitability, the recent decline may merely be a return to normal levels. (2) The importance of the decline in profitability depends on whether the cost of capital has fallen proportionally. If it has, then the falling rate of return need not, in itself, be cause for concern.

In this chapter we present the evidence on profitability and capital costs for U.S. manufacturing corporations and all nonfinancial corporations. We attempt to clarify the issues posed by this evidence, to uncover the longer-term trends, if there are any, and to provide additional evidence about causes and consequences.

Our essay is organized around three questions: (1) How have investors in U.S. corporations fared? (2) What has been the rate of return earned by corporations on their capital assets? (3) How have rates of return on real capital held by corporations behaved relative to capital costs?

We answer the first question by measuring the returns investors earned on their aggregate portfolio of equity and debt securities. We answer the second by examining rates of return on corporate capital assets. We answer the third by comparing rates of return with an approximate measure of the cost of capital. Most of our analysis covers the post–World War II period from 1947 or 1948 to 1981.

We direct our three questions to two major corporate sectors.[2] (1) All Nonfinancial Corporations (NFCs). For them we have the most reliable information, the longest run of data, and the greatest volume of detail. (2) All Manufacturing Corporations (MCs). MCs are the major subsector of NFCs. For MCs we have enough information to develop estimates comparable with NFCs. Our estimates for MCs are less accurate than those for NFCs, but they are good enough, we think, for meaningful comparisons.

Our major conclusions are set out here in brief summary form. Their implications, the path by which we reached them, and the caveats and qualifications that attach to them appear in the sections that follow.

1. Investors in NFCs and MCs have fared poorly since the middle 1960s. Indeed over the period 1966–81 they earned a negative average real return on their holdings of equity and debt. On the other hand they did extremely well in the earlier postwar period. Over the whole of the postwar period investors in NFCs enjoyed a return of 5.3 percent; for MC investors the annual return averaged 8.1 percent. The difference between returns on investments in NFCs and MCs is consistent with the greater volatility of MC returns.

2. The evidence for NFCs suggests long-run stability in corporate investors' rates of return. Over the period 1930–81 they earned an average rate of 5.2 percent, virtually the same as the average for 1948–81.

3. When the market value of NFC and MC equity and debt is related to the current replacement cost of corporate assets, the 1960s are seen as an unusually favorable period, with ratios well above the average for the whole of the postwar period. The years 1974–81, however, are characterized by the lowest ratios for the entire post-war period (and, for NFCs, for the period 1930–81 as well).

4. Over the years 1948–81, for both NFCs and MCs the value of corporate securities was, on average, only about 90 percent of the replacement cost of corporate plant, equipment, and inventories and, for NFCs, only 70 percent of corporate capital defined to include land and net non–interest bearing monetary assets as well as plant, equipment, and inventories.

5. Real rates of return on corporate capital for both NFCs and MCs were unusually high in the 1960s. Measured before corporate income tax, rates of return on corporate assets were lower in the last decade than in the early years of the postwar periods. On an after-tax basis, rates of return in the most recent decade have run at about the same level as in the 1950s, and substantially less than in the 1960s.

6. After-tax rates of return on corporate assets have been "held up" by declining effective rates of corporate tax.
7. Over the postwar period MCs enjoyed higher rates of return on corporate capital than NFCs, but over time, especially on an after-tax basis, the gap between them has narrowed.
8. We have not found a declining trend in profitability for either MCs or NFCs. When we take account of other factors that could affect corporate rates of return, time has no significant explanatory value.
10. The real cost of capital for NFCs has varied within a narrow range from 1952–76. Over this period fluctuations in the market value of NFCs have been much more closely related to changes in operating profitability than to changes in the capitalization rate. Since 1976, this relationship seems to have broken down, however.
11. For both NFCs and MCs there has been a rise in the postwar period in the debt to total capitalization ratio. For NFCs debt ran at about 20 percent of total capital up through 1969, and then rose to 30 to 35 percent currently. For MCs debt was a very small proportion of capitalization until 1965, but has grown since to about 25 percent.

Sources for the estimates in our report are cited briefly with each table and tabulated in Appendix 2B. Appendix 2A describes the methodology for our estimates for the manufacturing sector.

Returns to Investors

Introduction

In the discussion that follows we first describe and discuss our definitions, methodology, and results for NFCs. We then present comparable figures for MCs and compare the results for the two aggregates.

We are concerned with the profitability of the nonfinancial corporate sector in aggregate—that is, treated as one giant firm. NFCs, of course, do not account for the entire private sector, but they are the major part of it. More than half of Gross Domestic Product (GDP) originates in the NFC sector. NFCs account for more than 90 percent of corporate GDP and more than 60 percent of total business GDP. The current (1981) replacement cost of plant, equipment, and inventories held by NFCs exceeds $2.6 trillion; if the values of land and non–interest bearing net monetary assets are added, the current value of the total capital stock of NFCs is about $3.1 trillion.[3] The past performance and current economic health of this sector is clearly of interest and concern.

It is a widely accepted fact (a fact we confirm in the section entitled "Rates of Return on Capital Stock") that NFC profitability has declined sharply since the middle 1960s. Is this conclusive and unambiguous evidence of poor performance? Not entirely so. There are a number of difficulties.

1. The rate of return on capital can be estimated in virtually countless ways, some suggesting a more serious decline than others. The National Income and Products Accounts (NIPA) provide several different estimates of depreciation, for example. Each implies a different measure of NFC income, a different value for net capital stock, and a different rate of return.
2. What is to be included in corporate capital stock? Most estimates for NFCs, drawing on NIPA data, include only the current re- placement cost of plant, equipment, and inventories. Land and net non–interest bearing monetary assets should be included.
3. What about intangible assets? These include, for example, the extra value of a going concern over a random collection of physical assets, the value of cumulative outlays on research, marketing, and em- ployeee training, and the present value of future investment opportunities.[4]
4. In measuring after-tax returns how do we account for the tax lia- bility "deferred" by accelerated depreciation? Or, to put the ques- tion alternatively, how do we account for that portion of the stock that has been financed, in effect, by interest-free government loans?
5. In calculating operating income (the numerator of the profit rate) how can we take account of the interest component of the rental payments for the leased portion of corporate capital stock?

The problems implicit in these and similar questions should con- vince us that rates of return based on accounting data will never be free of ambiguities of definition and errors of estimation. Of course these estimates are indispensable for many purposes, including those we put them to later. But they are not an unambiguous measure for determining how NFCs fared.

There is an alternative. The value of the firm is not determined by the cumulative funds invested in it or by the net replacement cost of its stock of real capital, but by the stream of earnings investors expect it to generate. The value of this stream at any time can be observed directly by summing the market value of all of the firm's outstanding securities. That is the true value of *all* the firm's assets. The income realized in any particular period can be found by adding the cash pay- ments received by investors to the change in the market value of the firm's securities over the period, computed net of any new issues of securities. The rate of return earned by investors in that firm is found by dividing income by start-of-period market value.

In short, we propose as one answer to the question, "How well have NFCs performed?" the returns earned in capital markets.

There is good evidence that capital markets are efficient, in the sense of responding promptly and accurately to new information. We consider investors' returns on their investment in corporate securities to be the least ambiguous evidence on how well corporations have fared, even though some recent research may consider these returns excessively volatile.[5]

Rates of Return to Investors

Consider a portfolio containing all the debt and equity securities issued by NFCs. That portfolio's aggregate market value (MV) is the market's estimate of the present value of the stream of future earnings[6] that investors expect NFCs to generate.

An investment in this portfolio would have generated income in the form of cash interest and dividend payments and also in the form of capital gains and losses. Thus we can calculate the rate of return earned by the portfolio in year t by estimating total income for year t and dividing by MV_t, the portfolio's market value at the start of the year. Let this rate of return be R_t.[7]

Note that R_t is *not* the rate of return earned by NFC stockholders. We are concerned with the performance of the entire NFC sector, not with the return received by holders of claims on part of that sector's earnings.[8] Stockholders may have gained at the expense of debt-holders, or vice versa, but that is not relevant here.[9] It is important that our profitability measure be unaffected by shifts in capital structure.

Of course, not all NFC securities are publicly traded. Even for those that are, price data are not always conveniently available. (This is the case for most corporate bonds, for example.) Therefore it was necessary to work out a procedure for estimating MV_t[10] and R_t. Here a number of alternative procedures are possible, but we believe any careful estimates will show the same patterns across time.

Table 2–1 shows real rates of return[11] for NFCs for one- and four-year intervals between 1929 and 1981. The Rs are extremely volatile when measured annually, as column 1 suggests and column 2 measures. Hindsight, however, reveals a pattern.[12] Investors in NFC securities fared very well indeed after World War II and up to about 1965, but poorly after that. The contrast between the first and second halves of

Table 2–1
Real Return to Investors in Nonfinancial and
Manufacturing Corporations

Year	NFCs		MCs	
	R_R	σ^a	R_R	σ^a
1930	−14.3			
1931	−23.7			
1932	12.8			
1933	43.4			
1934	4.5			
1935	29.6			
1936	23.6			
1937	−22.1			
1938	21.6			
1939	2.8			
1940	−3.2			
1941	−13.4			
1942	0.8			
1943	12.9			
1944	13.3			
1945	25.5			
1946	−22.2			
1947	−5.4			
1948	0.0	13.5	−0.9	20.7
1949	16.5	7.1	22.5	11.1
1950	16.8	8.5	32.2	12.5
1951	9.4	10.1	20.4	13.8
1952	10.5	8.7	12.3	13.3
1953	0.8	7.3	−0.5	9.6
1954	40.3	8.2	58.7	12.3
1955	19.8	7.6	30.0	11.0
1956	2.6	11.2	7.7	14.9
1957	−10.6	9.5	−15.3	13.4
1958	33.8	4.9	41.2	6.2
1959	9.4	6.3	13.8	8.6
1960	0.6	11.0	−6.2	12.8
1961	22.0	7.4	23.4	8.8
1962	−7.8	15.5	−11.1	19.4
1963	15.4	7.3	20.6	9.9
1964	12.9	7.4	15.5	4.4
1965	9.3	8.0	15.9	9.1
1966	−10.7	9.3	−12.7	10.4
1967	16.9	10.5	26.9	11.9
1968	5.5	9.7	5.4	9.4
1969	−15.5	11.1	−14.8	11.9
1970	−0.4	16.6	−3.2	17.5
1971	11.1	11.1	11.9	12.1
1972	11.8	5.4	14.3	5.5
1973	−21.3	9.7	−21.9	9.5
1974	−30.8	16.3	−33.1	14.9
1975	21.5	13.4	18.0	14.1
1976	18.6	10.0	18.0	12.4
1977	−9.8	7.6	−12.3	7.5
1978	−4.3	11.3	−1.9	11.5
1979	−1.1	9.3	1.2	10.5
1980	8.2	14.5	11.2	12.2
1981	−12.6	13.8	−12.9	13.3

Table 2–1 *(continued)*

Year	NFCs		MCs	
	R_R	σ^a	R_R	σ^a
Four-year averages				
1930–31[b]	19.0			
1932–35	22.6			
1936–39	6.5			
1940–43	−0.7			
1944–47	2.8			
1948–49[b]	8.3	10.3	10.8	15.9
1950–53	9.4	8.7	16.1	12.3
1954–57	13.0	9.1	20.3	12.9
1958–61	16.5	7.4	18.1	9.1
1962–65	7.5	9.6	10.2	8.5
1966–69	−0.9	10.3	1.2	10.9
1970–73	0.3	10.7	0.3	11.2
1974–77	−0.2	11.8	−2.4	12.2
1978–81	−2.5	12.2	−0.6	11.9
Series average 1930–81				
Mean	5.2			
Standard				
Deviation	16.6			
Series average 1948–81				
Mean	5.3		8.1	
Standard				
deviation	15.2		18.8	

1. Annual returns to investors *(R)* are weighted averages of rates of return on debt and equity held from the beginning to the end of the year. The equity rate of return is the annual rate of return, including both dividends and capital gains, computed from the files of the Center for Research in Security Prices, University of Chicago. The debt return is the rate of return on a portfolio of long-term corporate bonds constructed by R. Ibbotson and R. Sinquefield, *Stocks, Bonds, Bills and Inflation* (Charlottesville, Va.: Financial Analysts Research Foundation, 1982), exhibit A–3, pp. 92–93. Unfortunately the maturity of this portfolio probably overstates the average maturity of the NFC debt. Consequently, the volatility of this debt return overstates the true volatility. The portfolio weights are the proportional contributions of debt and equity to the total estimated market value. See appendix table 2B2.

2. Real returns are found by subtracting annual percentage changes in the CPI, as reported by Ibbotson and Sinquefield, exhibit A–6, pp. 98–99.

3. Averages are arithmetic means of annual returns. Two-year averages are calculated for 1930–31 and 1948–49.

4. Each year's standard deviation (σ) is calculated from twenty-four *monthly* rates of return for that year and the preceding year.

[a]σ = monthly standard deviation, annualized.

[b]Two-year averages.

the 1960s is dramatic. The poor performance of the late 1960s continues through the 1970s. The four-year averages in table 2–1 show that investors in NFCs have earned, on average, a negative real rate of return from 1966 to 1981.[13] In the longer run, however, real returns to investors have been stable. The averages for 1930–81 and 1948–81 are virtually identical.

Table 2–1 also shows real rates of return to investors in manufacturing corporations, calculated by the same general procedures as for NFCs. Again we see a sharp contrast between the two halves of the postwar period: very high real returns through 1965 and very low returns afterwards. The manufacturing returns, however, are generally higher than the NFC returns, and also more volatile, particularly up to the early 1960s.

We have measured this volatility by a series of standard deviations, one for each year for both NFCs and MCs. Each year's figure is based on twenty-four monthly rates of return earned in that year and the previous one. These standard deviations for NFC returns reflect the *business* risk of a widely diversified portfolio of corporate assets. This portfolio is a closer approximation to the "market portfolio" of capital asset pricing theory than the stock market alone, since it includes bonds as well as stock returns, weighted by aggregate market values.

The portfolio underlying MC returns is less well diversified, however. Therefore table 2–1 includes an adjusted standard deviation for MCs that removes that part of MC business risk that could have been avoided by diversification.

There is no evident trend in the standard deviation series. We note the quiet period from the late 1950s to the mid-1960s and the similar volatility of the earliest and most recent of the postwar decades.

Since MCs seem riskier than NFCs, we would expect them to borrow less, as they do. Debt to market value ratios for MCs and NFCs are given in appendix tables 2B2a and b and plotted in figure 2–1. MCs had essentially no net debt in the early postwar period—in several years they were net *lenders* in aggregate. But their debt ratio has crept gradually upward and now stands at roughly one-quarter.

NFCs, on the other hand, started out the postwar period with debt-to-total market-value ratios of about one-fifth. There was no substantial change until the late 1970s, when debt-to-total market value ratios climbed above one-third.

Aggregate Market Value of NFC Securities

Most of the volatility of investors' rates of return reflects capital gains or losses: that is, changes in MV_t, the aggregate market value of NFC securities. We are also concerned with the level of MV_t. Of course, we expect MV_t to increase over time as corporations grow; we must adjust for that part of the movement in MV_t caused by inflation and the expansion in the scale of NFC operations. Therefore we express MV_t relative to two measures of the NFC capital stock: (1) The net replace-

Source: appendix 2B, table 2B2a and b.

Figure 2–1. K_M, Ratio of Market Value of Debt to Market Value of Debt and Equity for Nonfinancial and Manufacturing Corporations 1948–81

ment cost of depreciable capital and inventory expressed in current dollars.[14] (2) An "augmented" capital stock, including the items noted just above plus land at current value and net non–interest bearing monetary assets.

The ratio of market value to the net replacement cost of corporate assets (most commonly taken to be plant, equipment and inventory) is usually referred to as "Tobin's q."[15] This ratio is given in table 2–2 for the usual definition of the capital stock for both NFCs and MCs (designated q_A), and for NFCs on an augmented base (q_w). The ratios are plotted in figure 2–2. Table 2–2 also gives q on the standard base for NFCs from 1930–46. This is the only q that can be computed from our data for the prewar years.[16]

Table 2–2
q Ratio for Nonfinancial and Manufacturing Corporations

Year	Nonfinancial q_A	q_W	Manufacturing q_A
1930	1.4		
1931	1.1		
1932	0.9		
1933	1.0		
1934	1.2		
1935	1.4		
1936	1.5		
1937	1.2		
1938	1.1		
1939	1.2		
1940	1.1		
1941	0.9		
1942	0.8		
1943	0.9		
1944	1.0		
1945	1.1		
1946	1.1		
1947	0.9	0.6	
1948	0.8	0.6	0.6
1949	0.7	0.5	0.6
1950	0.8	0.6	0.6
1951	0.7	0.5	0.6
1952	0.8	0.6	0.6
1953	0.7	0.5	0.6
1954	0.8	0.6	0.7
1955	1.0	0.8	0.8
1956	1.0	0.7	0.9
1957	0.9	0.7	0.8
1958	0.9	0.7	0.8
1959	1.1	0.8	1.1
1960	1.1	0.8	1.1
1961	1.2	0.9	1.1
1962	1.1	0.8	1.1
1963	1.3	0.9	1.2
1964	1.4	1.0	1.4
1965	1.4	1.0	1.6
1966	1.3	1.0	1.5
1967	1.4	1.1	1.4
1968	1.3	1.0	1.6
1969	1.1	0.9	1.4
1970	0.9	0.7	1.2
1971	1.0	0.8	1.1
1972	1.1	0.9	1.2
1973	1.0	0.8	1.0
1974	0.8	0.6	0.5
1975	0.7	0.6	0.5
1976	0.8	0.6	0.7
1977	0.7	0.6	0.6
1978	0.6	0.5	0.6
1979	0.6	0.5	0.5
1980	0.5	0.5	0.5
1981	0.5	0.5	0.5

Table 2–2 *(continued)*

| Year | Nonfinancial | | Manufacturing |
	q_A	q_W	q_A
Four-year averages			
1930–33	1.1		
1934–37	1.3		
1938–41	1.1		
1942–45	1.0		
1946–47	1.0		
1948–51	0.8	0.6	0.6
1952–55	0.8	0.6	0.7
1956–59	1.0	0.7	0.9
1960–63	1.2	0.9	1.1
1964–67	1.4	1.1	1.5
1968–71	1.1	1.1	1.3
1972–75	0.9	0.7	0.8
1976–81	0.6	0.5	0.6
Series average 1930–81			
Mean	1.0		
Standard deviation	0.2		
Series average 1948–81			
Mean	0.9	0.7	0.9
Standard deviation	0.3	0.2	0.4

1. q is the ratio of market value *(MV)* to capital stock. *MV* is given in appendix tables 2B2a and 2B2b. Capital stock used to calculate q_A includes plant, equipment, and inventories at current replacement cost. The denominator of q_W also includes the current value of land and net non–interest bearing monetary liabilities.

2. Estimates of the capital stock as of the end of the year for NFCs and MCs appear in tables 2B3a and 2B3b of appendix 2B. Averages of year-end values are used as the denominator in calculating all qs. Averages of the values in table 2B2b of appendix 2B are used as the numerator for q for MCs. For NFCs however, market values as of the end of June in each year, not published in table 2B2 of appendix 2B, are the numerator.

A value of $q = 1.0$ means that the market value of the earnings stream generated by NFC assets is exactly equal to the net replacement cost of those assets. This is the value for q we expect to observe if the economy is in long-run equilibrium, if the definition of CS_t includes all income-producing assets, and if MV_t and CS_t are measured without error. Recognizing these ifs, we should not read too much significance into the absolute value of q. It is nevertheless odd to find q so far below 1.0 in the early postwar period and since 1974. If the estimates are anywhere near correct, it was far cheaper for firms to add capacity by purchasing other firms than by buying fresh plant, equipment, and inventory. In 1953, for example, it was possible to purchase an "average firm" for only 70 percent of the net replacement cost of its assets; in 1981, companies' market values were, on average, about half the current cost of their plant, equipment, and inventory.

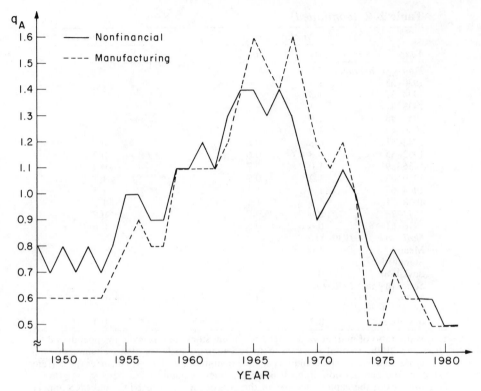

Source: table 2–2.

Figure 2–2. q_A, Ratio of Total Market Value to Total Replacement Cost of Fixed Capital and Inventories for Nonfinancial and Manufacturing Corporations 1948–81

The year 1965 was the turning point for q. Since then it has followed an erratic downward course to levels below those of the early postwar period. The high rates of return earned by investors in NFC securities over the 1946–55 period can be largely attributed to the recovery of q to a more "reasonable" level.

The capital bases used in computing q are discussed in more detail later. At this point we merely note that the choice of base used in calculating q does not affect its pattern over time.

Interpreting q

Despite its interest and the usefulness of the measure, the behavior of q is difficult to interpret and its meaning may be easily misunderstood.

Consider for example the following statement from the *Economic Report of the President* (1977, p. 28):

> If assets are valued in the market significantly above their replacement cost, corporations will be encouraged to invest in new equipment and thereby create capital gains for the owners of their securities.

Properly interpreted this statement is correct, but taken literally it is ambiguous. It could be misinterpreted as a prediction that firms will continue investing so long as the average q (which is what we observe) is greater than 1.

It is true that in long-run equilibrium both the average and the marginal q equal one. If all industries are competitive, and if the denominator of q correctly measures the value of all assets, including intangible ones, then any opportunities to make investments having positive net present values must last only for the short run. In this sense it is true to say that a q greater than 1 for some firms implies profitable investment opportunities for others.

On the other hand, an entrenched, profit-maximizing monopolist would have a continuing supply of positive net present value investments, and therefore would have a q greater than 1 even in long-run equilibrium. But not every firm with a high measured q is a monopolist: intangible assets, such as value created by expenditures on research and development, are reflected in the numerator but not the denominator of q. The observed q for such firms is overstated.[17]

The quotation we cited would be unambiguously correct if it referred not to the level of q but to a rise in that level. Because q reflects the expected profitability of corporate investment relative to the opportunity cost of capital, an increase in q should signal increased corporate investment.[18]

q for Manufacturing Corporations

The discussion of q has focused on NFCs. For them we think we have the best estimates and the longest run of data. For MCs, however, the story is much the same as for NFCs over the period for which we have data for both sectors, 1948–81. NFCs and MCs averaged about the same q over the period. The MC sector q showed the same pattern over time—rising from substantially below 1 over the postwar decade to a peak over 1.5 by the middle 1960s and declining suddenly in 1974 to about 0.5, remaining at that low level since. But the MC sector's q was more volatile than the NFCs.

The Absolute Value of q

As indicated in table 2–2 and figure 2–2, qs for NFCs and MCs have averaged 0.9 over the period 1948–81. But q measured on the augmented corporate capital base (NFCs only) averaged 0.7 over the postwar period.

Even our augmented base overstates q to the extent that capital assets have been created by advertising, research and development expense, and other "investments" that are treated as current expenditures for accounting purposes. On the other hand if an accelerated rather than straight line pattern of depreciation had been assumed in estimating plant and equipment, the estimated current value of corporate capital would be lower and q would tend to be higher, although on the augmented base the long-term average q would still be well below 1.0.

Conclusions

The first twenty postwar years were a generally favorable period for investors in U.S. corporations. Investors earned average rates of return on market value that seem, in hindsight, to be unusually generous. Much of this good performance can be traced to capital gains, as firms' market values appreciated relative to the net replacement cost of their assets. By 1965, aggregate market value was 50 percent larger than a greatly expanded base of inventory and plant and equipment.

There was a dramatic reversal of fortune in the next fifteen years. Real rates of return to investors were low, often negative, and averaged below zero. Aggregate market value fell to a level substantially below the asset base. These time patterns hold for MCs as well as for NFCs. MCs, however, generated higher average rates of returns to investors. They were also riskier. Of course, values observed in capital markets show us only the end result of a complicated process. Insights into earlier stages of the process must come from other measures of profitability.

Rates of Return on Capital Stock

In this section we examine corporate profitability estimated from annual measures of asset value and operating income developed by the Bureau of Economic Analysis of the Department of Commerce as part of the

National Income and Product Accounts (NIPA). In effect we are moving from capital market measures of return to measures akin to the book or accounting measures used by business firms. But our measures are based on income and capital stock estimates that are adjusted for price level changes.

The capital market rates of return are sufficient to tell us how well NFCs and MCs have fared, but they give no clue to the reasons for their good or bad performance in the capital markets. For example, we have no way of inferring from market value data whether the period of unusually high market values in the mid-1960s was the result of high operating profits, low capitalization rates for corporate securities, or a combination of both. The interpretation of capital market data requires information from other sources. Our discussion of corporate rates of return concentrates initially on the nonfinancial corporate sector. Then we take up the two component subsectors—manufacturing and non-manufacturing.

Many measures of rate of return can be derived from NIPA data. The one we emphasize most is the rate of return on capital stock, ROC_A, defined as the ratio of NFC operating income, that is, profits plus interest, to the net replacement cost of NFC plant, equipment, and inventories. But we also use a measure of profitability based on a broader concept of capital stock, ROC_W, which includes land and net non–interest bearing assets as well.

Following other investigators, we interpret ROC as the real rate of return on NFC capital stock. Of course, such an interpretation rests on a number of assumptions, some of which are not strictly true. Also, operating income equals real income only if there are no *real* holding gains on capital stock and inventory values rise at exactly the same rate as prices generally. Intangible assets, such as the value created by advertising and R&D expenditures, are not included in the capital base. Nor does operating income include the interest component of rental contracts.

Despite its imperfections, operating income as we measure it is an important indicator of corporate performance and a decent first approximation of real operating income. Moreover, our conclusions are insensitive to the exact definition of income, capital stock, or ROCs derived therefrom. (See Appendix 2C.)

Nonfinancial Corporations

Table 2–3 and figure 2–3 present three measures of the rate of return for NFCs, both before tax (BT) and after tax (AT).

Table 2–3
Estimates of Return on Capital for Nonfinancial Corporations 1929–81
(percent)

Year	$ROC_N(BT)$	Nominal t_y	$ROC_N(AT)$	$ROC_A(BT)$	Real t_y	$ROC_A(AT)$	$ROC_W(BT)$	Real t_y	$ROC_W(AT)$
1929	11.5	13.1	10.0	10.2	13.5	8.7			
1930	5.1	17.1	4.2	8.1	10.3	7.2			
1931	0.9	71.4	0.3	3.8	17.2	3.1			
1932	-2.2	-18.8	-2.6	-0.4	-99.9	-0.9			
1933	1.9	38.5	1.2	-0.6	—	-1.4			
1934	3.9	26.9	2.8	3.3	33.3	2.2			
1935	5.6	24.3	4.2	5.7	25.0	4.3			
1936	9.2	21.3	7.2	8.2	24.1	6.3			
1937	9.5	21.5	7.5	8.9	22.6	6.9			
1938	5.1	25.7	3.8	5.9	22.0	4.6			
1939	9.9	20.9	7.9	8.2	24.6	6.2			
1940	13.6	28.7	9.7	12.2	30.7	8.5			
1941	23.3	43.4	13.2	17.5	53.6	8.1			
1942	27.2	51.9	13.1	21.4	58.9	8.8			
1943	31.4	54.8	14.2	24.8	60.3	9.9			
1944	30.7	51.4	14.9	24.3	55.8	10.7			
1945	24.9	50.5	12.3	18.8	56.4	8.2			
1946	23.7	39.5	14.4	12.7	59.3	5.2	8.6	59.3	3.5
1947	26.4	36.7	16.7	14.3	52.7	6.8	10.1	52.7	4.8
1948	25.1	36.3	16.0	15.7	44.5	8.7	11.4	44.5	6.3
1949	18.3	36.2	11.7	13.3	38.9	8.1	9.7	38.9	5.9
1950	25.7	43.2	14.6	15.8	55.4	7.0	11.6	55.4	5.2
1951	23.3	52.6	11.0	15.8	61.4	6.1	11.7	61.4	4.5
1952	18.5	50.7	9.1	13.2	56.7	5.7	9.8	56.7	4.2
1953	18.2	50.3	9.0	12.7	59.1	5.1	9.4	59.1	3.8
1954	16.2	45.0	8.9	11.7	51.8	5.6	8.7	51.8	4.2
1955	20.1	44.0	11.2	14.6	50.6	7.2	10.9	50.6	5.4
1956	18.4	43.8	10.3	12.5	53.5	5.8	9.4	53.5	4.4
1957	16.6	42.6	9.5	11.4	51.5	5.5	8.6	51.5	4.2
1958	13.8	41.4	8.1	9.7	49.2	4.9	7.3	49.2	3.7

Year									
1959	16.6	42.0	9.7	12.4	47.9	6.4	9.2	47.9	4.8
1960	14.9	41.3	8.7	11.3	46.9	6.0	8.4	46.9	4.5
1961	14.2	41.8	8.3	11.4	46.2	6.1	8.4	41.2	4.5
1962	15.8	37.8	9.9	13.1	41.1	7.7	9.6	41.1	5.6
1963	16.5	38.0	10.3	14.1	40.7	8.3	10.3	40.7	6.1
1964	17.6	35.6	11.3	15.1	38.1	9.3	11.2	38.1	6.9
1965	19.1	34.5	12.5	16.4	36.9	10.4	12.4	36.9	7.8
1966	19.1	34.3	12.5	16.1	37.1	10.2	12.3	37.1	7.7
1967	17.1	32.9	11.5	14.3	35.7	9.2	11.0	35.7	7.1
1968	17.5	35.8	11.2	14.1	40.1	8.4	11.0	40.1	6.6
1969	16.3	35.2	10.5	12.3	41.1	7.3	9.8	41.1	5.7
1970	13.8	31.5	9.4	9.7	38.7	5.9	7.7	38.7	4.7
1971	14.5	31.0	10.0	10.3	37.2	6.4	8.3	37.2	5.2
1972	15.8	30.1	11.0	10.9	36.6	6.9	8.9	36.6	5.7
1973	17.4	29.4	12.3	10.8	39.4	6.6	8.9	39.4	5.4
1974	17.2	27.2	12.5	8.2	45.1	4.5	6.7	45.1	3.7
1975	16.2	25.8	12.0	9.0	35.2	5.8	7.4	35.2	4.8
1976	17.6	28.1	12.6	9.7	38.5	5.9	8.0	38.5	4.9
1977	18.7	27.4	13.6	10.5	36.9	6.6	8.6	36.9	5.4
1978	19.2	26.9	14.1	10.4	37.4	6.5	8.5	37.4	5.3
1979	18.8	25.1	14.1	9.1	38.7	5.6	7.5	38.7	4.6
1980	17.2	22.8	13.3	7.8	36.9	4.9	6.5	36.9	4.1
1981	16.9	20.4	13.5	8.3	30.4	5.8	6.9	30.4	4.8
Four-year Averages									
1929–33	3.4	24.3	2.6	4.2	−36.8	3.4			
1934–37	7.0	23.5	5.4	6.6	26.3	4.9			
1938–41	13.0	29.7	8.6	11.0	32.7	6.9			
1942–45	28.6	52.1	13.7	22.3	57.8	9.4			
1946–49	23.4	37.2	14.7	14.0	48.9	7.2	9.9	48.9	5.1
1950–53	21.4	49.2	10.9	14.3	58.2	6.0	10.6	58.2	4.5
1954–57	17.8	43.9	10.0	12.5	51.9	6.1	9.4	51.9	4.5
1958–61	14.9	41.6	8.7	11.2	47.6	5.9	8.3	47.6	4.4
1962–65	17.3	36.5	11.0	14.7	39.2	8.9	10.9	39.2	6.6
1966–69	17.5	34.5	11.5	14.2	38.5	8.8	11.0	38.5	6.8
1970–73	15.4	30.5	10.7	10.4	38.0	6.5	8.5	38.0	5.2
1974–77	17.4	27.2	12.7	9.4	38.9	5.7	7.7	38.9	4.7

Table 2–3 *(continued)*
(percent)

Year	$ROC_N(BT)$	Nominal t_s	$ROC_N(AT)$	$ROC_A(BT)$	Real t_s	$ROC_A(AT)$	$ROC_W(BT)$	Real t_s	$ROC_W(AT)$
1978–81	18.0	23.8	13.7	8.9	35.9	5.7	7.3	35.9	4.7
Series average 1929–81									
Mean	16.3	34.7	10.2	11.7	35.2	6.5			
Standard deviation	7.1	13.5	4.0	5.0	23.5	2.4			
Series average 1946–81									
Mean	18.1	36.0	11.5	12.2	44.1	6.7	9.3	44.1	5.2
Standard deviation	3.2	8.0	2.2	2.5	8.2	1.5	1.6	8.2	1.1

1. The before-tax rate of return is the ratio of (1) before-tax operating income of nonfinancial corporations to (2) the net replacement cost of nonfinancial corporations' inventory and capital equipment. Item (1) is calculated after straight-line depreciation on the net replacement cost of capital equipment, assuming asset life is 85 percent of lives published in the Department of Commerce's Bulletin F. Item (1) is before interest and does not include inventory profits. Item (2) is the average of inventory and fixed capital equipment values as estimated at the start and end of the calendar year. From 1958 on the inventory figure is the June quarter value in each year. The fixed capital component of item (2) is the NIPA estimate of the current cost of fixed nonresidential corporate capital. "Current cost measures are derived by valuing all assets in the stock at any specified period at the prices of that period. This is done by applying price indexes to the constant cost stock estimates to convert them to current cost estimates. In effect, the current cost stock is a measure of the replacement value of capital" (J.C. Musgrave, "Fixed Nonresidential Business Capital in the United States, 1925–75," *Survey of Current Business*, April, 1976, pp. 49–50.)

2. The basic data used in calculating entries in table 2–3 are in tables 2B3a and 2B4a in appendix 2B.

3. The after-tax rate of return is calculated from before-tax income, minus corporate income taxes as furnished in NIPA accounts (see sources in the first note above).

4. NIPA estimates are usually revised several times. Our estimates include the latest revisions as of December 1982.

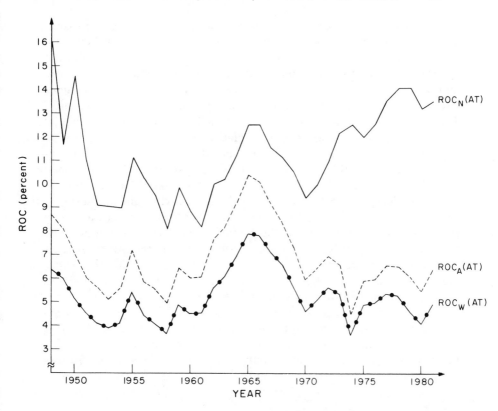

Source: table 2–3.

Figure 2–3. *ROC,* Return on Capital after Tax for Nonfinancial Corporations: Nominal *(N),* Real Standard Base *(A),* and Real
Augmented Base *(W)* 1948–81

1. ROC_N is a *nominal* rate of return, an approximation of the rate of
    return as measured by accepted accounting conventions.[19]
2. ROC_A is a *real* rate of return, for which profits are adjusted to
    reflect depreciation based on current replacement costs, nominal
    holding gains on inventory are eliminated, and physical capital
    stock—plant, equipment, and inventories—is valued at current
    replacement cost.
3. ROC_W is a *real* rate of return whose numerator is the same as
    ROC_A. The denominator, however,—the capital stock—is aug-
    mented by including land at current value and net non–interest
    bearing monetary assets.

Before-Tax Rates of Return. Look first at $ROC_N(BT)$. This measure includes nominal inventory profits in income, measures depreciation on the basis of historical cost, and values the capital stock at book, that is, at the acquisition cost of the plant, equipment, and inventories. The numerator of the ROC_N overstates real income because it includes nominal capital gains on inventories and understates real depreciation.[20] The denominator is understated because the historical cost of the capital stock is below the current cost of replacing it.

Therefore, ROC_N overstates real profitability and is not a meaningful measure of the rate of return. Note that $ROC_N(BT)$ averaged 16.3 and 18.1 percent for the periods 1929–81 and 1946–81, respectively, while $ROC_A(BT)$ ran at considerably lower values, averaging 11.7 and 12.2 percent for the same spans of years. Nor can anything meaningful be inferred from the behavior of ROC_N over time. The book profitability of NFCs has been about as high in the last eight years as in the twenty years from 1954 through 1973. In fact, by the ROC_N measuring rod NFCs are better off now (that is, during the most recent eight years) than in the "golden" 1960s.

But it is useful to present estimates of the ROC_N since the nominal measure suggests the substantial magnitude of error in measuring NFC profitability from corporate accounts and thus motivates an interest in the real rates of return. Incidentally, the $ROC_N(BT)$ and its after-tax equivalent come closest to the figure cited (not so frequently today as in the past) as the "normal" return on corporate investment—20 percent before tax and 10 percent after tax.

For the real story on corporate profitability we turn to the $ROC_A(BT)$. It averaged 11.7 and 12.2 percent for the postwar years. We concentrate on the latter period.

This cyclical and irregular series is marked by three distinct periods: a slow decline from 1946 to 1960, a rise over the 1960s, and then a pronounced fall in the 1970s to values that are lower than in any of the preceding years. Recent rates of return are well below long-run averages; note the four-year averages in table 2–3.

Before-tax profitability measured on augmented capital stock, $ROC_W(BT)$, shows the same pattern. The recent decline, however, does not seem to go so far below the "characteristic" value of the time series. The 1960s again stand out as a peak period.

Before-tax profitability can be taken to be a measure of the average productivity of capital in the NFC sector. The evidence suggests a significant decline in productivity in the last decade, but "eye-balling" is not sufficient to establish this. In a later section we make a more careful attempt to extract the trend, if there is any, in before-tax profitability.

After-Tax Rates of Return. We turn now to our estimates of the after-tax rate of return, which are also presented in table 2–3. Many consider the $ROC_A(AT)$ the most pertinent evidence in the debate on corporate profitability. Investors' claim is to after-tax profits. $ROC_A(AT)$ is the accounting counterpart to R, the market rate of return to investors on all NFC securities, and $ROC_A(AT)$ can be viewed as a proxy for the incentive to invest.

We compute after-tax income by subtracting corporate income tax payments to all levels of government from before-tax operating income.

After-tax book profitability—$ROC_N(BT)$—is higher now than it has been in most of the last half-century. But the picture for real after-tax profitability is quite different. It displays the same general pattern over time as real before-tax profitability, with rates of return in the 1970s running below the long-term average. There was a similar run of low rates of return from 1950 to 1961. But what stands out most dramatically in table 2–3 and figure 2–3 is the high level of $ROC_A(AT)$ in the 1960s.

The real after-tax rate of return on the augmented capital base is, of course, lower. But the same conclusion emerges. Look once more at the four-year averages: the "low" rates of return of the last dozen years are about the same as NFCs earned from 1946 to 1961; what is unusual are the high profit rates in the 1960s.

The historical record does not support the view that recent after-tax rates of return earned by NFCs have been uniquely low. In this respect there seems to be a difference between the before- and after-tax measures: the former suggest a remarkably low level of profitability in the late 1970s. But the latter suggest not that the profit rates of the most recent decade were abnormally low, but, rather, that profitability in the 1960s was unusually high. Of course this is only the picture one "sees." A more careful analysis of trends is undertaken below.

The Effective Rate of NFC Income Tax. The narrowing spread between before- and after-tax profitability reflects a downward drift in effective tax rates on NFCs. We measure the effective rate t_y by the ratio of Corporation Income Tax Payments to Operating Income (Profits plus Net Interest Payments). (The tax rate is the same for both ROC_A and ROC_W.) We note a gradual decline, starting in the early 1950s, becoming more pronounced in the 1960s, and continuing to the present. While uneven and irregular, the decline has been persistent and significant; compare 1951's effective tax rate of 61 percent with 1981's 30 percent.

In part this decline in effective rates reflects a decline in legislated rates, from 52 percent in 1952 to 46 percent currently.[21] But other factors explain most of the decline. Note the drop from 57 percent in

1952 to 41 percent in 1963, a period over which the federal government's legislated corporate tax rate—52 percent on taxable profits—was constant and state corporate tax rates, on average, rose.

The decline in effective rates has been partly the result of the increasing weight of net interest payments (which are not taxed at the corporate level) in operating income. As table 2–4 shows, for NFCs this fraction rose from less than 5 percent in the early postwar period to 30 percent in 1981. The deductibility of interest reduces the effective

Table 2–4
Ratio of Interest to Operating Income for Nonfinancial and Manufacturing Corporations
(percent)

Year	NFC	MC
1947	3.9	−0.3
1948	3.4	−0.1
1949	4.2	−0.2
1950	3.0	−0.7
1951	3.2	−0.4
1952	3.8	0.0
1953	4.2	0.0
1954	5.0	0.2
1955	4.0	−0.2
1956	4.5	0.1
1957	5.9	0.6
1958	8.2	1.6
1959	7.2	1.3
1960	8.6	1.4
1961	9.2	1.8
1962	9.0	1.9
1963	8.6	1.5
1964	8.4	1.8
1965	8.3	2.1
1966	9.3	3.3
1967	11.2	5.2
1968	12.1	5.9
1969	16.3	9.3
1970	24.4	17.6
1971	22.5	14.3
1972	20.8	12.4
1973	22.6	13.8
1974	31.8	20.9
1975	26.3	18.1
1976	21.6	12.4
1977	19.9	11.6
1978	20.6	10.9
1979	24.6	13.1
1980	29.9	16.8
1981	30.0	15.7

Sources: appendix tables 2B4a and 2B4b.

tax rate on real NFC income by as much as eighteen percentage points.[22] This reflects higher nominal interest rates as well as an increase in the debt-to-market value ratio: the ratio of debt to market value of all NFC securities rose from 0.19 in 1952 to over 30 percent in recent years.[23] Still, the effective tax rate declined between 1952 and 1963, when the debt ratio was substantially unchanged.

The decline in effective rates also reflects purposeful government policies, including acceleration of tax depreciation schedules, shortening of depreciable lives, last in first out (LIFO) inventory accounting, and the investment tax credit.[24] Although inflation increases effective tax rates (see 1974's 45 percent rate, for example), the growth in net interest payments relative to profits and the loss carry-back provision of the corporate tax have helped keep down the effective tax rate.

Thus for NFCs the tax incentives introduced over the postwar period served generally to keep the corporate income tax levied on nominal profits from becoming an increasing burden on real operating income, while the growing importance of the interest shield acted to lower the effective rate on real operating income. Only for the stretch of years from 1962 through 1966, when the debt interest shield was an essentially constant fraction of real operating income and the effective rate fell, can it be concluded that the tax incentives alone were sufficiently powerful to outweigh the upward pressure on effective rates created by taxation of nominal capital gains on inventory and plant and equipment. This is one explanation for the sharp rise of after-tax profitability in the early 1960s. Price stability over this period kept nominal capital gains low, thus permitting tax incentives to show up in lower effective rates of tax on real income.

Although the effective tax rate has drifted downward in the postwar period, that tendency is only part of the story. Bursts of inflation have sent corporate income tax liabilities up and after-tax profitability down. The results for 1974 are particularly dramatic. Hankin (1977) found (and we corroborate in the section entitled "Searching for Trends in Profitability") a significant negative correlation in the postwar period between the after-tax ROC and the rate of inflation, after adjustment for a time trend and the rate of change in GNP. This suggests a strong positive link between inflation and the effective tax rate. There was no significant association between inflation and before-tax ROCs.[25]

Manufacturing Corporations

The discussion in the previous section concentrating on NFCs has covered much of the ground for MCs as well. The patterns over time for returns to investors, *ROC*s, effective tax rates, and q are generally similar for NFCs and their manufacturing subsector. This suggests that a common process underlies profitability outcomes for both MCs and NFCs, a suggestion reinforced by the results of the regression analysis reported below.

But, as the estimates in table 2–5 indicate, there have been some differences between MCs and NFCs. The one that particularly stands out is the higher level of average before-tax profitability of NCs. Over the period 1947–81, $ROC_A(BT)$ for MCs averaged 2.4 percentage points more than for NFCs. This differential was roughly 3.3 percentage points up to the early 1970s but considerably smaller since. In the most recent four-year period, MCs had a lower rate of return before-tax than NFCs.

MCs' after-tax profitability was consistently higher than that of NFCs up to about 1970, but since then the two sectors have earned about the same after-tax rates of return (see figures 2–4).

The effective tax rate on MC profits has been higher than the tax rate for NFCs since the late 1950s. This explains the greater degree of convergence of after-tax profitability compared with profitability before tax for the two sectors.

Nonmanufacturing Corporations—NMCs. From the comparisons between MCS and NFCs one can infer the behavior of another sector— all NFCs except MCs, which we call nonmanufacturing corporations (NMCs). This sector is not as homogeneous as the Manufacturing sector. NMCs include the following industries: construction, mining, retail and wholesale trade, services, communications, transportation, and electrical utilities.

Two major differences between MCs and NMCs could affect relative profitability. First, regulated, or formerly regulated, industries make up a sizable proportion of all NMCs. Second, NMCs, to a greater extent than MCs, sell in the domestic U.S. market.

It is tempting to break out the data for NMCs and display them directly, rather than simply infer them from the differences between NFCs and MCs. We have yielded to this temptation, but alert the reader to treat the NMC estimates as, at best, suggestive. As explained earlier, the NFC estimates are derived primarily from the NIPA data. Good as these data are, they are subject to errors of estimation and differences of opinion as to appropriate methodology for estimation. Our measures for MCs are also based primarily on the NIPA, but several bold assumptions are required to calculate the estimates used in this chapter. Thus the estimates are probably subject to a greater degree of error than those for NFCs.

Our estimates for NMCs are obtained indirectly simply by sub-

Table 2–5

Return on Capital and Effective Tax Rate (T_p) for Nonfinancial, Manufacturing, and Nonmanufacturing Corporations 1947–81

Year	Nonfinancial			Manufacturing			Nonmanufacturing		
	$ROC_A(BT)$	t_y	$ROC_A(AT)$	$ROC_A(BT)$	t_y	$ROC_A(AT)$	$ROC_A(BT)$	t_y	$ROC_A(AT)$
1947	14.3	52.7	6.8	18.5	50.4	9.2	11.1	55.6	4.9
1948	15.7	44.5	8.7	19.4	41.8	11.3	12.9	47.7	6.8
1949	13.3	38.9	8.1	16.7	36.9	10.5	10.8	41.3	6.3
1950	15.8	55.4	7.0	21.3	54.6	9.7	11.8	56.5	5.1
1951	15.8	61.4	6.1	21.8	60.9	8.5	11.2	62.2	4.2
1952	13.2	56.7	5.7	17.1	55.7	7.6	10.2	57.8	4.3
1953	12.7	59.1	5.1	16.6	59.0	6.8	9.5	59.2	3.9
1954	11.7	51.8	5.6	13.8	54.4	6.3	10.1	49.2	5.1
1955	14.6	50.6	7.2	18.6	51.8	9.0	11.7	49.3	5.9
1956	12.5	53.5	5.8	15.4	52.8	7.3	10.3	54.2	4.7
1957	11.4	51.5	5.5	13.8	51.2	6.7	9.6	51.9	4.6
1958	9.7	49.2	4.9	10.6	50.1	5.3	9.1	48.6	4.7
1959	12.4	47.9	6.4	15.5	48.9	7.9	10.2	46.9	5.4
1960	11.3	46.9	6.0	13.6	49.0	7.0	9.8	45.1	5.4
1961	11.4	46.2	6.1	13.3	48.5	6.9	10.1	44.3	5.6
1962	13.1	41.1	7.7	15.5	44.3	8.6	11.5	38.3	7.1
1963	14.0	40.7	8.3	17.5	43.7	9.8	11.8	37.9	7.3
1964	15.0	38.1	9.3	18.6	41.4	10.9	12.8	35.1	8.3
1965	16.4	36.9	10.4	21.6	40.0	13.0	13.2	33.6	8.7
1966	16.1	37.1	10.2	21.0	41.5	13.0	13.0	32.4	8.8
1967	14.3	35.7	9.2	17.4	38.7	10.7	12.2	33.0	8.2
1968	14.1	40.1	8.4	17.2	44.0	9.6	12.0	36.3	7.7
1969	12.3	41.1	7.3	14.2	45.7	7.7	11.1	37.2	7.0
1970	9.7	38.7	5.9	9.7	43.5	5.5	9.6	35.6	6.2
1971	10.3	37.2	6.4	11.3	41.8	6.6	9.6	33.9	6.4
1972	10.9	36.6	6.9	12.8	41.6	7.5	9.8	32.7	6.6
1973	10.8	39.4	6.6	12.9	44.6	7.2	9.6	35.3	6.2
1974	8.2	45.1	4.5	8.7	52.1	4.1	8.0	40.5	4.7
1975	9.0	35.2	5.8	8.8	41.7	5.1	9.1	31.5	6.2

Table 2–5 *(continued)*

Year	Nonfinancial			Manufacturing			Nonmanufacturing		
	$ROC_A(BT)$	t_y	$ROC_A(AT)$	$ROC_A(BT)$	t_y	$ROC_A(AT)$	$ROC_A(BT)$	t_y	$ROC_A(AT)$
1976	9.7	38.5	6.0	10.9	45.6	6.0	9.0	33.4	6.0
1977	10.5	36.9	6.6	11.9	44.8	6.6	9.7	31.2	6.7
1978	10.4	37.4	6.5	11.5	44.4	6.4	9.7	32.4	6.5
1979	9.1	38.8	5.6	9.4	45.6	5.1	8.9	34.4	5.8
1980	7.8	36.9	4.9	6.2	48.5	3.2	8.8	31.9	6.0
1981	8.3	30.4	5.8	6.3	41.0	3.7	9.6	26.1	7.1
Four-year averages									
1947–49	14.5	45.4	7.9	18.2	43.0	10.3	11.6	48.2	6.0
1950–53	14.3	58.2	6.0	19.2	57.6	8.1	10.7	58.9	4.4
1954–57	12.5	51.9	6.0	15.4	52.5	7.3	10.4	51.1	5.1
1958–61	11.2	47.6	5.9	13.3	49.1	6.8	9.8	46.2	5.3
1962–65	14.6	39.2	8.9	18.3	42.4	10.6	12.3	36.2	7.9
1966–69	14.2	38.5	8.8	17.4	42.5	10.1	12.1	34.8	7.9
1970–73	10.4	38.0	6.5	11.7	42.9	6.7	9.7	34.4	6.3
1974–77	9.4	38.9	5.7	10.1	46.1	5.4	8.9	34.2	5.9
1978–81	8.9	35.9	5.7	8.4	44.9	4.6	9.2	31.2	6.4
Series average									
Mean	12.2	43.7	6.8	14.6	46.7	7.7	10.5	41.5	6.1
Standard deviation	2.5	7.8	1.5	4.3	5.8	2.4	1.4	9.8	1.3

Sources: appendix tables 2B3a, 2B3b, 2B4a, and 2B4b. Estimates for nonmanufacturing do not appear in these tables. They are obtained by subtracting the respective manufacturing entries from the nonfinancial entries.

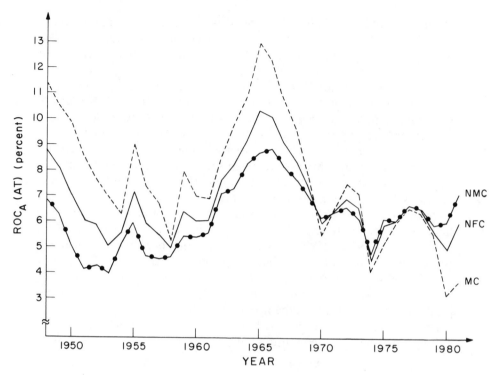

Source: table 2–4.

Figure 2–4. $ROC_A(AT)$, Return on Capital after Tax for Nonfinancial, Manufacturing, and Nonmanufacturing Corporations 1948–81

tracting MC from NFC values. The NMC numbers are, in a sense, doubly damned since they are subject to the errors of estimate that attach to both NFCs and MCs.

Nonetheless we present estimates for NMCs for two reasons: (1) If true, they tell an interesting story. (2) They should constitute a rough basis for evaluating the consistency of our MC estimates.

A comparison of *ROC*s as estimated for MCs and NMCs suggests both important similarities and major differences for the two sectors. In essence one gets the same picture as in the comparison between MCs and NFCs, but the similarities are not as strong and the differences are more apparent when the two component sectors of NFCs are compared.

MCs have enjoyed higher and more volatile rates of return both before and after tax. We infer from earlier data that there is a heavier weight of debt in the financial mix of NMCs. Finally, MCs have suffered considerably heavier effective rates of corporate tax, averaging close to 47 percent between 1947 and 1981, as against the NMC average of under 42 percent.[26]

The $ROC_A(BT)$ for NMCs in the 1970s was only slightly lower than in earlier periods, while in the last ten years the $ROC_A(AT)$ for NMCs was slightly above average for the whole of the postwar period, exceeded only (and not greatly) by the after-tax returns of the 1960s.

Thus the NFC aggregate appears to be composed of two distinctly different subsectors. MCs have been characterized by high rates of return, high risk, low debt, relatively high effective corporation income tax rates, and a substantial decline in profits in the last decade. NMCs have been less profitable on average and less volatile. They have had high debt, relatively low effective tax rates, and no sharp decline in profits in the 1970s. NMC profitability was higher, but not that much higher, in the 1960s than in the rest of the postwar years. In the last decade, NMCs have had higher rates of return than MCs.

Two cautions are appropriate at this point. First, we remind the reader of our concern with the accuracy of the NMC estmates. Second, whether profitability has declined or not cannot be established by "eye-balling" the data. More careful analysis is required.

Searching for Trends in Profitability

Our search for trends follows the framework developed first by Nordhaus (1974) and followed by a number of other studies since. Nordhaus sparked an interest in "trends" in profitability with his conclusion that the rate of return on capital in the postwar period (1948–70) showed "a definite downtrend from 1948 to the middle 1950s; a dramatic recovery from the late 1950s to the mid-1960s with a peak in 1965 or 1966; and a deterioration to a plateau by 1970" (pp. 180–81). He interpreted this as a postwar downtrend in corporate profitability, which reflected a steady decline in the opportunity cost of capital (205–08).

Later investigations using a more extensive run of substantially revised data have shown no consensus concerning the trend in profitability. And only a few have related their study of rates of return to the behavior of the cost of capital.[27] In this section we report on our exploration for trends in profitability with the help of a set of statistical tests originally developed by Hankin (1977). We are not testing whether profitability was lower in the 1970s than in earlier years, but whether time is a determinant of the process that generates rates of return. We adjust for other factors that determine profitability, and then ask whether the ROC is a declining function of time.

Table 2–6 presents the results of our search for trends in $ROC(AT)$. Lines 1 through 3 of panel A of the table, for example, report the results of successively regressing $ROC(AT)$ for NFCs on time alone, then on time and the annual percentage change in GNP, and, finally, on time, the annual percentage change in GNP, and the rate of inflation. The change in GNP is a rough correction for the business cycle, and the rate of inflation corrects primarily for the impact of inflation on the effective rate of corporate income tax.

The first equation in panel A is the equivalent of a simple time trend. As a function of time alone $ROC_A(AT)$ for NFCs trended downward, but the coefficient is not significant. In the second equation the $ROC(AT)$ is related to time *and* the percentage change in the level of economic activity. The latter emerges as a significant explanatory factor, while time remains insignificant. The third equation adds the rate of price change to the independent variables. Inflation, too, turns out to be a significant determinant of after-tax profitability for NFCs. The more rapid the rate of inflation, other things equal, the lower the $ROC_A(AT)$. Inflation, it appears, exercises its negative effect on profitability primarily through higher effective tax rates.

Note that in line 3 of panel A the sign of the coefficient on time is now positive, suggesting a slight upward trend in post-tax rates of returns for NFCs, but the coefficient is not significant. The trend is more strongly positive in equation 4 (but still not significant), in which a dummy variable picks up the low $ROC_A(AT)$s experienced in the 1970s.

We conclude that after-tax profitability for NFCs has shown neither a downward nor an upward trend in the postwar period. Variations around its average value can be explained, in large part, by changes in the level of economic activity and in the rate of inflation.[28]

Perhaps we should not search for long-term trends assuming an invariant profitability generating process. It could be that there has been a shift in that process; the economy of the 1970s and the determinants of profitability may be fundamentally different from before. The poor profitability record of the last decade is not fully explained by a slack economy and a brisk inflation. The dummy variable in equation 4 of panel A indicates that the ROC(AT)s for NFCs were 1.3 percentage points lower than they would have been in the years 1947–69, even after adjustments for inflation and the rate of change of GNP. But the coefficient of the dummy variable is not statistically significant.

Table 2–6
Regression Analysis of the After-Tax Rate of Return on Capital for NFCs, MCs, and NMCs 1947–81

Equation	Constant Term	Time	Independent Variables — Level of Economic Activity[a]	Inflation[b]	Dummy[c]	R^2
A. $ROC_A(AT) - NFC$						
1	7.54	−0.04				0.61
	(4.4)	(−0.6)				
2	6.34	−0.0	0.16[e]			0.73
	(3.3)	(−0.2)	(3.87)			
3	5.29	0.06	0.16[e]	−0.15[d]		0.77
	(3.3)	(0.82)	(4.31)	(−2.25)		
4	5.05	0.11	0.17[e]	−0.17[d]	−1.31	0.79
	(4.2)	(1.68)	(4.15)	(−2.41)	(−1.63)	
B. $ROC_W(AT) - NFC$						
1	5.42	−0.01				0.57
	(4.6)	(−0.18)				
2	4.55	0.01	0.12[e]			0.71
	(3.5)	(0.17)	(3.94)			
3	3.84	0.06	0.13[e]	−0.12[d]		0.75
	(3.5)	(1.28)	(4.40)	(−2.34)		
4	3.59	0.10	0.13[e]	−0.12[d]	−0.96	0.77
	(4.1)	(2.12)	(4.26)	(−2.46)	(−1.61)	
C. $ROC_A(AT) - MC$						
1	10.49	−0.16				0.67
	(4.5)	(−1.59)				
2	8.53	−0.12	0.27[e]			0.83
	(3.1)	(−1.12)	(5.45)			
3	7.22	−0.03	0.29[e]	−0.17[d]		0.85
	(3.4)	(−0.34)	(5.83)	(−2.07)		
4	6.71	0.04	0.29[e]	−0.20[d]	−1.74	0.86
	(4.2)	(0.49)	(5.68)	(−2.26)	(−1.69)	
D. $ROC_A(AT) - NMC$						
1	5.45	0.04				0.64
	(4.14)	(0.77)				
2	4.89	0.06	0.08			0.68
	(3.6)	(0.97)	(1.99)			
3	4.13	0.12[d]	0.09[d]	−0.15[d]		0.73
	(3.4)	(2.07)	(2.34)	(−2.27)		
4	3.91	0.16[e]	0.08[d]	−0.16[d]	−1.12	0.75
	(4.1)	(2.89)	(2.20)	(−2.36)	(−1.51)	

Note: t statistics in parentheses.
[a]Annual percentage change in real GNP.
[b]Annual percentage in PCE deflator.
[c]Zero for all years 1947–69, and one in every year from 1970 through 1981.
[d]Significant at 5 percent level.
[e]Significant at 1 percent level.
Regressions fitted by Cochrane-Orcutt method to correct for autocorrelation.

Panel B presents our regression results for the rate of return for NFCs measured on the augmented base—the $ROC_W(AT)$. The story is much the same as for $ROC_A(AT)$, and requires no additional discussion.

The four equations in panel C explain the $ROC_A(AT)$ for the manufacturing sector. Essentially the same picture emerges as for NFCs. However, $ROC_A(AT)$ for manufacturing is considerably more responsive to the rate of growth of GNP than its NFC counterpart. Also our equation has greater explanatory power (R^2) for MCs than for NFCs.

Finally, in panel D we present the results for NMCs, once again cautioning that the estimates for this sector are less reliable than for the other two. NMCs experienced a statistically significant rising trend in profitability. Both change in GNP and inflation affected NMC profitability in the same way as for MCs and NFCs, but the change in GNP was not as strong a determinant for NMCs as for MCs.

The dummy variables in all four panels of table 2–6 have negative coefficients. This tells us that the 1970s was a low profitability period. The coefficients are not significant, but even if they were, it would not prove a permanent downward shift in profitability. We could have fitted dummy variables to other subperiods—the 1960s, for example—and no doubt would have found significant coefficients, particularly as the periods of abnormally low or high rates of return can be picked by hindsight. But none of these previous episodes was a permanent shift.

Our equations explaining ROC are useful, a sort of multi-dimensional scatter diagram, but they are crude. After-tax profitability responds to more than inflation and the growth of GNP. At least some of these omitted variables could have been unfavorable in the 1970s. We have no way of knowing whether they will continue to be.

We conclude that the evidence does not support the hypothesis of a declining trend in corporate profitability after tax in the postwar period, but we admit our ignorance of the reasons for the corporate sector's poor profitability in the 1970s.

A similar exercise, but with somewhat dissimilar results, is summarized in table 2–7, which gives the regression results for before-tax profitability. In panel A, the significant declining time trend in equation 1 disappears when we add additional variables. The same happens with the equations for the $ROC_W(BT)$. But in panel C, a significant negative trend persists for manufacturing.

We conclude, then, that for the manufacturing sector rates of return before tax have declined secularly over time. But from the results in panels A, B, and D, there has been no declining trend in the $ROC(BT)$ for all nonfinancial corporations and for their nonmanufacturing sector.

In contrast with the $ROC(AT)$, inflation does not have an adverse

Table 2–7
Regression Analyses of Before-Tax Rates of Return on Capital for NFCS, MCs, and NMCs 1947–81

Equation	Constant Term	Time	Level of Economic Activity	Inflation	Dummy	R^2
A. $ROC_A(BT) - NFC$						
1	15.3	−0.18[a]				.68
	(9.69)	(−2.51)				
2	12.7	−0.13	0.36[b]			.91
	(6.2)	(−1.59)	(9.59)			
3	13.9	−0.20	0.36[b]	0.10		.92
	(4.6)	(−1.73)	(9.82)	(1.69)		
4	12.7	−0.11	0.35[b]	0.10	−1.64[b]	.93
	(5.9)	(−1.16)	(9.89)	(1.63)	(−2.16)	
B. $ROC_W(BT) - NFC$						
1	11.1	−0.10[a]				.58
	(10.1)	(−2.05)				
2	9.3	−0.07	0.28[b]			.89
	(6.4)	(−1.21)	(9.77)			
3	10.1	−0.12	0.27[b]	0.07		.90
	(5.1)	(−1.47)	(9.90)	(1.45)		
4	9.2	−0.05	0.27[b]	0.06	−1.27[a]	.92
	(6.2)	(−0.71)	(10.03)	(1.42)	(−2.24)	
C. $ROC_A(BT) - MC$						
1	20.4	−0.34[b]				.69
	(8.5)	(−3.05)				
2	16.4	−0.28[a]	0.63[b]			.92
	(5.6)	(−2.32)	(9.90)			
3	18.9	−0.42[a]	0.62[b]	0.19		.93
	(3.9)	(−2.22)	(10.27)	(1.84)		
4	16.8	−0.27	0.61[b]	0.18	−2.51	.94
	(4.7)	(−1.70)	(10.26)	(1.78)	(−1.99)	
D. $ROC_A(BT) - NMC$						
1	11.6	−0.06				.58
	(9.9)	(−1.19)				
2	10.2	−0.03	0.19[b]			.78
	(7.3)	(−0.54)	(5.41)			
3	10.4	−0.04	0.18[b]	0.02		.78
	(6.8)	(−0.61)	(5.29)	(0.34)		
4	9.9	−0.02	0.18[b]	0.01	−1.35	.80
	(9.6)	(−0.30)	(5.06)	(0.19)	(−1.92)	

Notes: t statistics in parentheses. Independent variables and statistical procedures are identical to those used in table 2–6.

[a]Significant at 5 percent level.

[b]Significant at 1 percent level.

effect on before-tax profitability. In fact, the sign on inflation is positive in the $ROC(BT)$ equations, although not significant. We conclude that inflation exercises its effect on rates of return through the tax levied on nominal profits.

Dummy variables for the 1970s are more strongly negative in table

2–7 than in table 2–6. Reservations about the interpretation of the dummy variable still apply, however.

Before-tax rates of return in manufacturing are more strongly affected by changes in GNP than in NMC as a whole. A given percentage change in GNP, on average, had over three times as great an effect on manufacturing as on nonmanufacturing rates of return.

In summary, then, we find a declining trend in before-tax rates of return over the period 1947–81 for the manufacturing sector, but not for all nonfinancial corporations or the nonmanufacturing sector. Of course, our findings depend on the periods examined. We feel the full postwar period to be the most appropriate for testing for long-run trends. Had we used data for a shorter run of years, however, say from 1961–81, we would have reported very different findings. We would under these conditions have found declining trends in after-tax returns for all but NMCs. And, in the after-tax equations, the rate of change of prices would not have exercised an effect on after-tax profitability. (See Appendix 2D for further discussion of this point.)

Returns on Net Worth

While both equity and debt finance corporate investment, stockholders are the "active" agents in the corporate investment decision; maximizing stockholder wealth is alleged to be the objective of corporate management. The last decade of poor equity returns (measured by dividends plus capital gains to stockholders) has raised a concern that corporations have failed to generate a sufficiently high return on stockholders' investment. We believe that rates of returns on assets, no matter how financed, are more relevant in assessing corporate performance. Equity rates of return are nevertheless of interest, particularly since in other chapters in this volume returns on equity are reported for a number of countries.

Stockholders own the assets of their company subject to the prior claims of lenders. Their net investment in the company consists therefore of corporate assets (which as before we will define to include the current value of plant, equipment, and inventories) minus the market value of corporate debt. The return on net worth is income generated for stockholders as a percentage of corporate net worth.

Stockholders' income equals inflation-adjusted profits, as reported in the NIPA, plus a "gearing adjustment" reflecting the decrease in the real value of debt caused by inflation. Lenders demand an inflation premium in interest payments to compensate for the expected loss in the real value of their claim. Stockholders pay the inflation premium but gain as the real value of the firms' liability falls. The inflation premium is (implicitly) subtracted from profits reported in the NIPA, but the offsetting gain is not added back. Our gearing adjustment corrects this error. This gearing adjustment is hardly a minor item. Consider the following mean rates of return on equity for NFCS.

| Period | Before Tax | | After Tax | |
	With Adjustment	Without	With Adjustment	Without
1946–81	15.0	13.9	8.2	7.1
1972–81	11.9	9.4	7.1	5.0

Without the gearing adjustment, average after-tax real rates of return to equity would be understated by one percentage point for the whole of the postwar period and two percentage points in the last decade.[29]

Table 2–8 shows real rates of return on equity, reflecting the gearing adjustment, for both NFCs and MCs. Their behavior over time roughly corresponds to patterns of returns calculated on total capital stock, particularly when after-tax rates of return are examined. The postwar

Table 2–8
Return to Net Worth for Nonfinancial and
Manufacturing Corporations

| | Nonfinancial | | Manufacturing | |
	$REG_A(BT)$	$REG_A(AT)$	$REG_A(BT)$	$REG_A(AT)$
1930	7.9	6.7		
1931	−3.1	−4.1		
1932	−9.6	−10.3		
1933	−7.6	−8.9		
1934	10.1	7.8		
1935	10.9	7.5		
1936	17.5	12.3		
1937	23.7	18.3		
1938	6.7	3.6		
1939	13.3	8.6		
1940	24.0	15.8		
1941	37.3	19.3		
1942	43.6	21.2		
1943	45.5	20.6		
1944	39.7	18.5		
1945	29.6	13.2		
1946	19.4	9.2		
1947	19.1	9.9		
1948	19.1	10.8	19.1	11.1
1949	15.2	9.0	16.5	10.5
1950	18.9	8.3	20.7	9.4
1951	19.1	7.7	20.8	8.0
1952	15.5	6.6	16.8	7.4
1953	14.8	5.9	16.6	6.8

Table 2–8 *(continued)*

	Nonfinancial		Manufacturing	
	REG$_A$(BT)	*REG$_A$(AT)*	*REG$_A$(BT)*	*REG$_A$(AT)*
1954	13.8	6.4	13.9	6.3
1955	17.5	8.4	18.7	9.0
1956	14.6	6.6	15.4	7.2
1957	13.3	6.4	13.9	6.8
1958	11.3	5.4	10.8	5.3
1959	14.7	7.3	16.1	8.2
1960	13.5	6.8	14.1	7.1
1961	13.7	6.9	13.8	7.0
1962	16.5	9.3	16.3	9.0
1963	18.1	10.3	18.4	10.3
1964	19.5	11.6	19.7	11.4
1965	21.7	13.3	23.2	13.8
1966	21.5	13.2	23.1	13.4
1967	18.2	11.2	19.5	11.7
1968	18.3	10.6	19.7	10.8
1969	15.7	8.8	16.2	8.5
1970	11.8	6.6	10.9	5.7
1971	12.9	7.6	13.4	7.4
1972	14.0	8.3	15.2	8.4
1973	14.8	8.6	15.8	8.4
1974	11.8	6.6	11.0	5.4
1975	11.3	7.1	10.3	5.9
1976	11.5	6.6	12.3	6.4
1977	13.1	8.0	13.5	7.2
1978	13.0	7.9	13.4	7.3
1979	11.2	6.7	10.8	5.9
1980	9.3	5.7	7.3	3.9
1981	8.9	5.7	6.6	3.8
Four-year averages				
1930–31	2.4	1.3		
1932–35	1.0	−1.0		
1936–39	15.3	10.7		
1940–43	37.6	19.2		
1944–47	27.0	12.7		
1948–49	17.2	9.9	17.8	10.8
1950–53	17.1	7.1	18.7	7.9
1954–57	14.8	7.0	15.5	7.3
1958–61	13.3	6.6	13.7	6.9
1962–65	19.0	11.1	19.4	11.1
1966–69	18.4	11.0	19.6	11.1
1970–73	13.4	7.8	13.8	7.5
1974–77	11.9	7.1	11.8	6.2
1978–81	10.6	6.5	9.5	5.3
Series average 1930–81				
Mean	16.1	8.6		
Standard deviation	10.1	5.8		
Series average 1948–81				
Mean	14.9	8.1	15.4	8.1
Standard deviation	3.3	2.1	4.1	2.4

Sources: appendix tables 2B2a, 2B2b, 2B3a, 2B3b, 2B4a, and 2B4b.

mean returns, however, were exactly the same for the two groups: 8.1 percent. Compare this figure to the mean rates of return generated by the common stocks of these firms:

Average Postwar Real Rate of Return	NFCs	MCs
On net worth (NIPA data)	8.1	8.1
Postwar average real rate of return to equity investors (capital market data)	8.3	9.0

The correspondence of the average returns to investors in corporate equity and the average return on net worth are almost exact for NFCs and close for MCs. But for these estimates net worth is defined as the excess of the value of plant, equipment, and inventory over the market value of debt. Had we included land and net monetary assets in the assets "owned" by stockholders, the average return on net worth would be about 6.5 percent. On the basis of the more inclusive definition, then, it appears that over the long pull equity investors earned more on their stock portfolios than corporations earned on net worth.

Because on either definition MCs and NFCs had the same average return, we are left with a question, however. MCs were, on average, more profitable than NFCs when returns on assets are examined. Why do we not see this extra profitability when returns to equity are examined? The reason is that MCs borrow less. What seems to have happened is this.

1. Assets held by MCs are riskier than those held by NFCs.
2. The rate of return on MC assets is, on average, correspondingly higher.
3. Because of this additional business risk, MCs borrow less.
4. Thus the sum of business and financial risk borne by equity investors is about the same for MCs and NFCs.
5. Therefore average equity rates of return are about the same for the two groups.

It appears that NFCs are less profitable than MCs when returns are calculated on firm value or total capital stock, but that NFCs "catch up" when equity returns are examined. But this simply reflects the NFCs' higher debt ratio. The extra average return earned by equity investors in NFCs is the reward for the extra risks created by financial leverage.

Searching for Trends in the Return on Net Worth

Tables 2–9 and 2–10 show the results of regression analyses of rates of return on net worth. Independent variables and statistical procedures are the same as used in tables 2–6 and 2–7. The return to equity before tax, *REG(BT)*, for NFCs shows no time trend, but is determined by the state of economic activity and inflation. This time inflation enters with a positive sign, since the magnitude of the gearing adjustment depends on the rate of inflation. Inflation, however, is not a significant variable for MCs. This probably reflects the lower debt ratio of the manufacturing sector.

For both NFCs and MCs, after-tax returns to equity, *REG(AT)*, show no trend. The inflation coefficients are small and insignificant for NFCs, but larger and close to significant for MCs. For NFCs the gains that stockholders enjoy at the expense of debt holders are to some extent canceled out by the higher taxes on the higher nominal corporate

Table 2–9
Regression Analyses of Rate of Return on Net Worth before Tax, with "Gearing Adjustment," NFCs, and MCs 1948–81

Equation	Constant Term	Time	Level of Economic Activity	Inflation	Dummy(70)	R^2
A. $REG_A(BT)$ – NFC						
1	17.51	−0.17				.57
	(6.21)	(−1.28)				
2	14.79	−0.13	0.50[b]			.85
	(4.16)	(−0.86)	(7.75)			
3	17.50	−0.29	0.47[b]	0.23[a]		.87
	(2.87)	(−1.25)	(7.89)	(2.26)		
4	14.95	−0.12	0.46[b]	0.22[a]	−2.61[a]	.89
	(3.45)	(−0.63)	(7.95)	(2.34)	(−2.19)	
B. $REG_A(BT)$ – MC						
1	19.55	−0.25				.53
	(6.37)	(−1.71)				
2	17.56	−0.27	0.68[b]			.88
	(3.74)	(−1.41)	(9.65)			
3	18.34	−0.31	0.67[b]	0.06		.88
	(3.50)	(−1.46)	(9.32)	(0.55)		
4	15.63	−0.11	0.65[b]	0.06	−3.32[a]	.90
	(4.08)	(−0.62)	(9.52)	(0.55)	(−2.35)	

Notes: *t* statistics in parentheses. Independent variables and statistical procedures are identical to those used in table 2–6.
[a]Significant at 5 percent level.
[b]Significant at 1 percent level.

Table 2–10

Regression Analyses of Rate of Return on Net Worth after Tax, with "Gearing Adjustment," NFCs, and MCs 1948–81

Equation	Constant Term	Time	Level of Economic Activity	Inflation	Dummy	R^2
A. $REG_A(AT) - NFC$						
1	7.29	0.01				.64
	(2.71)	(0.08)				
2	5.89	0.04	0.21[b]			.77
	(2.19)	(0.34)	(3.94)			
3	5.85	0.05	0.21[b]	−0.01		.77
	(2.17)	(0.37)	(3.84)	(−0.17)		
4	5.23	0.15	0.21[b]	−0.04	−2.27[a]	.79
	(3.10)	·(1.6)	(3.70)	(−0.44)	(−2.10)	
B. $REG_A(AT) - MC$						
1	9.09	−0.09				.61
	(3.18)	(−0.67)				
2	7.52	−0.06	0.27[b]			.77
	(2.42)	(−0.45)	(4.56)			
3	6.71	0.02	0.30[b]	−0.19		.79
	(2.98)	(0.23)	(4.93)	(−1.89)		
4	5.92	0.14	0.29[b]	−0.22[a]	−2.62[a]	.82
	(3.95)	(1.62)	(4.83)	(−2.18)	(−2.28)	

Notes: t statistics in parentheses. Independent variables and statistical procedures are identical to those used in table 2–6.

[a]Significant at 5 percent level.

[b]Significant at 1 percent level.

incomes, which are the result of inflation. For MCs, however, stock-holders' gains appear to have been almost completely offset by the extra tax created by inflation.

The Link between Real and Financial Markets

We have examined both physical and financial asset measures of NFC and MC profitability performance. We will now say what we can about the link between them. Over the long pull, we would expect the average real rate of return to corporate investors (R) and the corporations' rate of return on their physical assets (ROC) to be the same. Here are the long-run averages (1948–81) for each measure.

	Return to Investors (R)	Return on Capital Standard Base (ROC)	Return on Capital Augmented Base (ROC_W)
NFCs	5.3	6.8	5.2
MCs	8.1	7.7	—

For NFCs the averages match up well. The average *ROC* for the augmented base, 5.2 percent, is virtually equal to the rate of return to investors. The average *ROC* on the standard base is 1.6 percentage points higher, at 6.8 percent, but this "standard" *ROC* is less comparable to *R* than the *ROC* calculated on the augmented base: the market value of the firms' securities reflect the value of land and non-interest bearing monetary assets as well as plant, equipment and inventories.

The averages for MCs are not as comforting. The average "standard" *ROC*, at 7.7 percent, is 0.4 percentage points less than the average return to investors. The "augmented" *ROC*, if we had it, would be one to two percentage points lower still. Of course we are less confident of our profitability measures for MCs than for NFCs. Also we do not know whether this long run (1947–81) is long enough to insure convergence of the two measures of return. Nevertheless, we wish we knew why average returns were closer for NFCs than for MCs.

The Behavior of q, ROC, and the Cost of Capital

Further insights require a linking up of the physical and financial sectors. The most important issue here is how real rates of return on corporate investment have behaved relative to capital costs.

It is difficult to measure the opportunity cost of capital directly, because it is defined in terms of *expected* future returns on equity and debt securities. There is no simple way to infer these expectations from historical returns,[30] but estimates of *q* can provide useful insights into whether the rate of return on physical assets has declined *relative* to the cost of capital which we designate as ρ. If, for example, we observe a decline in *q*, we can infer that the ROC has declined relative to ρ.[31] And we can say this with reasonable confidence, since the market values of equity and debt incorporate investors' required rates of return and their expectations of future profitability.

We cannot use *q* to derive specific estimates of the rate of return on capital or the cost of capital for any particular year. But we can use it as a proxy for *changes* in the *spread* between present and anticipated profitability, on the one hand, and capital costs on the other.[32]

Values of *q* for NFCs and MCs were presented and discussed in an earlier section. Over the postwar period they averaged 0.9 for both NFCs and MCs, when capital stock is taken to be plant, equipment, and inventories only. We note again the gradual rise from well below 1 at the start of the period to substantially over 1 by the late 1960s, and the dramatic fall since.

Declining profitability would not depress stock and debt market values if capital costs declined proportionately; q does not depend solely on ROC, but on the ratio of ROC to ρ. Therefore we interpret the upward sweep in q in the first half of the postwar period as reflecting a rise in NFC and MC rates of return relative to their opportunity cost of capital, and the downward drift in the more recent years as indicating a decline in ROC relative to the opportunity cost of capital.

Can we go further and identify whether it was the ROC, the cost of capital, or both that were responsible for the observed changes in q? It is difficult to separate the effects of ROC and ρ on q, because we lack a good estimate of ρ. We can develop a simple rough measure, however. In table 2–11 we show ρ, the ratio of operating income to

Table 2–11

q and Capitalization Rate (ρ) for Nonfinancial and Manufacturing Corporations 1947–81

	Nonfinancial		Manufacturing	
	q_A	ρ	q_A	ρ
1947	0.9	7.6	—	—
1948	0.8	10.4	0.6	18.3
1949	0.7	12.0	0.6	19.3
1950	0.8	9.2	0.6	16.3
1951	0.7	8.4	0.6	14.3
1952	0.8	7.7	0.6	12.6
1953	0.7	7.5	0.6	11.7
1954	0.8	7.5	0.7	9.3
1955	1.0	7.2	0.9	10.5
1956	1.0	6.1	0.9	8.2
1957	0.9	6.2	0.8	8.6
1958	0.9	5.6	0.8	6.4
1959	1.1	5.8	1.1	7.5
1960	1.1	5.7	1.1	6.3
1961	1.2	5.2	1.1	6.1
1962	1.1	7.4	1.2	7.5
1963	1.3	6.6	1.2	8.2
1964	1.4	6.8	1.4	7.9
1965	1.4	7.7	1.6	8.0
1966	1.3	7.7	1.5	8.1
1967	1.4	6.7	1.4	7.4
1968	1.3	6.5	1.6	6.2
1969	1.1	6.4	1.4	5.5
1970	0.9	6.7	1.2	4.7
1971	1.1	6.2	1.1	5.9
1972	1.1	6.1	1.2	6.3
1973	1.0	6.5	1.0	7.1
1974	0.8	5.8	0.5	7.8
1975	0.7	7.9	0.5	10.3
1976	0.8	7.6	0.7	8.9
1977	0.7	9.5	0.6	10.5
1978	0.6	10.5	0.6	11.4
1979	0.6	10.1	0.5	10.5

Table 2-11 *(continued)*

	Nonfinancial		Manufacturing	
	q_A	ρ	q_A	ρ
1980	0.5	9.6	0.5	6.9
1981	0.5	10.2	0.5	8.3
Four-year averages				
1947–49	0.8	10.0	0.6	18.8
1950–53	0.7	8.2	0.6	13.7
1954–57	0.9	6.7	0.8	9.2
1958–61	1.1	5.6	1.0	6.6
1962–65	1.3	7.1	1.3	7.9
1966–69	1.3	6.8	1.5	6.8
1970–73	1.0	6.4	1.1	6.0
1974–77	0.7	7.7	0.6	9.2
1978–81	0.6	10.1	0.5	9.3
Series average				
Mean	0.9	7.7	0.9	9.3

Sources: appendix 2B, tables 2B2a, 2B2b, 2B3a, 2B3b, 2B4a, and 2B4b.

market value of equity and debt for NFCs and MCs from 1947 to 1981. We can think of this ratio as a generalized earnings-price ratio, where price is equal to the market value of debt and equity and earnings equals real operating income.

Figure 2–5 shows how ρ has changed over time for NFCs and MCs. Look at the plot for NFCs first. There are high values at the beginning and end of the series, and a trough of twenty years' relative stability, from the mid-1950s to the mid-1970s. During this period fluctuations of market value were more closely related to shifts in profitability than to shifts in the real cost of capital. Figure 2–6 shows the essentially parallel movements of q and *ROC* for NFCs during this period.

If we could stop history in 1976, we would have a neat story to tell for NFCs, in which investors capitalize real income at an essentially constant rate. Unfortunately ρ increased suddenly and dramatically in the late 1970s, so that the q for NFCs fell even faster than *ROC*. We have no solid explanation for this recent shift. There is no apparent increase in the risks borne by investors, for example—see the volatility measures presented in table 2–1. Neverthless, we can conclude that the recent low q's for NFCs reflect the failure of their capitalization rate or "cost of capital" to decline at an equal rate with after-tax profitability.

The capitalization rate for MC income has been generally higher than for NFC income. The higher level makes sense because MCs are riskier: the standard deviation of returns to investors is higher than for NFCs, and in addition MC income is more sensitive to the business cycle (see tables 2–6 and 2–7). The MC capitalization rate has also

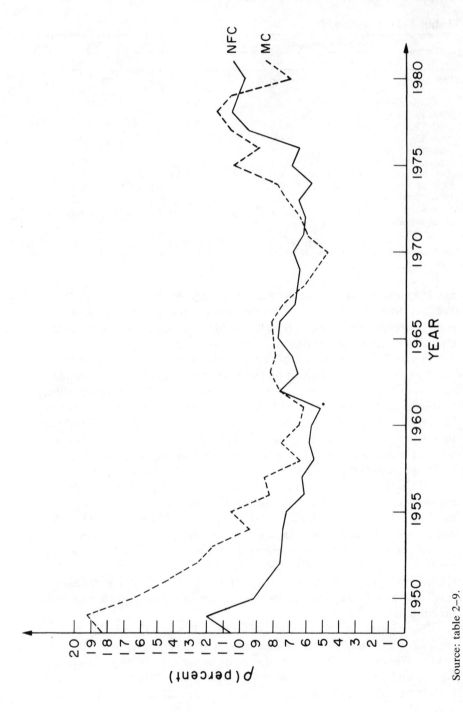

Source: table 2–9.

Figure 2–5. ρ, Capitalization Rates for Nonfinancial and Manufacturing Corporations 1948–81

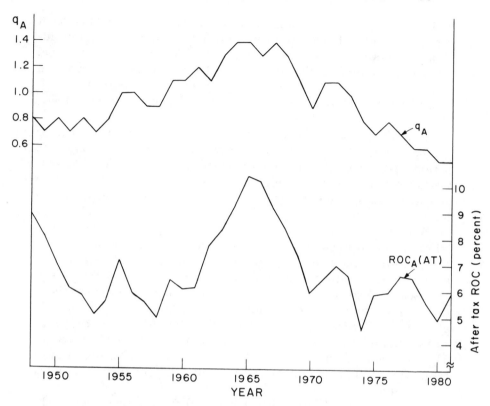

Source: q_A from table 2–2; $ROC_A(AT)$ from table 2–3.

Figure 2–6. The Relationship of $ROC_A(AT)$ and q_A for Nonfinancial Corporations

been less stable than the NFC rate, as figure 2–5 shows. The pattern of ρ over time is roughly the same for MCs as for NFCs, however.

Conclusion

There is no question that NFCs and MCs have fared poorly in the 1970s. This fact is obvious from the low real rates earned by investors in their securities. The poor performance is confirmed by declining operating profitability, a rising opportunity cost of capital in the last four years, and a decline in the ratio of the market value of corporate securities to the current replacement cost value of corporate assets.

Whether corporate performance in the most recent decade is viewed with alarm depends on what is viewed as normal. If we compare recent experience to the 1960s, recent performance is poor. The real profitability of NFCs and MCs was higher in the 1960s both absolutely and relative to the opportunity cost of capital. The problems encountered recently are not so bad, however, compared to the early postwar period. Compare the 1970s to the first twelve years of the postwar period (1948–59).

Over the postwar period we have found no evidence of a declining secular trend in NFC or MC rates of return on a before- or after-tax period. Had we limited our inquiry arbitrarily to the period 1961–81, we would have found declining trends for rates of return both before and after tax. We think the longer period is the more meaningful period for analysis, however.

Manufacturing seems to have taken a deeper profitability bath than NFCs in the aggregate. We have not analyzed the reasons for this, except to note the failure of effective rates of tax to fall as much for MCs as NFCs. But MCs also suffered a greater decline in $ROC(BT)$. One possible explanation is that profitability in manufacturing has been driven down by increasingly effective international competition—the economic resurgence of the European Common Market and Japan—to a greater degree than the other industries making up the NFC sector. This suspicion is reinforced by the rising trend in after-tax rates of return for NMCs and the inconsequential fall in their before-tax profitability.

Contrast the industries that compose manufacturing—chemicals, petroleum products, motor vehicles, primary metal products, fabricated metal products, and so on—with the rest of NFCs—wholesale and retail trade, transportation, communication, electric, gas and sanitary services, construction, and so on. The lists suggest a greater degree of international competition for the manufacturing sector than for non-manufacturing nonfinancial corporations, many of which are regulated and produce primarily for the home market.

Notes

1. Professors of Finance, Sloan School of Management, MIT. Parts of this chapter were adapted from Holland and Myers (1979). We are grateful to the Committee for Economic Development for permission to use this material. We also thank Lakshmi Shyam-Sunder for extremely competent research assistance, John Gorman of the Bureau of Economic Analysis, Department of Commerce, for generously supplying and explaining unpublished NIPA data on corporate profits and capital stock, and Stephen Taylor of the Board of Governors, Federal

Reserve Board, for a similar service with respect to the Federal Reserve Board *Flow of Funds* data.

Finally we want to thank Deans William F. Pounds and Abraham J. Siegel of the Sloan School of Management at the Massachusetts Institute of Technology for their continuing interest and support of our work.

2. We also report some results for nonmanufacturing corporations (NMCs), defined as all NFCs except MCs. Our estimates for NMCs are distinctly inferior, however, to those for the other two subsectors, and we do not analyze them in detail.

3. See Appendix table 2B3a below.

4. The stock market's current valuation of growth firms like Hewlett-Packard or Digital Equipment Corporation can only be explained by the present value of profitable future investment opportunities. Current earnings are insufficient to account for these firms' values, even if capitalized at high-grade bond yields.

5. For example, see Shiller (1981).

6. Earnings in this context are measured after taxes but before interest, since our portfolio contains debt as well as equity securities. We are using "earnings" loosely here: strictly speaking, we should subtract the present value of future investment outlays from the present value of the future earnings these outlays are expected to generate.

7. R can be expressed as a weighted average returns to creditors and stockholders.

$$R_t = R_t(D) \left(\frac{MV_t(D)}{MV_t} \right) + R_t(E) \left(\frac{MV_t(E)}{MV_t} \right)$$

where $R_t(D)$ = the rate of return earned in year t on a portfolio of *all* the net outstanding debt of NFCs. $R_t(D)$ includes interest receipts and capital gains or losses.

$Mv_t(D)$ = the market value of that debt portfolio at the start of year t.

$R_t(E)$ = the rate of return earned in year t on a portfolio of all the equity shares of all NFCs. $R_t(E)$ includes both dividends and capital gains.

$M_t(E)$ = the market value of that equity portfolio at the start of year t.

MV_t = the total market value of all NFC securities—$MV_t(D) + MV_t(E)$—at the start of year t.

Thus R_i is the rate of return earned on a portfolio of all securities issued by NFCs. It is the return to all bond and stockholders considered as a group.

8. R does not, however, measure the return earned by the government through taxation. In a sense MV understates the value to society of NFCs, because it does not include the present value of future taxes.

9. There is no reason for the past relative performance of stocks and bonds to affect firms' future capital investment decisions, for example.

10. Our procedures for estimating MV_t generally follow those developed by John Ciccolo (1975).

11. The real rate of return to investors *(R)* is equal to the nominal rate of return (that is, the annual return measured by the dollar magnitudes of each year) minus the percentage change in the Consumer Price Index.

12. We are *not* implying that there are meaningful trends or cycles in the rates of return shown in table 2–1. It is not possible to predict future Rs from the historical figures shown. It is only hindsight that allows us to interpret the history of rates of return.

13. Incidentally, this is a lower rate of return than over the period 1929–41, which encompasses the Great Depression and the lean economic years that followed. Over this period investors in NFCs earned an average real rate of return of 2.4 percent.

14. We use an average of starting and ending values of NFC capital stock and inventories. Thus capital stock *(CS)* for 1950 is a simple average of figures for the end of 1949 and the end of 1950. MV for NFCs is estimated as of mid-year—the end of the second quarter. This convention facilitates comparison to the rate of return measures presented below.

15. James Tobin has emphasized the importance of this ratio and employed it in theoretical and empirical work. See, for example, Tobin (1969).

16. There is one major surprise in the prewar data: q was higher in 1936 than it has been at any time since! And it fell below 1 only in the deepest Depression year. Overall q averaged 1.4 for 1929–41, which is higher than its average for the 1960s (1.2), the most profitable decade (except for the war years) of corporate earnings covered by our study. The immediate reasons for high q's in the 1930s is the actual shrinkage of the net replacement cost of capital stock in that period, combined with recovery in market value beginning in 1934. We have not identified a deeper reason. But the apparent magnitude of q warns against the characterization of all of the 1930s as a bleak time for all U.S. corporations.

17. Slippery issues are encountered as soon as one tries to specify exactly which assets should in principle go into the denominator of q. There is no reason for excluding assets just because they are intangible. But, as Fischer Black has pointed out to us, all of MV_t can in principle be traced to some tangible or intangible asset. Thus q might be interpreted as the ratio of the value of all assets to the value of tangible assets.

18. See Paddock (1981).

19. The comparison is not fully accurate, because current corporate accounting practice is not 100 percent historical cost accounting. Many firms use LIFO inventory accounting, for example.

20. Book income, however, may understate true *nominal* income because it does not include inflation-caused holding gains on fixed assets. If this source of nominal income exceeds the difference between historical and current cost depreciation, book income understates nominal income.

21. This is the top marginal rate of corporate tax, which applies to by far to the largest portion of corporate profits.

22. This calculation assumes that corporate earnings are sufficiently large to permit deduction of the full amount of net interest payments without reducing the firm's ability to utilize other deductions or credits. Recent research, however, suggests that this is not so, and therefore that our estimates overstate the degree to which the debt cushions the effective tax rate. See Joseph Cordes and Steven M. Sheffrin (1981, p. 427). Cordes and Sheffrin estimate (p. 429) that the marginal tax advantage of debt finance was 36 percent in 1976, well below the 46 percent implied by the marginal statutory rate.

23. See Appendix table 2B2a.

24. The sharp drop between 1980 and 1981 undoubtedly also reflects the accelerated capital recovery system and "safe harbor" leasing provisions of the Economic Recovery Tax Act of 1981.

25. We checked Hankin's finding by regressing the effective tax rate on the rate of inflation, the percentage change of GNP, time, and a dummy variable for the 1970s, using the general procedures described in the section entitled "Manufacturing Corporations." For the entire postwar period the tax rate was in all runs significantly positively associated with the rate of inflation, both for NFCs and MCs.

In a similar regression for the years 1961–81, however, there was no association between the effective tax rate and the rate of inflation. Since inflation was more brisk over the years 1961–81 we conclude that the heavier tax on higher nominal profits was outweighed by factors ameliorating the tax, for example, increased interest expenses and changes in the tax rules such as accelerated depreciation and the investment tax credit.

26. Early on in the postwar period, effective rates ran at about the same level for MCs and NMCs, but starting in 1962, a sharp difference developed, with NMCs enjoying the lower rate. For the period 1962–81, MCs had an average effective rate of 43.8 percent, while the average effective rates over this period for NMCs was 34.1 percent.

27. Since Nordhaus (1974), there have been numerous studies on trends in corporate rates of return. We have cited many of these in the references to this chapter. Despite varying definitions and methods, most of these studies draw on essentially the same data set and conclude that profitability in the 1970s has declined from the peak levels reached in the 1960s. Some have suggested that the decline is permanent and have called for remedial policy measures. See Nordhaus (1974) and Kopcke (1978, 1982), for example. Feldstein and Summers (1977) have argued that no conclusion can be reached without determining the causes of the documented decline. While Grimm (1982) and Nordhaus (1974) have modeled profits in relation to targeted mark-up rates, a complete structural model is lacking in the literature. Empirical work has explored the effects of labor costs, productivity, material prices, energy price shocks, and inflation. See for example, Feldstein and associates (1981) and Grimm (1982). With the exception of inflation, these factors do not appear to have significant explanatory power; consequently, most of the discussion has centered around the combined effects of inflation and taxation.

While many of the studies stress the distortionary effects of the taxation of nominal profits, some also recognize the countervailing effect of the tax deductibility of nominal interest payments. Hasbrouck's (1983) simulation, for example, highlights the possibility that, beyond a certain rate of inflation, the net tax burden may decline. Feldstein (1982) uses more comprehensive tax rates developed in Feldstein and others (1981), which include not only federal and state income taxes but also state and local property taxes as well as personal income and capital gains taxes, and argues that effective tax rates have risen. In our analysis we take account only of income taxes at the corporate level.

28. Our conclusions on NFCs are based on a more extensive statistical inquiry than appears in panel A of table 2–6. We tried other variables—rate of capacity utilization and lagged inflation—as substitutes for and in combination with those in the table and ended up with the same general results.

29. The gearing adjustment is less important for MCs because MCs relied less on debt finance. It became much more important for MCs, however, as their debt ratio increased steadily during the 1970s.

30. We believe Nordhaus (1977) is the first and one of the few

investigators who has attempted to measure and compare trends in the rate of return *and* the cost of capital. But his cost of capital measure is flawed by (1) the use of book, rather than market values, for debt and equity in his weighted average cost of capital measure, (2) an inappropriate adjustment for the tax shield provided by interest, (3) using a risk-free rate to measure the expected rate of return on corporate bonds, and (4) using the earnings-price ratio for the expected market rate of return on equity (see esp. p. 199). Assumption (4), or some equally simple rule of thumb, is perhaps unavoidable when dealing with aggregate data, but the first three assumptions can be improved upon.

31. The market value of a firm *(MV)* equals the capitalized value of the long-run average earnings from assets now in place (Y/ρ), plus the present value of growth opportunites *(PVGO)*. (In the derivation that follows Y is after-tax operating income.)

$$MV = \frac{Y}{\rho} + PVGO \tag{2.1}$$

The capitalization rate, ρ, is the equilibrium expected rate of return established in capital markets for this firm and others of equivalent risk. Earnings are equal to the return on capital times the real capital stock, *(CS)*. Thus $Y = ROC(CS)$, and

$$MV = CS\left(\frac{ROC}{\rho}\right) + PVGO \tag{2.2}$$

PVGO is the present value of future opportunities to invest at rates of return in excess of the cost of capital. Growth is worth nothing if expected *ROC* on future investment just equals ρ. If $ROC = \rho$ now and for the future, the market value of the firm just equals the value of its real capital. Thus q, the ratio of *MV* to *CS*, depends on the ratio of *ROC* to ρ:

$$q = \frac{MV}{CS} = \frac{ROC}{\rho} + \frac{PVGO}{CS} \tag{2.3}$$

where *PVGO* is a function of ROC/ρ and the rate of expansion of real capital stock.

Now, by identifying changes in q with changes in ROC/ρ, we are actually assuming a constant expected long-term rate of expansion in real capital stock. It is conceivable that q could vary as the result of changes in the expected rate of investment, even with *ROC* and ρ

constant. But we consider this unlikely, for two reasons. First, if ROC and ρ are constant, there is no obvious mechanism to account for changes in the real investment rate. If the real rate of investment increases as ROC/ρ increases, then that merely strengthens the relationship between q and ROC/ρ. Second, data presented below (figures 2–5 and 2–6) show that over a good part of the period 1947–81 fluctuations in MV can be largely accounted for by changes in ROC.

32. This approach does have its difficulties, however. There are problems in defining and measuring real capital, and in estimating market values. These problems are likely be particularly severe in cross-sectional comparisons for industrial breakdowns finer than MCs or NFCs. There is little meaning in comparing the qs of the drug and steel industries, for example, since so much of the drug industry's assets do not show on balance sheets. (Comparisons of these industries' ROCs would be just as suspect—perhaps more so). On the other hand, biases in estimating CS or MV are not likely to be volatile over time.

References

Board of Governors of the Federal Reserve System. *Balance Sheets for the U.S. Economy, 1945–81,* October 1982.

Brainard, W.C.; Shoven, J.B.; and Weiss, L. "The Financial Valuation of the Return to Capital." *Brookings Papers on Economic Activity* (Washington, D.C.: The Brookings Institution) 2 (1980):453–502.

Bulow, J. and Shoven, J. "Inflation, Corporate Profits and the Rate of Return to Capital." *Inflation: Causes and Effects.* Robert Hall, ed. Chicago: University of Chicago Press, 1982, pp. 233–59.

Chirinko, R. "The Not-So-Conventional Wisdom Concerning Taxes, Inflation and Capital Formation." *Proceedings of the Seventy-fifth Annual Conference on Taxation.* Columbus, Ohio: National Tax Association–Tax Institute of America, 1983, pp. 272–81.

Ciccolo, J. "Four Essays on Monetary Policy." Unpublished Ph.D. Dissertaton, Yale University, 1975.

Coen, R.M. "Depreciation, Profits and Rates of Return in Manufacturing Industries." Unpublished paper prepared for the Office of Tax Analysis, U.S. Treasury Department, April 1975.

Dausman, J.F. "Corporate Manufacturing Rates of Return, 1947–1976." Unpublished M.S. Dissertation, MIT, 1978.

Economic Report of the President. Washington, D.C.: U.S. Government Printing Office, January 1977 and January 1983.

Feldstein, M. "Inflation, Tax Rules and Investment: Some Econometric Evidence." *Econometrica* 50, no. 4 (July 1982):825–62.

Feldstein, M; Poterba, H.; and Dicks-Mireaux, L. "The Effective Tax Rate and the Pretax Rate of Return." National Bureau of Economic Research Working Paper, no. 740, August 1981.

Feldstein, M., and Summers, L. "Is the Rate of Profit Falling?" *Brookings Papers on Economic Activity* (Washington, D.C.: The Brookings Institution) 1 (1977):211–28.

———. "Inflation and the Taxation of Capital Income in the Corporate Sector." *National Tax Journal* 32 (1979):445–70.

Fellner, W. "Corporate Asset-Liability Decisions in View of the Low Market Valuation of Equity." *Contemporary Economic Problems, 1980.* Washington, D.C.: American Enterprise Institute for Public Policy Research, 1980, pp. 77–102.

Friend, I., and Hasbrouck, J. "The Impact of Inflation upon the Profitability and Valuation of U.S. Corporations." *Proceedings of the Conference on Savings, Investment and Capital Markets in an Inflationary Environment.* G. Szego and M. Sarnat, eds. Cambridge, Mass.: Ballinger, 1982.

Fullerton, D. "Which Effective Tax Rate?" National Bureau of Economic Research Working Paper, no. 1123, May 1983.

Goldsmith, R.W. "The Position of Institutional Investors and of Corporate Stock in the National Balance Sheets and the Flow of Funds Accounts of the United States of America, 1952–1968." *Institutional Investors and Corporate Stock.* R.W. Goldsmith, ed. New York: National Bureau of Economic Research, 1973.

Gonedes, N. "Evidence of 'Tax Effects' of Inflation under Historical Cost Accounting Methods." *Journal of Business,* April 1981.

Grimm, B.T. "Domestic Nonfinancial Corporate Profits." *Survey of Current Business.* Washington, D.C.: Bureau of Economic Analysis, U.S. Department of Commerce, January 1982, pp. 30–42.

Hankin, R. "The Impact of Inflation on Corporate Profitability." Unpublished S.B. Thesis, MIT, 1977.

Hasbrouck, J. "The Impact of Inflation upon Corporate Taxation." *National Tax Journal* 36, no. 1 (March 1983):65–81.

Hill, T.P. *Profits and Rates of Return.* Paris: Organization for Economic Cooperation and Development, 1979.

Holland, D.M., and Myers, S.C. "Trends in Corporate Profitability and Capital Costs." *The Nation's Capital Needs: Three Studies.* R. Lindsay, ed. Washington, D.C.: Committee on Economic Development, 1979, pp. 103–88.

———. "Profitability and Capital Costs for Manufacturing Corporations and All Nonfinancial Corporations." *American Economic Review Papers and Proceedings* 70 (1981):320–25.

Ibbotson, R., and Sinquefield, R. *Stocks, Bonds, Bills and Inflation:*

The Past and the Future. Charlottesville, Va.: Financial Analysts Research Foundation, 1982.

King, M., and Fullerton, D. "The Taxation of Income from Capital: A Comparative Study of the U.S., U.K., Sweden and West Germany—Comparisons of Effective Tax Rates." National Bureau of Economic Research Working Paper, no. 1073, February 1983.

Kopcke, R.W. "The Decline in Corporate Profitability." *New England Economic Review* (Boston: Federal Reserve Bank of Boston), May–June 1978, pp. 36–56.

———. "The Continuing Decline in Corporate Profitability and Stock Prices." *New England Economic Review* (Boston: Federal Reserve Bank of Boston), July–August 1982, pp. 5–17.

Liebling, H. *U.S. Corporate Profitability and Capital Formation: Are Rates of Return Sufficient?* New York: Pergamon Press, 1980.

Miller, M.H., and Modigliani, F. "Dividend Policy, Growth and the Valuation of Shares." *Journal of Business* 34 (1961):411–33.

Musgrave, J.C. "Fixed Nonresidential Business Capital in the United States, 1925–75." *Survey of Current Business,* April 1976, pp. 49–50.

Nordhaus, W.D. "The Falling Share of Profits." *Brookings Papers on Economic Activity* (Washington, D.C.: The Brookings Institution) 2 (1974):169–308.

Paddock, J. "Growth Opportunities and Corporate Investment Theory in Efficient Financial Markets." Alfred P. Sloan School of Management Working Paper, no. 1246–81, MIT, October 1981.

Scanlon, M. "Postwar Trends in Corporate Rates of Return." *Public Policy and Capital Formation* (Washington, D.C.: Board of Governors of the Federal Reserve System), April 1981, pp. 75–87.

Shiller, R. "Do Stock Prices Move Too Much to Be Justified by Subsequent Changes in Dividends?" *American Economic Review* 71, no. 2 (June 1981).

Tobin, J. "A General Equilibrium Approach to Monetary Policy." *Journal of Money, Credit and Banking* 1 (1969):15–29.

Tobin, J., and Brainard, W.C. "Pitfalls in Financial Model Building." *American Economic Review* 58 (1968):99–122.

U.S. Department of Commerce, Bureau of Economic Analysis. *National Income and Product Accounts of the United States, 1929–76. Supplement to Survey of Current Business,* September 1981.

———. *Survey of Current Business,* July and October 1982.

———. *Fixed Reproducible Tangible Wealth in the United States, 1925–79.* Washington, D.C., 1982.

Appendix 2A
Estimating Operating Income for Manufacturing Corporations

This appendix explains how we obtained before- and after-tax operating incomes for manufacturing corporations. The goal was to obtain figures comparable to those published in the National Income and Product Accounts (NIPA) for all nonfinancial corporations (NFCs). Therefore, we wanted income on an establishment basis—that is, income attributed to manufacturing establishments, not manufacturing companies. Manufacturing companies often have activities outside manufacturing. Also, companies classified outside of manufacturing may do some manufacturing on the side. Figures derived for establishments therefore reflect manufacturing activity more purely. Capital stock figures for manufacturing are for establishments.

We faced two major obstacles. First, many of the building blocks for operating income are available only for manufacturing companies. Second, no capital consumption adjustments were available for either manufacturing companies or establishments.

Table 2A1 summarizes how we circumvented these difficulties. Look first at the left-hand column headed "Variable," which shows the figures we need. We start with book (that is, historical cost) income, after interest but before taxes (BY). An inventory valuation adjustment *(IVA)* is *added* to remove inventory profits. (Note: Positive inventory profits imply a negative *IVA*.) Then a capital consumption adjustment *(CCADJ)* is added to adjust for the excess of tax return historical cost depreciation over estimated economic depreciation. (Economic depreciation is expressed in current dollars. When it exceeds tax return historical cost depreciation, as it has during most of the 1970s, *CCADJ* is negative. Adding it reduces book income.) Next, interest *(INT)* is added back to obtain before-tax operating income (YBT). Finally, income taxes *(TAX)* are subtracted to give after-tax operating income *(YAT)*.

None of these variables is directly available for manufacturing establishments. The figures that are available are not precisely the ones we want. *BY, IVA, INT,* and *TAX* are published for manufacturing companies. We now examine table 2A1 line by line.

1. The NIPA do give "profit-type return" for manufacturing establishments. This figures includes inventory profits and it covers all

Table 2A1
Calculating Operating Income for Manufacturing Corporations on an Establishment Basis

Variable	Symbol	Procedure[a]
(1) Book income, after interest but before tax[b]	BY	= Profit-type return for all manufacturing (after interest, incorporating IVA but not capital consumption adjustment) − IVA for all manufacturing − Profit-type return for noncorporate manufacturing
(2) Plus: Inventory valuation adjustment[b]	+ IVA	= IVA, company basis, for manufacturing corporations $\left(\dfrac{BY + \text{interest } (INT) \text{ from } (4)}{BY,\ \text{company} + \text{interest, company}\ \text{basis} \quad \text{basis}}\right)$
(3) Plus: capital consumption adjustment	+ $CCADJ$	= $\left(\begin{array}{l}\text{Capital consumption allowance} \\ (CCALL),\ \text{all manufacturing} - CCALL,\ \text{noncorporate} \\ \text{manufacturing}\end{array}\right) \times \dfrac{CCADJ \text{ for all NFC}}{CCALL \text{ with } CCADJ - CCADJ \text{ for all NFCs}}$
(4) Plus: interest[b]	+ INT	= Interest, company basis $\left(\dfrac{BY + INT - \text{Tax from } (5)}{BY,\ \text{company} + INT,\ \text{company} - \text{Tax, company}\ \text{basis} \quad \text{basis} \quad \text{basis}}\right)$
(5) Equals: operating income before tax	= YBT	= $BY + IVA + CCADJ + INT$
(6) Less: tax[b]	− TAX	= Tax, company basis $\left(\dfrac{BY}{BY,\ \text{company basis}}\right)$
(7) Equals: operating income after tax	= YAT	= $YBT - TAX$

[a] All variables on establishment basis unless otherwise noted.
[b] Directly available on a company basis.

manufacturing, not just corporations, but book income comparable to BY is given for noncorporate manufacturing.

Thus, we calculate BY by first reversing the inventory valuation adjustment. That is, the IVA for all manufacturing is subtracted, thus adding inventory profits back to "profit-type return." Then the profit-type return for noncorporate manufacturing is subtracted. The result is book income for corporate manufacturing establishments.

2. IVA is given for manufacturing *companies*. We assumed that the IVA for establishments was the same proportion of book income before interest and taxes, that is, of $BY + INT$, as for companies. Note that INT for establishments is calculated in line 4.

3. The NIPA capital cost adjustment adjusts tax return historical cost depreciation in two ways: (a) to bring tax return depreciation allowances, which reflect an accelerated pattern of writeoffs, into conformity with the historical cost basis equivalent of economic depreciation; and (b) to convert the historical cost equivalent of economic depreciation to a replacement cost basis. The sum of (a) and (b), therefore adjusts tax return depreciation to real economic depreciation.

The adjustment under (a) is usually a subtraction from tax return depreciation. The adjustment under (b) is usually an addition to economic depreciation at historical cost. When (a) exceeds (b), as in the 1960s, the sign of the capital consumption adjustment is positive; adding it back adjusts income for the excess of tax return depreciation over "true" depreciation. When, as since 1974, (b) exceeds (a) by a sufficient margin to make the sign of the capital consumption adjustment negative, adding the capital consumption adjustment corrects income for the excess of "true" depreciation over tax return depreciation.

The NIPA contain no capital consumption adjustment for manufacturing. We are only given the capital consumption allowance $(CCALL)$, which is historical cost depreciation from tax records. We were forced to assume that the ratio of $CCADJ$ to $CCALL$ was the same for manufacturing as for all NFCs. This is an extremely strong assumption.

4. Companies, not establishments, pay interest, but we allocated a fraction of company interest to establishments. The fraction is based on book income after taxes but before interest $(BY - TAX + INT)$ for companies and establishments. (The same ratio was used later in estimating market values to allocate company dividends to establishments.) Note that TAX is calculated in line 7.

5. YBT equals $BY + IVA + CCADJ + INT$.

6. A fraction of corporate taxes is allocated to establishments. The fraction is based on taxable book income, that is, BY, for establishments and companies.

Table 2A2
Calculating Operating Income for Manufacturing Corporations—
Illustration Using Data for 1967
(figures in billions of dollars)

Variable	Nonfinancial Corporations	Manufacturing Corporations
(1) BY	55.2	$34.2 = 35.2^d - (-0.8)^e - 1.8^f$
(2) IVA	-1.6	$-.7 = -.8\left(\dfrac{34.2 + 1.9^a}{39.3^g + 2.2^h}\right)$
(3) $CCADJ$	4.0	$2.0 = (18.1^i - 0.4^j)\left(\dfrac{4.0^k}{38.9^l - 4.0}\right)$
(4) INT	8.7	$1.9 = 2.2\left(\dfrac{34.2 + 1.9 - 14.5^b}{39.3 + 2.2 - 16.6^m}\right)$
(5) YBT	66.3	37.5^c
(6) TAX	27.7	$14.5 = 16.6\left(\dfrac{34.2}{39.3}\right)$
(7) YAT	38.6	23.0

Sources: all National Income and Product Account (NIPA) references relate to tabulations published in the *Survey of Current Business,* July 1982, for recent years and in the *National Income and Product Accounts of the United States, 1929–76, Statistical Tables,* for earlier years, except for d and i, which are unpublished and were obtained from the Bureau of Economic Analysis, Department of Commerce.
[a]From line (4).
[b]From line (6).
[c]Column does not add up exactly because of rounding.
[d]NIPA GDP by sector or industry of origin.
[e]NIPA table 6.18A lines 5 and 18.
[f]NIPA table 6.16A line 5.
[g]NIPA table 6.21A line 13/12.
[h]NIPA table 6.19A line 6.
[i]NIPA GDP by sector or industry of origin.
[j]NIPA table 6.17A line 7.
[k]NIPA table 1.13 line 16.
[l]NIPA table 1.13 line 20.
[m]NIPA table 6.22A line 13/12.

7. YAT equals $YBT - TAX$.

Table 2A2 illustrates the calculations using figures for 1967.

Appendix 2B
Basic Data

The notation in this appendix follows that of the common glossary appearing at the end of the first chapter in this volume. In some sections of our chapter, however (notes 7 and 31 in particular), we used a more general notation that was more convenient for expository purposes.

Table 2B1
List of Symbols Used in Tables

Tables 2B2a and 2B2b

S_1: Market value of stock at end of period 1

DM_1: Market value of debt at end of period 1

MV_1: Market value of investors' holdings at end of period $1 = S_1 + DM_1$

K_M: DM_1/MV_1

Tables 2B3a and 2B3b

$B + E$: Fixed nonresidential plant, equipment, and structures

G: Inventories

A: $B + E + G$

L: Land

M: Net monetary assets = currency and demand deposits + trade
credit − trade debt

W: $A + L + M$.

Tables 2B4a and 2B4b

P = Inflation-adjusted profits

I = Net interest payments

Y = Operating income

T = Income taxes

Table 2B2a
Market Values of Equity and Debt for Nonfinancial
Corporations 1929–81
($ billions)

	$S_1{}^a$	$DM_1{}^b$	MV_1	$K_M{}^c$
1929	103.1	26.7	129.7	.21
1930	83.9	27.7	111.6	.24
1931	40.1	25.1	65.2	.39
1932	38.1	17.5	55.6	.31
1933	45.4	30.2	75.6	.40
1934	51.3	35.3	86.6	.41
1935	67.5	38.0	105.5	.36
1936	63.0	43.2	106.1	.41
1937	39.1	43.6	82.7	.53
1938	58.1	38.6	96.7	.40
1939	49.4	40.4	89.8	.45
1940	47.7	37.6	85.3	.44
1941	38.4	38.9	77.3	.50
1942	49.1	38.6	87.7	.44
1943	55.1	35.0	90.1	.39
1944	64.1	32.8	96.9	.34
1945	89.4	34.8	124.2	.28
1946	89.4	24.8	123.2	.20

Table 2B2a *(continued)*

($ billions)

	$S_1{}^a$	$DM_1{}^b$	MV_1	$K_M{}^c$
1947	79.5	26.4	105.9	.25
1948	64.6	25.8	90.3	.29
1949	68.3	34.7	102.9	.34
1950	82.9	31.3	114.1	.27
1951	103.5	34.8	138.3	.25
1952	119.6	40.6	160.2	.25
1953	107.8	41.1	148.9	.28
1954	137.3	54.3	191.6	.28
1955	170.2	48.4	218.6	.22
1956	200.9	49.1	250.1	.20
1957	177.9	54.3	232.3	.23
1958	256.9	65.4	322.3	.20
1959	285.2	67.9	353.6	.19
1960	292.8	79.7	372.5	.21
1961	345.5	89.1	434.6	.21
1962	284.6	105.6	390.2	.27
1963	357.7	110.3	467.9	.24
1964	418.9	117.9	536.9	.22
1965	503.1	136.3	640.3	.21
1966	422.9	142.9	565.8	.25
1967	533.2	146.8	680.0	.22
1968	648.1	168.3	816.4	.21
1969	549.1	182.9	732.0	.25
1970	549.8	211.9	761.7	.28
1971	594.7	235.9	830.6	.28
1972	725.6	272.4	998.0	.27
1973	547.1^d	314.6	861.8	.37
1974	360.6^d	325.1	685.7	.47
1975	635.5	317.2	952.8	.33
1976	755.7	340.2	1095.9	.31
1977	627.8	416.3	1044.1	.40
1978	680.1	415.5	1095.5	.38
1979	695.8	440.6	1136.4	.39
1980	947.2	442.6	1389.8	.32
1981	1053.9	408.0	1461.9	.28

[a]Net dividend payments by NFCs were capitalized by yields computed from the Center for Research in Security Prices, University of Chicago. Annual dividend payments were used from 1929 to 1945 and quarterly payments from 1945 to 1981. Both annual and quarterly dividend payments were obtained from U.S. Department of Commerce, Bureau of Economic Analysis (1981), *National Income and Product Accounts of the United States, 1929–76. Supplement to Survey of Current Business,* September; *Survey of Current Business,* July, 1982, table 1.13, line 31.

[b]Net interest paid by NFCs was capitalized at the BAA corporate bond rate quoted in *Moody's Industrial Manual.* Annual interest payments were used from 1929 to 1945 and quarterly payments from 1945 to 1981. Both annual and quarterly interest payments were obtained from *National Income and Product Accounts of the United States; Survey of Current Business,* July, 1982, table 1.13, line 35.

[c]Figure 2–1 plots averages of year-end values of K_M.

[d]We have strong reservations about this estimate. It is based on a figure for dividends that appears to be unduly low.

Table 2B2b
Market Value of Equity and Debt for Manufacturing
Corporations 1947–81
($ billions)

Year	$S_1{}^a$	$DM_1{}^b$	MV_1	$K_M{}^c$
1947	51.7	−1.3	50.4	−.02
48	40.3	−0.6	39.7	−.02
49	45.5	−0.7	44.8	−.02
1950	56.0	−4.7	51.2	−.09
51	63.6	−3.0	60.6	−.05
52	64.2	0.1	64.2	.00
53	61.9	0.1	62.0	.00
54	86.5	1.2	87.7	.01
55	111.1	−1.4	109.7	−.01
56	116.7	0.2	116.8	.00
57	96.4	2.7	99.1	.03
58	128.7	6.1	134.8	.05
59	158.7	6.4	165.1	.04
1960	148.7	5.9	154.6	.04
61	167.4	7.8	175.2	.04
62	160.0	9.7	169.7	.06
63	193.4	9.3	202.7	.05
64	235.5	11.8	247.3	.05
65	298.3	16.8	315.1	.05
66	248.4	25.2	273.6	.09
67	310.8	34.0	344.8	.10
68	350.5	37.2	387.7	.10
69	287.0	47.2	334.1	.14
1970	261.0	58.4	319.4	.18
71	283.5	63.8	347.3	.18
72	332.2	67.9	400.1	.17
73	211.6^d	80.5	292.1	.28
74	66.4^d	86.2	152.6	.56
75	246.8	82.7	329.5	.25
76	285.4	78.5	363.9	.22
77	256.5	96.4	352.9	.27
78	264.4	99.1	363.5	.27
79	250.9	103.6	354.5	.29
1980	330.5	104.9	435.5	.24
81	377.0	61.0	438.0	.14

[a]Net dividend payments by MCs were capitalized by dividend yields computed from the Center for Research in Security Prices, University of Chicago data. The methodology for estimating annual dividend payments for MCs is described in appendix 2A.

[b]Net interest payments by MCs were capitalized at the BAA industrial bond rate quoted in *Moody's Industrial Manual*. The methodology for estimating annual interest payments for MCs is described in appendix 2A.

[c]Figure 2–1 plots average of year-end values of K_M.

[d]We have strong reservations about this estimate. It is based on a figure for dividends that appears to be unduly low.

Table 2B3a
Net Capital Stock of Nonfinancial Corporations 1928–81:
Standard Case—Straight-Line Depreciation; Service Lives—
85 Percent of Bulletin F
(current $ billions)

	$B+E^a$	G^b	A^c	L^d	M^e	W^c
1928	63.7	22.6	86.3			
1929	63.7	23.6	87.3			
1930	60.8	20.6	81.4			
1931	54.3	17.2	71.5			
1932	48.6	14.4	63.0			
1933	47.0	15.7	62.7			
1934	46.7	16.5	63.2			
1935	46.3	17.0	63.3			
1936	48.4	19.2	67.6			
1937	50.8	20.6	71.4			
1938	49.7	18.8	68.5			
1939	49.6	20.3	69.9			
1940	52.2	21.8	74.0			
1941	57.9	27.9	85.8			
1942	61.6	29.9	91.5			
1943	62.4	30.5	92.9			
1944	63.6	29.9	93.5			
1945	69.7	29.3	99.0	30.1	24.6	153.7
1946	87.7	41.1	128.8	33.3	22.2	184.3
1947	109.1	48.7	157.8	36.4	25.9	220.1
1948	125.1	53.7	178.8	38.3	26.9	244.0
1949	131.7	49.3	181.0	39.8	27.5	248.3
1950	145.8	60.1	205.9	41.7	30.5	278.1
1951	162.3	69.7	232.0	44.4	34.5	310.9
1952	172.4	70.8	243.2	47.4	36.5	327.1
1953	182.4	72.6	255.0	48.7	35.8	339.5
1954	189.5	71.1	260.6	51.4	38.6	350.6
1955	206.5	78.5	285.0	55.3	40.5	380.8
1956	230.8	86.6	317.4	62.2	41.5	421.1
1957	247.0	88.5	335.5	66.4	41.6	443.5
1958	255.2	86.8	342.0	71.0	45.3	458.3
1959	263.8	92.9	356.7	76.9	44.6	478.2
1960	270.3	95.9	366.2	80.9	45.5	492.6
1961	276.7	98.9	375.6	85.0	51.0	511.6
1962	286.6	104.3	390.9	90.5	55.1	536.5
1963	297.3	110.6	407.9	89.5	52.5	549.9
1964	313.1	117.5	430.6	91.9	53.1	575.6
1965	338.5	128.2	466.7	97.0	54.4	618.1
1966	374.8	144.8	519.6	101.2	55.3	676.1
1967	409.0	157.2	566.2	105.5	58.6	730.3
1968	449.7	169.3	619.0	103.5	62.4	784.9
1969	502.5	187.9	690.4	108.0	69.7	868.1
1970	555.8	197.3	753.1	112.7	71.4	937.2
1971	599.2	207.9	807.1	111.5	70.4	989.0
1972	645.7	225.9	871.6	122.8	76.7	1071.1
1973	730.8	276.3	1007.1	136.8	78.0	1221.9
1974	906.4	354.1	1260.5	162.5	117.2	1540.2
1975	994.8	349.7	1344.5	171.3	122.8	1638.5

Table 2B3a *(continued)*
(current $ billions)

	$B + E^a$	G^b	A^c	L^d	M^e	W^c
1976	1070.2	398.0	1468.2	186.1	133.7	1788.0
1977	1192.5	431.1	1623.5	206.1	150.7	1980.3
1978	1336.2	496.5	1832.7	233.9	159.3	2225.9
1979	1522.0	587.6	2109.6	266.1	182.8	2558.5
1980	1723.0	651.0	2374.0	293.6	203.4	2871.0
1981	1930.7	699.4	2630.1	308.2	204.7	3143.0

[a]Net stock of fixed nonresidential equipment and structures from J.C. Musgrave, "Fixed Nonresidential Business Capital in the United States, 1925–75," *Survey of Current Business,* April 1976, pp. 49–50, table A2, and unpublished data supplied to us by J. Gorman, J. Musgrave, and G. Silverstein of the Bureau of Economic Analysis, Department of Commerce.

[b]Unpublished data supplied to us as in a above.

[c]In computations for tables in the text the average of the beginning and end of year values was used.

[d]From *Balance Sheets for the U.S. Economy, 1945–81,* October 1982, table 705, line 6.

[e]Ibid. *M* was defined as currency and demand deposits, line 9, plus trade credit, line 17, less trade debt, line 38.

Table 2B3b
Estimated Net Capital Stock of Manufacturing Corporations
1946–81: Standard Case Straight-Line Depreciation; Service
Lives 85 Percent of Bulletin F
(current $ billions)

Year	$B + E^a$	G^b	A^c
1946	30.8	24.1	54.9
47	40.4	28.4	68.8
48	46.6	31.5	78.1
49	48.1	28.1	76.2
1950	52.6	34.1	86.7
51	59.2	42.2	101.4
52	62.7	43.2	105.9
53	65.2	45.1	110.3
54	67.6	43.1	110.7
55	73.4	47.5	120.9
56	82.3	53.1	135.4
57	87.5	53.4	140.9
58	88.7	51.7	140.4
59	89.8	54.0	143.8
1960	90.6	54.8	145.4
61	91.7	56.0	147.7
62	93.8	59.1	152.9
63	96.9	61.2	158.1
64	101.8	65.1	166.9
65	110.7	70.1	180.8
66	124.8	80.2	205.0
67	138.9	87.0	225.9
68	151.9	93.4	245.3
69	169.5	103.1	272.6
1970	184.8	106.7	291.5
71	194.9	108.1	303.0
72	207.0	114.8	321.8
73	229.2	138.8	368.0
74	284.6	187.1	471.7
75	311.0	187.6	498.6
76	335.2	205.1	540.3
77	377.9	222.4	600.3
78	427.9	251.7	679.6
79	497.1	303.6	800.7
1980	573.1	339.4	912.5
81	649.3	362.9	1012.2

[a]Net stock of fixed nonresidential equipment and structures from J.C. Musgrave, "Fixed Nonresidential Business Capital in the United States, 1925–75," *Survey of Current Business,* April 1976, table A2, and from unpublished data supplied to us as in appendix 2B, table 2B3a note a.

[b]Unpublished data supplied to us as in note a above.

[c]In computations for tables in the text the average of beginning and end of year values was used.

Table 2B4a
Operating Income of Nonfinancial Corporations 1929–81:
Standard Case Straight-Line Depreciation;
Service Lives 85 Percent of Bulletin F
(current $ billions)

Year	P^a	I^b	Y^c	T^d	$Y - T$
1929	7.5	1.4	8.9	1.2	7.7
1930	5.2	1.6	6.8	0.7	6.1
1931	1.1	1.8	2.9	0.5	2.4
1932	−2.0	1.7	−0.3	0.3	−0.6
1933	−2.1	1.7	−0.4	0.5	−0.9
1934	0.5	1.6	2.1	0.7	1.4
1935	2.0	1.6	3.6	0.9	2.7
1936	3.8	1.6	5.4	1.3	4.1
1937	4.6	1.6	6.2	1.4	4.8
1938	2.6	1.5	4.1	0.9	3.2
1939	4.2	1.5	5.7	1.4	4.3
1940	7.4	1.4	8.8	2.7	6.1
1941	12.7	1.3	14.0	7.5	6.5
1942	17.7	1.3	19.0	11.2	7.8
1943	21.8	1.1	22.9	13.8	9.1
1944	21.6	1.0	22.6	12.6	10.0
1945	17.1	1.0	18.1	10.2	7.9
1946	13.8	0.7	14.5	8.6	5.9
1947	19.7	0.8	20.5	10.8	9.7
1948	25.6	0.9	26.5	11.8	14.7
1949	22.9	1.0	23.9	9.3	14.6
1950	29.6	0.9	30.5	16.9	13.6
1951	33.4	1.1	34.5	21.2	13.3
1952	30.2	1.2	31.4	17.8	13.6
1953	30.0	1.3	31.3	18.5	12.8
1954	28.6	1.5	30.1	15.6	14.5
1955	38.3	1.6	39.9	20.2	19.7
1956	35.9	1.7	37.6	20.1	17.5
1957	34.9	2.2	37.1	19.1	18.0
1958	30.2	2.7	32.9	16.2	16.7
1959	40.1	3.1	43.2	20.7	22.5
1960	37.4	3.5	40.9	19.2	21.7
1961	38.3	3.9	42.2	19.5	22.7
1962	45.6	4.5	50.1	20.6	29.5
1963	51.2	4.8	56.0	22.8	33.2
1964	57.7	5.3	63.0	24.0	39.0
1965	67.7	6.1	73.8	27.2	46.6
1966	72.2	7.4	79.6	29.5	50.1
1967	68.8	8.7	77.5	27.7	49.8
1968	73.3	10.1	83.4	33.4	50.0
1969	67.5	13.1	80.6	33.1	47.5
1970	52.7	17.0	69.7	27.0	42.7
1971	62.1	18.0	80.1	29.8	50.3
1972	72.7	19.1	91.8	33.6	58.2
1973	78.6	23.0	101.6	40.0	61.6
1974	63.6	29.6	93.2	42.0	51.2
1975	86.1	30.8	116.9	41.2	75.7
1976	107.3	29.5	136.8	52.6	84.2
1977	129.5	32.1	161.6	59.6	102.0
1978	142.1	36.9	179.0	66.9	112.1

Table 2B4a (*continued*)
(*current $ billions*)

Year	P^a	I^b	Y^c	T^d	$Y - T$
1979	134.7	43.9	178.6	69.2	109.4
1980	123.0	52.4	175.4	64.8	110.6
1981	145.6	62.5	208.1	63.3	144.8

[a]Corporate profits with inventory valuation and capital consumption adjustments from *National Income and Products Accounts of the United States; Survey of Current Business,* July, 1982, table 1.13, line 27.
[b]Net interest payments from ibid., table 1.13, line 35.
[c]Operating income = $P + I$.
[d]Profit tax liability from *National Income and Product Accounts of the United States; Survey of Current Business,* July, 1982, table 1.13, line 29.

Table 2B4b

Estimated Operating Income of Manufacturing Corporations 1947–81
(*current $ billions*)

Year	P^a	I^a	Y	T^a	$Y - T$
1947	11.5	−0.03	11.5	5.8	5.7
48	14.3	0.0	14.3	6.0	8.3
49	12.9	−0.02	12.8	4.7	8.1
1950	17.4	−0.1	17.3	9.5	7.8
51	20.6	−0.1	20.5	12.5	8.0
52	17.7	0.0	17.7	9.9	7.8
53	18.0	0.0	18.0	10.6	7.4
54	15.2	0.1	15.3	8.3	7.0
55	21.6	−0.04	21.6	11.2	10.4
56	19.8	0.0	19.8	10.4	9.4
57	19.0	0.1	19.1	9.8	9.3
58	14.6	0.2	14.9	7.5	7.4
59	21.8	0.3	22.0	10.8	11.2
1960	19.4	0.3	19.7	9.7	10.0
61	19.2	0.4	19.5	9.5	10.0
62	22.9	0.4	23.3	10.3	13.0
63	26.8	0.4	27.2	11.9	15.3
64	29.7	0.5	30.2	12.5	17.7
65	36.8	0.8	37.6	15.0	22.6
66	39.2	1.3	40.5	16.8	23.7
67	35.6	2.0	37.6	14.5	23.1
68	38.0	2.4	40.4	17.8	22.6
69	33.3	3.4	36.7	16.8	19.9
1970	22.6	4.8	27.4	12.0	15.4
71	28.9	4.8	33.7	14.1	19.6
72	35.1	5.0	40.1	16.7	23.4
73	38.4	6.1	44.5	19.9	24.6
74	28.8	7.6	36.4	18.9	17.5
75	34.8	7.7	42.5	17.7	24.8
76	49.8	7.1	56.9	25.9	31.0
77	60.0	7.8	67.8	30.4	37.4
78	65.8	8.0	73.8	32.8	41.0
79	60.2	9.0	69.2	31.6	37.6
1980	44.2	8.9	53.1	25.8	27.3
81	51.2	9.5	60.7	24.9	35.8

[a]The methodology for estimating P, I, and T for MCs is described in appendix 2A.

Appendix 2C
Alternative Estimates
of Rate of Return

We think that the *ROC* estimates discussed in this chapter are reasonable and pertinent measures of profitability. They are based on the income and capital stock estimates chosen by the Bureau of Economic Analysis as their "preferred" or "standard" set. But they are derived, of course, from specific assumptions about depreciation patterns and service lives, specifically straight-line depreciation and 85 percent of the asset lives given in Bulletin F of the Internal Revenue Service.

While these conventions are considered reasonable, and the income and capital series based on them are widely used in studies of profitability, other possibilities cannot be ruled out.

Recognizing this, the Bureau of Economic Analysis has developed a series of alternative estimates of the current replacement cost of plant and equipment and of inflation-adjusted corporate profits. From this group we have chosen two. One assumes the same asset life as the "standard" assumption (85 percent of Bulletin F) but double-declining balance rather than straight-line depreciation; the other, like the "standard" case, assumes straight-line depreciation, but a different pattern of service lives, namely, 100 percent of Bulletin F up to 1940, then gradual decline to 75 percent by 1960, and a continuance at 75 percent from 1960 on.

These variations in underlying assumptions provide different estimates for operating income and the plant and equipment component of corporate capital. For example, for 1977 (mid-year), the current value of NFC plant and equipment is $1,131 billion under the standard assumption, $913 billion with double-declining balance depreciation, and $1,056 billion under the assumption of a declining pattern of service lives. After-tax operating income in 1977 was $102, $95.4, and $95.3 billion respectively. The alternative measures of the *ROC* do not vary as much as these numbers would suggest, however. The denominator of the *ROC* includes inventories, which are the same under all three alternatives, and in the expanded definition it includes also land and net non−interest bearing monetary assets, which also are the same for all the alternatives. Furthermore, differences in the denominator and numerator tend to be offsetting—more accelerated depreciation will lead both to lower profits and lower value of plant and equipment. Consequently, the estimated *ROC*s differ only slightly for the three alternatives. For 1978, for example, the estimated $ROC_A(AT)$ is 6.5

Table 2C1
Return on Capital for Nonfinancial Corporations Using
Different Depreciation Rules
(ROC_A)

	"Standard"Method: Straight-Line Depreciation; 0.85 Bulletin F Lives		Double-Declining Balance Depreciation; 0.85F of Bulletin F Lives		Straight-Line Depreciation; Changing Lives over Time from Bulletin F to 0.75 of Bulletin F	
	BT	*AT*	*BT*	*AT*	*BT*	*AT*
1929	10.2	8.9	11.8	10.2	9.6	8.3
1930	8.1	7.2	9.2	8.3	7.6	6.8
1931	3.8	3.1	4.3	3.5	3.6	3.0
1932	-0.4	-0.9	-0.4	-0.9	-0.1	-0.5
1933	-0.6	-1.4	-0.4	-1.3	-0.4	-1.1
1934	3.3	2.2	4.6	3.2	3.1	2.1
1935	5.7	4.3	7.3	5.6	5.0	3.8
1936	8.2	6.3	10.6	8.2	7.4	5.6
1937	8.9	6.9	11.0	8.6	7.8	6.0
1938	5.9	4.6	7.3	5.7	5.2	4.1
1939	8.2	6.2	10.2	7.7	7.2	5.4
1940	12.2	8.5	14.9	10.4	10.8	7.5
1941	17.5	8.1	20.6	9.7	15.5	7.2
1942	21.4	8.8	25.0	10.4	19.1	7.9
1943	24.8	9.9	29.2	11.7	22.1	8.8
1944	24.3	10.7	28.7	12.8	21.3	9.5
1945	18.8	8.2	22.0	9.7	16.5	7.1
1946	12.7	5.2	14.6	5.9	11.3	4.6
1947	14.3	6.8	16.0	7.4	12.8	6.1
1948	15.7	8.7	17.5	9.5	14.2	7.9
1949	13.3	8.1	14.7	8.8	12.0	7.4
1950	15.8	7.0	17.6	7.6	14.3	6.4
1951	15.8	6.1	17.6	6.5	14.4	5.5
1952	13.2	5.7	14.7	6.1	12.1	5.2
1953	12.6	5.1	14.0	5.4	11.5	4.6
1954	11.7	5.6	12.9	6.0	10.6	5.0
1955	14.6	7.2	16.4	7.9	13.4	6.5
1956	12.4	5.8	13.9	6.2	11.4	5.1
1957	11.3	5.5	12.5	5.8	10.3	4.8
1958	9.7	4.9	10.7	5.2	8.8	4.3
1959	12.4	6.4	13.9	7.0	11.3	5.6
1960	11.3	6.0	12.7	6.5	10.3	5.2
1961	11.4	6.1	12.8	6.7	10.3	5.3
1962	13.1	7.7	14.8	8.5	12.1	6.8
1963	14.0	8.3	15.9	9.3	13.1	7.5
1964	15.0	9.3	17.0	10.3	14.1	8.5
1965	16.4	10.4	18.4	11.4	15.6	9.6
1966	16.1	10.2	17.8	11.0	15.3	9.4
1967	14.3	9.2	15.6	9.8	13.7	8.6
1968	14.1	8.4	15.4	8.9	13.6	7.9
1969	12.3	7.3	13.4	7.6	11.9	6.7
1970	9.7	5.9	10.4	6.1	9.3	5.4
1971	10.3	6.4	11.2	6.8	10.0	6.0
1972	10.9	6.9	12.1	7.5	10.8	6.7
1973	10.8	6.6	11.9	6.9	10.7	6.3

Table 2C1 *(continued)*   *(p 111)*

	"Standard" Method: Straight-Line Depreciation; 0.85 Bulletin F Lives		*Double-Declining Balance Depreciation; 0.85F of Bulletin F Lives*		*Straight-Line Depreciation; Changing Lives over Time from Bulletin F to 0.75 of Bulletin F*	
	BT	*AT*	*BT*	*AT*	*BT*	*AT*
1974	8.2	4.5	8.8	4.6	8.1	4.2
1975	9.0	5.8	9.8	6.1	8.9	5.6
1976	9.7	6.0	10.8	6.5	9.7	5.8
1977	10.5	6.6	11.7	7.2	10.6	6.5
1978	10.4	6.5	11.6	7.1	10.5	6.4
1979	9.1	5.6	10.1	6.0	9.2	5.5
1980	7.8	4.9	8.7	5.3	7.9	4.9
1981	8.3	5.8	9.3	6.4	8.5	5.9
Four-year averages						
1929–33	4.2	3.4	4.9	4.0	4.1	3.0
1934–37	6.5	4.9	8.4	6.4	5.8	4.4
1938–41	11.0	6.9	13.2	8.4	9.7	6.1
1942–45	22.3	9.4	26.2	11.1	19.8	8.3
1946–49	14.0	7.2	15.7	7.9	12.6	6.5
1950–53	14.3	6.0	16.0	6.4	13.1	5.4
1954–57	12.5	6.1	13.9	6.4	11.4	5.4
1958–61	11.2	5.9	12.5	6.4	10.7	5.1
1962–65	14.6	8.9	16.5	9.9	13.7	8.1
1966–69	14.2	8.8	15.6	9.3	13.6	8.1
1970–73	10.4	6.5	11.4	6.8	10.2	6.1
1974–77	9.4	5.7	10.3	6.1	9.3	5.5
1978–81	8.9	5.7	9.9	6.2	9.0	5.7
Series average 1929–81						
Mean	11.7	6.5	13.2	7.3	10.8	5.9
Standard deviation	4.9	2.4	5.7	2.7	4.4	2.1
Series average 1946–81						
Mean	12.2	6.7	13.5	7.3	11.4	6.2
Standard deviation	2.5	1.5	2.8	1.7	2.1	1.4

Source: U.S. Department of Commerce, Bureau of Economic Analysis, *Fixed Reproducible Tangible Wealth in the United States*, 1925–79, Washington, D.C., 1982; U.S. Department of Commerce, *Survey of Current Business*, October 1982.

percent under the standard method, 7.1 percent for double-declining balance assumption, and 6.4 percent for the changing depreciable lives assumption. See table 2C1.

Table 2C1 shows clearly that the general time pattern of profitability is the same under all three bases of estimation. Double-declining balance gives *ROC*s slightly higher than the standard assumption; changing depreciable lives gives *ROC*s slightly below the standard case. Since the standard case falls between the others, we felt justified in using the standard case as the primary data for our study.

Appendix 2D
Regression Analysis
of Rate of Return
on Capital

As explained in the text we felt that, in a search for trends, the longer the period covered by the data the better. Therefore we ran our regressions for ROCs over the whole of the postwar period. Our findings reported in the section of the text, entitled "Searching for Trends in Profitability," depend, of course, on this choice.

For many of the other countries included in this volume rates of return were measured over a shorter span of years, characteristically 1961–81. Had we limited our investigation to this period, we would have had a very different set of findings. As summarized in tables 2D1 and 2D2, we would have reported a declining trend in profitability. Time, alone or in conjunction with the other independent variables, is negative and significant for all ROCs with the sole exception of $ROC_A(AT)$ for NMCs.

One of the reasons, then, why different investigators reach disparate conclusions about the trend of profitability is that their studies cover different periods. To illustrate with reference to the chapters in this volume: for the four countries for which the rate of return data substantially cover the postwar period—Canada, Italy, Sweden, and the United States—the authors reached the conclusion that there was no declining trend in profitability. For most of the other countries that had estimates only for the last twenty years or so the characteristic finding was a declining trend in profitability.

There is another feature of the regression in table 2D2 worth noting. Inflation plays no explanatory role in after-tax rates of return. Yet inflation and presumably therefore the overtaxation of profits were more pronounced in 1961–81 than for 1948–81. But also more pronounced for 1961–81, apparently, were the factors that tended to ameliorate the corporate income tax burden, namely, the growing importance of interest relative to profits and various modifications of the tax rules from 1961 on, for example, accelerated depreciation, investment tax credits, and so on.

Table 2D1
Regression Analysis of Rate of Return on Capital before Tax for NFCs, MCs, and NMCs 1961–81
(ROC(BT))

Constant Term	Time	Level of Economic Activity[a]	Inflation[b]	Dummy[c]	R^2
Panel A—$ROC_A(BT)$ – NFCs					
16.7	– .46[e]	—	—	—	0.85
(12.9)	(–4.66)	—			
15.3	–0.42[e]	0.32[e]	—	—	0.93
(11.7)	(–4.64)	(4.7)	—	—	
15.1	–0.48[e]	0.37[e]	0.14	—	0.94
(9.9)	(–4.04)	(4.03)	(0.74)	—	
14.7	–0.27[e]	0.30[e]	0.02	–2.03[d]	0.95
(14.1)	(–2.45)	(3.36)	(0.13)	(–2.65)	
Panel B—$ROC_W(BT)$ – NFCs					
12.5	–0.30[e]	—	—	—	0.80
(13.1)	(–4.10)	—	—	—	
12.5	–0.27[e]	0.26[e]	—	—	0.92
(11.3)	(–4.08)	(5.05)	—	—	
11.2	–0.31[e]	0.28[e]	0.10	—	0.92
(10.1)	(–3.57)	(4.19)	(0.67)	—	
11.1	–0.17	0.24[e]	0.02	–1.43	0.94
(13.3)	(–2.03)	(3.64)	(0.13)	(2.48)	
Panel C—$ROC_A(BT)$ – MCs					
21.9	–0.78[e]	—	—	—	0.83
(10.1)	(–4.72)	—	—	—	
19.5	–0.73[e]	0.60[e]	—	—	0.93
(9.3)	(–5.02)	(5.49)	—	—	
19.2	–0.79[e]	0.65[e]	0.16	—	0.94
(7.9)	(–4.17)	(4.35)	(0.48)	—	
19.1	–0.54[d]	0.56[e]	0.01	–2.63	0.95
(9.5)	(–2.76)	(3.82)	(0.05)	(–1.98)	
Panel D—$ROC_A(BT)$ – NMCs					
13.3	–0.25[e]	—	—	—	0.81
(15.3)	(–3.74)	—	—	—	
12.6	–0.22[e]	0.15[d]	—	—	0.87
(12.4)	(–3.12)	(2.78)	—	—	
12.3	–0.27[d]	0.19[d]	0.12	—	0.88
(10.1)	(–2.81)	(2.61)	(0.78)	—	
12.1	–0.05	0.10	–0.05	–1.99[e]	0.91
(17.9)	(–0.59)	(1.33)	(–0.29)	(–3.51)	

Note: *t* statistics appear in parentheses under the coefficients.

[a] Annual percentage change in real GNP.

[b] Annual percentage change in PCE deflator.

[c] Zero for all years 1947–69, and one in every year from 1970 through 1981.

[d] Significant at 5 percent level.

[e] Significant at 1 percent level.

Table 2D2
Regression Analysis of Rate of Return on Capital after
Tax for NFCs, MCs, and NMCs 1961–81
(ROC(AT))

Constant Term	Time	Level of Economic Activity[a]	Inflation[b]	Dummy[c]	R^2
Panel A—$ROC_A(AT)$ – NFCs					
10.2	-0.27^e	—	—	—	0.78
(11.2)	(−3.83)	—	—	—	
9.2	-0.23^e	0.21^e	—	—	0.87
(9.8)	(−3.56)	(3.48)	—	—	
9.1	-0.25^d	0.22^d	0.03	—	0.87
(8.3)	(−2.64)	(2.64)	(0.18)	—	
8.9	−0.10	0.17	−0.06	−1.36	0.89
(10.2)	(−1.02)	(1.93)	(−0.33)	(−1.90)	
Panel B—$ROC_W(AT)$ – NFCs					
7.6	-0.17^e	—	—	—	0.71
(11.3)	(−3.27)	—	—	—	
6.8	-0.14^e	0.17^e	—	—	0.83
(9.8)	(−2.97)	(3.61)	—	—	
6.7	-0.15^d	0.17^e	0.02	—	0.83
(8.2)	(−2.14)	(2.68)	(0.12)	—	
6.6	−0.05	0.13	−0.05	−0.95	0.86
(9.8)	(−0.68)	(2.04)	(−0.32)	(−1.72)	
Panel C—$ROC_A(AT)$ – MCs					
12.9	-0.48^e	—	—	—	0.83
(9.4)	(−4.59)	—	—	—	
11.4	-0.43^e	0.34^e	—	—	0.92
(8.6)	(−4.78)	(4.49)	—	—	
11.4	-0.44^e	0.34^e	−0.01	—	0.92
(7.5)	(−3.49)	(3.23)	(−0.02)	—	
11.2	−0.29	0.29^d	−0.09	−1.45	0.93
(8.5)	(−2.08)	(2.67)	(−0.38)	(−1.49)	
Panel D—$ROC_A(AT)$ – NMCs					
8.5	-0.13^d	—	—	—	0.62
(12.3)	(−2.14)	—	—	—	
7.8	−0.11	0.12^d	—	—	0.70
(9.9)	(−1.93)	(2.12)	—	—	
7.7	−0.12	0.14	0.05	—	0.70
(7.9)	(−1.47)	(1.72)	(0.28)	—	
7.7	0.05	0.06	−0.12	-1.57^d	0.75
(10.5)	(0.60)	(0.68)	(−0.63)	(−2.64)	

Note: *t* statistics appear in parentheses under the coefficients.

[a] Annual percentage change in real GNP.

[b] Annual percentage change in PCE deflator.

[c] Zero for all years 1947–69, and one in every year from 1970 through 1981.

[d] Significant at 5 percent level.

[e] Significant at 1 percent level.

3 Measures of Business Performance—The Swedish Case

Lars Bertmar

Objectives and Major Conclusions

Like companies in many other industrialized countries, most of the evidence concerning Swedish industry indicates that the 1970s were a decade of poor profit performance. Many regard the mid-1960s as the starting point of a downward trend. This has raised concern for the consequences of the decline for industrial growth. The evidence suggests that decline in profitability goes hand in hand with declining growth, the main trade-off being changes in the equity ratio (the ratio between owners' equity and total assets). And a decreased equity ratio might in itself serve as a check to growth through its impact on financial risks (Bertmar and Molin, 1977). The need for increased profitability has therefore become an often heard argument in the Swedish economic and political debate. Arguments have also been raised, however, that the long-run profitability has not decreased and that the performance during the 1970s, viewed from a long-run perspective, should not necessarily be of great concern (Bergström and Sodersten, 1979).

The purpose of this essay is to bring some clarity to the simple question: how has Swedish industry fared up to the late 1970s? This question can, however, lead to many different research designs. Ours centers around the following two main aspects: (1) How has Swedish industry fared in recent years compared with earlier periods? If there has been a decline in profitability, is it from an earlier stable level (in which case the decline might be alarming) or is it from an extraordinarily high level, returning the profitability back to more normal levels (in which case the decline may be not so alarming)? (2) Is the result concerning performance sensitive to our choice of data, measures of performance, and sample of companies? What are the most valid measures of profitability and other related variables?

The second question represents the type of question that usually gains very little attention. It will, however, be given a dominant role in this report for two reasons: first, the debate lacks precision and any effort to structure the discussion seems worthwhile and second, this utilizes a comparative advantage the "Swedish case" has over many

117

other countries. A number of Swedish researchers (Bertmar, Molin, Forsgaardh, and Sodersten) have devoted considerable effort in recent years to develop data of high quality that permit more careful estimates of profitability.

Questions are answered for two types of economic units, business groups, and corporations. A business group is a group of companies linked together by ownership. Most often this takes the form of one parent company's owning one or more subsidiaries. The business group thus corresponds to the "economic entity." We will concentrate on public business groups where the parent company is listed on the Stockholm Exchange.

If the performance of Swedish industry is studied in terms of the performance of *business groups,* "Swedish" is interpreted as "Swedish-owned." Foreign subsidiaries will be included along with domestic corporations, while foreign-owned companies in Sweden (that is, subsidiaries of foreign parent companies) are excluded.

The second type of unit we will study is Swedish *corporations.* Here, "Swedish" denotes corporations with residence in Sweden, despite the fact that they might be subsidiaries to foreign companies. Accordingly, foreign subsidiaries of Swedish parent companies are excluded. The emphasis is thus on entities responsible for domestic production rather than entities with domestic ownership.

Two main types of measures will be used: *market rates of return,* that is, the returns earned on the portfolio of equity and debt instruments by investors in companies, and *company rates of return,* that is, the returns earned by companies on their capital. The former are based on market data and can thus only be constructed for entities for which market data can be found, that is, business groups. The latter are based on firm accounting data adjusted in a number of ways. They can be constructed for business groups *and* Swedish corporations.

Two types of market rates of return will be used, return on all investors' holdings (debt, *D,* and stock, *S*) and return on stocks. Both measures will be expressed in both nominal and real terms, the difference being the rate of inflation (measured as the change in the Consumer Price Index, *CP*). All market measures are expressed before investors' taxes. The terms "Market rate of return" and "Return to investors" (or "Investors' return") will be used interchangeably.

Several types of company rates of return will be used. They include rates of return on assets (all assets or only nonmonetary assets) and on owners' equity, and they are expressed before as well as after company taxes. All company rates of return are expressed in real terms except for some measures for business groups, where nominal figures are also given.

Most descriptions concern *aggregate figures* for business groups and corporations, respectively. Some measures based on figures for individual firms will also be given.

The periods covered in the report are determined by the data available. They will be:

Entity	Market Rates of Return	Company Rates of Return
Business groups	Stock: 1949–82 All investors' holdings: 1967–80	All measures: 1967–80
Corporations	—	Aggregate: 1951–78 Individual firms: 1966–79

Our main conclusions are the following:

1. By all standards, Swedish industry has fared poorly since the early 1960s. Decreasing profitability has been accompanied by decreasing equity ratios (the ratio between owners' equity and total assets). In the 1970s the decrease has also been coupled with an increase in the rate of inflation.

2. The turning point as described by company rates of return came in the early 1960s rather than in the mid-1960s, as has commonly been believed. The turning point for the return on investors' holdings of stocks occurred at about the same time.

3. The turning points marked an end of increasing profitability. The decline since then is thus not a decline from stable levels but back from a peak. Whether or not the decline is bigger than the previous increase becomes a question we cannot answer because of lack of data for the 1940s. The overall conclusion as to the question of a falling trend for the whole period from the early 1950s thus becomes: not proven. Even returning to old levels, however, does not mean returning to old conditions. The equity ratio has been lowered and the evidence suggests increased financial risks. The paired reduction in profitability and reduced equity ratio should be of great concern. Moreover, the period studied ends with a dramatic decline in profitability, down to levels never previously experienced during the period studied, that is, since the early 1950s.

4. Examination of the most carefully adjusted data available, which is generally for the larger corporations (more than 200 employees), suggests a more marked decline since the mid-1960s. (These are the larger manufacturing companies; we do not know whether it is also true of other kinds of firms, nor can we assert that the smaller firms have behaved like the larger ones.) The more pronounced decline in profitability, which shows up in aggregations

of data carefully developed for individual larger firms, also shows up in the median corporation. Further, behind the aggregate there are substantial differences among companies.

Measures of Performance

Before analyzing the empirical data, let us devote some attention to the important question of how performance—more specifically, rate of return—of companies should be measured. Should we use market data or should we compute rates of return from accounting figures?

The determination of market rates of return is a clear-cut problem in principle. Investors' return consists of two parts, namely the change in the market value of the stock and the debt (or either component if one wants to measure the return to stocks—RS— or debt separately) of the company, plus distributed income (dividends and interest).

In symbols, Return to investors for company i, period t, is:

$$R_{it} = ((MV_{i,t} - MV_{i,t-1}) + \omega_{i,t} + I_{i,t})/MV_{i,t-1},$$

where

$$
\begin{aligned}
R &= \text{Return to investors} \\
MV &= \text{Market value of stock and debt} \\
\omega &= \text{Dividends} \\
I &= \text{Interest payments}
\end{aligned}
$$

The obvious appeal of measuring performance from the investors' point of view, and thus utilizing market data, might lead to the conclusion that accounting data, that is, company rates of return, are of no value for measuring performance. For at least two reasons this is not true.

First, the fact that economic changes that cause sudden changes in market values are not immediately and fully reflected in accounting measures does not mean that they are never reflected. In the long run company rates of return and capital market rates of return tend to tell the same story. Company rates of return can thus be used as a long-run proxy for capital market measures. This is an important feature in a country like Sweden, where the majority of the firms are not traded publicly. It also makes it possible to distinguish between the performance of Swedish-owned companies and of domestic production—a very important distinction for an open economy like the Swedish.

Second, company rates of returns are focused on management's ability. Performance *ex post* from the investors' point of view can, somewhat simplified, be said to be the function of two main factors, (changes in) expectations of future income (or rather distributable cash flow) and investors' required rate of return. Company rates of return are based on realizable income (a specific form of company measure, that is, historical cost accounting, is based on realized, rather than realizable, income), which for specific periods on the average should coincide with earlier expectations (but disregards changes in future expectations that occurred during the period). Company rates of return are also based in the short run on the assumption of constant required rates of return and only gradually adapt to new long-run required rates.

In these respects, company rates of return can be viewed as a measure that, to a greater extent than investors' return, focuses on factors over which management is supposed to exercise some influence—the questions of when, where, and what concerning investment, production, pricing, distribution, and so on. This leaves the measure unaffected by short-run changes in expectations or in required rates of return—factors that do influence the market rate of return. For example, a change in the way stockholders are taxed or in the interest rate is (through a change in the required rate of return) reflected in the *ex post* investors' return but not in the company rates of return— thus leaving the measure of management's ability unaffected.

Empirical measures of company rates of return have, however, received a rather bad reputation for use in economic analysis. There are at least three reasons for this. The first is the frequent lack of understanding of how company rates of return should be constructed. Second, the company rates of return are often based on historical costs that might cause invalid descriptions. And third, there are few examples of valid descriptions of company rates of return in *real* terms.

We will try to bring some clarity to the construction of company rates of return. As a basis for discussion, refer to figure 3–1.[1] The figure describes the firm in terms of how the capital invested and the income earned can be structured. It also gives examples of how different company rates of return can be constructed. The income concepts and the rates of return are in nominal terms.

The first principle to keep in mind is that of matching income and capital concepts. If a rate of return on a particular definition of capital is sought, an income concept should be used that includes the income earned by capital so defined. For example, suppose we are interested in the rate of return earned on total capital. Then total capital should be measured as total assets (or total equity) and income should be measured as operating income plus financial income (for example, in-

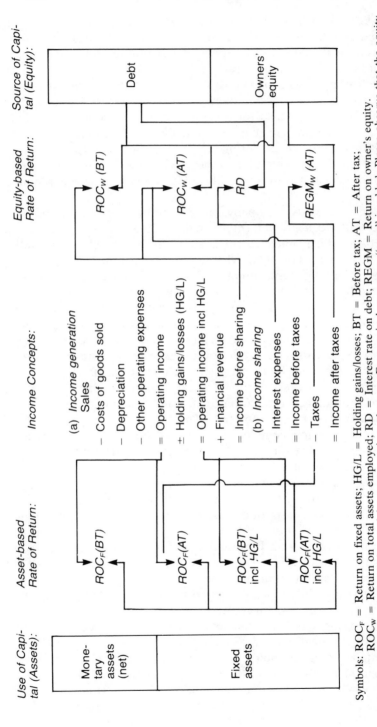

Symbols: ROC_F = Return on fixed assets; HG/L = Holding gains/losses; BT = Before tax; AT = After tax;
ROC_W = Return on total assets employed; RD = Interest rate on debt; REGM = Return on owner's equity.
In the text the symbols will be used for measures in real terms. For nominal measures, "nom" is added. Please observe that the equity
based rates of return (i.e. ROC_W and $REGM_W$) includes holding gains/losses.

Figure 3–1. Matching of Income and Capital Concepts When Constructing Corporate Rates of Return

terest earned on monetary assets). Many macroeconomic studies, lacking data on monetary assets, use physical capital (that is, fixed or nonmonetary assets) as the capital concept. In this case, the appropriate income concept to use is operating income (thus excluding financial income). Often this is calculated before real holding gains and losses, simply because of lack of data, and implies the assumption that real holding gains and losses tend to even out over the long run. (The term holding gain/loss is used throughout the chapter as an abbreviation for "holding gains and losses and realizable cost savings." By a nominal holding gain we mean a gain—loss, realizable cost saving—due to price movements on specific assets and with no consideration of changes in the general price level, measured by the *CP*. Take a piece of inventory as an example. The cost-of-goods-concept used in operating income is based on current costs, that is, the price at the time of the sale. The price differential between the time of purchase and of sale is a nominal holding gain—more precisely in this case it is a realized cost saving. By adjusting for changes in the *CP*, that is, by looking only at the difference between changes in the specific price for the goods and the *CP*, the holding gain is expressed in real terms.)

These are straightforward matters. Still, confusion stemming from bad matching of income and capital concepts is frequent. We will expand on this later but let us first consider the second principle concerning the selection of a basis for capital valuation (and thus measurement of income). That principle, too, is straightforward: current costs should be used, not historical costs, if valid descriptions of company rates of return are to be reached. The arguments are well known and shall not be repeated here; see, for example, *Financial Accounting Standards Board*.

Under some circumstances, however, company rates of return based on historical costs can be used as approximations for rates based on current costs. What is the rationale behind this? How can this statement be combined with the often heard argument that rates based on historical costs will overstate "true" rates (that is, rates based on current costs)? Here, confusion with the matching of income with capital gives the key. The argument refers to a rate of return based on capital valued at historical prices as a measure of return on capital, *ROC,* where capital is interpreted as fixed capital and income thus is defined as operating income (thus interpreted as ROC_F). If income is defined as operating income before holding gains/losses, when prices rise over time, the use of historical cost will overstate the income (mainly as the result of depreciation on historical cost) and understate capital. Both factors will work to overstate the "true" rate of return. Thus, it is said, historical costs cannot be used to approximate *ROC*.

The use of historical costs means, however, that some of the holding gains/losses are included in the income, namely those that are realized during the period.[2] The relevant comparison is thus operating income *including* holding gains/losses. In times of rising prices, the true income (that is, based on current costs and including holding gains/losses) is typically understated if historical costs are used, since unrealized holding gains/losses are left out. Since the capital is also understated, the errors partly offset each other. This means that rate of return based on historical costs under certain circumstances (approximately continuous growth; limited turbulence in the price movements, and so on) might be used as approximations to rates based on current costs and including holding gains/losses.[3]

Let there be no doubt, however, as to the preferences: current costs should be used if possible. But let the merits of historical costs be valued without confusion as to what kind of rate of return should be the basis for comparison. This can also be stated with respect to the third important criterion for the construction of company rates of return: that of real versus nominal rates. (As an important matter of terminology, the symbols used in figure 3–1 are from now on interpreted as *real* rates of return—the main type of measure used in the empirical parts. When we refer to a *nominal* rate, (nom) is added to the symbol.)

A nominal rate of return is constructed with no adjustments made for changes in the general price level, that is, inflation. The adjustments needed to construct a real rate of return are effects of a changing price level (measured by the *CP*) during the time capital is held. The *ROC* (based on current costs) before holding gains/losses (that is, ROC_F) is a real rate of return since all prices are expressed at the same point of time (current time) and since we do not want to account for the income effect of any holding activities, that is, effects of holding assets over time. For the rates of return derived from income concepts after operating income in figure 3–1 we have to distinguish between nominal and real measures (that is, $ROC_{F,incl\,HG/L,\,nom}$ versus $ROC_{F,\,incl\,HG/L}$, $ROC_{W,nom}$ versus ROC_W, $REGM_{W,\,nom}$ versus $REGM_W$, and so on): the measures are nominal if corrections are not made for changes in the general price level. If so done, it is a real rate of return (Johansson, 1977). (Please observe that in the construction of equity-based rates of return according to figure 3–1, the distinction between nominal and real is not only a matter with respect to holding gains/losses but also to financial revenue and interest expenses. If, for example, a nominal rate of return on total capital—fixed and monetary assets—is constructed, the nominal financial revenue is used together with nominal holding gains/losses and the operating income to form the denominator. If we want the corresponding real rate of return we must express the holding gains/losses *and* the financial revenue in real terms. This is done by deducting the "inflation loss," that is, change in the CP times the current value of the assets at the start of the period, from the nominal income. This can even more conveniently be expressed as nominal rate of return minus rate of inflation (that is, change in CP) equals real rate of return—given the rates are computed as continuously compounded rates; otherwise we need a small correction factor).

The distinction between real and nominal rates of return is, of course, of greatest importance. As an illustration, let us return to the rate of return based on historical costs and the question of its use for approximating ROC. As stated earlier, ROC as commonly defined in macroeconomic studies (that is, ROC_F) is based on operating income as an approximation for operating income including *real* holding gains/losses. The assumption is that real holding gains/losses tend to offset each other and that a rate based on operating income, ROC_F, will be a good proxy to the "true" real rate of return, $ROC_{F, incl HG/L}$. On the other hand, a commonly defined rate of return based on historical costs is usually constructed to show a *nominal* rate of return (including nominal *realized* holding gains and losses). *If* this measure can be used as a proxy for a nominal rate of return based on current costs (that is, $ROC_{F, incl HG/L,nom}$; see discussion above) it can only be meaningfully compared to ROC_F if the rate of inflation is deducted.

But once again, let there be no doubt as to the preferences: current costs should be preferred to historical costs (and, in this chapter, real measures will be preferred to nominal measures). But let the preferences be formulated from a relevant comparison of merits and not from confusions regarding the impact of holding gains/losses *or* the distinction between nominal and real rates of return.

Finally, one additional remark on the construction of corporate rates of return should be made. It concerns the treatment of taxes. Here, no obviously superior alternative exists. Throughout the next section and the section entitled "The Rate of Return in the Long Run," we have chosen to recognize only taxes actually paid and thus to consider any deferred taxes (not recorded as deferred taxes) as a part of income after taxes and the accumulated deferred taxes as a part of owners' equity. In the section entitled "Tests of Validity," we will show the effects of recognizing deferred taxes as expenses and accounting for the accumulated deferred taxes as a liability.[4]

The Performance of Swedish Business Groups

Investors' Return

Let us begin the empirical analysis by looking at the investors' return. We must then turn to entities that are valued at the market, i.e., business groups, and for which market values are observable, i.e., public groups that are listed at the Stockholm Exchange.[5]

Table 3–1 shows the rate of return to investors in stocks 1949–82.[6] The data are depicted in figure 3–2 and concern all financial and non-financial business groups. Looking at the whole period 1949–82 we cannot find any trend in the real rate of return to investors in stocks.

Table 3–1
Rate of Return to Investors in Stocks 1949–82
(percent)

Year	Nominal	Real	Inflation[a]
1949	9.5	9.5	0.0
50	31.3	23.3	8.0
51	17.9	3.1	14.8
52	− 9.8	−13.0	3.2
53	16.6	16.2	0.4
54	35.2	34.8	0.4
55	− .9	− 7.1	6.2
56	3.1	− 1.3	4.4
57	7.3	3.4	3.9
58	23.7	21.3	2.4
59	44.6	41.6	3.0
60	4.0	1.4	2.6
61	3.5	0.4	3.1
62	− 1.2	− 5.4	4.2
63	29.8	26.6	3.2
64	22.2	18.5	3.7
65	4.6	− 1.9	6.5
66	−16.2	−21.3	5.1
67	5.4	2.5	2.9
68	43.4	41.0	2.4
69	− 1.5	− 5.6	4.1
70	−14.2	−23.3	9.1
71	24.3	18.2	6.1
72	13.6	7.7	5.9
73	5.5	− 2.4	7.9
74	3.6	− 7.1	10.7
75	29.9	19.9	10.0
76	0.9	− 8.4	9.3
77	− 5.6	−18.9	13.3
78	20.1	13.5	6.6
79	2.8	− 8.4	11.2
80	25.0	11.7	13.3
81	62.3	53.0	9.3
82	39.4	29.4	10.0
Average	14.1	8.0	6.1
Slope 1949–82	.23	.00	
1949–60	.38	.67	
1961–78	.00	− .41	
1961–82	1.04	.61	

[a]Change in Consumer Price Index.

Percent

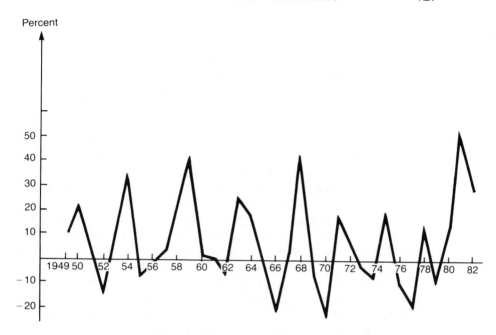

Figure 3–2. Real Return to Investors in Stocks 1949–82

But if we divide the period into parts, a positive trend of 0.67 percentage points per year can be applied to the years 1949–60, while a negative trend of −0.41 percentage points can be applied to the period 1961–78 (this period will be used later). Both trends are, however, not statistically significant because of the high volatility of the figures.[7]

The average real rate of return for the twelve-year period 1949–60 was 11.1 percent, compared to 3.0 percent for the eighteen-year period 1961–78 and 6.4 percent for the twenty-two-year period 1961–82.

To conclude, the real rate of return to investors in stocks has declined from a top at the end of the 1950s to the late 1970s, turning the average down to levels not experienced in the 1950s. The period of study is too short, however, to tell whether the trends since the end of the 1950s should be called "back to normal" or "down below normal."

Let us now turn to the most relevant market description of how the business groups have fared, the return on both debt and stocks (total capital). Conventionally, this rate of return, R, is measured with the help of market data for stocks and bonds, the latter being the measure of debt. The rationale for the use of bond data is twofold. First, there are no other observable market data. Second, debts other than bonds are assumed to be of negligible importance.

For Swedish industry, however, debts other than bonds are the dominant type of debt. To accept the bonds as the only measure of the value of debt could seriously affect the validity of the description. The proper alternatives are then to find a way to measure market values of all debts—although no explicit values can be observed—or to drop the idea of measuring total value.

We have chosen the first alternative because of the availability of necessary company data. The tool is to find implicit market values on debts from the market and accounting data that exist. This can be done if certain assumptions are introduced. Generally speaking, the market value of debt is defined as the present value of expected future payments where the current market interest rate is used as the discount rate. The assumptions and procedures used in the computations are discussed in the notes.[8] Of course alternative procedures are possible, but we believe any careful estimates will show the same pattern across time. The data needed for the computations, except the nominal market rate of interest, have been collected from FINDATA, a computerized data bank with data on business groups listed on the Stockholm Exchange. It enables us to provide estimates for 1967–80 (and thus, unfortunately, the period prior to 1967 cannot be studied for nonfinancial companies). They are shown in table 3–2, where market rate of return on stocks is shown along with market rate of return on debt and on total capital—stocks plus debts. We also give values for the equity-ratio to be discussed below. The figures concern groups listed all years during the period.[9] Except for the equity ratio, none of the trends is statistically significant. The main reason for this is the high volatility of the figures as a result of capital gains/losses in the numerator.[10]

Still, there are reasons to believe in a decreased return to investors if we look at five-year averages for the periods 1967–70 (only four years), 1971–75, and 1976–80: the average real return on total capital, R, was 2.1, -0.3 and -3.6, respectively.

Behind this development of R, different patterns for real returns on stocks and debts can be observed. The average return on stocks increased to 7.0 percent during the period 1971–75, from 4.8 percent during 1967–70, and then decreased sharply to -4.1 percent during 1976–80. The return on debts, on the other hand, had the opposite pattern. The average return decreased to -5.8 during the period 1971–1975 from -1.1 percent during 1967–1970 and then increased to -2.6 percent. The main reason behind these two opposite—but supplementing—patterns is the slow pace at which nominal interest rates on old debts adapted to a higher rate of inflation. Thus, heavy capital losses were induced by increased nominal market interest rates on new debt while interest income did not quickly adapt to new nominal interest

Table 3–2
Return to Investors in Swedish Business Groups, Aggregate Figures
(percent)

Year	Stocks		Debts		Total Capital		Equity Ratio
	Nominal	Real	Nominal	Real	Nominal	Real	
1966							61.2
1967	7.2	4.3	5.0	2.1	6.3	3.4	54.8
1968	41.5	39.2	15.7	13.3	29.8	27.4	59.0
1969	8.6	4.5	− 5.1	− 9.2	3.0	− 0.9	59.3
1970	− 19.6	− 28.7	− 1.7	− 10.8	− 12.3	− 21.4	49.5
1971	25.6	19.5	− 4.6	− 10.7	10.3	4.2	51.7
1972	15.5	9.6	13.4	7.5	14.5	8.6	49.8
1973	2.1	− 5.8	12.5	4.6	7.3	− 0.6	43.9
1974	− 0.2	− 10.9	4.2	− 6.5	2.3	− 8.5	39.5
1975	32.6	22.6	− 13.7	− 23.7	4.6	− 5.4	44.5
1976	0.6	− 8.7	14.8	5.5	8.5	− 0.8	38.4
1977	− 15.7	− 29.0	1.2	− 12.1	− 5.3	− 18.6	30.0
1978	16.1	9.5	− 0.7	− 7.3	4.3	− 2.3	33.4
1979	4.5	− 6.7	7.0	− 4.2	6.1	− 5.0	33.6
1980	27.8	14.5	18.5	5.2	21.9	8.6	32.3
Average							
1967–80	10.5	2.2	4.8	− 3.3	7.2	− 0.8	45.4
1967–70	9.4	4.8	3.4	− 1.1	6.7	2.1	56.8
1971–75	15.1	7.0	2.4	− 5.8	7.8	− 0.3	45.9
1976–80	6.7	− 4.1	8.2	− 2.6	7.1	− 3.6	33.5
Slope	− 0.26	− 1.03	0.32	− 0.37	− 0.09	− 0.78	− 2.25[a]

[a]Statistically significant, 5 percent level.

rate levels. By the end of the 1970s, when the market had become used to a new level of inflation, a larger share of total debts had adapted their interest rates to higher nominal levels.

The reason behind the average negative real rate of return on debts for the whole period as well as for the three parts of the period can also be found in capital losses. Nominal market interest rates rose successively from 8.0 percent in 1967 to 14.2 percent in 1980. The decreasing equity ratio (a pattern which is statistically significant) suggests increased financial risk of firms. As will be seen in the next section, however, the equity ratio decreased also when measured with data other than market data.[11]

Company Rates of Return

The purpose of this section is to see whether accounting information for business groups reveals the same picture of profit performance as the market data in the previous section. Accounting data, as they are published in annual reports, are based on historical costs, and we have therefore used certain correction factors in order to adjust the aggregate data components to current costs.[12] We will look at the aggregate of exactly the same sample of companies, and for the same period, 1967–80, and use the same set of data, that is, FINDATA, as in the analysis of investors' return in the previous part. Four types of measures are of concern[13] and are presented in table 3–3.

ROC_F = Return on fixed capital; before and after taxes.

ROC_W = Return on all capital employed (fixed and *net* monetary assets),[14] including real holding gains/losses, before and after taxes.

$REGM_W$ = Return on equity, including real holding gains/losses on fixed capital, "inflation losses" on net monetary assets, and "inflation gains" on debts, after taxes.

Table 3–3
Real Corporate Rates of Return for Swedish Business Groups, before Taxes (*BT*) and after Taxes (*AT*)
(percent)

	Rate of Inflation (a)	Real Rate of Return on Fixed Assets, ROC_F		Real Rate of Return on All Assets Employed, ROC_W, Including Holding Gains/ Losses		Real Rate of Return on Equity, $REGM_W$ AT (f)	Equity Ratio, EQ/W (g)
		BT (b)	AT (c)	BT (d)	AT (e)		
1966	5.1						77.1
1967	2.9	4.9	2.6	6.7	4.0	4.5	74.4
1968	2.4	6.3	3.5	6.9	4.5	4.3	73.2
1969	4.1	8.4	5.1	12.5	9.8	11.7	73.9
1970	9.1	5.8	3.1	4.9	2.6	3.3	72.9
1971	6.1	4.2	2.4	5.1	3.6	3.5	70.6
1972	5.9	4.1	2.1	6.7	4.9	5.9	70.2
1973	7.9	7.9	5.3	9.3	7.0	9.4	70.9
1974	10.7	10.5	8.2	8.9	6.8	9.8	72.2
1975	10.0	4.9	2.7	4.6	2.7	2.9	70.4
1976	9.3	2.3	0.7	0.7	− 0.8	− 2.2	67.9
1977	13.3	− 1.4	−2.9	− 4.1	− 5.5	− 7.8	65.1
1978	6.6	1.8	0.3	2.8	1.4	− 0.9	64.3
1979	11.2	3.3	1.6	3.2	1.7	2.0	66.5
1980	13.3	3.0	1.4	− 1.2	− 2.8	− 5.2	65.7
Average	7.9	4.7	2.6	4.8	2.9	2.9	
Slope		− 0.38	−0.28	− 0.71[a]	− 0.62[a]	− 0.83[a]	− 0.79[a]

[a]Statistically significant, 5 percent level.

EQ/W = Equity ratio; owners' equity as a percentage of all
capital employed (both factors at current costs).

The second variable, ROC_W, is the most relevant variable to describe
return on capital, but the ROC_F is included to make international comparisons possible.

The ROC measures are the company counterparts to the measures
of investors' return, R, in the previous section. Similarly, the $REGM_W$
is the company counterpart to investors' return on stocks and should
thus be defined after taxes.

The corporate rates of return reveal a similar general pattern as
the market data, but in a less dramatic way. The pattern is: decreasing
real rates of return and decreasing equity ratio.[15]

Further, it can be noted that the negative slope of the trend of
ROC_W is steeper than that of ROC_F, that is, the decline in profitability
is bigger when we take account of real holding gains/losses and net
monetary assets (and related financial revenue). The reason for this is
probably to be found in the latter factor than among holding gains/
losses. The same market imperfections as those discussed above concerning nominal interest rates on debts are present when it comes to
financial revenue on monetary assets. Average nominal interest rates
were not adjusted to the sudden changes in the rate of inflation that
occurred from 1973. This caused negative real rate of return on net
monetary assets.

Whether or not the downward sloping trend of ROC merely reflects
a poor profit performance or also a decreasing cost of capital is of
course of crucial importance. Empirical measures of cost of capital are
very difficult to find. A very rough estimate can be found by comparing
operating profit (after taxes) with the market value of firms' securities, that is, the market value of stocks and debts. This ratio is denoted
by ρ.

Values of ρ over time are depicted in figure 3–3 along with values
of $ROC_F(AT)$ and $ROC_W(AT)$. The trend of ρ is downward sloping
(but not statistically significant; see table 3–4) with a slope of minus
0.39 percentage points per year. The tentative conclusion is that the
reductions in profitability over time partly reflect a reduction in the
cost of capital.

ROC, however, has generally been lower than ρ—all years but one
with respect to $ROC_F(AT)$ and all years but four with respect to
$ROC_W(AT)$. The implication would be that although reduced profitability has been accompanied by a reduced cost of capital, the profitability has been lower than the opportunity cost of capital. This should
be reflected in values of Tobin's q, the ratio of market values of firms'

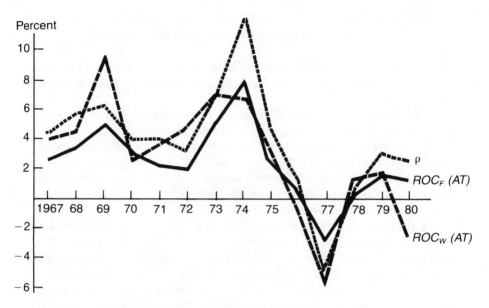

Figure 3–3. Return on Fixed Capital *(ROC_F)* and all assets employed *(ROC_w)*; Ratio of Operating Profit to Market Value of Firms' Securities (ρ)

securities to the current cost of their assets, lower than 1. In figure 3–4 values of q_F (ratio of market value of firms' securities to the current costs of fixed assets, that is, inventory, plant, equipment, and land) have been depicted along with values of q_w (ratio of firms' securities to total assets employed in business operations).

As expected, the *level* of q is lower than 1. Of course, there are a lot of reasons why the measured q might be lower than the true value. These factors have to do with the quality of the data, the techniques for measuring current costs, the technique used for finding implicit market values of debts, and so on. It is, however, highly unrealistic to conclude that the true q has been close to or higher than 1—rather, it has been lower than 1 and the market value of firms' securities has been lower than the current costs of firms' assets. In terms of business behavior this can be expressed as a lower profitability for investment activities than their opportunity cost, that is, investing in physical capacity could have been done more cheaply by acquiring other companies than by buying the assets.

One important reason for this behavior might be the "liberal" Swedish corporate tax system, wherein companies can postpone their tax payment as long as they keep investing in fixed assets.

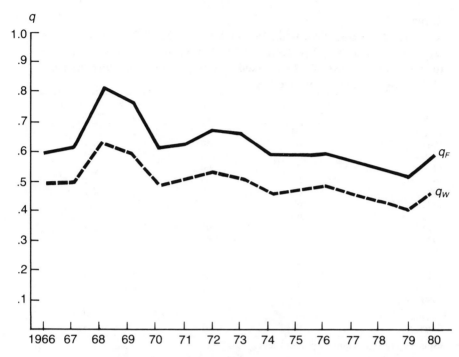

Figure 3–4. Tobin's q. Ratio of Current Cost of Fixed Assets *(q_F)* and All Assets Employed *(q_W)*, Respectively, to Market Value of Firm's Securities

Moreover, the trend of q has been downward sloping. Even if a reduced *ROC* is partly offset by a reduction in ρ, the reduction has been big enough to make the q decrease over time. Values of ρ and q are given in table 3–4.

Corporate Rate of Return for Domestic Corporations

Introduction

The previous discussion examined Swedish-owned business groups, for which market data are available—thus making it possible to compare their performance as measured by investors' returns with their performance according to company records. But a study of Swedish-owned business groups does not tell us how Swedish domestic industry has performed (by domestic industry we mean operations within the

Table 3–4
Ratio of Operating Profit to Market Value of Firms' Securities, That Is, "Cost of Capital," ρ. Ratio of Market Value of Firms' Securities to the Current Cost of Their Fixed Assets (q_F) and the Current Cost of All Their Assets Employed (q_W)

Year	q_F	q_W	"Cost of Capital" (Percent)
1966	.60	.49	
1967	.61	.49	4.4
1968	.81	.63	5.8
1969	.77	.60	6.3
1970	.61	.49	4.1
1971	.62	.50	4.1
1972	.67	.53	3.4
1973	.66	.52	7.9
1974	.59	.47	12.4
1975	.58	.47	4.7
1976	.59	.48	1.2
1977	.56	.46	− 4.9
1978	.55	.44	0.5
1979	.51	.41	3.0
1980	.59	.47	2.6
Average	.62	.50	4.0
Slope	− 1.08[a]	− .83[a]	− 0.39

[a]Statistically significant, 5 percent level.

country). This is something other than operations run by Swedish-owned companies. In the latter, operations of foreign subsidiaries are excluded and operations by Swedish subsidiaries of foreign companies are included. The performance as described earlier might actually be the result of (or despite) the poor (good) performance of foreign subsidiaries of Swedish companies and not the result of their domestic performance.

The purpose of this section is to measure and discuss the domestic rate of return. By focusing on domestic operations we abstract from the economic entities that are valued on markets where we can observe their values. There simply are no stock markets or other markets for external valuation of domestic operations (except for those cases where the company is solely operated domestically). If we want to study domestic operations, corporate rates of return are then the only available measures of performance. Further, these measures are available for legal entities (that is, corporations), which will constitute our sample.[16]

What are the uses of accounting information for units that by definition are not explicitly valued on any markets? We can see two main uses. First, it seems likely that return to investors—had it been possible to measure—in the long run would correspond to the accounting information as it did for business groups earlier. The purpose of accounting information (at least if based on current costs) is to respond to market prices—although the accounting techniques might cause the response to be lagged in time or to result in a smoothing of the effect of the turbulence of market prices, thus causing discrepancies with market measures in the short run.

A regression analysis run on real return on capital—that is, $ROC_A(BT)$ (see below)—"explaining" the real rate of return to investors in stock (see section entitled "Investors' Return") gives a statistically significant positive β-coefficient of 4.30 (percentage points) when return on capital is lagged one year—return on stocks $= f\ (ROC_A(BT)_{k+1})$. Second, corporate rates of return give measures of performance regarding activities over which domestic entities are supposed to have control. They give the basic pieces of information from which corporate decisions on growth supposedly are formed (Bertmar and Molin, 1977).

The main questions to be raised in this part are: How has the rate of return in domestic Swedish industry developed over the long run? And what has been the long-run behavior of equity ratios? These questions will be analyzed in the next section. In framing our answers we pay particular attention to how the descriptions change if we (a) look at different kinds of rates of return; (b) use measures including instead of excluding holding gains; (c) utilize data of highest available quality (possible for the later part of the studied period); and thereby (d) compute taxes including deferred taxes and change the definition of liabilities and owners' equity accordingly; (e) use different measures of total capital; and (f) analyze individual firms instead of the aggregate. These matters will be analyzed in the next two sections. They are examples of questions that should be asked in most discussions of trend in profitability but that for lack of data seldom are. In the Swedish case the possibilities exist for a richer analysis based on carefully developed corporation data. In the section entitled "Tests of Validity" we utilize a comparative advantage of the Swedish data, which are of sufficiently high quality and have a richness of detail that permit an analysis and deeper understanding of problems of data measurements and interpretation common to all countries.

The Rate of Return in the Long Run

Figure 3–5 gives before- and after-tax rates on return on capital, *ROC,* as it is conventionally defined in macroeconomic studies, that is, as operating profit—before *(BT)* and after *(AT)* deduction of taxes—as a percentage of the current cost (that is, replacement cost) of depreciable capital stock and inventories (that is, ROC_A). No consideration

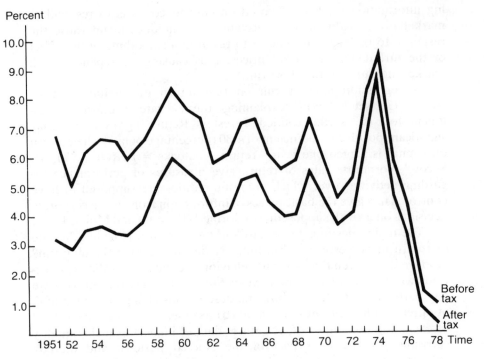

Figure 3–5. Rate of Return on Physical Capital 1951–1978

is given to holding gains/losses or financial income in the profit measure or to investment in net monetary assets or land in the measure of capital. (This will be done in the next section.) The data are primarily collected by the Swedish Statistical Bureau (SCB) and regard manufacturing industry. Although subject to all the limitations that characterize aggregate estimates of the capital stock, particularly, this series is still the longest run of profitability estimates available for Swedish industry.[17]

The interpretation of figure 3–5 is straightforward (see also table 3–5): $ROC_A(BT)$ during the period 1951–78 had a statistically significant downward sloping trend of 0.09 percentage points per year, but because of a falling tax rate (measured as paid-in taxes as a percentage of operating income) over time, we cannot find any trend in the $ROC_A(AT)$.

Behind the general pattern some details should be observed. The 1950s showed increasing rates of return; 0.22 and 0.31 percentage points yearly for $ROC_A(BT)$ and $ROC_A(AT)$ respectively during 1951–60 (both statistically significant). The turning point to a decreasing trend occurred in the late 1950s or early 1960s.[18] The rate of return was then almost stable until the mid-1970s. After 1976 the decline is dramatic—with the $ROC_A(AT)$ down to 0.2 percent in 1978—resulting in a decline for the entire period 1961–78 of -0.20 (statistically significant) and -0.11 (not statistically significant) percentage points per year for $ROC_A(BT)$ and $ROC_A(AT)$ respectively. This gives an ample background to the economic problems Sweden presently is facing.

The decline in the tax rate (expressed as a percentage of operating income) has occurred despite an increase in the statutory tax rate. The decline has several explanations, one of them possibly being the introduction of several means for companies to defer taxes, for example through formation of investment reserves from the late 1950s. Another main reason is the decrease in the equity ratio and the corresponding increase in interest expenses, which have reduced the portion of the before-tax ROC chargeable to income taxes.

Impact of Economic Activity

The decreasing ROC_A across time is, however, better explained by changes in economic activity than by the passing of time per se. This can be concluded after a regression analysis where three regression functions have been tested: (1) ROC_A as a function of time alone; (2) ROC_A as a function of time and economic activity, measured as the percentage change in real GNP; and (3) ROC_A as a function of time, economic activity, and rate of inflation, measured as the percentage change in Consumer Price Index.

As noted earlier, the regression of $ROC_A(BT)$ against time gives a significant F-value. But when change in GNP is introduced as an explanatory variable, this variable receives the statistical significance, the significance of time reduces, and the explanatory power of the regres-

Table 3–5
Regression Analysis of Before-Tax Return on Capital,
$ROC_A(BT)$ 1951–78

Equation	Variable			
	Time	Economic Activity	Inflation	R^2
(1)	-0.09			0.16
	(5.11[a])			
(2)	-0.05	0.58		0.51
	(2.29)	(17.39[a])		
(3)	-0.06	0.63	0.08	0.53
	(3.15)	(18.14[a])	(0.96)	

Note: F statistics appear in parentheses under the coefficients.
[a]Indicates significance.

sion equation increases substantially. Adding the rate of inflation, however, does not add any new insight.

The same relationships hold for $ROC_A(AT)$ but the F-values and R^2 are lower. As a matter of fact, regression of $ROC_A(AT)$ versus time alone gives us no indication of relationship whatsoever. (See table 3–6).

The conclusion closest at hand, then, is that return on capital has varied with the level of economic activity (but not with the rate of inflation) and *not* with time per se.

Including Real Holding Gains/Losses

The main pattern does not change if the measure of profitability is defined as including holding gains. This can be confirmed by studying figure 3–6, where we give descriptions of ROC_A, including holding gains/losses. The alternative measures are based on the same data set as used above.

The decline in a trendline applied to the data is very similar to that for ROC_A.[19] For the whole period 1954–78 it is -0.08 and -0.02 percentage points per year for the before- and after-tax measure (both are not statistically significant) compared to -0.13 and -0.04 percentage points respectively for $ROC_A(BT)$ and $ROC_A(AT)$. The levels of return are also similar. The main impact of including real holding gains/losses is that the outcome fluctuates slightly more around the trendlines. The methodological conclusion then indicates that we could stay with the traditional measure, that is, ROC_A excluding real holding gains/losses, as long as we are interested in the long-run performance. But for short-run descriptions it becomes important to consider the real

Table 3–6
Regression Analysis of After-Tax Return on Capital,
$ROC_A(AT)$ 1951–78

Equation	Time	Economic Activity	Inflation	R^2
		Variable		
(1)	0.00			0.00
	(0.00)			
(2)	0.04	0.55		0.38
	(1.26)	(15.56[a])		
(3)	0.03	0.58	0.05	0.39
		(15.03[a])	(0.36)	

Note: F statistics appear in parentheses under the coefficients.
[a]Indicates significance.

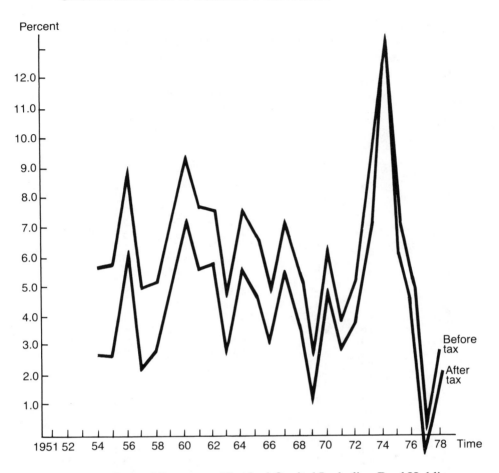

Figure 3–6. Rate of Return on Physical Capital Including Real Holding
         Gains and Losses 1954–1978

holding gains/losses. The numbers behind figures 3–5 and 3–6 are shown
in table 3–7.

Income Sharing

Let us conclude the analysis of the long-term performance of Swedish
corporations by adding a description of how income has been shared—
specifically the real rate of return on owner's equity after tax,
$REGM_o(AT)$. By so doing we will give the accounting counterpart of

Table 3–7
Corporate Rates of Return and Equity Ratio in Swedish
Corporations 1951–78: Aggregate Figures
(percent)

Year	ROC_A BT	ROC_A AT	ROC_A, Including Real HG/L BT	ROC_A, Including Real HG/L AT	REGM_O AT	Equity Ratio
1951	6.8	3.2	n.a.	n.a.	n.a.	63
1952	5.0	2.9	n.a.	n.a.	n.a.	65
1953	6.2	3.5	n.a.	n.a.	n.a.	66
1954	6.6	3.7	5.7	2.8	2.7	67
1955	6.6	3.5	5.8	2.7	0.6	65
1956	6.0	3.4	8.8	6.2	5.3	65
1957	6.5	3.8	5.0	2.2	1.5	65
1958	7.4	5.1	5.2	2.9	2.6	66
1959	8.3	6.0	7.4	5.1	5.3	65
1960	7.7	5.6	9.4	7.2	6.7	63
1961	7.4	5.2	7.8	5.6	5.7	63
1962	5.8	4.0	7.6	5.8	5.6	64
1963	6.1	4.2	4.7	2.7	2.7	64
1964	7.2	5.2	7.6	5.6	5.5	63
1965	7.3	5.4	6.7	4.5	4.3	60
1966	6.1	4.4	4.8	3.1	2.9	58
1967	5.6	4.0	7.1	5.5	5.8	59
1968	5.9	4.0	5.5	3.7	4.4	58
1969	7.2	5.5	2.7	1.0	.6	54
1970	5.9	4.6	6.2	4.9	4.6	52
1971	4.5	3.6	3.9	3.0	1.9	54
1972	5.2	4.0	5.3	4.1	4.1	54
1973	7.7	6.5	8.3	7.1	7.4	54
1974	9.6	8.7	13.5	12.6	13.2	56
1975	5.8	4.7	7.3	6.2	5.5	54
1976	4.2	3.3	5.4	4.5	3.4	56
1977	1.4	0.8	0.0	− 0.7	− 3.1	53
1978	0.9	0.2	2.9	2.2	3.0	53
Average 1954–78	6.1	4.4	6.2	4.4	4.1	60
Slope of linear trend; percentage points per year						
1951–78	− .09[a]	.00	n.a.	n.a.	n.a.	− .56[a]
1954–78	− .13[a]	− .04	− .08	− .02	.03	− .64[a]
1951–60	.22[a]	.31[a]	n.a.	n.a.	n.a.	− .04
1954–60	.29	.44[a]	.38	.53	.67	− .39
1961–78	− .20[a]	− .11	− .12	− .03	− .07	− .66

[a]Statistically significant; 5 percent level.

the long-term market rate of return on shares described earlier under
the heading "Company Rates of Return" (although based on aggregate
data and concerning a different business entity—the corporation rather
than the business group).

In order to cover the longest possible time span we have to rely on aggregate figures of relatively poor quality. Thus holding gains/losses on net monetary assets and land are not accounted for. We denote the measure $REGM_O$.[20]

$REGM_O(AT)$ is depicted in figure 3–7. The general pattern for $REGM_O(AT)$ is similar to that of ROC_A, meaning an increased rate of return during the 1950s (slope = 0.67 percentage points per year 1954–60; not statistically significant) and a declining rate of return since then (slope = −0.07 percentage points per year 1961–78; not statistically

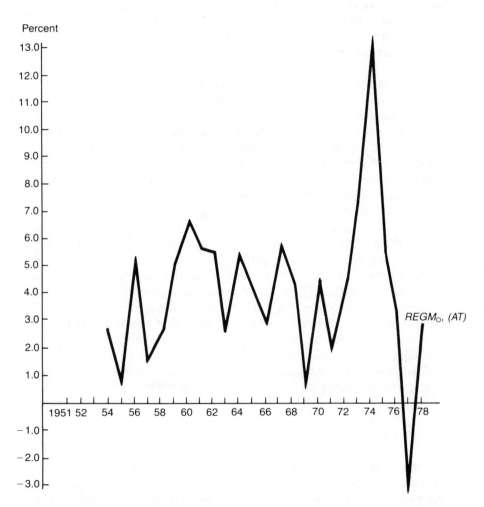

Figure 3–7. Real Rate of Return on Owner's Equity after Tax 1954–1978

significant). For the whole period 1954–78, however, the trend is slightly positive (0.03 percentage points per year; not statistically significant).

It can be noted that the turning point for $REGM_O(AT)$ occurred in the late 1950s or early 1960s, that is, approximately at the same time as for investors' return on stocks (cf. figure 3–2).

The spectacular increase in $REGM_O(AT)$ in 1974 deserves some comments. Behind this is a structural change combined with a temporary one. The temporary change has to do with changes in the tax system that were made specifically for 1974.[21] This added to an extraordinary $REGM_O(AT)$, since we define taxes as taxes payable. The structural change has to do with changes in the equity ratio. It decreased from 67 percent in 1954 to 53 percent in 1978 (see table 3–7). Implied in this decrease are higher fluctuations in $REGM_O(AT)$, other things being equal.

The relation between a decreased equity ratio over time and trends in rates of return should be given an additional comment. It has to do with the implied growth rates. The decrease in equity ratio was concentrated in the period prior to the 1970s. Thus it decreased from 67 percent in 1954 to 54 percent in 1969 and was thereafter almost constant, ending at 53 percent in 1978 (but see the validity tests in the next section). At the same time we can observe both ROC_A and $REGM_O(AT)$ falling more sharply in the 1970s than earlier after the turning point in the late 1950s. Why? Should not falling profitability correspond to decreased equity ratio? The answer lies with the real rate of growth in capital. Prior to the 1970s the rate of growth was high enough to result in decreasing equity ratio despite a comparatively high real rate of return. In the 1970s the growth rate declined to levels where even a decreasing $REGM_O(AT)$ could not make the equity ratio fall further.

This is an "economic" explanation behind the changes in the equity ratio. It should, however, be kept in mind that the analyses in this section are based on aggregated data of comparatively poor quality. The impact of a switch to data of higher quality will be shown next.

The values for the equity ratio together with numbers for the variables previously discussed are summarized in table 3–7.[22]

Tests of Validity

The last section of this chapter will be devoted entirely to discussing the validity of the conclusions reached in the previous section.[23] For this purpose we will utilize data of the highest quality available. The data set—called the KKR-bank—has been established by the Economic Research Institute at the Stockholm School of Economics (EFI) and concerns all Swedish corporations with more than 200 employees, that is, approximately 400 corporations. Together, these companies account for almost 70 percent of domestic industrial employment.

The main differences compared with the data used in the previous section are the following: (a) The objects of study are the individual corporations that make up the aggregate rather than the aggregate itself. (b) The data are arranged so as to guarantee a consistent measurement of each year and every company over time. This includes data of equal quality for all companies and all years. It means that "technical" problems—mergers, for example,—are analyzed and treated in a consistent manner. (c) For each corporation, individually assigned depreciation rates are used. (d) Current costs are used as the valuation basis. (e) In the income measurement, all holding gains or losses are isolated from the operating income. Among other things, this demands not only current cost data regarding total inventories, but also different kinds of inventories, that is, supplies, work in progress, and finished goods. (f) Land is included among the assets. No real holding gains/losses are recognized on land.[24]

One way of giving an overall picture of the quality and the details in the KKR-bank is to mention that for all companies and all years, it includes the same kind of details on such items as current costs that are required to be disclosed in annual reports by larger U.S. corporations since 1980 according to *FASB* 33.

The high standards formulated for the data have made it impossible to expand the period of study further back than to 1966. The data set is presently updated to 1979.

We will concentrate on three variables, real return on capital, real return on owners' equity, and the equity ratio. Real return on capital is measured before tax while real return on equity is measured after tax. The equity ratio is included in order to indicate the changes in capital structure accompanying the trends in profitability.

Our validity analysis will cover two main dimensions, corresponding to items (c) through (f) in the section entitled "Corporate Rate of Return for Domestic Corporations." The first regards the impact on the description of different data sets and different ways of operationalizing variables. The second regards differences between descriptions for the aggregate and for individual firms. Table 3–8 summarizes the first dimension. Along with the data and measures used in the previous section, two alternative measures are given. Both are based on the KKR-bank. In the first alternative, land and net monetary capital are included (this was not done in the previous section). In the second alternative (not relevant with respect to *ROC*), deferred taxes are recognized as liabilities and tax expenses are defined including the taxes

Table 3–8
Impact on Measures of Substituting the Data Set and Definitions Used: Aggregate Numbers (*percent*)

Year	Real Return on Capital before Tax		Real Return on Owners' Equity after Tax			Equity Ratio		
	(a) Previously Described; $ROC_A(BT)$	(b) Including Land and Net Monetary Assets; $ROC_W(BT)$	(c) Previously Described; $REGM_O(AT)$	(d) Including Land and Net Monetary Assets; $REGM_W(AT)$	(e) Deferred Taxes = Liability	(f) Previously Described	(g) Including Land and Net Monetary Assets	(h) Deferred Taxes = Liability
1966	6.1	6.3	2.9	3.3	3.6	58	76	43
67	5.6	6.2	5.8	2.9	3.5	59	75	43
68	5.9	6.1	4.4	1.9	3.3	58	73	42
69	7.2	7.8	0.6	4.3	4.5	54	72	42
70	5.9	3.1	4.6	-0.6	-1.2	52	71	40
71	4.5	3.9	1.9	0.4	0.3	54	68	37
72	5.2	5.4	4.1	3.0	2.4	54	66	36
73	7.7	8.6	7.4	9.0	6.4	54	65	36
74	9.6	8.8	13.2	9.0	5.4	56	66	34
75	5.8	3.8	5.5	1.5	0.6	54	66	33
76	4.2	2.1	3.4	-0.9	-0.2	56	64	32
77	1.4	-4.2	-3.1	-10.2	-8.9	53	61	31
78	0.9	0.8	3.0	-6.2	-3.0	53	59	30
(79)		(2.1)		(-1.1)	(-2.9)		(60)	(31)
Average 1966–78	5.4	4.5	4.1	1.3	1.3	55	68	37
Slope 1966–78	-0.28	-0.53[a]	-0.06	-0.63	-0.59[a]	-.33[a]	-1.31[a]	-1.20

[a]Statistically significant; 5 percent level.

deferred each period (and capital includes net monetary assets and land). The difference between the previous figures and the figures based on the KKR-bank—that is columns (a) versus (b), (c) versus d, and (f) versus (g)—then depends on three factors: (a) the sample: the KKR-bank does not include companies smaller than 200 employees; (b) the quality of the data; (c) what has been included in the capital measure (only fixed assets—excluding land—in the previous section).

Table 3–8 can be interpreted as follows: the use of data of higher quality does not substantially change the picture of a declining ROC: see columns (a) and (b). For $REGM(AT)$, the data of higher quality give a lower average than previously described, and a downward-sloping trend—contrary to what has been shown earlier: see columns (c) and (d). This picture still holds if the definition of tax expense is altered: see columns (d) and (e). In all cases, however, the trends are not statistically significant.

As to the effect on the equity ratio of the use of data of higher quality, table 3–8 gives clear indications: the decrease in the equity ratio becomes more accentuated: see columns (f) and (g). If the definition of owner's equity is altered (deferred taxes are excluded from owner's equity) the trend does not change but, of course, the level of the ratio becomes lower: see columns (g) and (h).

The general conclusion thus becomes: the use of data of higher quality does not contradict the conclusions previously drawn on falling trends in real rates of return during the period 1966–78. Behind the general pattern, substantial differences can occasionally be found between different measures for specific years. Let us only pinpoint one difference, namely regarding $REGM(AT)$ in 1973 and 1974. Recall the spectacular outcome of $REGM_o(AT)$ in 1974 according to figure 3–5. When data of higher quality are used, the outcome for 1974 is not as spectacular any more—although still high—and it is not higher than for 1973. The implication of this is that great caution should be exercised in accepting and "explaining" the findings from and basing decisions on relatively poor aggregate data. For further discussion on this topic, see Johansson, 1974.

Our final test of validity concerns a comparison between measures for the aggregate and measures for individual firms that make up the aggregate. This is done in table 3–9, where the aggregate numbers based on the best available data (the KKR-bank) are compared with the value for the median firm based on the same data. To indicate the dispersion within the aggregate, the twenty-fifth and seventy-fifth percentiles are also given. The variables selected are $ROC_w(BT)$ and $REGM_w(AT)$ The aggregate figures thus correspond with the figures given in table 3–8, columns (b) and (d), respectively.

Table 3–9
Comparison between Measures for the Aggregate and for Individual Firms
(percent)

Year	$ROC_w(BT)$				$REGM_w(AT)$			
	Aggregate	Median	25th Percentile	75th Percentile	Aggregate	Median	25th Percentile	75th Percentile
1966	6.3	6.7	1.5	14.7	3.3	2.1	−3.5	9.9
67	6.2	7.3	2.3	13.7	2.9	2.6	−2.7	10.1
68	6.1	5.5	0.1	13.6	1.9	0.7	−6.6	9.3
69	7.8	6.6	1.7	12.8	4.3	2.3	−4.5	9.4
70	3.1	2.9	−2.3	8.6	−0.6	−1.4	−9.1	5.4
71	3.9	4.1	−0.9	8.7	0.4	−0.9	−8.4	5.7
72	5.4	5.7	1.4	11.8	3.0	3.3	−3.6	10.1
73	8.6	8.3	2.9	15.3	9.0	8.1	1.2	16.5
74	8.8	7.0	0.9	15.8	9.0	6.8	−1.5	17.7
75	3.8	3.3	−2.9	9.2	1.5	0.0	−8.8	6.6
76	2.1	3.4	−4.4	9.6	−0.9	0.6	−10.3	8.3
77	−4.2	−2.1	−9.8	4.4	−10.2	−6.9	−20.3	0.8
78	0.8	1.6	−4.7	9.4	−6.2	−3.4	−17.3	6.4
79	2.1	2.8	−3.1	9.6	−1.1	−0.1	−9.9	8.0
Average	4.3	4.5	−1.2	11.2	1.2	1.0	−7.5	8.9
Slope	−0.49[a]	−0.42[a]	−0.58[a]	−0.42[a]	−0.57	−0.31	−0.84[a]	−0.22

[a]Statistically significant, 5 percent level.

As can be seen in table 3–9, analyzing the median firm instead of the aggregate gives a slightly different picture. The average values are lower and the slopes of the trendlines are more negative (decreasing). As a general remark one might add that the difference between the aggregate and the median value should foster great caution when basing analysis on aggregate data. This is true for all kinds of measures of profitability and refers to descriptions of long-term trends as well as analysis of changes from year to year and absolute levels for individual years.

Notes

1. The figure and the discussion are based on the assumption that total capital of the company is defined excluding non–interest-bearing liabilities. By "debt" is thus meant interesting-bearing liabilities and by "nonmonetary assets" monetary assets less non–interest-bearing liabilities.

2. The difference between depreciation (or costs of goods sold) measured at historical costs and measured at current costs equals realized holding gains/losses.

3. The degree of approximation depends on many factors, including lives of assets, growth rate, the manner in which specific prices increase over time, and asset structure. Great caution should be exercised when using historical costs as a basis for descriptions over time. See also note 15.

4. The treatment of taxes in the manner indicated is mainly for pedagogical reasons. The Swedish corporate tax system is comparatively liberal in that it gives the firm many different opportunities to postpone tax payments. Writing down inventories, accelerated depreciation techniques, and different kinds of investment reserves are the main examples. It has turned out to be very difficult to describe the special features of the Swedish tax system to an international forum not specifically interested in the taxation of firms. "Economic" arguments for concentrating on actually paid taxes can easily be raised, but the perhaps the most crucial supporting argument for the purposes of this chapter is that of avoiding a difficulty that is mainly Swedish.

5. We will concentrate on companies on the so-called AI-list at the Stockholm Exchange.

6. The values for nominal rate of return during the period 1965–82 have been developed by Aktiv Placering, Skandinaviska Enskilda Banken, Stockholm. The values for 1949–64, which have never before been published, have been constructed with "Affärsvärldens general

index" as a first input. The index, which started in 1949 with a consistent methodology, describes the market value of all companies' stocks. Figures for aggregate dividends have been constructed on the assumption that the aggregate figure has increased over time in a linear fashion and that the slope of this trend coincides with a regression line applied to the stock index. The procedure assumes an average ratio of aggregate dividends to market value of stock that is the same for 1949–64 as for 1965–82.

7. The spectacular real rate of return during 1981 and 1982 is partly the effect of a substantial reduction in taxes for private investors.

8. We define the aggregate market value of debt at the beginning of period t, $M(L_t)$, as:

$$M(L_t) = E(I)_t/i_t,$$

where

$$E(I)_t = \text{Expected interest earned during period } t$$
$$i_t = \text{Nominal market rate of interest.}$$

The simple formulation implies an infinite rather than finite income stream. The fact that loans are repaid is thus—for the aggregate—viewed as a tool for changing nominal rates over time rather than as reflecting an intention that the lending is to be abandoned.

The formulation further implies that the expected interest earned is constant over time. The actual expectations of course concern interest earned on loans given at a specific point of time, t, but fluctuations in interest earned over time are a function of fluctuations in the market interest rate. At a specific point in time, the interest rate is i_t and the expectations derived from that interest are given and assumed constant, $E(I)_t$.

As to the actual measurement of the components, i_t is perhaps the more difficult. Generally speaking, i_t is the (weighted) average of the market rate on the "bank loan" market and the bond market. These rates change over time and differ between companies and between loans to the same company (because of the risk involved). What we can observe are rates required by the market for the loans actually given. As a result of different kinds of regulations, the differences in risks are, however, mainly accounted for by means other than differences in interest rates—leaving very small differences in interest rates between companies and between markets. We will therefore use the market interest rate on long-term industrial bonds as the base for our measure of average market rate on all debt. To account for the higher interest normally required on other types of loans, we have added two percentage points to the bond rate.

The expected interest earned—the numerator of the ratio—consists of two main parts. The first regards loans where the face interest rate is given and is constant over time. Examples are bonds and some bank loans. Expected interest earned on these loans can be computed by the market with a very high degree of accuracy. The second part regards loans where the face interest rate changes over time. These fluctuations reflect changes in the market interest rate. At the beginning of period t, this market interest rate is i_t and the expected interest earned during period t becomes a function of i_t. Since i_t only takes one value, that is, the value for the aggregate, the second part of the expected interest earned can also be computed with a high degree of accuracy.

The solution we have selected is therefore to define $E(I)_t$ as the actual interest earned during the period I_t. As actual and expected interest earned coincides as to the first type of debt, the possible difference between $E(I)_t$ and I_t becomes primarily a matter concerning the second type of debt and thus a function of changes in the market interest rate *within* period t. In addition, there is a variance that is the result of interest on new net borrowing. Both variances are presumably small compared to I_t and should not interfere too much with the validity of long-term descriptions.

Finally, in order to simplify the computations, let us assume that all retirements, A_t, and issuance of new debts, N_t, are being made at the end of the period, implying that the recorded interest expenses should be interpreted as the interest expense for the liabilities, L_t, at hand at the beginning of the period. Then, the market rate of return on debt, $R(L)_t$, can be expressed as:

$$R(L)_t = (M(L_t) - M(L_{t-1}) - (N_t - A_t) + I_t)/M(L_{t-1}).$$

9. FINDATA is managed by the Economic Research Institute at the Stockholm School of Economics. The sample consists—with two exceptions—of all listed nonfinancial companies that can be studied over the whole period. When this study originally was planned, the intention was to cover the period 1967–78. Forty-five companies were selected. Later, the period was extended to 1980 and during 1979 and 1980 two companies left the Stockholm Exchange and must therefore be excluded from the sample. The figures for 1979 and 1980 therefore cover forty-three companies. Together they account for approximately 40 percent of industrial employment in Sweden.

10. The figures of table 3–2 differ slightly from the figures in table 3–1 because in table 3–2 the sample is smaller (excludes financial companies and companies that cannot be studied all years in the period; see note 9).

11. Measured as a percentage of book value, the market value of debts decreased from 97.2 percent in 1966 to 83.9 percent in 1978. The market value of stocks was 49.7 percent of the book value of owners' equity—as measured in table 3–3 (that is, including deferred taxes)—in 1966 and decreased to 39.2 percent in 1978.

12. Except for the last years in the studied period, financial statements typically give no information on current costs. Historical costs have then been used, but adjusted to current costs through correction factors applied directly to the aggregated historical cost figures. These correction factors consist of ratios between current cost and historical cost figures, collected from a data set (the KKR-bank; see section entitled "Tests of Validity"), where data for individual corporations—rather than business groups—have been collected. These data include both historical cost and current cost figures. Our experiences from data collection give us reason to believe that this way of approximating current costs for the aggregate of business groups should give a valid picture, but we have no way of testing the validity of the technique.

13. Among the ROC measures, ROC_W is most accurately computed because all that is needed are two adjustments of the basic historical cost data. Thus, the change in unrealized holding gains/losses is added to the numerator of the historical costs ratio and in the denominator the assets valued at current costs are substituted for historical cost figures, that is, accumulated unrealized holding gains/losses are added to the historical cost figures; see note 12.

The ROC_F measures are based on depreciation over the economic life of assets and on current costs calculated for each business group by Aktiv Placering, Skandinaviska Enskilda Banken, Stockholm. As to the holding gains/losses on inventory, CP has been used as the price index since there is no appropriate alternative index for individual business groups or industries to utilize. In the long run, changes in CP should be a valid description of price movements in inventory. But for individual years the technique might have caused slight shifts of profits between adjacent years. This means that the validity of ROC_F is less than that of ROC_W.

14. By net monetary assets is meant monetary assets less non–interest-bearing liabilities (mostly current liabilities). This means that the debt concept used in the denominator coincides with the concept of debt used in the section entitled "Investors' Return" to calculate the market value of debt. Please observe that the numerator of ROC_W, but

not that of ROC_F, includes real financial revenue (since net monetary capital is included in the denominator).

15. Referring to the methodological discussion in the section entitled "Measures of Performance," it might be of some interest to compare measures based on historical costs with those based on current costs. The relevant comparison is one where the nominal rate based on historical costs is adjusted for the rate of inflation and compared to the real rate on all assets employed, based on current costs and including holding gains/losses (column e in table 3–3). The picture for measures after tax (percent) is shown in table 3–10. As expected, the description based on historical costs gives a slightly lower average rate of return, but the slope of the trendline is close to that of current costs, and it is statistically significant.

16. Some legal units might have operations abroad that are not run in the form of subsidiaries and that consequently will be included in the corporations studied. But such units should be excluded if "domestic operations" were to be operationalized literally.

17. The data in the section entitled "The Rate of Return in the Long Run" have most kindly been made available by Jan Sodersten at the University of Uppsala, who also has made the computations of the depreciable capital stock from national account data (produced by the Swedish Statistical Bureau). The procedure for measuring depreciable capital stock has been the perpetual inventory model. The sample includes manufacturing firms with more than fifty employees. Unfortu-

Table 3–10
Real Rate of Return after Tax on All Assets Employed

Year	Historical Costs	Current Costs
1967	3.9	4.0
1968	7.0	4.5
1969	6.6	9.8
1970	2.1	2.6
1971	0.7	3.6
1972	2.0	4.9
1973	4.6	7.0
1974	5.5	6.8
1975	1.2	2.7
1976	−1.2	−0.8
1977	−6.1	−5.5
1978	−0.2	1.4
1979	0.5	1.7
1980	0.4	−2.8
Average	1.9	2.9
Slope	−.54[a]	−.62[a]

[a]Statistically significant, 5 percent level.

nately, it has not been possible within the time limits of this research project to collect data later than 1978.

18. To pinpoint the turning point is partly a matter of taste. Should it be set before or after the peak of the business cycle (1959), that is, should it be set at 1958 or 1960? We have chosen the latter alternative.

19. In figures 3–6 and 3–7 nothing is plotted for the years 1951–53 because of the lack of data.

20. Owners' equity is computed by deducting liabilities from assets as computed in ROC_A. This means that land is excluded from the asset concept, which in turn leads to an undervaluation of owners' equity. Consequently, real holding gains/losses on land are excluded from the numerator. The total effect is that $REGM_O$ should be slightly lower than the "correct" variable, $REGM_W$. We can make no assessment of the development of the deviation across time.

21. Following the price turbulence and increase in the rate of inflation that accompanied the oil shock in 1973 came very high nominal accounting profits reported by companies in 1974. In order to prevent taxation of temporary windfall gains, special rules were employed to lighten the tax burden. This resulted in the lowest effective tax rate (taxes payable as a percentage of operating income) ever experienced during the period under study.

22. As to the *level* of the equity ratio, the figure probably underestimates the true level for two reasons. First, total capital (the denominator) is defined as including monetary capital instead of net monetary capital (this is a procedure chosen by Jan Sodersten in his computations; see note 17). At the same time land is excluded from the assets but the net effect on total capital should be that the data on assets are higher than what they would be if measured including net monetary capital and land. The second reason is that owners' equity is slightly underestimated for the reasons explained in note 20.

23. In Bertmar (1979), the focus for comparisons was the kind of data used in the section of this report entitled "The Rate of Return in the Long Run" on the one hand, and the kind of data used in the section entitled "Tests of Validity" on the other hand. The comparison was initiated by an article on rates of return, based on the first kind of data (Bergström and Sodersten, 1979). The numbers presented in that article do, however, differ from the numbers presented in the first of the two sections just mentioned. The reason for this is that in computing the numbers used in this chapter, separate indexes for building and machinery have been used while a weighted index was used in (Bergström and Sodersten, 1979).

24. The KKR-bank is described by Bertmar and associates (1979). As to the valuation of land it has been assumed that the prices of land

(that is, its current cost) change with the Consumer Price Index. This is an arbitrary choice—as would be any other choice—but is governed by the idea that, since any method for valuation of land can be disputed, we should measure real profits as if there were no real holding gains/ losses on land.

References

Bergström, V., and Sodersten, J. "Nominal and Real Profit in Swedish Industry." *Skandinaviska Enskilda Banken Quarterly Review*, 1–2/ 79.

Bertmar, L., and Molin, G. *Capital Growth, Capital Structure and Rates of Return*. Stockholm: EFI, 1977 (summary in English).

Bertmar, L., et al. *Wages, Profitability and Equity Ratio* Stockholm: EFI, 1979 (in Swedish).

Bertmar, L. "Profit Measurement: A Chaotic Picture." *Skandinaviska Enskilda Banken Quarterly Review*, 3–4/79.

Brealy, R., and Myers, S. *Principles of Corporate Finance*. New York: McGraw-Hill, 1981.

Ciccolo, J. "Four Essays on Monetary Policy." Unpublished Ph.D. Dissertation, Yale University, 1975.

Copeland, T., and Weston, F. *Financial Theory and Corporate Policy*. Reading, Mass.: Addison-Wesley, 1979.

Financial Accounting Standards Board, Statement 33.

Handelsbanken, Common Stock Return. Published Yearly.

Holland, D., and Myers, S. "Trends in Corporate Profitability and Capital Costs." In Robert Lindsay, ed. *The Nations Capital Needs: Three Studies*. Washington, D.C.: Committee for Economic Development, 1979, pp. 103–88.

———. "Profitability and Capital Costs for Manufacturing Corporations and All Nonfinancial Corporations." *American Economic Review*, May 1980, pp. 320–25.

Johansson, S.-E. "Profits and Inflation." *Swedish Association of Banks*, 1974 (only in Swedish).

———. "Measures of Profitability during Inflation." *Skandinaviska Enskilda Banken Quarterly Review*, 3–4/77.

Rundfelt, R. "Effektiv avkastning på aktier." IUI 1975 (only in Swedish).

Statens Offentliga Utredningar. SOU 1965: 72 (only in Swedish).

———. SOU 1978: 13 (only in Swedish).

The Profitability of United Kingdom Industrial and Commercial Companies 1963–1981

Norman P. Williams

Introduction

This chapter summarizes and updates a number of articles[1] published in the *Bank of England Quarterly Bulletin* in recent years that have examined trends in the profitability of United Kingdom non–North Sea industrial and commercial companies (that is, excluding the profits earned through the extraction of petroleum and natural gas). It describes some of the conceptual and methodological aspects of measuring these indicators and examines trends in them over the period 1963–81. Particular emphasis is put on (1) pretax historic cost and real rates of return on trading assets; (2) the relationship between post-tax returns on trading assets and the cost of capital (as summarized by Tobin's valuation ratio, q), which is thought to be an important influence on the volume of private industrial investment; and (3) pretax returns to the equity stake in trading assets that are related to returns on all trading assets by the levels of interest rates and capital gearing. While measures of profitability relate to non–North Sea industrial and commercial companies, the availability of data requires that estimates of the cost of capital, q, and capital gearing relate to all industrial and commercial companies.

National accounts data, compiled by the Central Statistical Office, are used in this chapter, in contrast to the company accounts data used in studies of the profitability of United Kingdom industrial sectors by Williams (1979 and 1981). (Another chapter in this volume—Williams [1984]—summarizes the company accounts based studies of the profitability of United Kingdom industrial sectors and describes the differences, mostly minor, between the two studies, which have been mainly enforced by the data.) The classification "industrial and commercial companies" comprises those privately controlled corporate enterprises,

The author acknowledges the benefits of numerous helpful discussions with colleagues in the Economics Division of the Bank of England.

other than those classified as financial companies, that are organized (with a few exceptions) for profit and are resident in the United Kingdom. (Certain government-controlled companies and companies that are subsidiaries of the National Enterprise Board are included. Unincorporated businesses are excluded and are classified within the personal sector.) The profits of the United Kingdom branches and subsidiaries of overseas parent companies are included, and the profits of the overseas branches and subsidiaries of United Kingdom parent companies are excluded. So far as possible, the profits of industrial and commercial companies' financial activities (nontrading income) are excluded.

Conceptual and Methodological Aspects of Measurement

Pretax Rates of Return on Trading Assets

The trading assets of companies are defined for these purposes as the net capital stock (that is, net of accumulated depreciation) of buildings, plant and machinery, vehicles, plus stocks and work-in-progress. Land and monetary working capital are excluded.[2] The national accounts allocate fixed assets to sectors on the basis of ownership, rather than use, so that distortions are likely to have arisen with the rapid growth of leasing by financial institutions to industrial and commercial companies in recent years, though the impact is, at present, unlikely to be large. Earnings are defined as gross trading profits, plus rent,[3] less capital consumption (valued at either historic cost or at current cost) and, for current cost measures of profitability, stock appreciation. This earnings stream is gross of interest payments, but net of nontrading income (other than rent) and income earned abroad, thus ensuring consistency with the measure of trading assets.

Alternative definitions of pretax rates of return on trading assets, which incorporate different valuations of the assets of the business, can then be derived. Traditional accounting practice has been to value the capital stock and capital consumption at, or close to, historic cost: such a measure can be expressed as:

$$\frac{GTP + R - CCH}{FH + W}, \tag{4.1}$$

where

GTP = gross trading profits;
R = rent;
CCH = capital consumption at historic cost;
FH = net capital stock at historic cost; and
W = book value of stocks and work-in-progress.

But the profit measured on a historic cost basis will overstate the surplus generated by a business after provision for the maintenance of the real value of its assets at a time of inflation. A more appropriate measure of the pretax rate of return generated by the total trading assets of a business involves: (1) the revaluation of fixed assets—and, consistently, capital consumption—at current, or replacement, cost; (2) the deduction of "holding gains" on stocks—stock appreciation or, as referred to in the accounting literature, the "cost-of-sales adjustment"—which are imputed to profits if costs are calculated on a historic, rather than a current, basis; and (3) the deduction from profits of a monetary working capital adjustment (MWCA) to reflect the erosion of the real value of monetary working capital in the form of net trade credit extended (or a credit to profits if credit received exceeds credit extended). In practice, the calculations presented here do not incorporate an MWCA (data on net trade credit are, however, available from end-1966): this omission is unlikely to compromise seriously the estimates of rates of return since net trade credit extended has been a very small portion of total trading assets.

A pretax real rate of return on trading assets,[4] measured in accordance with current cost accounting principles, can then be measured as:

$$\frac{GTP + R - CCR - SA}{FR + W^5} \qquad (4.2)$$

where

CCR = capital consumption at replacement cost;
SA = stock appreciation; and
FR = net capital stock at replacement cost.

An alternative measure of the real rate of return could be derived by valuing assets at constant purchasing power, thus crediting to profits any gains arising from company holding assets that have risen in price faster than general inflation.[6]

Posttax Real Rates of Return on Trading Assets

The calculation of a posttax real rate of return on trading assets[7] is inevitably complicated because of the frequent changes in the system of United Kingdom company taxation, because no single posttax rate of return is suitable for all purposes, and because the national accounts provide no balance sheet data on deferred taxation for industrial and commercial companies.[8] As a simplification, this chapter will describe the calculation of posttax returns for the period since 1973, when the "imputation" system of corporation tax has been in force.[9] Under this system, tax is levied at a single rate (at present 52 percent) on qualifying income. Companies pay advance corporation tax (ACT) when they make a qualifying distribution of dividends. This payment of ACT can be set against their overall liability to corporation tax within certain limits; the balance is their "mainstream" liability. In the hands of the shareholders, the dividend carries a tax credit equivalent to the basic rate of income tax (which has varied between 30 percent and 35 percent during the period of this study), and the shareholder is regarded as having paid income tax at that rate on the sum of the dividend and the tax credit.[10] The allowances that can be offset against accounting profits in deriving taxable profits have been more generous during the 1970s than previously. Important features of the present system are the availability of initial capital allowances of 100 percent for plant, machinery, ships, and aircraft, and of 75 percent for industrial buildings,[11] the availability of stock relief,[12] and the tax-deductibility of interest payments.

Two types of tax adjustment are presented: the "backward-looking" adjustment computes the deferred tax liability by reference to the allowances in force when the capital was acquired; and the "forward-looking" adjustment assesses the liability by reference to the allowances currently available. (The relative merits of these measures are discussed below.)

The derivation of a posttax rate of return on trading assets involves not just the deduction of tax accruals from profits but also the deduction of deferred tax liabilities—which may be regarded as that part of a business financed by the government—from trading assets. A liability to deferred tax may arise in a number of ways. The most important are the availability of accelerated depreciation allowances and of stock relief, and the revaluation surpluses on fixed assets for which a tax charge will arise if the gains are realized through disposal.[13] By way of illustration, if a company takes advantage of accelerated capital allowances on purchasing a machine and subsequently sells the asset, a tax liability arises in respect to the asset if it should be sold for more than its tax-written-down value. The revaluation of fixed assets to replacement cost also gives rise to a potential tax liability on the capital gains which would be realized through the disposal of the assets.

There is a separate calculation of the deferred tax liability for the backward-looking and forward-looking treatments of tax. The backward-looking approach attempts to assess a company's tax liability if it should sell all of its assets at their replacement value. Considering fixed assets first, the contingent tax liability depends on the depreciation that has been allowed over the life of those assets and can be written as:

$$c \ (FR \ - \ TWDVF) \tag{4.3}$$

where

$$c = \text{corporation tax rate; and}$$
$$TWDVF = \text{tax-written-down value of fixed assets.}$$

Fixed assets net of this liability can then be expressed as:

$$FR \ - \ c \ (FR \ - \ TWDVF) \tag{4.4}$$

or, equivalently, as:

$$(1 \ - \ c) \ FR \ + \ cTWDVF \tag{4.5}$$

$TWDVF$ is calculated in the following way. In comparing two successive years, $TWDVF$ is increased by the value of gross fixed investment in the later year but reduced by the value of (a) any investment grants received; and (b) statutory depreciation allowances. Thus $TWDVF$ at the end of year t is estimated as:[14]

$$TWDVF_t \ = \ TWDVF_{t-1} \ + \ G_t \ - \ GR_t \ - \ SD_t \tag{4.6}$$

where

$$G = \text{gross fixed investment;}$$
$$GR = \text{investment grants paid; and}$$
$$SD = \text{statutory depreciation.}$$

Under the original stock relief scheme, the deferred tax liability arising from stock relief was deducted from trading assets. This liability represented the contingent "clawback," or the government's equity stake in the value of a firm's stocks: hence, $c \ (W - TWDVS)$ was deducted from W, where $TWDVS$ was the tax-written-down value of stocks. But under the new scheme announced in the 1981 Finance Act, clawback only occurs in exceptional circumstances (see above). Since, therefore, there is effectively no deferred tax liability, W enters the measure of trading assets.

The current valuation of trading assets, net of deferred tax liabilities calculated on a backward-looking basis, can be written as:

$$CB = (1 - c)(FR + W) + c\ TWDVF \qquad (4.7)$$

where

> CB = backward-looking tax-adjusted replacement cost trading assets.

The remaining step is the calculation of posttax earnings. The available statistics on tax paid by companies are not used because they include taxes on nontrading income. On the other hand, the method of estimation presented here is defective in assuming that all tax relief and allowances are fully offset against taxable profits even though this has not been the case recently (see below). Each year's tax liability is computed by reference to existing and previous tax codes so that allowance is made for the impact of past investment incentives on companies' tax assessments. It is assumed, as a simplification, that all interest and dividend payments are liable to income tax at the basic rate, rather than the weighted average of all the relevant marginal rates, which is conceptually more appropriate.

Companies' mainstream tax liability, calculated on a backward-looking basis and having regard to the current system of stock relief only, is:

$$\begin{aligned} c\ (GTP + R - INT) - c\Delta ASI \\ \cdot\ W_{t-1} - t\ GDIV - c\ SD - GR + (c\ AFY + GR)\ N/G \end{aligned} \qquad (4.8)$$

where

> INT = gross interest payments;
> t = basic rate of income tax;
> $GDIV$ = gross dividend payments, including those classified as profits due abroad;
> $t\ GDIV$ = advance corporation tax (ACT);
> AFY = all first-year depreciation allowances (first-year allowances, initial allowances and investment allowances);

N = net investment (that is, $G - CCR$).[15]; and
ASI = stocks price index used in calculating stock relief.[16]

or, equivalently:

$$c\ (Y + SA + CCR - INT) - c\Delta ASI$$
$$\cdot\ W_{t-1} - t\ GDIV - c\ SD - GR + (c\ AFY + GR)\ N/G. \quad (4.9)$$

The tax liability of shareholders and interest recipients is:

$$t\ (GDIV + INT). \qquad (4.10)$$

The backward-looking rate of return can then be derived as:

$$\frac{(1 - c)Y - c\ (SA + CCR) + c\Delta ASI \cdot W_{t-1}}{(1 - c)(FR + W) + c\ TWDVF}$$
$$- \frac{(t - c)INT + c\ SD + GR - (c\ AFY + GR)N/G}{(1 - c)(FR + W) + c\ TWDVF} \qquad (4.11)$$

But posttax returns calculated with a backward-looking adjustment may not be a very good indicator of the prospective returns from a new investment, especially if the corporate tax system has been as subject to change as the United Kingdom's. The prospective returns will be influenced by the current tax rate and system of investment allowances, and will only be affected by tax allowances on earlier investment if these are large enough to prevent a company from taking (immediate) advantage of new investment allowances. The forward-looking rate of return attempts to produce a measure more relevant to investment decisions. The capital base is expressed as:

$$CF = (1 - \alpha)\ FR + W \qquad (4.12)$$

where

CF = forward-looking tax-adjusted capital base; and
α = present value of all tax allowances (including normal depreciation) per unit of investment.

Corresponding to this measure of the capital base, tax accruals are calculated by applying the present value of current investment incentives per unit of investment, α', to replacement investment, CCR, in the year in question. Tax reliefs stemming from investment allowances are limited to replacement investment alone because it is the rate of return on the existing capital stock which is to be measured. The measure α' differs from α because tax allowances vary among buildings, plant, machinery, and vehicles, and these components have different weights in capital consumption, CCR, and the capital stock, FR. The discount rate used in these calculations is the yield on five-year British government stocks, adjusted for the rate of corporation tax.

Companies' mainstream tax liability is:

$$c\,(GTP\,+\,R\,-\,INT)\,c\Delta ASI\cdot W_{t-1}\,-\,\alpha'\,CCR\,-\,t\,GDIV \quad (4.13)$$

or, equivalently:

$$c\,(Y\,+\,SA\,+\,CCR\,-\,INT)\,-\,c\Delta ASI$$
$$\cdot\,W_{t-1}\,-\,\alpha'\,CCR\,-\,t\,GDIV. \quad (4.14)$$

Taking account of the tax liability of shareholders and interest recipients as well, the forward-looking rate of return is:

$$\frac{Y\,-\,c\,(Y\,+\,SA\,+\,CCR\,-\,INT)\,+\,c\Delta ASI\cdot W_{t-1}}{(1\,-\,\alpha)\,FR\,+\,W}$$
$$+\,\frac{\alpha'CCR\,+\,t\,GDIV\,-\,t(GDIV\,+\,INT)}{(1\,-\,\alpha)\,FR\,+\,W} \quad (4.15)$$

or, equivalently:

$$\frac{(1\,-\,c)\,Y\,-\,c\,SA\,+\,c\Delta ASI\cdot W_{t-1}}{(1\,-\,\alpha)\,FR\,+\,W}$$
$$+\,\frac{(\alpha'\,-\,c)\,CCR\,-\,(t\,-\,c)\,INT}{(1\,-\,\alpha)\,FR\,+\,W} \quad (4.16)$$

Cost of Capital and Valuation Ratio (q)[17]

Flemming and associates (1976b) present a general measure of the cost of capital to a company, combining the cost of both equity and debt finance. The overall cost of capital is the rate at which the company's future earnings are discounted by the capital market in valuing the securities on which those earnings will accrue—whether in the form of interest, dividends, or retained profits. This discounted value of the future earning of a company is the sum of the market values of its equity, preference shares, long-term debt, and bank borrowing, and the cost of capital is the discount rate at which this financial valuation equals the present value of future posttax real earnings. Expectations of future earnings are, of course, unobservable; and relevant future earnings are restricted to those on the existing volume of capital. For these purposes, expected posttax real earnings in all future years on the existing capital stock (and any replacements) are proxied by earnings in the current year. The ratio of current forward-looking posttax real earnings to the financial valuation of companies then gives a measure of the posttax real cost of capital. The cost of capital can be expressed as:

$$\frac{FPRP}{FVIC} \qquad (4.17)$$

where

$FPRP$ = forward-looking posttax real profits—the
numerator of the rate of return in (4.15);[18] and
$FVIC$ = financial valuation of industrial and
commercial companies.

Estimates of the financial valuation were derived in the following way. The market values of ordinary shares, preference shares, and long-term loans were estimated by dividing the corresponding dividend or interest flows by the yield on such assets as measured by the appropriate "Financial Times" stock market indexes. The stock of bank advances is added to the value of these liabilities, and the total obtained represents the market valuation of earnings, whether from domestic physical assets, financial assets, or overseas assets. For a comparison with the rate of return on domestic physical assets, only a valuation of earnings from the first set of assets is relevant. The total financial valuation is therefore reduced by the value of companies' liquid assets. The market value of ordinary shares is multiplied by the ratio of United Kingdom trading income to the sum of United Kingdom trading and overseas income in an attempt to exclude the market valuation of overseas assets. The financial valuation of industrial and commercial companies can then be expressed as:

$$(MVOS \cdot PIUK) + MVPS + MVDL + BADN - LQAN \qquad (4.18)$$

where

$MVOS$ = market valuation of ordinary shares;
$PIUK$ = proportion of income arising in the United Kingdom;

$MVPS$ = market valuation of preference shares;
$MVDL$ = market valuation of debentures and loan stock;
$BADN$ = bank advances; and
$LQAN$ = liquid assets.

The incentive to invest might be supposed to depend on the relationship between prospective profitability and the cost of capital. Of the measures of profitability developed earlier, the forward-looking posttax real rate of return on trading assets is the most appropriate because its treatment of taxation takes account of current investment incentives. It will be remembered that this rate of return is based on current earnings rather than on expected future earnings. The cost of capital has also been measured by reference to current, rather than expected future, earnings, and so the relationship between these measures of the rate of return and the cost of capital can be summarized as the ratio of the financial valuation to the forward-looking tax-adjusted capital base. The valuation ratio (or q) thereby derived can be written as:

$$\frac{FVIC}{(1 - \alpha)\ FR - W} \tag{4.19}$$

Pretax Rates of Return on the Equity Stake and Capital Gearing

So far we have concentrated on the rate of return generated by the total trading assets of a business; that is, we have derived a measure of profitability which is independent of the financing "mix" between equity and debt. The owners of a business, however, will normally be more interested in the return on the equity stake in trading assets. In this chapter, we will concentrate solely on pretax returns to the equity stake. Posttax returns to the equity stake estimated from a sample of company accounts are presented in Williams (1984).

A pretax historic cost rate of return on the equity stake in trading assets can be derived from the corresponding return on all trading assets by deducting net interest payments (i.e. net of interest receipts) from earnings to give historic cost equity earnings, and deducting net debt from the historic valuation of total trading assets to give the equity stake in those assets. This return can be written as:

$$\frac{GTP + R - CCH - NINT}{FH + W - DEBN} \tag{4.20}$$

where

$$NINT = \text{net interest payments; and}$$
$$DEBN = \text{net debt.}[19]$$

$$DEBN = NVDL + NVPS + BADN - LQAN \qquad (4.21)$$

where

$NVDL$ = nominal value of debentures and loan stock; and
$NVPS$ = nominal value of preference shares.

Nominal returns on debt have typically been lower than those returns earned by total trading assets for the aggregate of companies;[20] the corollary is that the extent to which nominal returns on equity exceed those on debt depends on the capital gearing (at historic cost) of the business. Capital gearing is the extent to which a business is financed by debt; a historic valuation can be expressed as:[21]

$$\frac{DEBN}{FH + W}. \qquad (4.22)$$

The derivation of a pretax real rate of return on the equity stake in trading assets from the corresponding return on all trading assets involves the two adjustments required for the calculation of historic cost equity returns from returns on total trading assets (see above), but also allowance for the erosion of the real value of both the gross debt and the liquid assets of a business through inflation. The adjustment (the "gearing adjustment") is normally an addition to the profits of industrial and commercial companies since their gross debt normally exceeds their liquid assets, and may be regarded as that part of the nominal interest payment which is an early repayment of capital. It may be calculated as the accrued gain (referred to below as the "natural" gearing adjustment) to the equity stake:

$$p \cdot DEBN \qquad (4.23)$$

where

p = rate of inflation, here calculated as the change in
the retail price index between successive Decembers.

Alternatively, it may be calculated as the realized portion of the current cost adjustments to the earnings of total trading assets (i.e. stock appreciation, and the adjustments to depreciation and monetary working capital)[22]. This latter approach is consistent with the prudential conventions of accountants and is recommended in the current cost accounting standard, SSAP 16[23]. The SSAP 16 adjustment is here calculated as:

$$KGRN \left[SA + (CCR - CCH) \right] \qquad (4.24)$$

where

$$KGRN = \text{capital gearing at replacement cost, that is, } \frac{DEBN}{FR + W}.$$

A pretax real rate of return on the equity stake on trading assets (with either a "natural" or an SSAP 16 gearing adjustment) can be derived as:[24]

$$\frac{GTP + R - SA - CCR - NINT + GRAJ}{FR + W - DEBN} \qquad (4.25)$$

where

$$GRAJ = \text{gearing adjustment.}$$

Results

Pretax Rates of Return on Trading Assets

The main features of the rates of return shown in table 4–1 and figure 4–1 are the increasing divergence of historic cost and real pretax rates of return, especially during the 1970s, and the sharp fall in the real measure since the early 1970s. The historic cost return averaged about 15 percent in the years 1963–72; it then increased, exceeding 20 percent on average during the period from 1974 to 1979, before falling to 13¼ percent (the lowest recorded) in 1981. The impact of accelerating *current* rates of inflation is shown by a comparison of this return with one from which stock appreciation has been deducted: for instance, the returns gross and net of stock appreciation diverged sharply between 1972 and 1974 as raw material and wage costs increased sharply, but

Table 4–1
Rates of Return on Trading Assets: Non–North Sea
Industrial and Commercial Companies
(percent)

Year	Pretax Historic Cost	Pretax Historic Cost, Net of Stock Appreciation	Pretax Real	Posttax Real (Backward-looking)
1963	15.9	15.4	11.4	7.4
1964	16.6	15.9	11.9	7.8
1965	15.8	15.0	11.2	7.3
1966	14.2	13.4	9.9	5.9
1967	13.6	13.3	10.0	5.8
1968	14.8	13.3	10.1	5.7
1969	14.9	13.3	9.9	6.0
1970	14.4	12.2	8.6	5.2
1971	15.2	13.2	8.9	6.1
1972	16.8	14.5	9.3	6.5
1973	19.7	15.2	9.1	8.1
1974	20.0	12.0	6.0	6.6
1975	18.4	12.1	5.2	3.9
1976	20.4	13.5	5.5	5.5
1977	21.1	16.7	6.9	7.2
1978	21.1	17.6	7.2	7.1
1979	20.4	14.2	5.2	6.3
1980	15.6	11.7	3.6	4.2
1981	13.2	10.2	2.7	3.8

the divergence had narrowed appreciably by 1978 as a result of slower inflation.

The pretax real rate of return on trading assets, which also reflects the effect of *cumulative* inflation over the life of the capital stock, diverged increasingly from the historic cost rate of return, especially during the mid-1970s, when inflation was most rapid. The real rate of return, which was on a modest downward trend between the early 1960s and early 1970s, fell sharply in the mid-1970s (from 9 percent in 1973 to 5¼ percent in 1975): after a modest recovery, to 7¼ percent in 1978, there was a further sharp decline to 2¾ percent in 1981, the lowest yet. The principal factors underlying this most recent sharp fall in the real rate of return are the decline in demand and the deterioration in UK competitiveness, which restricted the ability of companies to pass on cost increases in the domestic market and reduced export margins.[25] However, the latest figures in particular may have been understating profitability; for instance, redundancy payments are treated as current spending in the national accounts and hence reduce profits, but they are in some ways akin to capital spending since they secure future profits

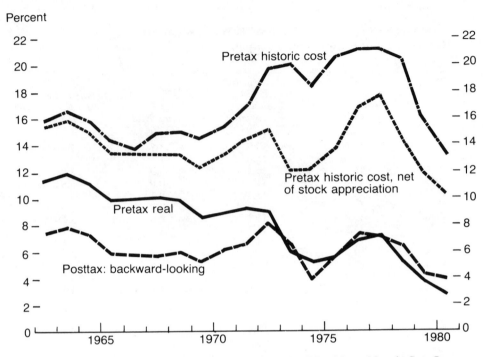

Figure 4–1. Rates of Return on Trading Assets: Non–North Sea Industrial and Commercial Companies

by raising labor productivity; local authority rates, which have recently grown more sharply than labor and raw material costs, are treated as a current cost, unlike income taxes levied by the central government, which are deducted after pretax profits have been struck; and the installation of labor-saving and energy-saving technology in recent years may have been accompanied by the accelerated scrapping of outmoded capital (Bank of England, 1982).

Posttax Returns, the Cost of Capital
and the Valuation Ratio (q)

The (backward-looking) posttax real rate of return on trading assets—the preferred measure of realized posttax profitability as it takes account of the system of allowances in force when new physical investment was undertaken—has been much better sustained than its pretax equivalent as tax allowances have become more generous.[26] In 1978, for instance, the posttax return was within 1 percent of the highest level recorded. The posttax return, however, in common with other measures, fell to a new low in 1981. The measure of posttax profitability described above assumes that all tax reliefs and allowances are fully offset against taxable profits, but as the value of these concessions has grown and pretax profitability has fallen, an increasing number of firms have not paid corporation tax and have thus accumulated unused tax reliefs and allowances. These have been estimated to amount to some £30 billion and to have increased recently by some £5 billion a year: about one-third of the total is attributable to stock relief and most of the remainder to capital allowances.[27] Therefore, the measures presented here overstate actual posttax profitability because tax payments made by companies have exceeded the estimated notional tax liabilities, which assume that allowances have been fully used.

Estimates of the cost of capital and the valuation ratio (q) are shown in figure 4–2. Since 1976, the cost of capital has been higher (by about 2 percent on average) than previously, possibly reflecting a number of sources of increased uncertainty, including rates of inflation, which have been generally higher and more variable. The rise in the cost of capital to 8.5 percent in 1981 from 5.5 percent in 1980 reflects the short-run favorable impact on posttax profits of moving to the new stock relief scheme, which was not reflected in corresponding increases in market valuations of companies (perhaps because the markets had never expected the clawback of stock relief would be allowed to be fully effective, or because the market took into account the loss of relief on future physical stockbuilding), and the effect of increased real interest rates in depressing market valuations.

Having generally remained above unity, albeit on a declining trend, q fell sharply in 1974. In spite of a recovery up to 1979, q has remained below unity and fell back to a new low in 1981. Recent econometric work has provided some support for the role of q in explaining private industrial investment, although it has not been possible to demonstrate that this approach is clearly superior to alternative accelerator and neoclassical models (Jenkinson, 1981). In fact, private industrial investment has been relatively buoyant in 1980 and 1981 considering the very low levels of q (and also of output), and this may have something to do with deficiencies in the measurement of q. Recent changes in technology and the relative costs of energy and labor have widened the disparity between returns on the existing capital stock and on new investment, with the result that the average rate of return on existing assets has become an increasingly poor indicator of the inducement to invest. In addition, the argument above that the capital stock is being increasingly overestimated implies that measures of q will be biased downward.

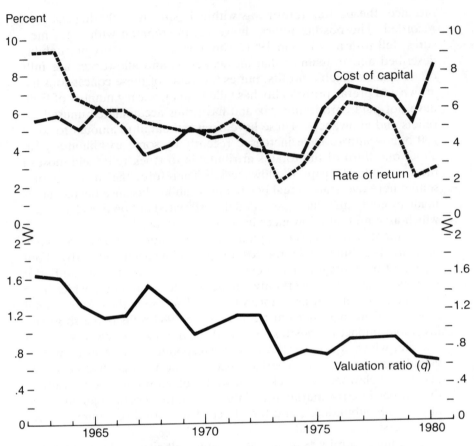

Percent

^a The rate of return covers non–North Sea industrial and commercial companies alone, but the cost of capital and *q* cover all industrial and commercial companies.

Figure 4–2. Rate of Return, Cost of Capital, and Valuation Ratio *(q)*^a

*Rates of Return on the Equity Stake,
and Capital Gearing*

Pretax historic cost returns on the equity stake (table 4–2) exceeded the corresponding return on total trading assets until 1979, but since then, with an increase in nominal interest rates and a reduction in the historic cost profitability of trading assets, the return to the equity stake has in fact been less than the return on trading assets overall.

The pretax real rate of return on the equity stake (with a "natural" gearing adjustment) was generally higher than the return on trading

Table 4–2
Rates of Return on the Equity Stake in Trading Assets: Non–North Sea Industrial and Commercial Companies
(percent)

		Pretax Real	
Year	*Pretax Historic Cost*	*"Natural"[a]*	*SSAP 16[a]*
1963	16.6	11.6	11.5
1964	17.9	12.9	12.4
1965	17.5	12.4	11.8
1966	16.2	11.2	10.6
1967	15.1	10.9	10.5
1968	16.5	11.7	10.7
1969	16.4	10.9	10.2
1970	15.9	10.2	8.9
1971	16.9	10.6	9.1
1972	18.8	10.5	9.5
1973	21.7	10.0	8.9
1974	22.2	7.9	5.4
1975	19.2	7.9	4.5
1976	20.6	6.1	4.9
1977	23.0	7.5	6.4
1978	23.0	7.1	6.7
1979	21.4	5.3	4.2
1980	15.1	3.1	1.9
1981	12.1	1.9	1.2

[a]Rates of return calculated with "natural" and SSAP 16 gearing adjustments, respectively.

assets during the 1960s and 1970s. Even though real interest rates were positive during the 1960s, they were lower than real returns on trading assets, and in the mid-1970s real interest rates were substantially negative as nominal interest rates did not compensate lenders for the effects of inflation in eroding the real value of their financial assets. So far in the 1980s, real returns on the equity stake have been lower than those on trading assets as a result of the sharp increase in real interest rates: this effect was only partly mitigated by reduced capital gearing. In 1981, the real return to the equity stake was 2 percent. Returns with an SSAP 16 gearing adjustment have been lower than with a "natural" gearing adjustment throughout the period under study.

The impact of revaluing physical assets at current cost is shown by a comparison of capital gearing as measured at historic and replacement valuations. In 1974, when historic cost capital gearing was at a peak, the replacement cost measure was 17¾ percent, below the levels experienced between 1966 and 1972 (table 4–3): replacement cost capital gearing has more than halved since 1974, and in 1981 it stood at 8¼ percent.

Table 4–3
Capital Gearing: Industrial and
Commercial Companies
(percent)

Year	Historic Cost	Replacement Cost
1963	16.1	13.1
1964	18.2	14.9
1965	21.2	17.5
1966	27.3	22.7
1967	25.8	21.7
1968	24.9	21.1
1969	24.8	20.9
1970	25.8	21.3
1971	24.4	19.5
1972	23.5	18.0
1973	22.9	16.4
1974	26.7	17.8
1975	24.4	15.3
1976	21.7	13.1
1977	20.8	12.4
1978	17.2	10.2
1979	17.0	9.9
1980	18.4	10.4
1981	15.1	8.3

Notes

1. J.S. Flemming et al. (1976a and 1976b), T.A. Clark, and N.P. Williams (1978). In addition, a series of annual supplementary notes have updated these estimates: the latest appeared in the June 1982 edition of the *Bank of England Quarterly Bulletin.*

2. The exclusion of land is the more troublesome. No reliable estimates are available in the national accounts, although land held by all companies was estimated to account for one-sixth of total trading assets on the above definition (Revell and Roe, 1971, and Walker, 1974). The company accounts-based analyses of United Kingdom profitability (Williams, 1984) include land and net trade credit extended (that is, net of credit received) within trading assets; land is not separately identifiable in the balance sheet data used, while the net credit extended by the sample of companies never exceeded 7.5 percent (in 1968) of the book value of trading assets during the period under study from 1961–77, and net credit received never exceeded 3 percent (in 1977).

3. An adjustment to include the rental income obtained by the letting of property.

4. This measure is equivalent to the measure $ROC_A(BT)$ in the common glossary.

5. National accounts estimates of the conceptually appropriate replacement valuation of stocks and work-in-progress are unavailable, but even at times of rapid United Kingdom cost inflation, the turnover of stocks is fast enough to imply only a modest divergence from the book valuation.

6. Clark and Williams (1978) showed that, for the aggregate of companies and the period examined, specific price indexes for fixed assets and stocks frequently diverged appreciably from "general" price indexes in the short run, but that such divergences were small over the longer term.

7. This measure is equivalent to the measure $ROC_A(AT)$ in the common glossary, except that account is taken of tax accruals, rather than payments, and deferred tax is deducted from current cost trading assets.

8. The company accounts-based work reported by Williams (1984b) had access to the deferred tax provisions published in companies' balance sheets, and the corresponding accruals in the profit and loss accounts. Even so, the calculation of a posttax real rate of return (in that case on the equity stake in trading assets) consistent with the backward-looking basis presented here is difficult because, with assets typically valued at less than replacement cost, the published deferred tax provision is unlikely to measure the tax liability on disposal of the assets of the business.

9. A summary tabulation of the UK corporate tax system for the years 1961–77 appears in Williams (1984). Fleming et al. (1976a) give details of the calculations under earlier tax regimes.

10. Shareholders pay additional income tax on their dividend receipts if their marginal tax rate exceeds the basic rate of income tax. If their marginal rate is less than the basic rate (certain institutions, such as charities and pension funds, are exempt from income tax), then they receive a tax rebate.

11. An increase from the rate of 50 percent, which had been in force since 1972, took effect from the time of announcement in March 1981.

12. The stock relief scheme was introduced in 1974, allowing relief on any change in the value of stocks and work-in-progress (because of either a rise in price or volume) in excess of 10 percent of gross trading profits net of short-term interest payments and, later, capital allowances. The percentage was increased to 15 percent from 1975–76. Relief was recovered by way of a tax charge if the book value of stocks fell (the "clawback"). The 1981 Finance Act introduced a new scheme, which applied to periods of account ending on or after November 14, 1980. Under this scheme, relief is calculated on the basis of the book value of stocks (at the start of the period of account) multiplied by the

increase in an index of the price of stocks. Broadly speaking, therefore, relief is restricted to the effect of inflation on the value of stocks. There is no clawback provision, except where a business ceases operation or the scale of its operations becomes small by comparison with the recent past.

13. Other sources of such liabilities, and certain aspects of the accounting treatment of them, are described in Williams (1984b).

14. Flemming et al. (1976a) describe the assumptions made to provide an initial estimate of TWDVF.

15. The term N/G is included so that tax relief on net investment does not form part of the return on the existing stock of trading assets.

16. The credit arising from the new stock relief scheme is expressed as $c\Delta ASI \cdot W_{t-1}$. When ASI falls, no relief is given, nor is any tax liability incurred.

17. The cost of capital is equivalent to the measure ρ in the common glossary, except that the real profits stream is net of tax accruals on a forward-looking basis. The valuation ratio (q) is equivalent to q_A in the common glossary, except that the denominator is the (forward-looking) tax-adjusted current cost measure of trading assets.

18. This measure of earnings relates to all industrial and commercial companies so as to be consistent with the financial valuation.

19. The data from which the estimates of net debt are derived relate to all industrial and commercial companies. An estimate for non–North Sea companies has been hypothesized on the simplifying assumption that net debt finances non–North Sea and North Sea trading assets—at replacement cost—in proportion to their respective magnitudes (that is, capital gearing is the same in both sectors).

20. Though the reverse has been true in some industrial sectors during recent years (for example, vehicles, and shipbuilding and marine engineering, in which historic cost returns on trading assets have frequently been under 10 percent; see Williams, 1984b).

21. This measure is equivalent to K_k in the common glossary.

22. For the reason stated above, the MWCA is excluded from this calculation, though it is included in the company accounts-based study of Williams (1984); the exclusion is unlikely to compromise seriously the estimates of the SSAP 16 gearing adjustment.

23. Institute of Chartered Accountants in England and Wales (1980).

24. The measure with a "natural" gearing adjustment is equivalent to $REGM_O(BT)$ in the common glossary, except that net trade credit is excluded from the equity stake in trading assets and, consistently, the earnings stream does not incorporate an MWCA.

25. An econometric analysis, based on an historic cost-plus pricing rule, has been partly successful in explaining real rates of return in the

United Kingdom in terms of changes in the rate of cost inflation, capacity utilization, and trend factors (see Williams, 1984).

26. The role of stock relief, which was not introduced until November 1974 with retrospective effect from 1973–74, in sustaining posttax real returns was particularly important; during much of 1974, the backward-looking posttax real rate of return calculated on the basis of the tax provisions then current was negligible.

27. See the Green Paper on Corporation Tax (HMSO, 1982).

References

Bank of England. "Profitability and Company Finance." *Bank of England Quarterly Bulletin* 22, no. 2 (1982):243–50.

Clark, T.A., and Williams, N.P. "Measures of Real Profitability." *Bank of England Quarterly Bulletin* 18, no. 4 (1978):513–22.

Flemming, J.S.; Price, L.D.D.; and Ingram, D.H.A. "Trends in Company Profitability." *Bank of England Quarterly Bulletin* 16, no. 1 (1976a):36–52.

Flemming, J.S.; Price, L.D.D.; and Byers, S.A. 1976b. "The Cost of Capital, Finance and Investment." *Bank of England Quarterly Bulletin* 16, no. 2 (1976b):193–205.

Green Paper on Corporation Tax (HM Stationery Office, Cmnd 8456, January 1982).

Institute of Chartered Accountants in England and Wales. Current Cost Accounting, Statement of Standard Accounting Practice, no. 16, 1980.

Jenkinson, N.H. "Investment, Profitability and the Valuation Ratio." Bank of England Discussion Paper, 1981.

Revell, J., and Row, A.R. "National Balance Sheets and National Accounting—A Progress Report." *Economic Trends* (HMSO) 211 (1971):8–19.

Walker, J.L. "Estimating Companies' Rate of Return on Capital Employed." *Economic Trends* (HMSO) 253 (1974):30–46.

Williams, N.P. 1979. "The Profitability of UK Industrial Sectors." *Bank of England Quarterly Bulletin,* 19(4):394–401.

———. "Influences on the Profitability of Twenty-two Industrial Sectors." Bank of England Discussion Paper, no. 15, 1981.

———. "UK Industrial Sectors's Rates of Return." In D.M. Holland, ed. *Measuring Profitability and Capital Costs.* Lexington, Mass.: LexingtonBooks, D.C. Heath & Co., 1984.

5 United Kingdom Industrial Sectors' Rates of Return

Norman P. Williams

Introduction

The previous chapter in this volume (Williams, 1984) analyzed trends in the profitability of United Kingdom non–North Sea industrial and commercial companies from 1963 to 1981 using aggregate national accounts data. This chapter applies a similar conceptual framework to the estimation of rates of return in different sectors of United Kingdom industry over the period 1961–77, using the published accounts of over 1,000 large listed companies as aggregated and presented in the Department of Industry's "Business Monitor MA3: Company Finance"[1] (hereafter referred to as BM). This chapter avoids a repetition of much of the common framework for measuring rates of return. There are, however, a number of differences (most of them enforced by the data) between the two chapters: the chief ones are the different practices adopted by accountants and national accounts statisticians in writing off physical assets; the use of both a broader definition of trading assets (including land and net trade credit extended) and of published data on companies' tax accruals and deferred tax liabilities, in the company accounts based study; and the coverage of the company accounts study, which is restricted to large listed companies and includes indistinguishably the overseas activities of the sample, but excludes the United Kingdom operations of foreign-owned companies. (Appendix 5C describes more fully the characteristics of the sample of companies.)

This study shows that the pretax real profitability of United Kingdom industrial sectors has varied greatly, the more so in the later years examined, when some have earned pretax real returns of over 10 percent, while others have sustained losses; and the downward trend has been widespread, though there have been exceptions. This pattern is common to real pretax returns on trading assets and on the equity stake in those assets: returns on the equity stake have, however, been higher in most, though not all, sectors to an extent that chiefly reflects the capital gearing of trading assets at replacement cost. There has also been a downward trend in the posttax real rate of return on the equity stake in most sectors, with many sustaining losses in the later years.

An econometric analysis provides evidence that the acceleration of cost inflation in the 1970s—together with an adherence to pricing policies that have not paid full regard to current costs—was an important factor leading to the depressed level of profitability in the most recent years studied.

Pretax Recorded Profitability

This section presents estimates of pretax recorded rates of return on companies' total trading assets and on the equity stake alone.

Trading Assets

The measurement of the pretax recorded rate of return on trading assets differs in two main ways from the corresponding historic cost measure in Williams (1984). First, the recorded rate of return is based directly on companies' published accounts and thus incorporates revaluations to fixed assets (and to depreciation provisions): the historic cost measure calculated from national accounts data is calculated by applying a perpetual inventory model, based on assumed physical asset lives, to prior gross investment flows and may thus be regarded as a "true" historic cost measure.[2] Second, trading assets have been defined as including land and net trade credit extended in this study, whereas data limitations prevent the inclusion of these items in national accounts-based studies. (A full specification of the measures presented in this chapter is available in appendix 5B.)

The recorded rate of return on the trading assets of the entire sample of manufacturing, distribution, and service industries fluctuated in the 12–15 percent range between 1961 and 1971, but then increased to average about 17 percent from 1972 onward. The return in manufacturing industry was, on average, around 3 percent lower than in distribution and service industries during the 1960s. During the 1970s, this measure of the rate of return in manufacturing industry rose, and rose by more than in distribution and service industries: since 1974, the rate of return averaged just over 17 percent in both broad aggregate groupings (table 5–1).

At the more disaggregated level of individual industrial sectors, there have been significant differences in recorded rates of return on trading assets and in their trends during the period examined (see table 5–1). During the period 1974–77, the average recorded rate of return was in the 15–20 percent range in twelve of the twenty-two industrial

Table 5–1
Pretax Recorded Rates of Return on Trading Assets and on the Equity Stake in Illustrative Sectors
(percent)

| | Manufacturing | | | | | | | | | | Distribution and Services | | | |
| | Total | | Tobacco | | Electrical Engineering | | Vehicles | | Bricks, Pottery, Glass, Cement, etc. | | Total | | Miscellaneous Services | |
Years	Trading Assets	Eq-uity	Trading Assets	Eq-uity	Trading Assets	Eq-uity	Trading Assets	Eq-uity	Trading Assets	Eq-uity	Trading Assets	Eq-uity	Trading Assets	Eq-uity
1961–65	13.1	15.5	13.2	19.1	13.5	16.2	12.2	14.3	17.6	19.8	16.3	19.3	16.6	20.9
1966–69	12.3	15.0	14.8	19.3	13.1	16.6	11.8	14.3	14.1	16.6	15.1	18.3	14.4	18.7
1970–73	14.3	18.1	17.8	26.4	17.8	22.0	9.8	10.8	16.4	20.5	17.4	22.5	13.9	18.9
1974–77	17.2	20.2	20.6	28.7	22.0	24.1	8.9	5.1	15.0	16.7	17.2	20.4	13.5	16.6

sectors, but the return averaged about 10 percent or less in shipbuilding and marine engineering (indeed, there were losses in this sector in some years), vehicles, and clothing and footwear, but averaged 22 percent in electrical engineering and rather higher in leather, leather goods and fur. The upward trend in the recorded rate of return in the 1970s described above was particularly marked in chemical and allied industries, electrical engineering, leather, leathers goods and fur, timber, furniture, etc. But there was a clear downward trend in the return in the shipbuilding and marine engineering, vehicles, clothing and footwear, and miscellaneous services sectors.

Equity Stake

The recorded rates of return on the equity stake for the entire sample of manufacturing, distribution, and service industries exceeded the returns on trading assets, reflecting both the extent to which the returns generated by trading assets exceeded those accruing to the equity stake[3] and changes in capital gearing as recorded in companies' balance sheets (table 5–2).

In most sectors, the rate of return on the equity stake exceeded that on trading assets. In the vehicles industry, however, the return to the equity stake was lower than that on trading assets during part of the 1970s, because of the very low returns on trading assets, lower in fact than the prior claim of the debt stake: in 1975, the equity stake sustained losses, even though trading assets as a whole were generating a modest profit. There was a modest amount of sectoral variation in the returns accruing to the debt stake[4] (perhaps reflecting risk and,

Table 5–2
The Relationship between Recorded Rates of Return on Trading Assets and on the Equity Stake: Manufacturing, Distribution and Services
(percent)

Years	Rates of Return: Recorded		"Implied" Nominal Rate of Interest		Capital Gearing: Recorded
	Trading Assets	Equity	On Gross Debt	On Net Debt	
1961–65	13.8	16.5	5.4	6.3	22.2
1966–69	13.6	16.8	6.9	7.4	28.1
1970–73	15.1	19.2	7.7	8.5	32.0
1974–77	17.2	20.3	10.4	11.5	29.1

with nominal interest rates rising on average over the period, differences in the structure and age composition of the debt), but differences in capital gearing as recorded in companies' balance sheets were more pronounced. Two examples illustrate the effects of differences in capital gearing on the relationship between recorded returns on the equity stake and on total trading assets. For instance, in the period 1974–77 (see table 5–3), the recorded return on the equity stake exceeded that on trading assets by 3 percent in the miscellaneous services industry, in which capital gearing was 45 percent, but the margin was 1.5 percent in the bricks, pottery, glass, cement, etc. industry, in which capital gearing was under 23 percent. The effect of changes in capital gearing can also be significant: the recorded rate of return on the equity stake in manufacturing industry exceeded that on trading assets by 2.5 percent or more in each year from 1970 to 1977, when capital gearing fell from 33 percent to 25 percent, but the margin fell from 4 percent to 1 percent over the same period in electrical engineering, in which capital gearing fell from 33 percent to 7 percent.

Pretax Real Profitability

Trading Assets

The calculation of a real rate of return on trading assets from the recorded return involves[5] the following deductions from recorded profits: (1) stock appreciation (sometimes referred to as a "cost-of-sales adjustment"); (2) a depreciation adjustment (that is, an adjustment of published depreciation provisions on to a current cost basis); (3) a monetary working capital adjustment (applied to the net trade credit extended of a business). It also involves the revaluation of physical assets on to a current cost basis.

The conceptual basis of these adjustments was discussed in Williams (1984) and the derivation of these adjustments is described in appendix 5A. The adjustments have been applied to the accounts of each industrial sector and broad aggregate, rather than company by company.

The pretax real rate of return on trading assets of the entire sample of manufacturing, distribution, and service companies exceeded 10 percent throughout the 1960s. The return was rather lower (averaging about 10 percent), and showing a more marked downward trend in manufacturing than in distribution and services (in which the return averaged 13.5 percent). The real rate of return declined sharply in both broad industrial groupings between 1972 and 1975, though more so in manufacturing, in which the return fell to just 2 percent. The real rate

Table 5–3
Recorded Capital Gearing in Illustrative Sectors
(percent)

Years	Manufacturing					Distribution and Services	
	Total	Tobacco	Electrical Engineering	Vehicles	Bricks, Pottery, Glass, Cement, etc.	Total	Miscellaneous Services
1961–65	22.4	38.5	24.4	20.9	13.2	21.0	26.3
1966–69	28.3	29.0	30.2	29.8	23.5	26.0	32.7
1970–73	32.2	38.0	26.9	33.9	28.8	31.2	39.4
1974–77	28.7	41.6	14.2	38.0	22.8	29.6	45.0

Table 5–4
Pretax Real Rates of Return of Trading Assets in Illustrative Sectors
(percent)

Years	Manufacturing					Distribution and Services	
	Total	Tobacco	Electrical Engineering	Vehicles	Bricks, Pottery, Glass, Cement, etc.	Total	Miscellaneous Services
1961–65	10.3	10.3	9.8	12.6	14.8	13.9	11.2
1966–69	9.2	11.0	9.2	10.6	11.8	12.9	11.2
1970–73	7.3	13.7	11.3	4.4	10.1	12.1	9.3
1974–77	3.7	7.2	8.9	−5.1	3.3	7.7	5.2

of return recovered between 1975 and 1977, especially in manufacturing industry, in which it rose to 6 percent. A framework within which these trends, at both the aggregate and sectoral level, can be analyzed is presented in the section of this chapter entitled "An Econometric Analysis of Trends in Profitability." It is suggested that the sharp fall in real profitability in the mid-1970s reflected, to a significant extent, the acceleration of cost inflation (exacerbated, no doubt, by price controls and an adherence to historic cost accounting conventions) and falling capacity utilization. The impact of the current cost adjustments in depressing real profitability was more pronounced in manufacturing than in distribution and service industries (figure 5–1): in 1975, for instance, when pretax recorded rates of return on trading assets were roughly the same in both sectors, the real return was 2 percent in manufacturing compared with 7¾ percent in distribution and services.

The downward trend in aggregate profitability is mirrored in most sectors (table 5–4, and the results for all twenty-two sectors shown in appendix 5D): for instance, the real return at least halved in fourteen of the twenty-two sectors between 1961–65 and 1974–77. The fall was particularly sharp (10 percent or more) in vehicles, metal goods not elsewhere specified, clothing and footwear, and bricks, pottery, glass, cement, and so on. In two sectors (electrical engineering and leather, leather goods, and fur), however, the real return on trading assets was, in general, higher during the 1970s than the 1960s. Real profitability fell sharply in all sectors (except leather, leather goods, and fur) in the mid-1970s, though the timing of the fall varied, perhaps depending on the incidence of cost inflation and cyclical factors. There have been marked differences in real returns on trading assets between sectors throughout the 1960s and 1970s (table 5–4). In the years 1974–77, when the real return for the entire sample averaged about 5 percent, an average return of between 3 percent and 7 percent was earned in just ten of the twenty-two sectors. Three sectors (metal manufacture, shipbuilding and marine engineering, and vehicles) sustained losses over the period 1974–77 as a whole, and other sectors (notably textiles) sustained losses in some of the latest years studied. But the real return on trading assets averaged 10 percent in retail distribution in 1974–77 and was higher in leather, leather goods, and fur.

The Equity Stake

The pretax real rate of return on the equity stake in trading assets[6] can be derived from its recorded counterpart by making the current cost adjustments described above as being necessary to estimate a real rate

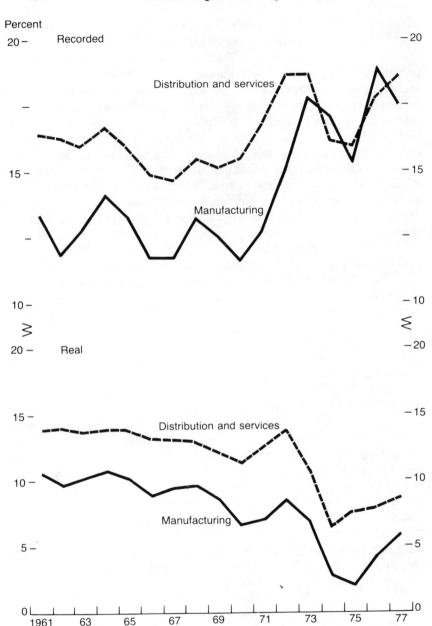

Figure 5–1. Pretax Recorded and Real Profitability of Trading Assets: Manufacturing, and Distribution and Services

of return on trading assets and, in addition, crediting a gearing adjustment to equity profits. Two alternative estimates of the gearing adjustment are presented here: a "natural" adjustment, which credits to equity profits the whole of the accrued gain resulting from the erosion of the real value of debt, and an SSAP 16 adjustment,[7] which credits only realized gearing gains (calculated as the debt-financed portion of stock appreciation, and of the current cost adjustments to depreciation and monetary working capital)[8] to equity profits.

"Natural" Gearing Adjustment. The pretax real rate of return on the equity stake (with a "natural" gearing adjustment) for the entire sample of companies fluctuated between 12.5 percent and 16 percent during 1961–73 and then fell sharply, to average about 9 percent from 1974 onward. Throughout this period, the return was lower in manufacturing (in which there was also evidence of a downward trend in the 1960s and early 1970s) than in distribution and services (figure 5–2). In the period 1974–77, the return averaged 7.5 percent in manufacturing, compared with 13 percent in distribution and services.

The real rate of return on the equity stake (with a natural gearing adjustment) for the entire sample of companies exceeded the return on trading assets throughout the 1960s and 1970s, although the differential varied as a result of movements in real returns on trading assets, real interest rates, and capital gearing at replacement cost.[9]

Real returns on the equity stake (with a natural gearing adjustment) exceeded those on trading assets in most sectors (table 5–5). Exceptions were shipbuilding and marine engineering, and vehicles in those years in which real returns on trading assets were particularly low. Sectoral differences in the relationship betwen real returns on equity (with a natural gearing adjustment) and on trading assets were heavily influenced by differences between sectors in levels of, and trends in, current cost capital gearing (table 5–6). For instance, in the period 1974–77, the real equity return was higher in the tobacco industry than in electrical engineering (15½% compared with 12%) in spite of the lower returns on trading assets (7% compared with 9%), chiefly because current cost capital gearing was nearly three times higher (34% compared with 13%). Further, between 1970–73 and 1974–77, the real return on equity was better sustained than the real return on trading assets in the miscellaneous services sector than in bricks, pottery, glass, cement, etc. (tables 5–4 and 5–5), partly because of little change in the capital gearing of the former at a time when gearing fell a good deal in the latter.

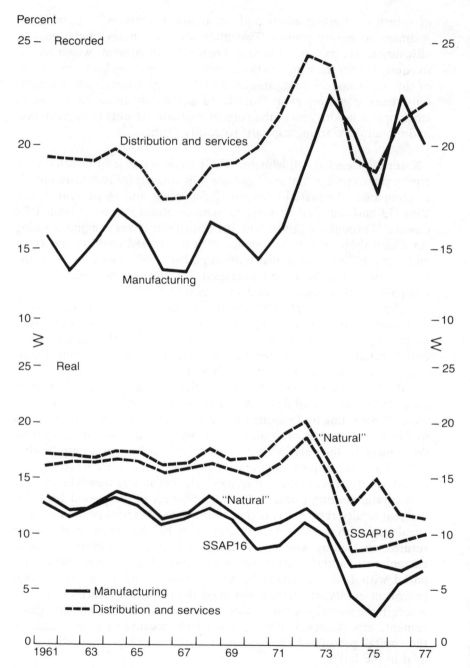

Figure 5–2. Pretax Recorded and Real Profitability of the Equity Stake: Manufacturing, and Distribution and Services

Table 5-5
Pretax Real Rates of Return on Equity (with a "Natural" Gearing Adjustment) in Illustrative Sectors
(percent)

	Manufacturing					Distribution and Services	
Years	*Total*	*Tobacco*	*Electrical Engineering*	*Vehicles*	*Bricks, Pottery, Glass, Cement, etc.*	*Total*	*Miscellaneous Services*
1961–65	12.8	16.3	12.4	16.6	16.8	17.0	13.9
1966–69	12.1	15.5	12.7	15.1	14.8	16.6	15.3
1970–73	11.0	23.9	16.3	7.1	14.3	18.1	15.4
1974–77	7.3	15.3	11.8	-6.3	6.1	12.8	11.8

Table 5-6
Capital Gearing at Replacement Cost in Illustrative Sectors
(percent)

	Manufacturing					Distribution and Services	
Years	*Total*	*Tobacco*	*Electrical Engineering*	*Vehicles*	*Bricks, Pottery, Glass, Cement, etc.*	*Total*	*Miscellaneous Services*
1961–65	20.7	37.2	22.8	25.1	12.3	19.5	20.7
1966–69	26.6	28.2	29.9	33.6	22.5	25.2	28.9
1970–73	28.2	35.5	26.1	34.5	24.9	28.8	34.0
1974–77	22.3	34.2	12.8	33.8	17.6	23.5	32.4

SSAP 16 Gearing Adjustment. Trends in real returns to the equity stake have been similar whether the calculation is based on a natural or an SSAP 16 gearing adjustment. Returns with an SSAP 16 gearing adjustment have, however, been lower throughout.

The sectoral estimates show a high degree of variation in real returns to equity (table 5–7). In the period 1974–77, when returns with an SSAP 16 gearing adjustment averaged just over 6 percent, the return was in the range of 4 to 8 percent in just ten of the twenty-two sectors: while some sectors (for instance, electrical engineering and retail distribution) earned an average return of over 10 percent, others (for instance, metal manufacture and vehicles) sustained losses. The intersectoral variability of real equity returns increased during the period under study and was rather greater than the variability of real returns on trading assets. Sectoral differences in the extent of the current cost adjustments were not great but were, nevertheless, great enough to have possible implications for the efficiency of capital markets. For instance, the real return on equity (with an SSAP 16 gearing adjustment) in leather, leather goods, and fur exceeded that in the tobacco industry during the years 1974–77 (14.5 percent compared with 11.5 percent), even though the recorded return on the equity stake was higher in the tobacco industry than in any other sector.

Posttax Real Rates of Return

The rates of return discussed above have been measured before tax, but the owners of companies are normally more interested in the posttax returns of the business. This section measures the posttax real rate of return accruing to the equity stake in trading assets, whether those returns are distributed (as dividends) or retained within the business.

The system of corporate taxation in the United Kingdom has undergone major changes during the period examined. Up to 1965, profits—whether retained or distributed—attracted a flat-rate profits tax and income tax at the basic rate. Corporation tax was introduced in 1965 and has been in force since. The "classical" system, which applied until 1973, imposed a flat rate of corporation tax on companies' taxable profits, and shareholders were additionally liable to income tax on their dividends. The classical system of taxation discriminated, thereby, in favor of profit retentions as compared with dividends,[10] and in favor of debt, as compared with equity, financing by allowing interest payments to be deducted from profits in assessing a liability to corporation tax. In 1973, the classical system was replaced by the "imputation" system. Companies now pay advance corporation tax (ACT) when they

Table 5-7
Pretax Real Rate of Return on Equity (with an SSAP 16 Gearing Adjustment) in Illustrative Subsectors
(percent)

| | | | Manufacturing | | | | Distribution and Services | |
| | | | Electrical | | Bricks, Pottery, | | | Miscellaneous |
Years	Total	Tobacco	Engineering	Vehicles	Glass, Cement, etc.		Total	Services
1961–65	12.4	15.6	12.1	16.1	16.6		16.5	13.4
1966–69	11.4	15.2	12.5	14.4	14.0		15.9	14.2
1970–73	9.7	20.6	15.2	5.4	12.8		16.4	12.4
1974–77	4.9	11.3	10.5	−8.9	3.9		9.2	5.4

Table 5–8
Corporate Tax System[a]
(percent)

Financial Year	Tax System	Corporate Tax Rate	Investment Allowances			Initial Allowances		
			Plant and Machinery	Industrial Buildings	Cars	Plant and Machinery	Industrial Buildings	Cars
1961/62	Profits tax and income tax	53.75	20	10	0	10	5	30
1962/63	"	"	30	15	"	"	"	"
1963/64	"	"	"	"	"	"	"	"
1964/65	"	"	"	"	"	"	"	"
1965/66	Classical	40.00	0	0	"	0	15	0
1966/67	"	"	"	"	"	"	"	"
1967/68	"	42.50	"	"	"	"	"	"
1968/69	"	45.00	"	"	"	"	"	"
1969/70	"	42.50	"	"	"	"	"	"
1970/71	"	40.00	"	"	"	"	30	"
1971/72	"	"	"	"	"	35	40	"
1972/73	"	"	"	"	"	55	50	"
1973/74	Imputation	52.00	"	"	"	100	"	"
1974/75	"	"	"	"	"	"	"	"
1975/76	"	"	ᶜ "	"	"	"	"	"
1976/77	"	"	"	"	"	"	"	"
1977/78	"	"	"	"	"	"	"	"

[a]This table presents a highly simplified summary of the system of investment incentives that have been available nationally. No account is taken of special regional schemes. Certain timing points (such as changes in investment incentives taking effect part of the way through a financial year) are not explicitly incorporated.

[b]Short-term interest is treated as an operating cost.

[c]Though allowances of 25 could still be claimed on plant and machinery purchased before 1973/74.

make a qualifying distribution. This payment of ACT can be set against their overall liability to corporation tax, the balance being their "mainstream" liability. In the hands of the shareholders, the dividend carries a tax credit equivalent to the basic rate of income tax, and the shareholder is regarded as having paid income tax at that rate on the sum of the dividend and the tax credit.[11]

There have been, in addition to these changes in the system of corporate taxation in the United Kingdom, numerous changes both in the rate at which tax is charged on taxable profits, and in the allowances which can be offset against accounting profits in deriving taxable profits (table 5–8). The most important changes during the period under study have been the nationwide extension of more generous initial capital allowances (which were increased to 100 percent for plant, machinery, ships, and aircraft in 1972, and to 50 percent for industrial buildings in

Table 5–8 *(continued)*

| Depreciation Allowances | | | Investment Grants | | | Other Allowances | |
Plant and Machinery	Industrial Buildings	Cars	Plant and Machinery	Industrial Buildings	Cars	Long-Term Interest[b]	Stock Relief
30	2	15	0	0	0	100	0
"	"	"	"	"	"	"	"
"	4	"	"	"	"	"	"
"	"	"	"	"	"	"	"
"	"	"	20	"	"	"	"
"	"	"	25	"	"	"	"
"	"	"	"	"	"	"	"
"	"	"	20	"	"	"	"
"	"	"	"	"	"	"	"
25	"	25	"	"	"	"	"
"	"	"	0	"	"	"	"
"	"	"	"	"	"	"	"
0[c]	"	"	"	"	"	"	$\Delta BVST - 0.1 GTPR'$[d]
"	"	"	"	"	"	"	"
"	"	"	"	"	"	"	$\Delta BVST - 0.15 GTPR''$[e]
"	"	"	"	"	"	"	"
"	"	"	"	"	"	"	"

[d]The relief was equal to the change in the book value of stocks ($\Delta BVST$) less a deduction of 10 percent of "trading profits" ($GTPR'$), that is, profits adjusted for tax purposes, excluding non-trading income and before deducting capital allowances.

[e]The relief is equal to the change in the book value of stocks ($\Delta BVST$) less 15 percent of trading profits after deducting capital allowances ($GTPR''$).

1974) and the retrospective introduction of stock relief in 1974. (There have been changes since 1977, notably the amended stock relief provisions discussed in Williams, 1984.)

The profits chargeable to tax for a particular period often differ appreciably from the accounting profit for the period. Systematic differences between accounting and taxable profits arise because certain types of income are tax free and/or because certain expenditure is allowable for tax purposes. There are, however, also "timing differences" between accounting and taxable profits, the result of the inclusion of items in the financial statements of a different period from that for taxation. Timing differences have become increasingly important during recent years owing to the availability of accelerated depreciation allowances (where the allowable depreciation charge exceeds the related charge in the financial statement) and of stock relief, and the revaluation surpluses on fixed assets for which a tax charge will arise if the gains are realized through disposal.[12] By way of illustration, if a company takes advantage of accelerated depreciation allowances on purchasing a machine and subsequently sells the asset, a tax liability arises in respect to the asset if it should be disposed of for more than its tax-written-down value (which is calculated by reference to the statutory depreciation allowances in force and not to accelerated depreciation allowances). Deferred taxation arising from the operation of accelerated depreciation allowances and stock relief is treated in a company's financial statements as a "transfer to deferred taxation" in the profit and loss account at the time the tax liability is deferred (i.e. when the allowance is claimed), and a deferred tax liability is shown on the balance sheet until the liability is fully written off.[13]

There are, however, circumstances—quite apart from the retrospective introduction of stock relief[14]—in which there will be a credit to the deferred tax balance without any corresponding transfer in the profit and loss account. The chief instance arises on the revaluation of a fixed asset in a company's balance sheet, which has as its counterpart a revaluation surplus among the company's liabilities. In order to allow for a potential tax liability on disposal of the asset, part of the revaluation surplus may be credited to the deferred tax balance. The total liability to deferred tax may be regarded as the government's "equity stake" in a business, and the tax accrual (including the transfer to deferred tax) as the return on that stake.

Unlike the method applied to national accounting data described in Williams (1984), following Flemming et al. (1976), in which estimates of tax accruals and deferred tax are derived using a simplified model of the tax system, posttax returns are estimated here using published data on tax accruals and deferred tax from companies' accounts. A posttax real rate of return to the private equity stake could be calculated from its pretax counterpart by (1) the deduction of tax accruals (including transfers to deferred tax balances) from pretax real equity profits; and (2) the deduction of deferred tax liabilities from the current cost equity stake in trading assets.

Published accounting data, however, have been inappropriate for the calculation of such a rate of return. Accounting provisions for tax accruals[15] (including transfers to deferred tax balances) are conceptually appropriate for the task. But the exclusion from the published deferred tax provision of the full tax liability contingent on the disposal of physical assets in excess of their tax-written-down value (because assets have not been revalued in the balance sheet to current cost) implies that a measure of the posttax return calculated using those provisions as published will understate the "true" injection of government capital into the business.[16] Estimates that take account of contingent tax liabilities calculated in this way are presented below as posttax real rates of return to the equity stake on a "disposal basis";[17] these rates of return are derived as if the assets of the business were sold at replacement cost at the end of each accounting period, and repurchased at the start of the next accounting period. This rate of return is probably better calculated with a "natural," rather than with an SSAP 16, gearing adjustment because the conceptual basis of that adjustment and the treatment of taxation outlined above appear to be more consistent in that they attempt to measure accruing income and accruing changes in the government's equity stake, respectively.

Such a treatment of deferred taxation is radically different from that suggested in SSAP 15.[18] Even prior to its publication, some companies had not accounted for deferred tax in circumstances where assets were unlikely to be disposed of and/or where it was unlikely that the value of stocks would be reduced and/or where the existence of a continuing capital spending program were likely to imply the indefinite postponement of any deferred tax liability; that is, those companies were, in general, making provision for likely, rather than potential, future tax liabilities. Such accounting practices were not, however, standard during the period of this study. For that period, the BM data cannot be used to generate likely deferred tax liabilities and, therefore, to derive a posttax rate of return in accordance with the principles of SSAP 15. Many companies have reduced substantially their deferred tax balances since the publication of SSAP 15, and it seems likely that a posttax return calculated just by deducting published tax accruals (other than transfers to deferred tax balances)[19] from pretax real equity profits, while making no adjustment to the pretax current cost equity stake,[20] would correspond more closely to the principles of SSAP 15 than a measure that took full account of the deferred tax accounting adopted by the BM sample; for convenience, such a measure is called a posttax real rate of return to the equity stake on a "going concern basis."[21] The conceptual basis of this adjustment for tax is probably more consistent with an SSAP 16 than with a "natural," gearing adjustment in that the former includes realized gains in income and the going concern treatment of taxation approximates the government's equity stake in the business by likely, rather than potential, future tax liabilities.

Posttax real rates of return on the equity stake were on a downward trend during the period of this study for the entire sample of manufacturing, distribution, and service companies, whether the tax treatment was on a disposal or a going concern basis and using either a "natural" or an SSAP 16 gearing adjustment (table 5–9). The posttax

Table 5–9
Posttax Real Rates of Return on the Equity Stake in Trading Assets, and Deferred Tax Balances: The Entire BM Sample
(percent)

Years	Disposal Basis Tax Treatment		Going Concern Basis Tax Treatment		Deferred Tax Balances[a] as Percentage of Pretax Current Cost Equity Stake in Trading Assets
	"Natural" Gearing Adjustment	*SSAP 16 Gearing Adjustment*	*"Natural" Gearing Adjustment*	*SSAP 16 Gearing Adjustment*	
	(1)	(2)	(3)	(4)	(5)
1961–65	7.6	7.0	7.3	6.8	3.8
1966–69	6.5	5.7	6.4	5.7	2.4
1970–73	6.4	4.7	6.8	5.3	10.0
1974–77	2.9	−0.7	4.7	2.0	24.9

[a]Published deferred tax balances, plus contingent tax liabilities calculated on the assumption that all physical assets are disposed of at current replacement cost.

real rate of return on a disposal basis with a natural gearing adjustment averaged 3 percent in the years 1974–77 as compared with 7.5 percent in 1961–65; on a going concern basis, with an SSAP gearing adjustment, it averaged 2 percent in 1974–77 as compared with 7 percent in 1961–65. Of these two preferred measures—columns (1) and (4) in table 5–9—returns on a disposal basis generally exceeded those on a going concern basis by about 1 percent;[22] the tendency of returns with a natural gearing adjustment to exceed those with an SSAP 16 gearing adjustment more than offset the greater incidence of tax during the 1970s on a disposal, than on a going concern, basis: see columns (1) and (3) in table 5–9. The share of deferred tax balances (including the theoretical contingent tax liability calculated as described earlier in this chapter) rose from under 4 percent in the 1960s to 25 percent in the mid-1970s.

Posttax rates of return were consistently lower in manufacturing industry than in distribution and service industries, by about 5.5 percent on a disposal basis and 4 percent on a going concern basis during the 1970s (figure 5–3). The incidence of tax—as implied by the difference between the corresponding measures of pretax and posttax returns—appears to have fallen on a going concern basis (though not on a disposal basis) in manufacturing industry between the 1960s and 1970s, but on both going concern and disposal bases in the distribution and service industries it was a good deal lower in 1974–77 than previously. The incidence of tax on both disposal and going concern bases was greater in distribution and services than in manufacturing industry during the period to 1973 but was broadly similar in both groupings from that date.

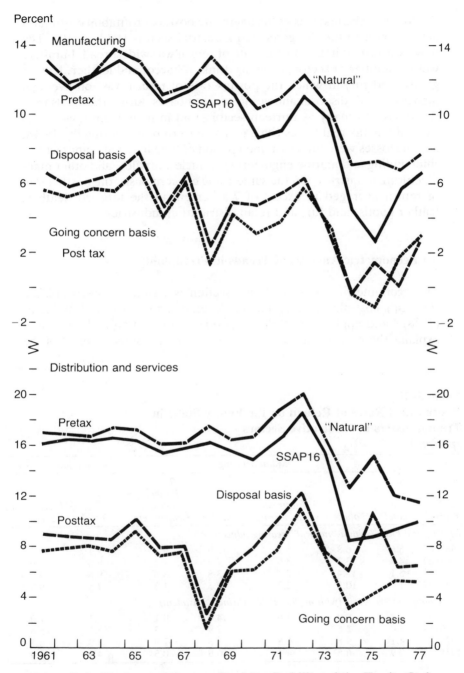

Figure 5–3. Pretax and Posttax Real Profitability of the Equity Stake: Manufacturing, and Distribution and Services

Many of the features of the aggregate posttax profitability estimates are common to the disaggregated industrial sectors (table 5–10). The downward trend in the posttax rate of return was widespread, but there were a number of sectors (such as drink, tobacco, and leather, leather goods, and fur) in which the posttax rate of return was, on average, higher on both disposal and going concern bases during the 1970s than the 1960s. As many as thirteen sectors—all in manufacturing—experienced posttax real losses (on a going concern basis) during the 1970s, and the losses were for a sustained period of time in metal manufacture, shipbuilding and marine engineering, vehicles, textiles, and other manufacturing industries. On the same going concern basis, the posttax rate of return averaged in excess of 7.5 percent in the tobacco, leather, leather goods, and fur, and retail distribution industries.

An Econometric Analysis of Trends in Profitability

The econometric analysis of this section is based on the simplified (historic) cost-plus pricing model developed in Clark and Williams (1978)[23] and applied by Williams (1981). An equation is derived that explains the pretax real rate of return of trading assets in terms of the

Table 5–10
Posttax Real Rates of Return on the Equity Stake in Trading Assets in Illustrative Sectors
(percent)

		Manufacturing				Distribution and Service	
Years	Total	Tobacco	Electrical Engineering	Vehicles	Bricks, Pottery, Glass, Cement, etc.	Total	Miscellaneous Services
(i) Disposal basis (with a "natural" gearing adjustment)							
1961–65	6.6	6.8	5.1	13.0	9.8	9.1	8.7
1966–69	4.7	3.2	3.6	7.9	7.2	6.4	6.9
1970–73	5.1	13.4	7.1	3.8	8.8	9.6	9.7
1974–77	1.0	10.5	2.2	− 12.5	1.3	7.5	9.8
(ii) Going concern basis (with an SSAP 16 gearing adjustment)							
1961–65	5.8	6.0	4.6	14.4	9.1	8.1	7.0
1966–69	4.0	2.6	3.3	7.9	6.3	5.7	5.6
1970–73	4.1	9.8	6.8	3.3	7.9	8.3	6.7
1974–77	0.9	6.5	4.1	− 10.0	0.5	4.5	1.9

level of capacity utilization and the rate of (labor and raw material) cost inflation.[24] This approach is a development, incorporating the role of cost inflation, of an analysis of US profitability by Feldstein and Summers (1977); trend factors are included in the estimating equation.

Table 5–11 shows the results of estimating such an equation for manufacturing industry and for nine illustrative sectors for which satisfactory data could be obtained. The explanatory performance of these regressions is reasonably good (with the exception of electrical engineering), and there is little evidence of autocorrelation, except in the case of vehicles.

The prior expectation was that the coefficients would be negative on the terms for both cost inflation (implying that an acceleration of growth in costs reduces real profitability) and capacity utilization (which enters the equation in reciprocal form, implying that real returns would benefit from a rise in capacity utilization). The coefficients on the costs term are, in all cases, of the expected sign, and are generally significant. But the hypothesis of the relationship between capacity utilization and profitability is less clearly supported by the data; the coefficient is negative in only seven of the ten equations and, even then, frequently insignificant. The time trends are negative and significant in all of the equations, except for electrical engineering. The constant terms differ from unity, often significantly, perhaps reflecting some misspecification of the underlying relationships. These results provide some support for the framework for explaining trends in real profitability, which has been considered here, and, in particular, suggest an important role for changes in the growth of costs. A clear feature is the better statistical performance of the equation for manufacturing industry than of those for its components; this may reflect the greater consistency of the industrial coverage of the dependent and independent variables among a highly aggregated grouping than among the sectors, which are bedeviled by the diversification of companies allocated to each BM sector.

Figure 5–4 illustrates the acceleration of cost pressures in manufacturing industry in the 1970s. The sharp acceleration in 1973 and 1974 was initially a reflection of faster growth in raw materials costs (table 5–12). In spite of the sharp deceleration of raw materials cost inflation in 1975, cost inflation remained rapid in the face of an acceleration in the growth of unit labor costs. There was also a sharp fall in capacity utilization, totaling 12 percent, between 1973 and 1975. The acceleration of cost inflation and fall in the capacity utilization in the mid-1970s were common to each of the nine sectors for which regression results are presented. (Illustrative trends are shown in table 5–13.)

Table 5–11
Econometric Results "Explaining" Real Pretax Rates of Return on Trading Assets 1961–77[a]

	Constant	Time Trend[b]	Change in Costs[c]	Reciprocal of Capacity Utilization	$\bar{R}^2$	DW
1 Manufacturing	0.392 (9.2)	-0.002 (3.9)	-0.207 (9.6)	-0.081 (2.3)	0.96	1.69
2 Food	0.344 (1.2)	-0.005 (3.2)	-0.109 (1.0)	-0.117 (0.4)	0.77	1.84
3 Chemicals and allied industries	0.417 (3.5)	-0.003 (3.6)	-0.118 (2.7)	-0.190 (1.9)	0.78	1.88
4 Metal manufacture	0.248 (3.3)	-0.003 (2.6)	-0.160 (2.9)	-0.024 (0.5)	0.75	2.21
5 Nonelectrical engineering	0.143 (2.2)	-0.002 (2.6)	-0.188 (4.5)	0.125 (2.9)	0.84	2.17
6 Electrical engineering	0.278 (2.3)	0.004 (2.6)	-0.343 (3.7)	0.163 (1.8)	0.43	1.87
7 Vehicles	0.813 (3.3)	-0.006 (2.6)	-0.492 (4.4)	-0.170 (0.9)	0.82	2.72
8 Metal goods not elsewhere specified	0.135 (1.9)	-0.007 (8.0)	-0.042 (0.9)	0.010 (0.2)	0.89	1.52
9 Textiles	0.339 (3.6)	-0.005 (3.6)	-0.086 (1.2)	-0.151 (2.7)	0.81	1.74
10 Paper, printing, and publishing	0.265 (3.5)	-0.003 (4.0)	-0.153 (3.4)	-0.005 (0.1)	0.79	1.82

Note: t statistics are in parentheses.
[a]The dependent variable is profits as a proportion, rather than as a percentage, of trading assets.
[b]Zero in the center of the estimation period.
[c]Year-on-year change in costs.

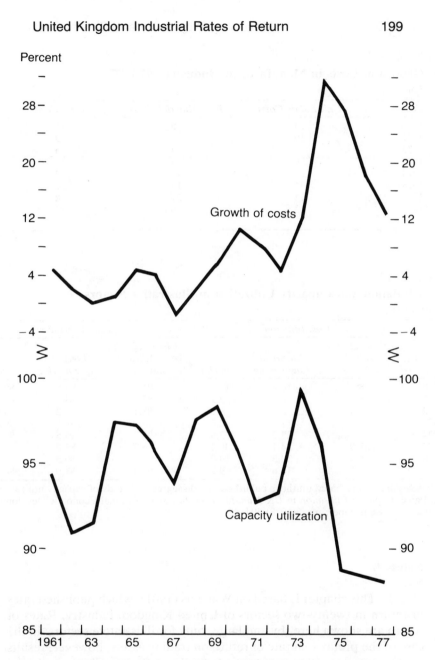

Figure 5–4. Growth of Costs, and Capacity Utilization: Manufacturing

Table 5–12
Growth of Costs in Manufacturing Industry 1970–77
(percent)

Year	Unit Labor Costs	Raw Material Costs	Total Costs
1970	13	5	11
1971	10	5	9
1972	5	4	5
1973	6	33	12
1974	24	49	32
1975	34	15	27
1976	14	27	18
1977	12	15	13

Table 5–13
Cost Inflation and Capacity Utilization in Illustrative Sectors
(percent)

	Cost Inflation			Capacity Utilization[a]		
Year	Chemicals and Allied Industries	Electrical Engineering	Vehicles	Chemicals and Allied Industries	Electrical Engineering	Vehicles
1970	8.8	10.4	17.6	91.6	90.6	89.7
1971	8.4	6.9	9.2	87.7	88.8	82.7
1972	1.4	3.0	8.0	88.1	90.2	83.9
1973	5.9	7.3	12.6	95.2	98.8	90.0
1974	33.9	23.2	22.9	97.7	95.5	89.0
1975	32.9	24.1	36.1	86.7	85.0	81.1
1976	6.8	20.3	19.0	92.5	80.6	80.2
1977	12.7	14.6	9.2	92.4	81.0	84.3

[a]These estimates are based on those published in a disaggregated study of capacity utilization by M. Panić, *Capacity Utilisation in UK Manufacturing Industry,* National Economic Development Office Discussion Paper, no. 5(1978):394–401.

Notes

1. This chapter is based on Williams (1981), which published rates of return in twenty-two sectors of United Kingdom industry. Rates of return are shown here, by and large, only for illustrative sectors: in the case of the pretax real rate of return on trading assets, however, results are presented for all twenty-two industrial sectors, as well as some broad aggregates. The Department of Industry has published an edition of the Business Monitor, based on slightly different industrial classifications and a larger sample of companies, covering the years to 1980 since this study was completed.

2. Clark and Williams (1978) presented some estimates of recorded and "true" historic cost rates of return on trading assets, the latter derived using the technique of appendix 5A, which, among other things, calculates true historic cost measures. The discrepancy of these two measures was estimated to be about 3 percent for the entire sample of companies.

3. The relevant return to the equity stake in this context is an "implied" nominal rate of interest on net debt, calculated as interest payments (net of interest receipts) as a percentage of debt (net of liquid assets).

4. As shown in Williams (1981).

5. This measure is equivalent to $ROC_w(BT)$ in the common glossary, except that cash (along with other liquid assets) is netted off against gross debt in deriving net debt (that is, $NTML$ in appendix 5B).

6. This measure is equivalent to $REQ_w(BT)$ in the common glossary, except that cash (and other liquid assets) is netted off against gross debt (see appendix 5B).

7. As proposed in the accounting standard SSAP 16: see Institute of Chartered Accountants in England and Wales, 1980.

8. SSAP 16 does not provide for any adjustment where there is an excess of monetary assets over monetary liabilities (that is, where capital gearing is negative, as has been the case in shipbuilding and marine engineering in the years 1973–77 and in some earlier years). The SSAP 16 gearing adjustment of each industrial sector is calculated by reference to the sector's overall capital gearing and does not, therefore, take account of any individual companies in that sector that hold net monetary assets; in such circumstances, the SSAP 16 adjustment has been understated.

9. The influence of these factors in determining the relationship between returns on total trading assets and on the equity stake alone was discussed further in Williams (1981 and 1984).

10. Though retentions, when realized, were liable to capital gains tax, the effective rate of tax on capital gains was lower than the basic rate of income tax.

11. Shareholders only pay additional income tax on their dividend receipts if their marginal tax rate exceeds the basic rate of income tax. If their marginal rate is less than the basic rate (certain institutions, such as charities and pension funds, are exempt from income tax) then they receive a tax rebate.

12. Other "timing differences" are attributable to (1) surpluses on the sale of fixed assets subject to rollover relief; (2) ACT, which cannot be recovered out of the current corporation tax liability but which is carried forward to be recovered out of future "mainstream" corporation

tax liabilities, can be deducted from the deferred tax provision in the financial statement subject to certain restrictions; (3) short-term timing differences arising from the partial use of the cash basis for tax purposes and the accruals basis in financial statements; and (4) trading losses (discussed further in Williams, 1981).

13. In practice, of course, even if an asset is sold and the deferred tax becomes payable, the total tax payable in that year may still be zero if capital allowances and stock relief are sufficient to reduce taxable income to zero.

14. When stock relief was introduced in November 1974 with retrospective effect for companies with financial year-ends after March 31, 1973, companies transferred sums from current taxation liabilities to deferred taxation reserves in their balance sheets, without corresponding entries in their profit and loss accounts.

15. The estimates of tax accruals in the BM sample of accounts include current United Kingdom and overseas tax, prior-year tax adjustments, and transfers to deferred tax balances; aspects of the treatment of the latter item are dealt with in the text. Prior-year adjustments should, on certain grounds, be allocated to the year's earnings to which they relate, but, in practice, the sums involved are sufficiently small not to compromise the estimates presented here. Capital receipts (for instance, investment and regional grants) are added back to equity profits, thus preserving a symmetrical treatment between periods when investment grants have, and have not, represented a part of the government-financed inducement to invest. The published tax accrual includes shareholders' imputed basic rate income tax prior to 1967 and from 1973. In the interim, an estimate of the (basic rate) income tax due on dividends has been added to the published tax accrual.

16. This contingent tax liability was calculated in the national accounts study of Williams (1984) as the tax that would be payable if a company disposed of its assets at their current replacement value.

17. This measure is equivalent to $REQ_w(AT)$ in the common glossary, except that tax accruals rather than payments are deducted from earnings, and deferred tax (including contingent liabilities) is deducted from the equity stake: see also above the respect in which the pretax real return on the equity stake differs from $REQ_w(BT)$.

18. The Institute of Chartered Accountants in England and Wales, 1978.

19. Including shareholders' imputed basic rate income tax prior to 1967 and from 1973, and an estimate of the (basic rate) income tax due on dividends during the interim (as described above).

20. That is, both transfers to deferred tax balances, and those bal-

ances themselves, are constrained to zero (that is, it is assumed that no deferred tax liabilities are likely to be payable ultimately).

21. This measure is equivalent to $REQ_w(AT)$ in the common glossary, except that tax accruals rather than payments are deducted from earnings: see also the above respect in which the pretax real return on equity differs from $REQ_w(BT)$.

22. All estimates subsequently presented on a disposal basis incorporate a "natural" gearing adjustment, and those on a going concern basis an SSAP 16 gearing adjustment (that is, the bases preferred on conceptual grounds above).

23. See the appendix by Jenkinson in Clark and Williams (1978).

24. See Williams (1981) for a derivation and discussion of the model.

References

Clark, T.A., and Williams, N.P. "Measures of Real Profitability." *Bank of England Quarterly Bulletin* 18, no. 4 (1978):513–22.

Feldstein, M., and Summers, L. "Is the Rate of Profit Falling?" *Brookings Papers on Economic Activity,* no. 1 (1977):211–28.

Flemming, J.S.; Price, L.D.D.; and Ingram, D.H.A. "Trends in Company Profitability." *Bank of England Quarterly Bulletin* 16, no. 1 (1976):36–52.

Institute of Chartered Accountants in England and Wales. *Accounting for Deferred Taxation, Statement of Standard Accounting Practice.* No. 15, 1978.

———. *Current Cost Accounting, Statement of Standard Accounting Practice.* No. 16, 1980.

Panić, M. *Capacity Utilisation in UK Manufacturing Industry.* National Economic Development Office Discussion Paper, no. 5, 1978.

Williams, N.P. "The Profitability of UK Industrial Sectors." *Bank of England Quarterly Bulletin* 19, no. 4 (1979):394–401.

———. "Influences on the Profitability of Twenty-two Industrial Sectors." *Bank of England Discussion Paper,* no. 15, 1981.

———. "The Profitability of United Kingdom Industrial and Commercial Companies 1963–1981." In D.M. Holland, ed. *Measuring Profitability and Capital Costs.* Lexington, Mass.: LexingtonBooks, D.C. Heath and Co., 1984.

Appendix 5A[1]
The Inflation
Adjustment of
Company Accounts[2]

The inflation adjustment of companies' published accounts[3] involves the estimation of (1) a current valuation of net fixed assets; (2) a current valuation of depreciation; (3) stock appreciation; (4) a monetary working capital adjustment; and (5) a gearing adjustment. A current valuation of net fixed assets is obtained as the difference between the current valuations of gross fixed assets and cumulative depreciation. Calculation of a current valuation of gross fixed assets in year t requires that the value of assets dating from each previous year $(t - k)$ should be adjusted from historic cost to current prices,[4] which is here accomplished by applying an estimated price change derived from fixed asset price indexes produced by the Central Statistical Office. As a preliminary, however, it is necessary to determine the portion of the historic value of gross fixed assets in any particular year that is attributable to assets acquired in each previous year.

Suppose investment of $£a_{t-k,o}$ takes place in year $(t - k)$. This will typically be composed of assets with different (accounting) lives. The gross value (at historic cost) of the assets installed in year $(t - k)$ that remain on the balance sheet in subsequent years will therefore decline as each component is written off until by, say, year $(t - k + n)$ all have been written off. (Note that n is not necessarily the same for the assets installed in different years.) For example, in table 5A1, $£a_{t-n,4}$

Table 5A1
At Historic Cost

Years	$t - n$	$t - n + 1$	$t - n + 2$	$t - n + 3$	$t - n + 4$ ....t	
$t - n$	$a_{t-n,0}$	$a_{t-n,1}$	$a_{t-n,2}$	$a_{t-n,3}$	$a_{t-n,4}$	$a_{t-n,n}(=0)$
$t - n + 1$		$a_{t-n+1,0}$	$a_{t-n+1,1}$	$a_{t-n+1,2}$	$a_{t-n+1,3}$	$a_{t-n+1,n-1}$
$t - n + 2$			$a_{t-n+2,0}$	$a_{t-n+2,1}$	$a_{t-n+2,2}$	$a_{t-n+2,n-2}$
$t - n + 3$				$a_{t-n+3,0}$	$a_{t-n+3,1}$	$a_{t-n+3,n-3}$
$t - n + 4$					$a_{t-n+4,0}$ ·········· $a_{t-n+4,n-4}$	
$\vdots$						
t						$a_{t,0}$
Total	$t - n$	$t - n + 1$	$t - n + 2$	$t - n + 3$	$t - n + 4$	t

205

represents the gross value (at year $t - n$ prices) of assets dating from year $(t - n)$ still on the balance sheet at the end of year $(t - n + 4)$. In practice, $£a_{t-k,i}$ is unlikely to be very different from $£a_{t-k,o}$ for small values of i because few assets will be written off in the first few years.

A method is now required for estimating the way in which the gross (historic) value of assets dating from each year declines over time. Total write-offs in a given year can be derived as the difference between the annual depreciation provision in the year and the change in cumulative depreciation from beginning to end-year. It has been assumed here that the total should be allocated to assets of different vintages in proportion to the value in the opening balance sheet of cumulative depreciation on assets of each vintage. At best, this is a rough approximation; in particular, it is likely to imply that too high a proportion of the assets written off are of recent vintage. Whatever the rule adopted, once the allocation is made, then it is possible to derive each column of the matrix from the immediately preceding one.

In calculating the price changes appropriate to assets of each vintage, the asset compositions of investment in each year—so far as they are represented by the conventional distinctions in the national accounts among "plant and machinery," "vehicles, ships and aircraft," and "new buildings and works"—have been taken into account. For a particular industry's total investment, the asset composition can be determined from national accounts data, and the same proportions have been assumed for investment by the BM companies assigned to the industry. These proportions, which typically vary from year to year, have been used to weight together price indexes (in many cases specific to a particular industry or group of closely related industries) for the three categories of asset. This leads to a series of indexes, specific to both industry and vintage, with which to adjust gross assets—and, as noted above, cumulative depreciation—to current prices.

Ideally, the matrix would begin with the year of acquisition of the oldest assets still on the balance sheet in the first year for which inflation-adjusted accounts have been constructed (1961 in this instance). In practice, neither BM data nor suitable information on the prices of fixed assets are available before 1948. A price change (here 50 percent) must therefore be assumed between the "average" date of installation of the gross capital stock on the balance sheet in 1948, and end-1948. The effect of this arbitrary assumption on the calculated real rate of return will clearly become less important as the proportion of old assets on the balance sheet declines. (By 1961, for example, the proportion of pre-1949 assets, measured at current cost, is estimated to have fallen to about one-third for the sample as a whole.)

The fixed assets acquired each year will be depreciated over their (accounting) lives; and the total of depreciation provisions made on assets still on the balance sheet—"cumulative depreciation"—clearly relates to assets of different vintages. As in the case of gross fixed assets, the age composition must be determined before current valuation can be derived, and much the same method can be used. During year t, cumulative depreciation attributable to assets of a particular vintage $(t - k)$ will be increased by the component of year t depreciation and reduced by the component of year t write-offs, attributable to assets acquired in year $t - k$. Write-offs have again been allocated to assets of different vintages in the way set out above, that is, according to the age composition of cumulative depreciation (at historic cost) in the opening balance sheet. Current-year depreciation has been assigned according to the age composition of historic cost net fixed assets. The price indexes used to convert the vintage components of cumulative depreciation to current prices are the same as those for gross fixed assets.

A current valuation of the annual depreciation charge is easily calculated once the age composition of the charge has been established, as indicated above. Because depreciation notionally arises *through* the year, the price indexes used for the conversion differ slightly from those applied to the beginning and end-year stocks; but they have been constructed along the same lines.

Of the adjustments mentioned at the start of this appendix, it remains to calculate stock appreciation, the monetary working capital adjustment, and, for returns to the equity interest, a gearing adjustment.

Stock appreciation has been calculated as the residual between the change in the book value of stocks and the current value of the physical change in stocks, the latter being taken as the difference between opening and closing book values when both are converted to mid-year prices. Price indexes that are specific both to the stocks held by each industry (or group of closely related industries) and to the average accounting year of companies allocated to each BM industry have been used.

The monetary working capital adjustment is readily calculated by applying the percentage change in a "general" price index to the companies' net trade credit position, adding the result to profits if there is a net receipt of credit and subtracting it if there is a net extension of credit. The calculation has been based on the change in the retail price index between successive Decembers.[5]

Both "natural" and SSAP 16 gearing adjustments are calculated and the result is credited to equity profits. The natural adjustment is derived as the change in the real value of net debt at a time of changing prices,[6] while the SSAP 16 adjustment is calculated as the geared portion[7] both of stock appreciation and of the adjustments to depreciation (from a historic to a current valuation) and monetary working capital.

The adjustments described above would be necessary irrespective of the source of company accounting information. In addition, however, certain adjustments are required because of two specific characteristics of the BM sample. Though confined to a fixed group of companies for periods of about five years, the BM sample does change slightly over time because of mergers, acquisitions, bankruptcies, and so on, so that, for example, the value of gross fixed assets in the opening balance sheet of one year is not generally the same as in the closing balance sheet of the previous year. In addition, the data do not distinguish within the total of gross fixed assets those that have been revalued.

The discontinuities in balance sheet totals do not present much difficulty when the objective is to calculate a series of ratios (for example, rates of return or gearing), which are scale free. At each discontinuity—for example, in the case of gross fixed assets—the procedure has been simply to scale the calculated components attributed to each vintage, and the calculated total, by the ratio of the "recorded" totals. The same procedure has been used for cumulative depreciation.

The conversion to current prices cannot be based directly on the recorded figures (that is, the BM data) because these include, indistinguishably, the effects of asset revaluations. It is clearly invalid to apply fixed asset price indexes if the "historic data" do not, in fact, reflect historic costs. For stocks of fixed assets and cumulative depreciation, revaluation effects can, in principle, be eliminated by deriving series of calculated figures as accumulations of flows, albeit with adjustments for changes in coverage between years. But it must be supposed that the recorded flows of depreciation and write-offs themselves reflect revaluations in previous years; and first, therefore, an attempt must be made to adjust these flows to reflect "true" historic costs. As a preliminary, total revaluations during a particular year have been derived as the change over the year in recorded gross fixed assets less the difference between fixed investment and "recorded" write-offs. It has then been assumed that this total is attributable to gross fixed asssets of each vintage in proportion to the cash amounts of the differences between true historic cost and current valuations (in the closing balance sheet) of gross fixed assets of the vintage. For each vintage, a tally is kept, year by year, of the proportion of the recorded value of gross fixed assets attributable to revaluation; and, in each year, the calculated components of depreciation and write-offs attributed to the vintage have been scaled down by the revaluation proportion derived from the previous end-year.

Appendix 5B
Technical Definitions

This appendix sets out the definitions of rates of return presented in this chapter. The derivation of the inflation-adjusted items was described in appendix 5A.

Pretax Recorded Rate of Return on Trading Assets

$$\frac{GTPR - DPRB}{NFAB + STKB + NTCE}$$

where:

$GTPR$ = gross trading profits (less charges for the hire of plant and machinery);
$DPRB$ = depreciation at book value;
$NFAB$ = net tangible fixed assets at book value;
$STKB$ = stocks and work-in-progress at book value; and
$NTCE$ = net trade credit extended.[8]

(All balance sheet items are expressed as an average of the beginning and end-year totals.)

Pretax Recorded Rate of Return on the Equity Stake in Trading Assets

$$\frac{GTPR - DPRB - INTN}{NFAB + STKB + NTCE - NTML}$$

where:

$INTN$ = net interest payments;[9] and
$NTML$ = net monetary liabilities.

$$NTML = DHFC\,[BOVD + STLN + DVID + CRTX + LTLN + PRSH] - [IBGS + ILAL + TXRC + TRBL + CASH]$$

where:

$BOVD$ = bank overdrafts and loans;
$STLN$ = short-term loans;
$DVID$ = dividends and interest due;
$CRTX$ = current taxation;
$LTLN$ = long-term loans;
$PRSH$ = preference shares;
$IBGS$ = investments: British government securities;
$ILAL$ = investments: local authority loans;
$TXRC$ = tax reserve certificates/deposit accounts;
$TRBL$ = Treasury bills; and
$CASH$ = cash, etc.

$$DHFC = (NFAR + STKB + NTCE)/NFAR + STKB \\ + NTCE + GDWL + IUSB + IBGS + ILAL \\ + IOLS + IULS + TXRC + TRBL + CASH$$

where:

$DHFC$ = debt hypothecation factor;[10]
$NFAR$ = net tangible fixed assets at replacement cost;
$GDWL$ = goodwill;
$IUSB$ = investment in unconsolidated subsidiaries;
$IOLS$ = investments: other listed securities; and
$IULS$ = investments: unlisted securities.

Pretax Real Rate of Return on Trading Assets

$$\frac{GTPR - DPRR - STAP - MWCA}{NFAR + STKB^{11} + NTCE}$$

where:

$DPRR$ = depreciation at replacement cost;
$STAP$ = stock appreciation; and
$MWCA$ = monetary working capital adjustment.

Pretax Rate of Return on the Equity Stake in Trading Assets ("Natural" and SSAP 16)

$$\frac{GTPR - DPRR - STAP - MWCA - INTN + GRAJ}{NFAR + STKB + NTCE - NTML}$$

where:

$GRAJ$ = gearing adjustment (alternately, "natural" and SSAP 16).

Posttax Real Rate of Return on the Equity Stake in Trading Assets

Disposal Basis

$$\frac{GTPR - DPRR - STAP - MWCA - INTN}{NFAR + STKB + NTCE - NTML - DFRT}$$
$$+ \frac{GRAJ - TXAC - TRDT + OTCR}{NFAR + STKB + NTCE - NTML - DFRT}$$

where:

$TXAC$ = tax accruals (excluding transfers to deferred taxation), that is, $UKTX + OVTX + PYTA + ITDV$

where:

$UKTX$ = current United Kingdom taxation;
$OVTX$ = overseas taxation;
$PYTA$ = prior year tax adjustments; and
$ITDV$ = income tax on dividends.

$TRDT$ = transfer to deferred taxation;
$OTCR$ = other capital receipts; and
$DFRT$ = deferred taxation, calculated as published provisions plus $[c \cdot (NFAR - NFAB)]$

where:

c = rate of corporation tax on retained earnings.

$TRDT$ and published deferred tax provisions are constrained to zero until 1968,[12] and based on the available accounting data for the period 1969–77.

Going Concern Basis. As disposal basis, except $TRDT$ and $DFRT$ are zero for the whole period 1961–77.

Appendix 5C
The Business Monitor
Sample of Company
Accounts[13]

The estimates of profitability in this chapter are based on the published accounts of more than 1,000 large listed companies, as presented in the Department of Industry's *Business Monitor MA3: Company Finance*. The present size criteria for inclusion in the sample are net assets of at least £5 million or gross income of at least £500,000 in 1973. An earlier article[14] indicated a number of reasons for interpreting profitability estimates derived from this source—on that occasion, at the aggregate level—with caution, and it may be useful to reiterate them. First, the financial behavior and performance of the relatively large companies within the BM sample—although covering about 60 percent of gross fixed assets and investment in the case of manufacturing industry, but rather less in distribution and services—may not be wholly representative of the company sector as a whole. Second, the sample excludes companies operating "mainly" overseas, but a significant element of overseas activity nevertheless remains in the sample from the overseas branches and subsidiaries of companies operating principally in the United Kingdom. In addition, the sample excludes the United Kingdom activities of companies operating mainly overseas, which, in some cases, are very substantial. Third, the profitability estimates presented in this chapter for a given calendar year relate to accounting years ending between April 6 of that year and April 5 of the following year. In practice, however, this qualification is not of great importance because about 70 percent of listed companies' accounting years end in the fourth and first calendar quarters.[15]

The interpretation of the disaggregated profitability estimates presented in this chapter requires rather more caution than is the case with aggregate profitability estimates. Companies within the BM sample have been allocated to industries according to their principal activity, but, with many diversified companies included within the sample, any one industry as presented in the BM inevitably includes some activities that do not rightfully belong therein and excludes some that do.[16] There are, of course, differences among industrial sectors in the extent to which the results are compromised by the diversification of companies and by the inclusion only of large listed companies operating mainly in the United Kingdom. The results presented in this chapter for some (especially the smaller) sectors will be heavily influenced by the performance of individual companies.

Appendix 5D

Table 5D1
Pretax Real Rates of Return for Twenty-Two Industrial Sectors and Broad Aggregates
(percent)

Year	Manufacturing, Distribution, and Services	Manufacturing										
		Total	Food	Drink	Tobacco	Chemicals and Allied Industries	Metal Manufacture	Nonelectrical Engineering	Electrical Engineering	Shipbuilding and Marine Engineering	Vehicles	Metal Goods Not Elsewhere Specified
1961	11.4	10.6	13.9	9.8	10.1	10.3	8.8	10.7	7.7	5.8	11.6	13.5
1962	10.7	9.7	14.0	9.6	11.1	9.8	5.9	8.9	10.0	2.6	10.1	12.7
1963	11.2	10.3	13.2	9.4	9.4	10.2	5.4	9.5	14.6	2.7	14.9	13.3
1964	12.2	10.8	13.9	9.4	11.8	12.0	6.5	9.1	7.5	0.2	11.6	13.4
1965	11.9	10.2	13.8	9.1	8.9	11.3	6.4	8.9	9.3	-7.0	14.6	12.6
1966	10.7	8.9	11.3	8.8	10.2	9.4	4.2	8.3	9.2	-1.8	11.2	11.0
1967	11.1	9.5	10.9	9.7	11.5	9.1	6.8	9.4	9.6	1.9	9.1	11.3
1968	11.5	9.7	10.3	9.1	9.9	11.3	6.6	8.4	9.2	3.4	12.4	8.8
1969	10.5	8.7	8.4	8.3	12.5	10.6	4.5	7.3	8.6	-4.4	9.8	9.1
1970	7.7	6.6	5.8	9.7	12.4	5.8	4.2	4.8	9.4	-2.7	-0.1	8.8
1971	8.5	7.0	6.0	10.5	13.9	5.0	4.5	5.2	10.1	-8.3	5.5	9.1
1972	10.0	8.5	8.3	11.4	10.8	6.7	4.1	7.5	14.5	4.5	4.9	6.5
1973	8.1	6.9	1.6	10.6	17.5	5.0	1.3	7.7	11.1	-15.3	7.1	2.7
1974	3.8	2.7	6.5	4.0	-0.7	3.0	-2.3	0.9	6.1	-0.7	-9.5	2.9
1975	3.7	2.0	3.5	4.2	3.2	2.0	-0.7	2.8	5.7	-8.1	-10.1	4.5
1976	5.3	4.3	6.5	6.8	13.4	4.2	-2.1	5.5	10.9	-2.5	-0.1	2.5
1977	6.7	5.9	5.7	6.7	12.7	6.5	3.5	6.7	13.0	0.1	-0.6	3.7

Table 5D1 *(continued)*

| | Manufacturing | | | | | | | | Con- | Distribution and Services | | | |
Year	Textiles	Leather, Leather Goods, and Fur	Clothing and Footwear	Bricks, Pottery, Glass, Cement, etc.	Timber, Furniture, etc.	Paper, Printing and Publishing	Other Manufacturing Industries	Total	struction	Transport and Communication (Excluding Shipping)	Wholesale Distribution	Retail Distribution	Miscellaneous Services
1961	10.1	6.5	16.4	15.1	10.1	12.1	9.4	13.9	12.9	7.9	11.0	18.4	12.3
1962	8.3	5.9	15.1	13.6	8.4	11.3	9.0	14.1	13.8	9.6	10.7	18.7	11.5
1963	8.7	8.9	12.5	14.2	10.3	11.2	10.2	13.8	14.3	10.7	11.4	17.2	12.0
1964	11.6	9.0	15.3	16.5	10.9	11.6	11.4	14.0	16.0	10.2	11.3	18.0	10.7
1965	10.8	8.6	14.6	14.4	11.9	12.0	9.9	13.9	15.1	9.6	11.6	18.3	9.6
1966	9.4	7.4	14.4	12.1	10.2	10.2	9.3	13.2	11.9	9.4	10.7	17.8	10.4
1967	9.9	9.6	16.7	13.2	11.3	9.8	10.7	13.1	12.8	10.4	9.7	17.7	10.4
1968	9.7	9.5	14.3	12.4	9.4	10.0	9.6	13.0	12.3	10.4	10.5	16.5	11.3
1969	8.7	9.4	14.7	9.5	7.3	8.5	7.9	12.2	10.7	8.8	9.7	14.7	12.7
1970	6.6	13.5	11.4	9.2	5.9	5.6	6.7	11.3	8.4	9.2	9.8	14.2	9.3
1971	5.8	9.7	13.0	8.4	10.9	6.1	7.6	12.6	11.7	7.6	9.8	16.4	9.7
1972	4.2	1.4	12.5	12.0	19.1	8.9	7.6	13.8	8.9	7.9	10.9	20.1	10.5
1973	5.8	19.2	11.2	10.8	7.8	8.7	2.5	10.8	2.2	10.9	8.0	17.7	7.8
1974	4.8	19.3	5.7	1.9	6.3	2.9	-0.7	6.5	2.3	4.9	6.4	9.3	5.0
1975	-0.3	10.5	4.7	2.0	11.1	2.2	3.1	7.7	8.0	6.7	7.4	10.3	4.1
1976	-1.0	6.0	3.0	4.5	4.4	4.8	3.6	8.0	11.1	3.8	5.5	10.0	5.1
1977	2.9	12.9	3.4	4.7	8.8	8.7	2.6	8.7	8.6	2.9	9.0	10.4	6.7

Notes

1. Appendices 1 through 3 are reproduced from Williams (1981).

2. Alastair Clark contributed particularly to developing and programming the technique of inflation adjustment used in this paper.

3. In practice, the published accounts of many companies seem, during the period of this study, to have incorporated a partial adjustment of net fixed assets and depreciation from a historic to a current valuation; hence the difference between recorded and "true" historic cost rates of return referred to above. It will be readily seen that true historic cost estimates are a product of the method of inflation adjustment outlined below.

4. But, for reasons outlined above, such a process of revaluation cannot be applied directly to the figures recorded in company accounts.

5. Thus incorporating a timing difference as compared with the price indexes used to calculate stock appreciation based on the "average" accounting year of companies allocated to each industry. In practice, companies' accounting years—with about 70 percent of listed companies' accounting years ending in the fourth and first calendar quarters—are such that the method adopted is not thought to invalidate the resulting estimates.

6. Based on the same price index as in the calculation of the monetary working capital adjustment.

7. That is, net debt (net monetary liabilities, as defined in appendix 5B) as a percentage of the current valuation of trading assets (net tangible fixed assets, stocks, and net trade credit extended).

8. That is, net of trade credit received.

9. That is, net of interest receipts.

10. It is assumed that gross debt finances trading and nontrading assets in proportion to their respective magnitudes; that is, a "neutral" assumption about the hypothecation of debt has been used. Consistently, therefore, gross interest payments have been scaled by the debt hypothecation factor in the calculation of net interest payments. There is a case for applying different debt hypothecation factors—based, alternately, on recorded and current valuations of trading assets—in the calculation of recorded and real equity profitability. It can be seen that, as an approximation, debt hypothecation factors based on current valuations of trading assets have been used in both sets of calculations.

11. Measured at book value, rather than at replacement cost, to preserve an element of consistency with national accounts estimates of profitability. The two valuations do not differ significantly, even at times of rapid inflation, because of the rapid turnover of stocks.

12. These items are constrained on the grounds that deferred tax

provisions are an unknown, and probably small, part of the "future tax reserves" item of the BM sample prior to 1969. (The major part of future tax reserves comprises corporation tax and income tax due on January 1 of the fiscal year following the companies' balance sheet dates.) An extension of calculations made in Flemming and associates (1976), p. 47, suggests that the major part of companies' deferred tax liability prior to 1969 has been taken account of in these estimates by the calculation of the contingent tax liability on assets if they should be sold at their current replacement value.

13. This appendix is based on one published in Williams (1979), p. 401.

14. Clark and Williams (1978).

15. The fixed asset and retail price indexes used in certain of the inflation adjustments are based on calendar, rather than accounting, years. Such timing points have been more important in recent years, when the rate of inflation has been high and changing rapidly, though the stock price indexes, which are specific to each sector, reflect the average accounting years of companies in each sector.

16. This difficulty is mitigated to some extent by the exclusion of the most highly diversified companies from the individual sectors considered in this chapter.

6

Profitability in Britain and France 1956–1975: A Comparative Study

Mervyn King and
Jacques Mairesse

Introduction

The aim of this chapter was to conduct a comparative analysis of profitability—or rates of profit or rates of return—in British and French manufacturing industry. In recent years, interest in the fortunes of profits has been great and there have been a number of studies in profitability in individual countries. A major problem with empirical studies on this kind is to know how to evaluate the figures that emerge. One possible comparison is with profitability in neighboring or economically related countries. Such was the motive for this study.

Comparative studies are notoriously difficult because of the problems involved in obtaining genuinely comparable statistics. The authors had previously worked on questions of profitability in their respective countries and embarked on this joint venture only when it was felt that data existed or could be found that made comparisons feasible. We discuss some of the difficulties involved but to our knowledge this study is perhaps the first to make a detailed comparison of measures of profitability in more than one country.

We chose to examine profits in manufacturing industry. This sector is of key importance to the growth of output and productivity in the economy as a whole and we were interested in the *ex post* profitability of domestic manufacturing production. To look outside manufacturing would introduce the vagaries of the fortunes of property companies and banks, the behavior of the principal nationalized industries supplying power, transport, and communications, and the problem of agriculture, for which it is difficult to differentiate wages from profits. Hence, we shall concentrate on manufacturing, and only on domestic production. Our concern is with the profitability of domestic produc-

This study was financed by the Centre National de la Recherche Scientifique (ATP Internationale no. 2604). We are grateful to L'Institut National de la Statistique et des Etudes Economiques in Paris and to the Central Statistical Office in London for help with data, especially to H. Delestré and R. Armitage, and we thank J.M. Chanut and M. Patel for their help.

tion, although for an individual company the profits it earns from its overseas operations may be of crucial importance.[1] For example, in the United Kingdom in recent years, profits from overseas subsidiaries have been as large as domestic corporate profits. Consequently, the ability of companies to pay dividends is not determined solely by domestic profitability.

In the next section, we begin by examining the evidence on profitability in manufacturing industry as a whole. By "manufacturing" we shall mean "all manufacturing excluding both food, drink, and tobacco and metal manufacture." The reason for excluding the food, drink, and tobacco industry group is that in France a high proportion of profits in that group is earned by unincorporated businesses, the taxation of which is different from that of companies, and for which the data are less reliable. Metal manufacture is excluded because we feel it desirable to exclude the effects of the nationalization of the steel industry and the price controls of preceding years in the United Kingdom. This definition of manufacturing we shall maintain throughout.

Next we turn to a brief examination of the experience of three subgroups of manufacturing corresponding to "intermediate" goods, "investment" goods, and "consumer" goods. The precise definitions of these three sectors are set out in the appendix (table 6A1). Further disaggregation would raise serious problems about comparability and the quality of the data.

In the section entitled "The Robustness of the Estimates" we summarize the main results of two further investigations in which we tried to ascertain the robustness of our estimates on profitability with respect to major revisions in national accounts figures and the large uncertainties about the service lives used in deriving the fixed capital stock and capital consumption estimates.

In the section entitled "An Econometric Analysis" we present some econometric tests of hypotheses about changes in profit rates. For example, has there been a statistically significant declining trend in the rate of profit? A word of caution, however, is in order here. The profit rates we calculate are average realized rates of return obtained by comparing an annual flow of profits to an estimate of the value of the capital stock at the midpoint of the year. These figures do not correspond directly to any behavioral variable or to the *ex post* internal rate of return on any particular investment project. Hence, our econometric results are not tests of behavioral hypotheses about the determinants of profitability but more exact ways of summarizing the data. In this context, we feel such an exercise to be valuable simply because the behavior of profitability is a subject concerning which people have been tempted to draw strong, and possibly misleading, conclusions from visual inspection of the data.

In table 6–1, we present the list of the basic variables for which data were collected and we define the transformed variables on profitability that we will be discussing. In appendix 6A, we explain the definitions and sources of the basic data themselves and we give the basic and transformed variables for manufacturing as a whole in the United Kingdom and France over the twenty years of the study period, 1956–1975 (table 6A2).

Profitability in Manufacturing Industry

We consider first our results for the manufacturing industry as a whole. The "real" rate of profit before tax *(T1)* is defined as the ratio of gross trading profits net of both capital consumption and stock appreciation to the sum of the value of net fixed capital stock at current replacement cost and the book value of stocks. The midyear value of capital is used. The real rate of profit after tax *(T2)* is similarly defined, with profits measured after deduction of corporate tax liabilities.[2] The former is

Table 6–1
List of Variables

United Kingdom		France
Basic variables		
R1	Gross trading profits	Excedent brut d'exploitation
R2	Capital consumption	Amortissement
R3	Stock appreciation	Appreciation sur stocks
R4	Taxes	Impôts
R5	Interest payments	Intérêts
R6	Dividends	Dividendes
R7	Income from employment	Charges salariales
R8	Net fixed capital stock	Capital fixe net
R9	Value of stocks	Stocks
R10	Gross fixed investment	Formation brute de capital fixe
R11	Stockbuilding	Variation de stocks
R12	Capacity utilization	Utilisation de capacité
Transformed variables		
T1	Rate of profit before tax	Taux de profit avant impôts
T2	Rate of profit after tax	Taux de profit apres impôts
T3	Share of profits before tax	Part du profit avant impôts
T4	Share of profits after tax	Part du profit apres impôts
T5	Effective tax rate	Taux effectif d'impôts
T6	Ratio of interest to capital	Ratio intérêts/capital
T7	Ratio of dividends to capital	Ratio dividendes/capital
T8	Self-financing ratio	Taux d'autofinancement
T9	Growth Rate of capital	Taux de croissance du capital
T10	Ratio of stocks to fixed capital	Ratio stocks/capital fixe
T11	Ratio of depreciation to fixed capital	Ratio d'amortissement/capital
T12	Ratio of stock appreciation	Ratio d'appreciation sur stocks/stocks

often said to measure the "social" rate of return on capital, although this is not necessarily true because of, first, the substantial degree of monopoly in a number of manufacturing industries and, second, the use, directly or indirectly, of certain services provided below cost by public sector capital (for example, the use of roads). Moveover, the *ex post* average rate of return may not provide a good guide to the future marginal rate of return that society might reasonably expect on additional investment. But it does not seem unreasonable to suppose that long-run changes in the rate of return we calculate would indicate a change in the social productivity of capital. The rate of profit after tax measures the return to the suppliers of finance (both equity and debt) before payment of personal income taxes. This might be compared with the real rate of interest before tax on a financial asset to give an indication of the differential between returns on real and on financial assets. The real profit rates in manufacturing over the period 1956–75 are shown in table 6–2 and figures 6–1 and 6–2.

Table 6–2
Real Profit Rates in Manufacturing, United Kingdom and France 1956–75
(percent)

	Pretax T1		Posttax T2	
	United Kingdom	France	United Kingdom	France
1956	8.7	9.9	5.1	6.6
1957	8.6	10.0	5.1	6.9
1958	8.5	10.0	5.8	6.1
1959	8.6	9.1	5.6	5.2
1960	9.2	10.9	6.0	7.2
1961	7.7	10.3	5.3	6.8
1962	7.3	9.6	5.1	6.5
1963	8.0	9.5	5.8	6.5
1964	8.7	10.1	6.2	7.1
1965	7.8	9.7	6.4	6.7
1966	6.5	9.6	5.4	7.1
1967	6.6	9.3	5.7	6.8
1968	6.4	10.1	5.0	7.8
1969	5.5	11.5	4.2	9.2
1970	4.2	11.5	3.3	8.7
1971	4.6	10.6	3.3	8.3
1972	4.9	12.3	3.4	9.7
1973	3.5	11.8	3.8	8.9
1974	−0.6	10.8	1.5	7.4
1975	−0.6	5.2	1.3	3.1

Source: see appendix 6A.

Note: the posttax profit rates in the United Kingdom before stock relief are 1973: 2.1; 1974: −1.6; and 1975: −1.0.

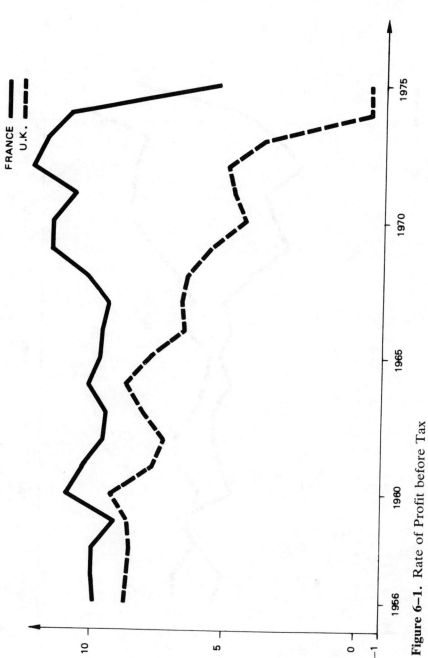

Figure 6–1. Rate of Profit before Tax

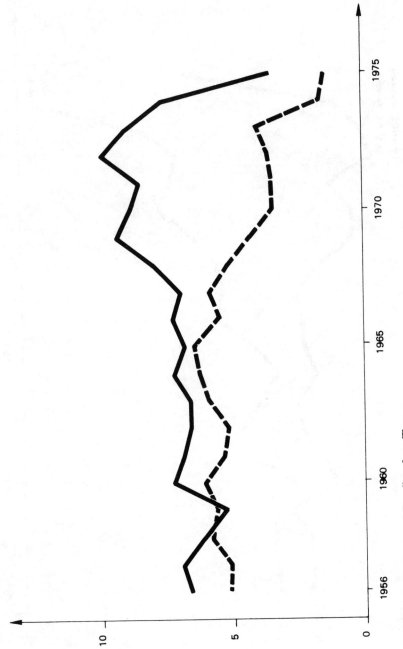

Figure 6–2. Rate of Profit after Tax

If we look at the *pretax profit rate (T1),* we see a striking difference between the two countries. In France, there is no evidence of any downward trend in profitability (if anything, the trend appears to be slightly upward), whereas in the United Kingdom there appears to have been a falling rate of profit over the period culminating in negative profitability in the recession years of 1974 and 1975. In France, the impact of the oil crisis and the resulting recession appears only in 1975.

The figures for the *posttax profit rate (T2)* show a rather different picture. In France, posttax profitability appears to have risen toward the end of the period before the sharp fall in 1975. In the United Kingdom there was a period of quite remarkable stability in the posttax profit rate between 1956 and 1968, when the profit rate fluctuated between 5 and 6 percent, rising to levels just above 6 percent only in the peak years of 1960, 1964, and 1965. Between 1969 and 1971, the profit rate fell to a level between 3 and 4 percent, where it remained until the recession of 1974–75. We shall defer discussion of the significance of these trends until the section entitled "An Econometric Analysis," where we examine some econometric results.

It is clear that the level of profitability is higher in France than in the United Kingdom (although the difference is less marked if we look at the posttax profit rate) and that the gap between the two countries is very striking from 1969 onward. Indeed, one of the features of the results appears to be the very close similarity in the posttax profit rate between the two countries until the period after 1968, when the trends in the two countries diverge.

The remaining figures (6–3 through 6–12) show the behavior of the other transformed variables (*T3* to *T12*) for manufacturing as a whole.

The *share of profits before tax (T3)* falls quite dramatically in the United Kingdom whereas in France it follows an upward trend until 1975. In France, the *share of profits after tax (T4)* follows a trend similar to that of the pretax share, whereas in the United Kingdom the share after tax is remarkably constant until after 1969, when it falls in two discrete jumps to the very low values of 1974 and 1975. It is interesting that until the end of the 1960s the share of profits after tax in the United Kingdom was actually higher than that in France. During the same period the rate of profit after tax was slightly below that in France.

The *effective tax rate (T5)* in the two countries, defined as the ratio of taxes to trading profits net of both capital consumption and stock appreciation, shows a similar downward trend. From levels of above 30 percent in the late 1950s, the effective tax rate falls in both countries fairly steadily, to reach levels of about 20 percent in the early 1970s. From then on in France, the rate appears to rise as the level of profits

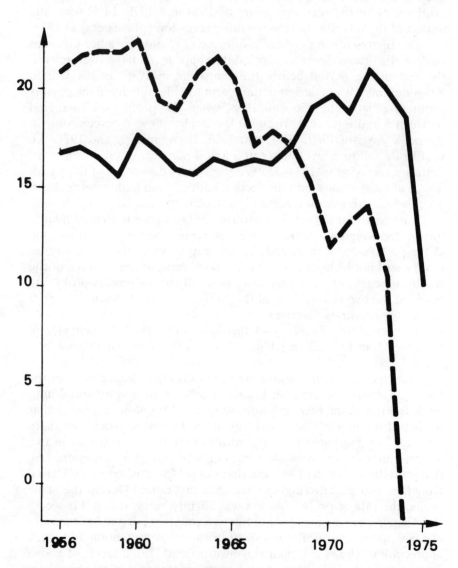

Figure 6–3. Share of Profits before Tax

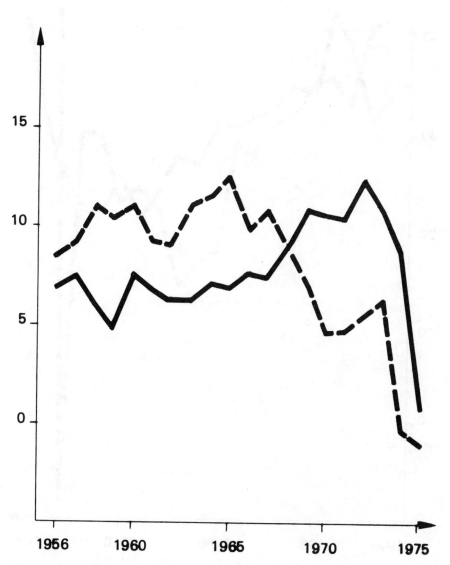

FRANCE ▬▬
U.K. ▬ ▬

Figure 6–4. Share of Profits after Tax

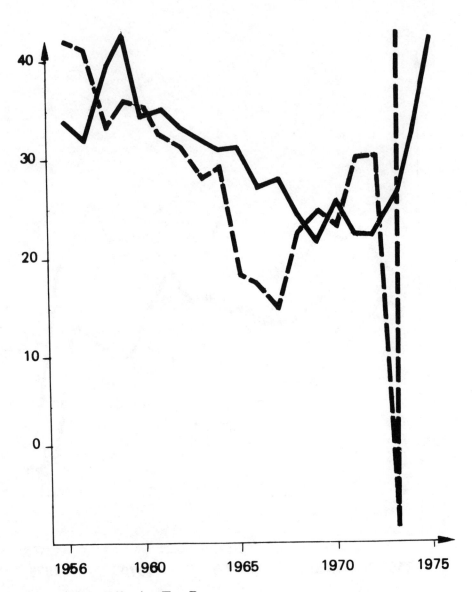

Figure 6–5. Effective Tax Rate

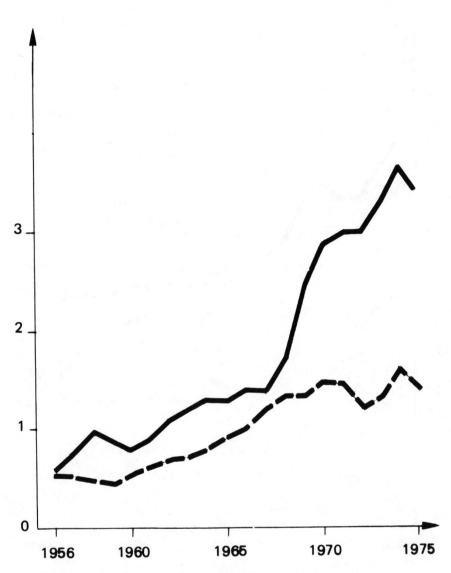

FRANCE ▬▬

U.K. ▬ ▬

Figure 6–6. Ratio of Interest to Capital

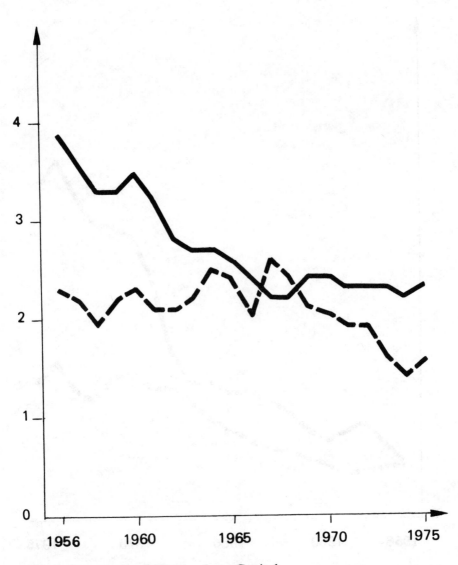

Figure 6–7. Ratio of Dividends to Capital

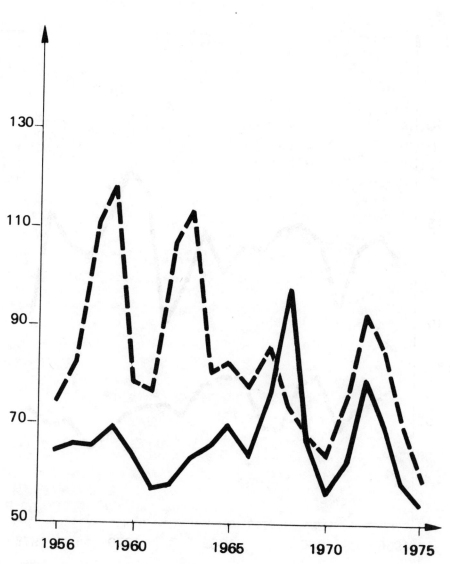

FRANCE ▬▬▬
U.K. ▬ ▬

Figure 6–8. Self-Financing Ratio

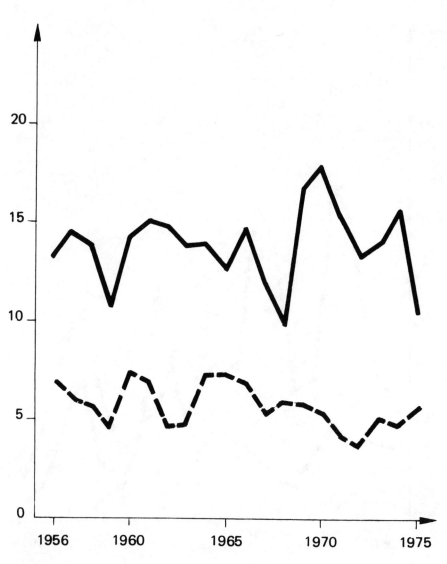

Figure 6–9. Growth Rate of Capital

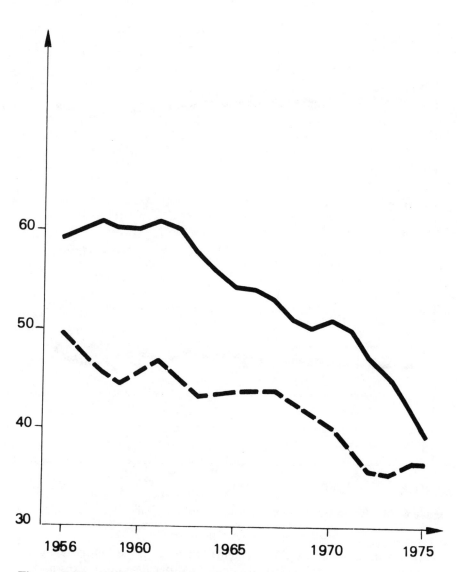

Figure 6–10. Ratio of Stocks to Fixed Capital

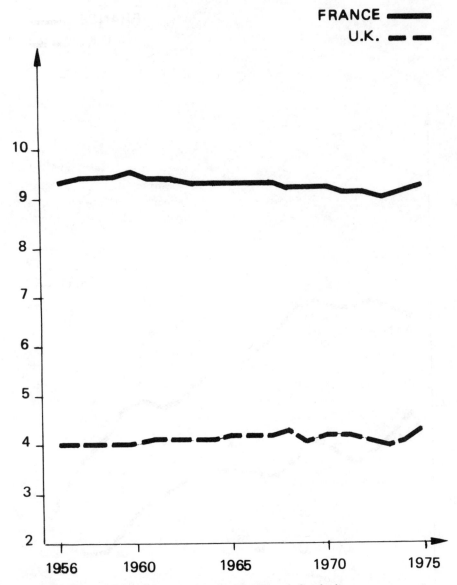

Figure 6–11. Ratio of Depreciation to Fixed Capital

falls (and with an unindexed tax system), whereas in the United Kingdom the tax rate becomes virtually undefined because both taxes and
profits fall to very low values. Subsequent to 1975, it is possible to show
that although profits recovered, tax payments have virtually disap-

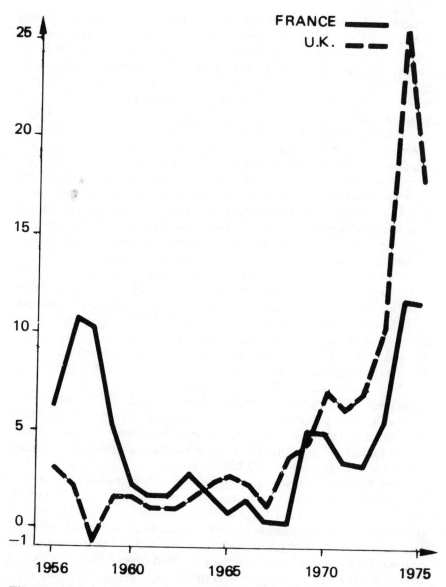

Figure 6–12. Ratio of Stock Appreciation to Stocks

peared. For the average industrial company in Britain, corporation tax has virtually been abolished.

On the financing side, the figures show that the *ratio of interest payments to capital (T6)* has risen at the same time the *ratio of dividends to capital (T7)* has fallen. These trends are much more marked in France than in the United Kingdom and reflect the growing importance of debt finance. Nevertheless, it is difficult to detect much of a trend in the behavior of the *self-financing ratio (T8),* which is defined here as the ratio of gross trading profits minus taxes, dividends, and interest payments to the value of gross investment and the increase in the book value of stocks.

There is no evidence of any trend in the underlying *growth rate of capital (T9)* in manufacturing, although it is obvious that this rate is much higher in France than in the United Kingdom. In both countries, there has been a steady fall in the *ratio of stocks to fixed capital (T10).* This is an interesting phenomenon for which we find it difficult to propose a simple explanation. At least one possible interpretation is that the investment incentives to fixed capital have gradually increased over the postwar period, whereas incentives to stock building have remained unchanged, and indeed (until the introduction of stock relief in 1974 in the United Kingdom) an increasing rate of inflation provided a disincentive to hold stocks because of the taxation of stock appreciation (only partially offset by the tax-deductibility of interest payments).

The *ratio of depreciation to fixed capital (T11)* is nearly constant in the two countries, but also very different: 4 percent in the United Kingdom as against 9.5 percent in France. Such a gap indicates that the average service life of fixed capital in the United Kingdom must be about double that in France. Although it is accepted that industrial equipment and structures are much older in the United Kingdom than in France, it is possible that this difference of average service life is overstated and only partly real. In the section entitled "The Robustness of the Estimates" we consider what would be the effects of assuming shorter service lives in the United Kingdom.

The figure of the *rate of stock appreciation to stocks (T12)* shows how rapidly stock prices increased in the period after 1972. The introduction of stock relief in 1974 in the United Kingdom not only removed the bulk of stock appreciation from corporate taxation but also extended free depreciation to physical investment in stocks. This redressed the balance between the fiscal incentives to fixed capital and to stocks. It is possible that this factor accounts for the halt in the fall in the ratio of stocks to capital evident in the United Kingdom from 1972 onward.

The Disaggregated Picture

We turn now to a brief look at profitability on a more disaggregated level to see if the trends apparent in manufacturing as a whole persist when we examine individual industries. The real profit rates before and after tax (*T1* and *T2*) for the three sectors of "intermediate," "investment," and "consumer" goods in France and the United Kingdom are shown in figures 6–13 to 6–16; they are also given in appendix 6A.

The evolution of profitability in the three sectors is more or less similar and parallel to that for manufacturing as a whole. In France the sectoral rates of profit intersect one another and tend to be very roughly equal. In the United Kingdom the consumer goods sector shows the highest average profit rate and the investment goods sector the lowest; both rates are relatively stable and differ by about 2 or 3 percent. The profit rate of the intermediate goods sector is more variable and fluctuates between the rates of the two other sectors. In both countries the consumer goods sector seems to have weathered the storm of the 1974–75 recession rather better than the intermediate and investment goods sectors.

The Robustness of the Estimates

One of the main problems when measuring profitability, and especially when trying to assess its evolution over time or when trying to compare its magnitude between sectors or countries, is the robustness of the estimates, or conversely their sensitivity to various errors and uncertainties. Stock appreciation is very difficult to measure and is all the more imprecise to the extent that inflation is more rapid. Capital consumption (or depreciation) and net fixed capital stock are computed by the permanent inventory method on the basis of past series of gross fixed investment, and they thus depend on assumptions about the average service lives and, more generally, the time profiles of replacement and depreciation.

Our estimates for France have been based on the so-called "1962 base year national accounts." Since these estimates, detailed figures going back to 1960 have also become available from the "1971 base year national accounts." Regarding these two national accounts data sets, there have been not only drastic revisions in the evaluations themselves, but also many minor changes and a few major ones in the nomenclature of agents and industries and the conceptual and practical definitions of operations and variables. We have been able to recalculate our profit rates based on the new national accounts, taking care of the major changes in nomenclature and definition. These new estimates thus differ from the previous ones because of the revisions in the underlying data and the changes in nomenclature and definitions for which we could not make any correction. Comparison of the two

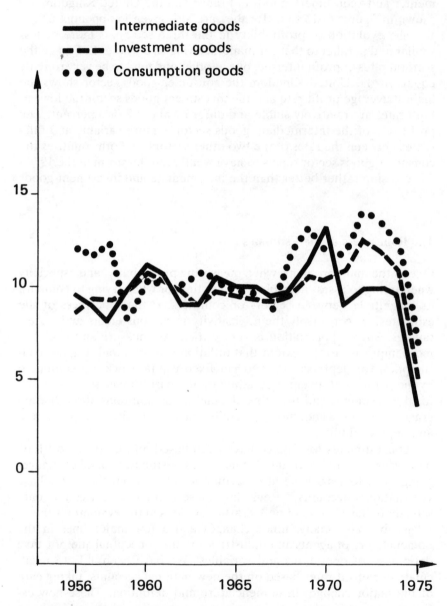

Figure 6–13. Rate of Profit before Tax

FRANCE

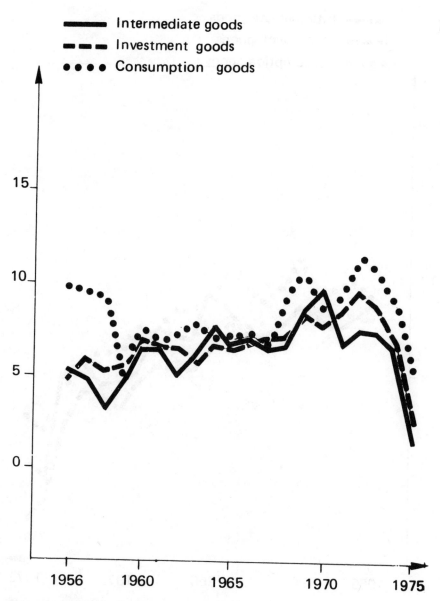

Figure 6–14. Rate of Profit after Tax

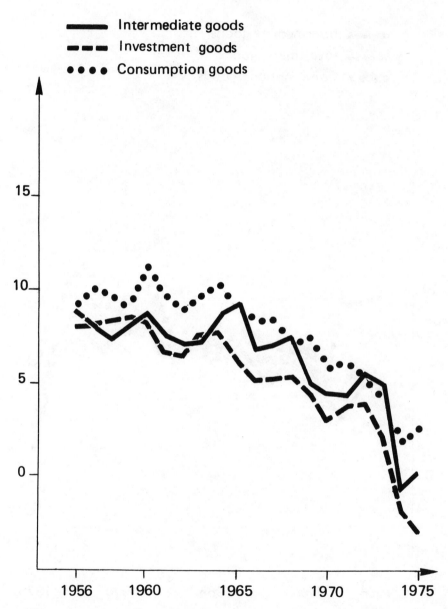

Figure 6–15. Rate of Profit before Tax

U.K.

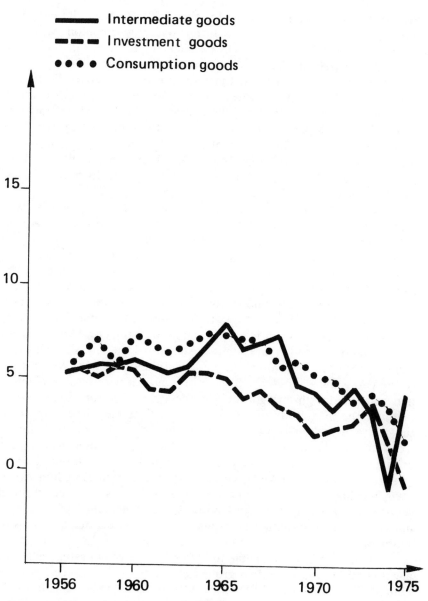

Figure 6–16. Rate of Profit after Tax

sets of data gives us an idea of the sensitivity to measurement errors and inconsistencies in the basic variables.

The two sets of before- and after-tax profit rates (*T1* and *T2* base year 1962 and 1971) are presented in figures 6–17 and 6–18 (and given also in appendix 6A). Their evolution over the common period of estimation, 1960–75, appears to be parallel and they differ in magnitude by at most 1 percent. This is rather fortunate and due largely to offsetting discrepancies between the numerators (profits) and denominators (capital) of the profit rates. The differences between the national accounts in base year 1971 and base year 1962 are of about 15 to 20 percent for gross profits; they vary from 5 to 20 percent for net fixed capital stock and capital consumption, and from 10 to 40 percent for the values of stocks. As regards stock appreciation the discrepancies are erratic and formidable for some years, ranging from half (− 80 percent) to triple (+ 200 percent).

The permanent inventory method used for the evaluation of fixed capital stock and consumption in the two countries differs in two respects: first in the exact implementation of the method, second in the supposed average service lives. The differences in method are more conventional than genuine, but seem to have little influence on the capital estimates themselves. In the United Kingdom past investments by industrial sectors are known for a number of different asset types; for each of these types a fixed service life and straight-line depreciation are assumed. In France it is only possible to distinguish two groups of assets: buildings and nonresidential structures on one side and machinery, vehicles, and other equipment on the other side. Within each of the two groups a log-normal distribution of service lives is assumed and combined with straight-line depreciation. Contrary to the exact method, the magnitude of average service lives has direct impact on the capital estimates. As we can see from the ratio of depreciation to fixed capital *(T11)*, the average service life in the United Kingdom is as much as double that of France. Such a difference can only be real in part, since the average service life for the United Kingdom would seem too high. It is then important to assess the way a reduction in service lives would change the United Kingdom estimates of fixed capital stock and consumption and thus ultimately affect our estimates of profit rates.

Actually we have been able to obtain the series of past investments aggregated for the same two groups of assets as for France from the United Kingdom Central Statistical Office. Thus we were able to recalculate the United Kingdom capital estimates using the same per-

FRANCE

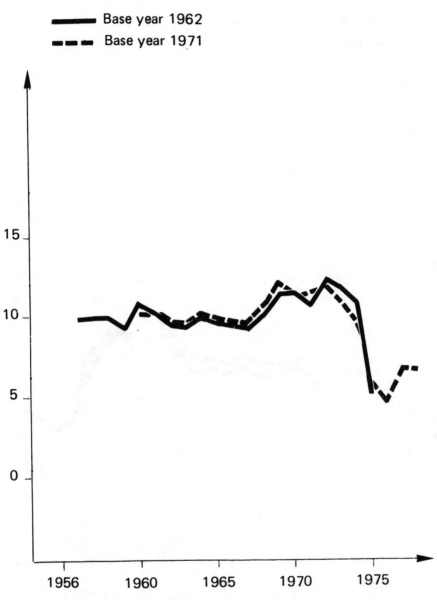

Figure 6–17. Rate of Profit before Tax

FRANCE

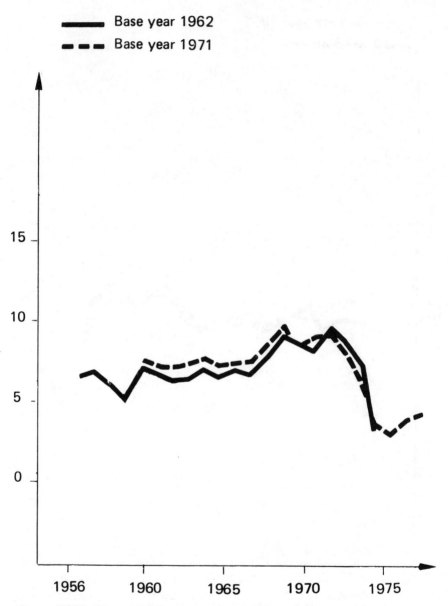

Figure 6–18. Rate of Profit after Tax

manent inventory method as for France, but with two alternative sets of service lives. In the first alternative we assumed that the service lives in the United Kingdom were longer than those in France by about 25 percent, and in the second that they were the same. For France the average service life for machinery and equipment (in most manufacturing industries) is supposed to be sixteen years, and the extreme service lives "at the 5 percent level of approximation" that served to set practical limits on the range of the distribution are about four and forty years. For buildings and structures the average service life is thirty-five years and the extreme service lives are ten and eighty years (again in most industries).

The alternative capital estimates we have computed are given in appendix 6A. The differences between the two sets and the official figures are remarkably stable. The two alternative estimates of net fixed capital stock are respectively smaller than the official ones by about 30 and 40 percent, and the two corresponding estimates of capital consumption are respectively larger than the official ones by about 25 and 35 percent. Thus, as before, there is a large offset between the changes in the numerator and denominator of the profit rates. We can see from figures 6–19 and 6–20, which plot our alternative and official estimates of the pretax and posttax profit rates (*T1* and *T2*) as well as the official ones, that these different rates remain rather close. Shorter service lives tend to augment the profit rates, but even when we apply French service lives to the United Kingdom the increase is at most 2 to 3 percent for the pretax rate and 1 to 2 percent for the posttax rate. In any case the general picture of falling profitability since the mid-1960s prevails for the United Kingdom.

An Econometric Analysis

We have examined some extremely simple regression models of the behavior of profitability. It would be an exaggeration to consider this as serious hypothesis testing, since we are really trying to do no more than find a more exact way of describing the data. All the regressions reported in this section were run over the period 1956–73 so that we could use the fitted equations to predict the years 1974 and 1975. There were three reasons for this: first, the usual one of wanting to predict outside the estimation period; second, the period after 1973 was one of an unusually deep recession and this provides a good test of how well our capacity utilization variable has been captured in the model;

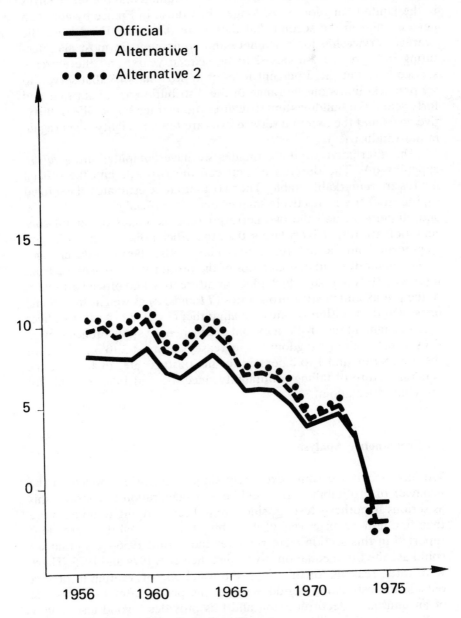

Figure 6–19. Rate of Profit before Tax

U.K.

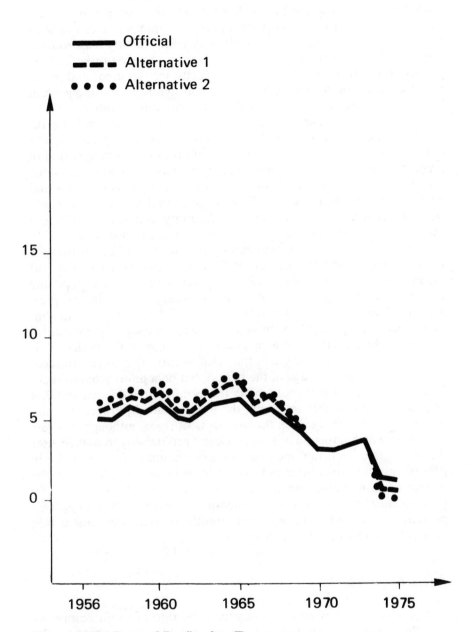

Figure 6–20. Rate of Profit after Tax

finally, the unanticipated increase in energy costs in 1973–74 may have rendered part of the capital stock economically obsolete and hence would lead us to expect lower than predicted rates of return in 1974 and 1975. Each equation was estimated by both ordinary least squares (OLS) and by maximum likelihood estimation of a first-order autoregressive error process. Only the OLS results are reported, and in the few cases in which the first-order process was significant at the 5 percent level this is indicated by an asterisk on the equation number.

We tested for the influence of three variables on the level of profitability. The first was a simple linear time trend to test the popular notion that there has been a falling rate of profit over a long period of time. The second variable was a dummy variable that took the value zero between 1956 and 1968 and the value of unity between 1969 and 1975. Visual inspection of the data suggests that this variable might well capture some of the variation in profitability, and there are differing explanations as to why it might be significant in the two countries. In Britain the story would be something like the following. In the late 1960s inflation started to increase and initially firms were very slow off the mark to realize that the traditional practice of historic cost pricing would be an inadequate rule of thumb in order to maintain real profitability. There is some independent evidence of this. By the time "inflation accounting" had been brought home to companies, price control had been introduced and was maintained throughout the period. It is difficult to assess the strength of the price controls that were enforced, particularly toward the end of the period, but on a priori grounds there is reason to suspect that profitability fell as inflation increased and that companies were unable to recoup the lost ground. In France, the significance of the 1968 events themselves is obvious, although it is less evident in which direction one might expect profitability to change after that date. The important increase in wages should cause a decrease in profits; however, measures in favor of firms were also taken, and the overall economic outcome was a strong recovery. The final variable included in the regression was a measure of capacity utilization (expressed as a percentage of capacity currently utilized), the construction of which is explained in appendix 6A.

Pretax Profitability

The results for the regressions in which the rate of profit before tax was the dependent variable are shown in tables 6–3 and 6–4. The standard errors of the estimates of the parameters are shown in paren-

Table 6–3
Pretax Profit Rate—Aggregate Manufacturing

Equations	Time	DUM	$(CU)_t$	$(CU)_{t+1}$	R^2	DW
United Kingdom						
1.	−0.306				0.841	1.09
	(0.033)					
2.	−0.314		0.093		0.853	1.18
	(0.034)		(0.082)			
3.	−0.323			0.220	0.913	1.45
	(0.026)			(0.062)		
4.	−0.352		0.085	0.220	0.939	1.52
	(0.025)		(0.055)	(0.054)		
5.	−0.214	−1.450	0.059		0.908	1.87
	(0.045)	(0.505)	(0.068)			
6.	−0.261	−0.929	0.059	0.163	0.940	1.76
	(0.041)	(0.466)	(0.057)	(0.061)		
France						
1.	0.107				0.383	1.34
	(0.034)					
2.	0.037		0.318		0.630	1.73
	(0.035)		(0.101)			
3.	0.049			0.230	0.502	1.92
	(0.044)			(0.121)		
4.	0.018		0.273	0.114	0.654	1.84
	(0.040)		(0.110)	(0.114)		
5.	−0.015	1.413	0.124		0.736	2.43
	(0.038)	(0.594)	(0.120)			
6.	−0.022	1.326	0.114	0.057	0.742	2.45
	(0.040)	(0.631)	(0.124)	(0.106)		

theses. For the United Kingdom, a time trend or a dummy variable is essential in order to explain the behavior of pretax profitability, whereas in France a reasonably good explanation can be obtained by assuming that the profit rate was equal to a constant plus a term measuring the degree of capacity utilization. The time trend is the more dominant influence in the United Kingdom, but even with a time trend there is room for a dummy variable representing a further decline in profitability in the period after 1969. In France, the only evidence of a trend over time is in the significance of the dummy variable showing that in the French case profitability was higher in the period 1969–73 than in the preceding period. Whereas the United Kingdom is characterized by a continuously declining rate of profit, France appears to have had a stable profit rate between 1956 and 1968, with an increase after that. In both countries the capacity utilization term is significant although it is interesting that the values that influence profitability are the utilization in both the current period and the following period. Lagged

Table 6–4
Pretax Profit Rate by Manufacturing Sector

	Time	DUM	$(CU)_t$	$(CU)_{t+1}$	R^2	DW
United Kingdom						
Intermediate goods						
4.	−0.257		0.207	0.265	0.783	1.67
	(0.038)		(0.092)	(0.095)		
6.	−0.111	−1.934	0.161	0.145	0.884	1.92
	(0.052)	(0.573)	(0.071)	(0.080)		
Investment goods						
4.	−0.378		−0.038	0.213	0.934	1.77
	(0.028)		(0.070)	(0.069)		
6.	−0.354	−0.334	−0.038	0.196	0.936	1.87
	(0.048)	(0.523)	(0.071)	(0.076)		
Consumer goods						
4.	−0.294		0.064	0.023	0.741	1.05
	(0.051)		(0.093)	(0.023)		
6.	−0.307	0.055	0.074	0.124	0.766	1.33
	(0.051)	(0.046)	(0.092)	(0.088)		
France						
Intermediate goods						
4.	0.025		−0.022	0.275	0.164	1.78
	(0.076)		(0.265)	(0.272)		
6.	−0.014	1.391	−0.219	0.148	0.200	1.89
	(0.092)	(1.805)	(0.371)	(0.322)		
Investment goods						
4.*	0.054		0.055	0.161	0.556	1.02
	(0.058)		(0.149)	(0.157)		
6.	0.025	1.746	−0.153	0.108	0.634	1.10
	(0.057)	(1.051)	(0.188)	(0.151)		
Consumer goods						
4.	0.054		0.448	0.079	0.409	1.28
	(0.070)		(0.189)	(0.190)		
6.	−0.105	2.644	0.318	0.056	0.608	2.21
	(0.086)	(1.031)	(0.168)	(0.161)		

*First-order autogressive process significant at 5 percent level.

values of the capacity utilization variable always had the wrong sign. One explanation for this may be that the variable measuring capacity utilization is defined in terms of output, and this may lag behind the factor determining profitability. This is by no means inevitable since increases in stocks as a result of falling sales would nevertheless show up in profits because profits include the increase in the book value of stocks. Even though our measure of profitability subtracts stock appreciation, it still includes physical investment in stocks as a sale. Nevertheless, the significance of future levels of capacity utilization is quite striking, particularly in the case of the United Kingdom and for posttax profitability.

There are significant differences between the sectors. In the United

Kingdom for the intermediate goods sector, a dummy variable seems to perform better than a time trend, the capacity utilization terms have the correct sign, and the current level of utilization is significant. The results for this sector in France are uniformly disappointing. Capacity utilization is not significant (and current levels have the wrong sign) and there is no evidence of a trend or a break in behavior after 1968. The model for the United Kingdom in the investment goods sector is fairly satisfactory, with clear evidence of a time trend and the influence of next period's capacity utilization. In France, however, capacity utilization is again insignificant as are the time trend and dummy variables, although there is some evidence of an increase after 1968. The results for the consumer goods sector are less satisfactory for the United Kingdom, although more so for France. The influence of capacity utilization does not really show up in the United Kingdom results although it does for those in France.

In both countries the quantitative impact of changes in capacity utilization is roughly similar. The sum of the coefficients on the capacity utilization variables tends to lie between 0.2 and 0.3 for both the United Kingdom and France. The effect of a fall in capacity utilization of six percentage points (the sort of change that occurs over a trade cycle) would result in a fall in the rate of profit of about 1.5 percentage points.

These regression equations were estimated over the period 1956–73, and the predictions of the best equation for each group for the years 1974–75 are shown in table 6–7. The equations selected to generate the predictions were chosen on the basis of which equation gave the least unsatisfactory explanation in our own minds, but were not chosen as the equations that necessarily yielded the best predictions. For the United Kingdom, all equations overpredict the level of profitability in 1974, and to some extent this carries through in 1975, although here the predictions for the intermediate and consumer good sectors are extremely good. The poor prediction is for the investment goods sector, in which the estimates overpredict profitability by about 3.5 percentage points in both 1974 and 1975. The predictions of the profit rates in France in 1974 are quite good, although in 1975 (the year in which profitability fell quite sharply) all equations overpredict profitability by a substantial amount.

Posttax Profitability

The regressions in which the dependent variable was the posttax rate of profit are shown in tables 6–5 and 6–6. The rate of profit after tax in the United Kingdom is affected by the introduction in 1974 of stock

Table 6–5
Posttax Profit Rate—Aggregate Manufacturing

Equations	Time	DUM	$(CU)_t$	$(CU)_{t+1}$	R^2	DW
United Kingdom						
1.*	−0.156				0.483	0.50
	(0.040)					
2.*	−0.163		0.073		0.500	0.63
	(0.042)		(0.101)			
3.*	−0.178		0.057	0.220	0.659	0.67
	(0.036)		(0.087)	(0.086)		
4.		−2.281	0.007	0.089	0.832	1.73
		(0.287)	(0.060)	(0.060)		
5.	−0.035	−1.962	0.019	0.111	0.839	1.57
	(0.046)	(0.514)	(0.063)	(0.067)		
France						
1.	0.182				0.671	1.56
	(0.032)					
2.	0.110		0.326		0.828	1.93
	(0.031)		(0.088)			
3.	0.084		0.265	0.156	0.856	2.19
	(0.033)		(0.091)	(0.095)		
4.		1.096	0.177	0.179	0.835	2.01
		(0.553)	(0.123)	(0.101)		
5.	0.066	0.616	0.191	0.129	0.867	2.42
	(0.037)	(0.583)	(0.115)	(0.098)		

*First-order autoregressive process significant at 5 percent level.

relief, which reduced the burden of tax on stock appreciation and was extended retrospectively to 1973. Since this could not have affected behavior in 1973, the equations are estimated over the period 1956–73 for the rate of profit after tax, but before any allowances given for stock relief. The predictions using this model are then compared with the rates of profit after tax including the effects of stock relief.

There is one interesting difference between the two countries in the results. Whereas in the United Kingdom a much better explanation can be found for the behavior of pretax profitability, the opposite is true in France, where the estimated equations for the rate of profit after tax are more satisfactory than the equivalent equations for pretax profit rates.

The first point to note is that as far as the United Kingdom is concerned a time trend is insignificant and provides no explanatory power at all for total manufacturing. Instead, there is a highly significant dummy variable showing that, as can be seen from the figures in the earlier part of the chapter, there was a discrete fall in the posttax rate of profit at the end of the 1960s from which there is little evidence of a recovery. But there are some significant differences among the sectors. The intermediate goods sector has a significant dummy variable

Table 6–6
Posttax Profit Rate by Manufacturing Sector

	Time	DUM	$(CU)_t$	$(CU)_{t+1}$	R^2	DW
United Kingdom						
Intermediate goods						
3.	−0.122		0.179	0.302	0.460	1.18
	(0.050)		(0.122)	(0.124)		
5.	0.117	−3.170	0.102	0.105	0.850	1.80
	(0.049)	(0.545)	(0.068)	(0.076)		
Investment goods						
3.*	−0.224		−0.045	0.197	0.780	0.67
	(0.034)		(0.084)	(0.083)		
5.	−0.120	−1.424	−0.046	0.124	0.865	1.68
	(0.045)	(0.498)	(0.068)	(0.072)		
Consumer goods						
3.*	−0.133		0.016	0.015	0.301	0.68
	(0.061)		(0.111)	(0.028)		
5.*	−0.150	0.069	0.029	0.140	0.375	0.98
	(0.061)	(0.055)	(0.109)	(0.105)		
France						
Intermediate goods						
3.	0.177		−0.052	0.273	0.593	1.63
	(0.067)		(0.235)	(0.241)		
5.	0.180	−0.124	−0.035	0.284	0.593	1.64
	(0.084)	(1.638)	(0.337)	(0.292)		
Investment goods						
3.	0.145		−0.023	0.201	0.845	1.97
	(0.042)		(0.108)	(0.114)		
5.	0.126	1.142	−0.159	0.167	0.867	2.15
	(0.043)	(0.779)	(0.140)	(0.112)		
Consumer goods						
3.*	0.065		0.421	0.113	0.395	0.91
	(0.074)		(0.199)	(0.199)		
5.	−0.093	2.626	0.292	0.090	0.577	1.64
	(0.093)	(1.110)	(0.181)	(0.173)		

*First-order autoregressive process significant at 5 percent level.

and an insignificant time trend; for the investment goods sector there is evidence of both a dummy variable and a significant time trend suggesting that for this sector there has been a much sharper fall in profitability; and for the consumer goods sector the estimated equation is so poor that it is difficult to come to any conclusion about the behavior of posttax profitability in this sector.

The behavior of posttax profitability in France has been very different. Again, the time trend and dummy variables seem to be significant, but in this case they have a positive sign reflecting the quite sharp increase in posttax profitability experienced in the period since the mid-1950s. For total manufacturing, both the time trend and dummy variable play some part in explaining the upward shift in profitability, and the effects of the capacity utilization variable can clearly be seen. Looking at the disaggregated data reveals that, for the intermediate and investment goods sector, the time trend is more important than the effects of the dummy variable, and further, that for these sectors, current capacity utilization has the wrong sign and it is next period's capacity utilization that plays the more significant role. In contrast, for the consumer goods sector, the dummy variable is the significant influence and current capacity utilization is quantitatively more important than next period's level of utilization.

The predictions shown in table 6–7 point to accurate predictions for 1974 and also, as far as the United Kingdom is concerned, for 1975 (with the exception of a significant underprediction for the intermediate goods sector). The predictions for France for 1975 are generally too high and the errors for this year are of the same order of magnitude as for the predictions of pretax profitability.

Conclusions

The main aim of this exercise was to produce a data set from which comparisons of profitability could be made on the basis of common definitions. We are under no illusions that there are still problems with our results, but these derive largely from the errors involved in estimating values of such variables as capital stock and stock appreciation. We have tried to overcome most of the problems involved in producing a comparable series of estimates but doubtless some remain. We have found that profit rates in France have been only slightly modified by the major revision of French national accounts from the 1962 base year to the 1971 base year. We have shown also that profit rates in the United Kingdom are not significantly affected by the large uncertainty about the service lives of fixed capital assets.

The behavior of profitability in, and the principal differences between, France and the United Kingdom can be seen by looking at the figures given in the chapter. If anything, there is a slight tendency for the real rate of profit to increase in French manufacturing from 1956 to 1974, while it is falling since the mid-1960s in the United Kingdom. It would be interesting to relate our measures of real profitability to financial variables, but since this is a first attempt, the econometric results presented here do no more than summarize the data in a form suggesting that there are distinct dangers in drawing sweeping conclusions from a visual inspection of the data. Disaggregation of the data seemed to make it more, not less, difficult to obtain plausible-looking fitted equations.

Table 6–7
Predictions of Profit Rates

	Equation Number	1974			1975		
		Actual	Forecast	Error	Actual	Forecast	Error
Pretax							
United Kingdom							
Intermediate goods	6	−0.64	2.50	−3.14	0.45	0.28	0.17
Investment goods	4	−1.95	1.55	−3.50	−3.05	0.75	−3.80
Consumer goods	6	1.87	3.58	−1.71	2.66	2.83	−0.17
Aggregate	6	−0.60	2.37	−2.97	−0.59	1.44	−2.03
France							
Intermediate goods	4	9.40	7.78	1.62	3.70	7.99	−4.29
Investment goods	6	10.70	10.46	0.24	5.00	11.70	−6.70
Consumer goods	6	12.30	11.78	0.52	7.20	9.13	−1.93
Aggregate	5	10.80	11.49	−0.69	5.20	10.46	−5.26
Posttax							
United Kingdom							
Intermediate goods	4*	−0.71	1.35	−2.06	4.29	−0.58	4.87
Investment goods	5	1.57	1.24	0.33	−0.74	1.02	−1.76
Consumer goods	5	3.50	2.66	0.84	1.75	2.48	−0.73
Aggregate	5	1.46	2.22	−0.76	1.31	1.90	−0.59
France							
Intermediate goods	3	6.50	5.80	0.70	1.80	6.53	−4.73
Investment goods	3	6.90	7.51	−0.61	2.60	7.85	−5.25
Consumer goods	5	9.00	8.98	0.02	5.10	6.52	−1.42
Aggregate	3	7.40	7.83	−0.43	3.10	5.76	−2.66

*Equation not tabulated in table 6–6.

Notes

1. Our figures *do* include profits made on export sales; they do not include profits on overseas production in foreign branches and subsidiaries.

2. A detailed discussion of the computation of tax liabilities will be found in appendix 6A. They are defined as corporation tax payments

net of advance corporation tax (in the UK) and avoir fiscal (in France). When calculating posttax rates of profit, no adjustment was made to the capital base to reflect accelerated depreciation as suggested in the *Bank of England Quarterly Bulletin,* March 1976. This was because the necessary data were not available on a disaggregated basis and experiments suggested that the differences involved were small. The problem is not so important for France.

References

Charpin, J.M. "L'Utilisation des capacités de production de 1951 à 1973." *Economie et Statistique,* no. 55 (1974).

Delestré, H., and J. Mairesse, "La rentabilité des sociétés privés en France 1956–75." Paris: Dossier Statistique, INSEE, 1978.

Feldstein, M.S., and L. Summers, "Is the Rate of Profit Falling?" *Brookings Papers on Economic Activity,* no. 1 (1977).

Griffin, T. "The Stock of Fixed Assets in the United Kingdom: How to Make Best Use of the Statistics." *Economic Trends,* October 1976.

King, M.A. "The UK Profits Crisis: Myth or Reality?" *Economic Journal,* March 1975.

———. *Public Policy and the Corporation.* London: Chapman and Hall, 1977.

———. *Profits in a Mixed Economy.* London: Macmillan, 1979.

Mairesse, J. "L'Evaluation du Capital fixe Productif." Paris: Les Collections de L'INSEE, 1972.

Saglio, A., and B. Tabuteau, "L'Utilisation des capacités production dans l'industries." *Economie et Statistique,* no. 21 (1971).

Appendix 6A
The Data

In this appendix, we describe the definitions of the variables and the construction of the data. Table 6A1 lists the industries covered by the study and shows the disaggregation of "manufacturing" into three subgroups for "intermediate," "investment," and "consumer" goods. For reasons explained in the text, we decided to exclude food, drink, and tobacco and metal manufacture from our definition of manufacturing. In both countries, the petroleum and natural gas industries are excluded because they are extractive industries, and so our figures do not include the very rapidly growing North Sea activities in the United Kingdom. A certain amount of refining activity that does constitute manufacturing is included in the intermediate goods sector in the United Kingdom but excluded in France because it proved impossible to differentiate it from the extractive activities. The figures involved are small and we do not think any serious bias results from this omission. Sim-

Table 6A1
Industrial Coverage

United Kingdom	France
Group 1 *Intermediate goods* Chemicals and Allied Industries Coal and Petroleum products Bricks, pottery, glass, etc.	*Biens intermédiaires* Chimie; verre. Materiaux de construction Metallurgie des non fereux

Group 2 *Investment goods*
Mechanical engineering
Instrument engineering
Electrical engineering
Shipbuilding and marine
  engineering
Vehicles
Metal goods not elsewhere
  specified
	Biens d'equipement
	Première transformation des
	  métaux
	Industries mécaniques
	Industries electriques
	Automobile
	Industries navale, aeronautique
	  et armement

Group 3 *Consumption goods* Textiles Leather, etc. Clothing and footwear Timber, furniture, etc. Paper, printing, and publishing Other manufacturing industries	Textiles, habillement, et cuir Bois, papier, presse Industries diverse

Total All Manufacturing excluding
  food, drink and tobacco and
  metal manufacture
	Ensemble de l'industrie *sauf*
	  industrie agricole et
	  alimentaire, et siderurgie

ilarly, in principle, "metallurgie des non fereux" should be moved from the intermediate to the investment goods sector but the available data preclude this. Again, the figures involved are very small.

The basic and transformed variables for which data were collected and computed are listed in table 6–1 in the text. The values of the basic and transformed variables for manufacturing as a whole for the United Kingdom and France appear in table 6A2. Data for the three subsectors of manufacturing are available from the authors, but real profit rates by sectors for France and the United Kingdom appear in table 6A3. The alternative estimates of profit rates based on the "1971 base year national accounts" for France and computed assuming shorter service lives of capital for the United Kingdom are given in table 6A4.

The definitions of the twelve basic variables and their sources are as follows.

R1: Gross trading profits. This is the trading profit made on domestic production (including production for export) by companies before any allowance for depreciation or stock appreciation.

UK: 1956–60: National Income and Expenditure 1967, table 35.
1961–65: National Income and Expenditure 1972, table 31;
1966–75: National Income and Expenditure 1977, table 5.8.
For 1974 and 1975 an estimate for profits in "bricks, pottery, etc." was made by assuming that in those years they increased at the same rate as profits in the rest of group 1.

France: Delestré and Mairesse (1978); better estimates for 1957 and 1958 were incorporated into our series.

R2: Capital consumption. This is an estimate of the fall in value at current replacement cost of the existing capital stock. Each asset type is assumed to have a fixed service life and is depreciated (on a straight-line basis) evenly over that period. The series is constructed to be consistent with the series for net capital stock at current replacement cost. Details of the service lives may be found in Griffin (1976) and Mairesse (1972). The assumed service lives are shorter in France than in the United Kingdom and this is reflected in the much higher ratio of capital consumption to the capital stock in France as shown by the values of the ratio of depreciation to fixed capital *(T11)*.

UK: Central Statistical Office.

France: Delestré and Mairesse (1978).

Table 6A2(1)
Raw Data for Manufacturing as a Whole—United Kingdom[a]

	R1	R2	R3	R4	R5	R6	R7	R8	R9	R10	R11	R12
1956	1428	310	115	417	65	258	3719	7669	3810	626	183	96.1
1957	1504	338	86	439	67	276	3843	8481	4049	685	91	96.1
1958	1449	364	-42	361	66	246	3980	9076	4166	653	97	92.4
1959	1622	375	68	415	64	297	4160	9483	4236	619	16	95.5
1960	1793	392	72	460	80	327	4516	9871	4512	690	403	98.9
1961	1669	429	56	373	99	328	4863	10464	4895	833	238	96.4
1962	1688	453	49	361	113	338	5023	11147	5057	788	-22	93.8
1963	1913	482	67	374	123	376	5155	11815	5143	759	77	93.5
1964	2215	515	125	449	145	448	5623	12598	5479	917	405	98.8
1965	2251	567	160	266	183	479	5845	13643	5992	1091	343	98.4
1966	2133	613	152	219	218	425	6562	14727	6463	1183	292	97.6
1967	2182	643	80	200	272	584	6628	15354	6762	1118	80	95.2
1968	2443	699	252	320	315	571	7135	16425	7048	1251	165	98.6
1969	2514	759	339	338	353	543	7849	18335	7593	1184	344	99.1
1970	2665	858	583	271	427	577	8931	20630	8310	1383	203	96.8
1971	3003	975	547	433	470	617	9676	23268	8882	1537	-144	94.0
1972	3460	1071	660	510	437	661	10372	26076	9358	1392	-77	93.9
1973	4008	1187	1405	-122	536	633	12059	29571	10529	1628	383	99.2
1974	4470	1447	3317	-1008	788	682	14975	35762	13078	2253	111	95.7
1975	4370	1896	2833	-1151	881	903	18300	44183	16186	2527	828	87.7

[a]R1 to R11 in 10^6 English pounds; R12 in percent.

Table 6A2(2)
Raw Data for Manufacturing as a Whole—France[a]

	R1	R2	R3	R4	R5	R6	R7	R8	R9	R10	R11	R12
1956	9707	3121	1329	1749	336	2038	25927	33139	19788	4803	2406	95.0
1957	11940	3525	2408	1869	505	2165	28937	37267	22507	5774	3031	96.2
1958	13193	3941	2584	2569	662	2202	33329	41533	25451	6359	2858	94.4
1959	12394	4335	1414	2819	679	2386	35634	45510	27527	6643	1293	92.0
1960	14045	4736	657	2941	608	2746	39788	49505	29935	7877	3524	94.0
1961	14942	5242	512	3171	829	2835	44782	55054	33756	9568	4038	94.1
1962	16019	5879	580	3103	1075	2842	50276	62093	37646	11284	3662	95.2
1963	18394	6662	1150	3311	1396	3043	56522	70865	41007	12539	3061	96.2
1964	20784	7420	854	3781	1642	3287	62680	79156	44341	13752	3607	95.0
1965	21579	8177	360	3954	1792	3541	66660	87191	47552	14407	2822	93.5
1966	23904	9002	764	3709	2062	3520	71648	95855	51991	16141	6065	94.8
1967	25039	9883	205	4031	2307	3600	76488	105256	56243	17305	2440	93.8
1968	28162	10596	191	4058	2943	3776	82619	113466	58181	15901	1433	94.4
1969	37392	11884	3311	4582	4611	4573	92446	127992	64353	21324	10911	97.7
1970	43779	13905	3841	6481	6570	5439	104984	149547	76487	27748	13357	97.2
1971	46455	15986	2950	5918	7705	5898	117684	172934	87025	32142	7711	97.0
1972	56869	18057	3062	7606	8753	6800	132843	196825	93921	32780	6069	97.7
1973	64864	20537	5664	9511	10920	7604	154038	224549	102302	35858	10694	99.5
1974	81458	25449	13693	13406	14493	8678	185955	275960	116802	44331	18303	97.8
1975	68065	29843	14703	9762	15408	10391	213826	321993	126849	43732	1794	89.6

[a]R1 to R11 in 10^6 Francs; R12 in percent.

Table 6A2(3)
Transformed Data for Manufacturing as a Whole—United Kingdom
(percent)

	T1	T2	T3	T4	T5	T6	T7	T8	T9	T10	T11	T12
1956	8.7	5.1	21.2	13.6	41.5	0.6	2.2	74.5	7.0	49.7	4.0	3.0
1957	8.6	5.1	21.9	14.3	40.7	0.5	2.2	83.6	6.2	47.7	4.0	2.1
1958	8.5	5.8	22.1	16.1	32.1	0.5	1.9	109.6	5.7	45.9	4.0	-1.0
1959	8.6	5.6	22.1	15.5	35.2	0.5	2.2	120.3	4.6	44.7	3.9	1.6
1960	9.2	6.0	22.7	16.1	34.6	0.6	2.3	79.4	7.6	45.7	4.0	1.6
1961	7.7	5.3	19.6	14.3	31.5	0.6	2.1	77.1	7.0	46.8	4.1	1.1
1962	7.3	5.1	19.1	14.1	30.4	0.7	2.1	107.4	4.7	45.4	4.1	1.0
1963	8.0	5.8	20.9	16.1	27.4	0.7	2.2	115.1	4.9	43.5	4.1	1.3
1964	8.7	6.2	21.9	16.7	28.5	0.8	2.5	81.0	7.3	43.5	4.1	2.3
1965	7.8	6.4	20.7	17.7	17.4	0.9	2.4	82.8	7.3	43.9	4.2	2.7
1966	6.5	5.4	17.3	14.9	16.0	1.0	2.0	78.1	7.0	43.9	4.2	2.3
1967	6.6	5.7	18.0	16.0	13.7	1.2	2.6	88.1	5.4	44.0	4.2	1.2
1968	6.4	5.0	17.3	14.1	21.5	1.3	2.4	74.2	6.0	42.9	4.3	3.6
1969	5.5	4.2	15.3	12.1	23.9	1.4	2.1	68.5	5.9	41.4	4.1	4.5
1970	4.2	3.3	12.0	9.6	22.1	1.5	2.0	64.1	5.5	40.3	4.2	7.0
1971	4.6	3.3	13.3	9.8	29.2	1.5	1.9	76.4	4.3	38.2	4.2	6.2
1972	4.9	3.4	14.3	10.5	29.5	1.2	1.9	93.7	3.7	35.9	4.1	7.0
1973	3.5	3.8	10.5	11.3	-8.6	1.3	1.6	86.7	5.0	35.6	4.0	13.3
1974	-0.6	1.5	-2.0	4.5	342.8	1.6	1.4	70.5	4.8	36.6	4.0	25.4
1975	-0.6	1.3	-2.0	4.1	320.6	1.5	1.5	60.4	5.6	36.6	4.3	17.5

Table 6A2(4)
Transformed Data for Manufacturing as a Whole—France
(percent)

	T1	T2	T3	T4	T5	T6	T7	T8	T9	T10	T11	T12
1956	9.9	6.6	16.9	11.9	33.3	0.6	3.9	65.4	13.6	59.7	9.4	6.7
1957	10.0	6.9	17.2	12.5	31.1	0.8	3.6	66.0	14.7	60.4	9.5	10.7
1959	10.0	6.1	16.7	11.0	38.5	1.0	3.3	65.8	13.8	61.3	9.5	10.2
1959	9.1	5.2	15.7	9.7	42.4	0.9	3.3	69.6	10.9	60.5	9.5	5.1
1960	10.9	7.2	17.9	12.6	34.0	0.8	3.5	64.3	14.4	60.5	9.6	2.2
1961	10.3	6.8	17.0	11.8	34.5	0.9	3.2	57.4	15.3	61.3	9.5	1.5
1962	9.6	6.5	16.0	11.4	32.5	1.1	2.8	58.0	15.0	60.6	9.5	1.5
1963	9.5	6.5	15.8	11.4	31.3	1.2	2.7	63.5	13.9	57.9	9.4	2.8
1964	10.1	7.1	16.6	12.2	30.2	1.3	2.7	66.3	14.1	56.0	9.4	1.9
1965	9.7	6.7	16.4	12.0	30.3	1.3	2.6	69.9	12.8	54.5	9.4	0.8
1966	9.6	7.1	16.5	12.7	26.2	1.4	2.4	63.6	15.0	54.2	9.4	1.5
1967	9.3	6.8	16.4	12.5	27.0	1.4	2.2	75.7	12.2	53.4	9.4	0.4
1968	10.1	7.8	17.4	13.9	23.4	1.7	2.2	99.2	10.1	51.3	9.3	0.3
1969	11.5	9.2	19.4	16.0	20.6	2.4	2.4	66.5	16.8	50.3	9.3	5.1
1970	11.5	8.7	19.9	15.7	24.9	2.9	2.4	56.3	18.2	51.1	9.3	5.0
1971	10.6	8.3	19.0	15.5	21.5	3.0	2.3	62.9	15.3	50.3	9.2	3.4
1972	12.3	9.7	21.2	17.5	21.3	3.0	2.3	80.4	13.4	47.7	9.2	3.3
1973	11.8	8.9	20.1	15.9	24.6	3.3	2.3	70.5	14.2	45.6	9.1	5.5
1974	10.8	7.4	18.5	13.5	31.7	3.7	2.2	58.8	15.9	42.3	9.2	11.7
1975	5.2	3.1	9.9	6.0	41.5	3.4	2.3	54.0	10.1	39.4	9.3	11.6

Table 6A3
Real Profit Rates by Sectors
(percent)

| | INTERMEDIATE GOODS | | | | INVESTMENT GOODS | | | | CONSUMER GOODS | | | |
| | PRE-TAX T1 | | POST-TAX T2 | | PRE-TAX T1 | | POST-TAX T2 | | PRE-TAX T1 | | POST-TAX T2 | |
	UK	FRANCE	UK	FRANCE	UK	FRANCE	UK	FRANCE	UK	FRANCE	UK	FRANCE
1956	8.1	9.6	5.1	5.3	8.9	8.5	5.1	4.9	9.1	12.1	5.1	9.8
1957	8.1	9.1	5.4	4.8	8.1	9.3	4.4	6.0	10.0	11.8	6.2	9.6
1958	7.4	7.9	5.7	3.3	8.4	9.3	5.1	5.3	9.8	12.3	7.1	9.3
1959	8.1	9.7	5.6	4.7	8.6	9.6	5.6	5.5	9.1	7.9	5.6	5.3
1960	8.8	11.3	5.9	6.6	8.4	10.8	5.4	7.2	11.3	10.7	7.4	7.7
1961	7.6	10.7	5.5	6.6	6.7	10.3	4.4	6.7	9.8	10.2	6.7	6.9
1962	7.1	9.0	5.3	5.1	6.5	9.7	4.3	6.6	9.1	9.9	6.4	7.3
1963	7.3	9.0	5.6	6.2	7.6	8.9	5.4	5.8	9.8	10.7	6.9	7.8
1964	8.8	10.5	6.9	7.7	7.9	9.8	5.3	6.7	10.3	10.3	7.4	7.2
1965	9.4	9.9	8.0	6.7	6.3	9.6	5.1	6.6	9.0	9.7	7.4	7.0
1966	6.9	9.9	6.7	7.1	5.2	9.4	4.0	6.9	8.5	9.5	6.9	7.2
1967	7.1	9.4	6.9	6.6	5.4	9.3	4.4	6.9	8.6	9.0	7.0	6.7
1968	7.5	9.5	7.3	6.8	5.4	9.5	3.5	7.2	7.2	11.7	5.7	9.6
1969	4.9	11.3	4.5	8.8	4.7	10.7	3.1	8.4	7.6	13.2	6.0	10.7
1970	4.6	13.5	4.2	10.0	3.1	10.4	1.9	7.8	5.0	11.6	5.0	8.9
1971	4.4	9.0	3.3	6.8	3.9	10.8	2.3	8.5	6.3	11.7	5.0	9.5
1972	5.6	9.9	4.5	7.5	4.1	12.7	2.6	9.8	5.5	14.1	3.8	11.5
1973	4.9	9.9	3.5	7.4	2.4	11.9	3.7	8.8	4.1	13.5	4.3	10.7
1974	-0.6	9.4	-0.7	6.5	-1.9	10.7	1.6	6.9	1.9	12.3	3.5	9.0
1975	0.4	3.7	4.3	1.8	-3.0	5.0	-0.7	2.6	2.7	7.2	1.7	5.1

Table 6A4
Alternative Estimates in France and in the United Kingdom

FRANCE			UNITED KINGDOM								
REAL PROFIT RATES USING 1971 BASE YEAR NATIONAL ACCOUNTS			ALTERNATIVE ESTIMATES USING AVERAGE SERVICE LIVES								
			EQUAL TO THE FRENCH ONES				LONGER THAN THE FRENCH ONES			
	T1	T2		T1	T2	R2	R8	T1	T2	R2	R8
1960	10.4	7.6	1956	10.3	5.6	391	5151	10.9	5.9	415	4381
1961	10.1	7.3	1957	10.5	5.8	429	5344	10.9	5.9	455	4818
1962	9.6	7.2	1958	10.1	6.5	461	6055	10.6	6.8	497	5179
1963	9.7	7.4	1959	10.3	6.3	477	6211	11.0	6.6	506	5312
1964	10.3	7.8	1960	11.1	6.9	498	6480	11.8	7.3	529	5541
1965	9.8	7.4	1961	9.0	5.9	537	6988	9.6	6.1	572	5982
1966	9.5	7.5	1962	8.5	5.7	570	7445	9.0	5.8	609	6379
1967	9.7	7.6	1963	9.5	6.6	608	7943	10.0	6.9	649	6797
1968	10.6	8.5	1964	10.5	7.3	638	8319	11.2	7.6	681	7114
1969	12.3	9.7	1965	9.2	7.5	699	9054	9.8	7.8	746	7753
1970	11.3	8.6	1966	7.5	6.1	760	9872	7.8	6.3	814	8471
1971	11.5	9.1	1967	7.6	6.5	798	10311	8.0	6.7	854	8855
1972	12.0	9.3	1968	7.3	5.5	867	11150	7.6	5.7	929	9575
1973	11.0	8.3	1969	6.2	4.5	945	12124	6.4	4.6	1014	10417
1974	9.7	6.6	1970	4.5	3.3	1078	13732	4.6	3.2	1157	11814
1975	5.8	3.9	1971	5.0	3.2	1234	15601	5.1	3.1	1324	13410
1976	4.7	3.2	1972	5.4	3.5	1367	17290	5.5	3.4	1463	14803
1977	6.8	4.3	1973	3.4	3.8	1559	19931	3.4	3.8	1664	16978
1978	6.7	4.6	1974	-2.0	0.6	1911	25052	-2.6	0.4	2033	21253
1979	7.5	5.1	1975	-1.9	0.6	2415	30655	-2.4	0.3	2558	26326

R3: Stock appreciation. This is a measure of the increase in the value of stocks arising solely from an increase in the price of stocks and not from an increase in the volume of stocks held. It is very difficult to measure and the data for stock appreciation are probably the most unreliable data in the study.

UK: Central Statistical Office.

France: Delestré and Mairesse (1978); improved estimates for 1957 and 1958 were available and these were incorporated into our series.

R4: Taxes. This is an estimate of the corporate tax liability on domestic trading profits. In the United Kingdom it is an estimate of the liability incurred on the profits earned in any given year; in France the figure relates to payments of taxes during the year. By "corporate tax liability" we mean the difference between profits and dividends, interest, and retained earnings all measured before deduction of personal income or capital gains taxes. In other words, under the classical system of corporation tax our definition corresponds to liabilities of corporation tax. Under the imputation system, currently used in both France and Britain, the definition is corporation tax liabilities minus advance corporation tax (avoir fiscal in France).

In France the figures of tax on domestic trading profits can be closely approximated by total tax payments because corporate income from abroad is small and few taxes are levied on it. Therefore we have taken figures for tax payments from Delestré and Mairesse (1978) and subtracted estimates of avoir fiscal supplied by INSEE.

In Britain the position is much more complicated. The available data on corporate tax liabilities relate to total liabilities on income from all sources because that is how the liability is calculated. But a large fraction of total income derives from sources other than domestic gross trading profits, and so to answer the hypothetical question of what would be the tax liability accruing on a given level of trading profits one has to construct a model to compute the value of this tax liability. The model used is that set out in King (1975) to which the reader is referred for details. The tax liability is that of the company and is defined to exclude the shareholders' income tax liability on their dividends and also their capital gains tax liability arising on the disposal of shares. Again this requires a model because the published data do not afford a consistent series on this basis. Investment grants, which replaced some tax allowances for investment during the period 1966–70, are considered as negative taxes.

The effective tax liability T is given by

$$T = t(P - D) + t_d G - S$$

where

$P =$ gross trading profits;
$D =$ tax deductions comprising both tax allowances for depreciation and investment, and interest payments;

G = gross dividends (that is, before
    deduction of income tax);
S = accruals of investment grants;
t = the basic rate of corporation tax;
t_d = a tax discrimination variable
    measuring the differential tax imposed
    on dividends versus retentions
    (see King, 1975).

The values of the tax rates were taken from appendix A of King (1977). Profits are as shown in R1. Tax deductions comprise tax allowances and interest payments. The former are equal to the difference between gross and net profits as given in the Blue Book in the same tables as the source for R1. No data on interest payments by the total of manufacturing companies are available, but there are data on payments by quoted companies. Moreover, these are disaggregated by industry. Therefore, we have assumed that the ratio of interest payments to gross trading profits in each of our industrial sectors was the same as that for quoted companies in the same sectors. Data on this ratio were obtained from *Business Monitor* ME (various issues) and *Economic Trends* (April 1972). (For years before 1971 an adjustment was made to allow for short-term interest payments, which had been excluded from the figures. The data were supplied by J.A. Beath and were based on the assumption that the interest rate on short-term borrowings was Bank Rate plus 2 percent. From 1971 the official figures include short-term interest payments.)

The same treatment was adopted to obtain estimates of gross dividends. The ratio of dividends to profits for quoted companies was taken from the sources just cited and adjusted to a consistent series for gross dividends (in some years dividends are shown in the official statistics net of standard rate income tax).

The remaining component of the effective tax liability is the value of investment grants received. The methods for calculating this is the same as that described in King (1975). The data were obtained from *Trade and Industry* (January 1973). No allowance has been made for Regional Development Grants and hence the tax liability is likely to be overstated.

R5: Interest payments. These include both short- and long-term interest payments out of trading profits.

UK: The estimates were obtained by multiplying the series for the ratio of interest payments to profits described in the section on taxation by the values of profits in R1.

France: Delestré and Mairesse (1978)

R6: Dividends. This comprises dividends on ordinary and preference shares measured before deduction of personal income tax (that is, dividends including tax credits or avoir fiscal).

UK: The estimates were obtained by multiplying the series for the ratio of dividends to profits described in the section on taxation by the values of profits in R1.

France: Delestré and Mairesse (1978).

R7: Income from employment. This consists of wages and salaries plus employers' contributions, that is, total cost to the employer of the labor force during the year.

UK: 1965–60: 1967 Blue Book tables 17 and 18.
1961–65: 1972 Blue Book tables 17 and 18.
1966–75: 1977 Blue Book tables 3.1 and 3.3.
In each case it was necessary to estimate employers' contributions by assuming that the ratio of the contributions to wages and salaries was the same in each of the three sectors as in manufacturing as a whole.

France: Delestré and Mairesse (1978).

R8: Fixed capital stock. The estimates are for the value of net capital stock at current replacement cost. They are derived from permanent inventory models assuming fixed service lives for different asset types (see, for example, the description in R. Maurice, ed., *National Accounts Statistics: Sources and Methods,* 1968). The figures available relate to the value of the capital stock at the end of each calendar year, and for our purposes we took the value for a particular year to be the arithmetic average of the end-year values. The capital base includes plant, machinery, and buildings but excludes land.

UK: Central Statistical Office.

France: Mairesse (1972) and Delestré and Mairesse (1978).

R9: Book value of stocks. This is the nearest we can get to an estimate of the value of stocks at replacement cost. As with R8 the value was taken to be the average of the end-year values of the preceding and current years. Total capital employed in each sector is the sum of R8 and R9.

UK: Central Statistical Office.

France: Mairesse (1972) and Delestré and Mairesse (1978).

R10: Gross fixed investment. This is the value at current prices of gross investment in all fixed assets.

UK: National Income and Expenditure (various issues as for R1).

France: Delestré and Mairesse (1978).

R11: Stock building. This is the value at current prices of the increase in the physical volume of stocks.

UK: Central Statistical Office.

France: Delestré and Mairesse (1978).

R12: Capacity utilization. In order to test the hypothesis that profitability depends upon capacity utilization we needed a measure of the degree of capacity utilization. Moreover, these indexes were required for each of the three sectors. No published data were available for the United Kingdom, but in France an index had been constructed in INSEE and this was used as the basis for our French series. Consequently, the two series have been constructed by rather different means (see below), but we do not think this is an important problem in testing the hypothesis we examined in the section of this chapter entitled "An Econometric Analysis." Both series were expressed as a percentage of capacity currently utilized.

UK: Wharton indexes were constructed for each of the industries listed in table 6A1. This was done by linking the peaks of the index of industrial production for each industry by logarithmic interpolation. The individual indexes were then aggregated to form indexes for each of the three sectors shown in table 6A1, and for manufacturing as a whole, using net output weights taken from the Censuses of Production. Further details may be found in King (1979).

France: Our series is based on the existing measure of the degree of capacity utilization in different industries calculated from the responses of firms to the regular business survey conducted by INSEE every four months. The following questions are posed.

"By how much could you increase production using only your existing plant and labor force?" "Could you produce more by hiring more labor?" "If so, by how much could you increase your production in total using your existing plant?" The answers to these questions are used to construct weighted series for capacity utilization in different sectors. These series have been compared with others, such as those based on the Wharton method, and a close correlation has been found between them. It should be noted that the survey asks for quantitative answers and does not use qualitative responses to construct the index (as happens in countries using the balance between "yes" and "no" answers to the question, "Are you working below capacity?").

The degree of capacity utilization, R12, is defined formally by

$$R12 = \frac{100 + U^{min}}{100 + U} \times 100$$

where

$U =$ the weighted average of the answers to the third question given above, "by how much could you increase your production in total using your existing plant?"

$U^{min} =$ the minimum answer given to this question in the past, which occurred in fact in 1973. For further information see Charpin (1974) and Saglio and Tabuteau (1971).

7

The Rate of Return in German Manufacturing Industry: Measurement and Policy Implications

Horst Albach

The Problem

In the 1960s the discussion about profitability of business started from the observation that profits were too high because of monopolistic market structure. Today's discussion starts from the fact that industrial profitability suffered an alarming decline in the 1970s. Profitability of capital has dropped to rates earned on financial assets, and real profitability was lower in many years of the decade between 1970 and 1981 than real interest. We will call this phenomenon the profitability gap.

The basic pattern of the present situation is not very dissimilar to that in the late 1920s, when real wages rose significantly at the expense of profits. This led to a significant decline in equity financing, to investment financing with short-term credit in the hope of further growth, and eventually to the liquidity crisis culminating in the Great Depression. During the 1970s the collapse of the Bretton Woods System made it obvious that real wages had risen extremely high in many countries. Rising inflation and export-driven growth had covered up the deterioration of economic conditions. The firms had prevented sharp losses in the rate of return on equity by the use of leverage. In order to restore monetary stability, the central banks have reduced monetary expansion. As a consequence interest rates rose significantly. Creditors demanded higher interest rates on the international money markets in order to shelter credit from erosion by inflation and the risk of devaluation. The yardstick for investment in real assets was made longer and longer. Investment volume declined. Productivity increase was slowed down as a consequence of smaller vintages added to productive capacity, and real rates of profit declined further. The profitability crisis is manifest in many sectors of the European economy, and in parts it has developed into a liquidity crisis.

I have benefited from the comments of my associates at the Institut für Gesellschafts- und Wirtschaftswissenschaften, Universität Bonn: Willi Koll, Manfred Schleiter, Bernd Geisen, and Erlfried Baatz. Particular thanks are due to Karl-Heinz Burg for computational and editorial assistance.

Economic development in Europe seems to be in a vicious circle. In order to master the problems of economic change, of unemployment, and of declining productivity, the economies need risk capital. The returns on risk capital, however, seem to decline steadily. Thus it becomes less and less attractive for private and institutional investors to hold equity. The firms resort to credit financing of investments in fixed assets, and the banking institutions develop new forms of industrial credit and of leasing of equipment to meet the rising demand for long-term credit financing of manufacturing industry. This, of course, increases financial risk for equity holders. The risk premium on equity capital rises. The declining returns on equity prove less and less adequate to cover the risk premia. New investment in risk-bearing assets and in R&D has become inadequate.

Economic policy has in the past tried to break this vicious circle by shifting part of the business risk to the government. Investment incentives, fast tax write-offs, loss carry-backs as well as government subsidies for R&D outlay are all intended to share the business risk incurred by the firms' investment in plant and equipment.

If government participation in the losses is not adequate to offset the losses in returns from government participation in the profits through taxation, then clearly the firms will tend to reduce business risk. There are two ways for companies to do this: by diversification and by shifting investment to less risky assets. Firms in Germany have resorted to both ways in order to keep risk under control in an unstable environment.

In this chapter we will show that (1) the rate of return on total capital has declined. This is explained by increased competition and by lower business risk due to changes in asset structure. (2) The rate of return on equity has declined. The reduction in business risk could account for this development also. (3) Financial risk has increased. Rising interest rates on debt capital and increasing debt-equity ratios are evidence of this fact.

Methodology and Data

The following empirical analysis of the hypotheses advanced will be based on data of German manufacturing firms from various sources. The sources will be explained first. Then we will comment briefly on the statistical methods used to analyze the data.

There are many sources of information on the profitability of German manufacturing corporations, but there are no national accounts available for Germany that cover the entire manufacturing sector and provide data on the profitability of manufacturing industry in such detail as was considered necessary in order to make international comparisons possible.

All the data available are derived from company financial reports. In our opinion two major sources of information are most suited for the investigation of profitability. The data banks of the Federal Statistical Office and of the Business Economics Institute of Bonn University contain the data of the annual financial reports of German corporations. There are 873 (in 1977) German corporations in manufacturing industry. They represent about 30 percent of total employment and about 45 percent of total sales in manufacturing. Small and medium-sized companies do not have to publish financial reports. Their tax returns are not available for analysis. We have to assume that the financial reports of German manufacturing corporations adequately reflect trends in the development of all the manufacturing firms. Caution is required, however, in the interpretation of the level of profits. Other sources indicate that small firms have higher profitability than large corporations (which is partly the result of different accounting methods) and that medium-sized firms have lower profits than either larger or smaller firms. The restriction to the financial reports of corporations has the advantage that the empirical analysis will be more conclusive with respect to the valuation of firms by the stock markets.

The data of the Federal Statistical Office[1] are published annually in the *Statistical Yearbook*. The time series based on this publication cover all corporations (without financial institutions such as banks and insurance companies) throughout the period 1961 to 1979. The capital market statistics used in the analysis were taken from sources published by the Central Bank. In particular we used the aggregate share prices of German corporations as computed by the Central Bank.[2]

The Bonn Sample is a collection of financial reports at the Business Economics Institute of Bonn University. At present 222 industrial corporations with a quotation on the stock market are covered by the Bonn Sample. Individual data are available for the years 1961 through 1981. Information not available from the financial reports is taken from newspapers and other sources. In particular, stock prices of the companies in the Bonn Sample are taken from stock exchange publications. The 222 industrial corporations are broken up into branches of industry as follows: Automobile Industry (6), Electrotechnical Industry (11), Iron and Steel Industry (9), Chemical Industry (21), Machinery Industry (28), Others (147).

The data of the Federal Statistical Office as well as those of the Bonn Sample are from financial reports published annually according to German corporation law. Two major revision of publication requirements were put into effect in the Corporation Act of 1959 and the

Corporation Act of 1965, respectively. Until 1959 corporations were not required to publish sales. They reported sales net of purchases of raw materials. Furthermore the 1959 act required corporations to report expenses and other income in more detail. For these reasons we limit the present analysis to years beginning in 1961, the first year for which the new requirements became effective.

The Corporation Act of 1965 brought significant changes in the standards of valuation. Strict rules for the valuation of depreciation allowances and inventories were passed. They stressed the principle of consistency as well as the principle of cautiously reporting equity and profits. Historical cost reporting prevails throughout. The valuation of inventories is based on moving averages, but due provision for inflationary price increases can be made by charging the difference from current cost to inventory reserves. The definitions of capital and profits are based on the format of the balance sheet as prescribed by German law. The appendix gives details. They follow as closely as accounting laws permit the conventions that were agreed upon by the group of international experts in this report in order to carry out a comparison of international profitability developments.

The Federal Statistical Office publishes aggregate data. The individual entries in the financial reports are summed and further aggregated on the assumption of proportionality to sales to yield the total entry. Ratios are derived from aggregate data. The Bonn Sample contains data of the individual firms, thus offering the opportunity to analyze the distribution of profitability for each year. So we compute ratios for the sample as a whole as averages of ratios. We thus have unweighted averages, but weighted averages calculated from the ratio of aggregated profits to aggregated capital are also given. This makes comparisons with the data of the Federal Statistical Office for a major aggregate possible and allows us to compare the weighted and the unweighted averages of the Bonn Sample. By doing so we will try to describe the influence of firm size on the development of profitability.

Real data were computed from the nominal data. Inflation accounting has a long history in German accounting theory. Its beginnings date back to the early 1920s. The method used here applies replacement cost indexes[3] to individual items in the balance sheet and takes estimates of useful lifetimes of equipment into account in arriving at current cost valuation.[4] The same method is used for nominal data of the Federal Statistical Office as well as for the data in the Bonn Sample.

Profitability on a more aggregate basis is computed for the German manufacturing sector from national accounts by the German Council of Economic Advisors, which reports a profit margin defined as "gross income from entrepreneurial activity and from property" divided by the value of production in the manufacturing sector. Gross income is measured in constant prices, and so is production value.[5]

Some German institutes of economic research have tried to compute profitability from national accounts. The Deutsches Institut für Wirtschaftsforschung (DIW) computed a nominal rate of profitability for the entrepreneurial sector (without housing rentals but inclusive of agriculture).[6] The Rheinisch-Westfälisches Institut für Wirtschaftsforschung (RWI) computed a real rate of profits on fixed assets for manufacturing industry.[7] We have also used national accounts to compute profitability for the period 1961 to 1980. These figures are comparable to results by Holland and Myers.[8] Profitability is defined as gross domestic income from entrepreneurial activity and from property in the manufacturing sector (inflation adjusted) divided by the sum of net fixed assets at current cost and inventories at book value. From the German national accounts we can also derive a profit margin defined as nominal income from entrepreneurial activity and property income divided by the nominal value of production in the manufacturing sector. Table 7–1 shows the two time series for the period 1961 to 1980.

Table 7–1
Profitability in the Manufacturing Sector

Year	Real Rate of Return before Taxes	Nominal Profit Margins
1961	19.5	9.9
1962	17.0	9.1
1963	15.8	8.8
1964	16.5	9.3
1965	16.0	9.1
1966	14.3	8.4
1967	14.8	8.8
1968	17.4	9.3
1969	16.9	9.7
1970	14.8	8.7
1971	13.6	8.3
1972	12.9	7.8
1973	12.9	7.6
1974	11.4	6.7
1975	9.9	6.0
1976	11.4	6.4
1977	11.2	6.3
1978	11.5	6.4
1979	11.7	6.5
1980	9.4	5.3

Source: Computed from national accounts. See: Volkswirtschaftliche Gesamtrechnungen, Fachserie 18, Reihe S.5, Revidierte Ergebnisse 1960–81, Wiesbaden, Stuttgart und Mainz, 1982.

Since the data in table 7–1 are the only reliable figures to be derived from national accounts and since they cannot be broken down further, we have to resort to the data of the Federal Statistical Office and to those in the Bonn Data Bank for further analyses. The results are given below.

Since we are interested in the development of the rate of return in the German manufacturing sector we will first present the time series of annual data from the Federal Statistical Office and from the Bonn Sample. We consider these time series to be the raw material from which to derive further hypotheses about trends. In the second part we analyze the major factors that influence the development of the rate of return by regression analysis. In the final section an econometric multi-equation model of the firm, which was estimated from the data of the Bonn Sample, is used to explain the rate of return and to make a forecast of profitability in manufacturing industry for the years 1983 and 1984. This forecast is used to bring forth the conditions for improved corporate profitability in the 1980s.

The Results

The Return on Capital

The basis of our analysis is a time series of profitability. We present rates of return in the German manufacturing sector in this section. Capital includes total assets employed in business operations, so that tangible and intangible assets, financial assets, inventories, and other current assets are included. We define the nominal rate of return in accordance with German accounting law. The real rate of return is calculated under the concept of identical replacement of assets. There-fore costs have to be calculated and deducted at their current instead of their historical values. The difference between current costs and historical costs is called "inflationary gain" (or loss) and is charged against nominal profit. Adjustments were also made for the current cost of maintaining inventories and for replacing depreciable assets together with the calculation of total real assets at current cost.[9]

The Nominal Rate of Return on Capital. The nominal rate of return in the German manufacturing sector shows a marked decline over the years 1961 to 1981. Profitability of total capital invested in all manu-facturing corporations dropped by roughly 25 percent during the two decades. Table 7–2 shows the time series. Three points merit additional emphasis. The time series of weighted returns shows a less marked decline of profitability than the unweighted figures of the manufacturing corporations. The bigger corporations have obviously been in a better

Table 7–2
Nominal Rate of Return on Total Capital

	Before Taxes			After Taxes			Effective Tax Rate		
	Manufacturing Corporations		Nonfinancial	Manufacturing Corporations		Nonfinancial	Manufacturing Corporations		Nonfinancial
Year	Unweighted	Weighted	Corporations	Unweighted	Weighted	Corporations	Unweighted	Weighted	Corporations
1961	12.7	11.9	9.4	5.5	5.7	4.4	56.6	53.0	53.2
1962	12.3	11.9	8.9	5.4	5.7	4.3	56.0	51.8	52.0
1963	12.2	12.0	8.9	5.5	6.0	4.5	55.1	49.8	49.9
1964	12.3	12.7	9.4	5.4	6.2	4.6	56.2	51.5	50.5
1965	11.7	11.3	9.1	5.7	6.1	5.0	50.8	46.7	44.8
1966	10.9	10.5	8.3	5.8	5.9	4.9	46.9	43.4	41.7
1967	9.9	9.6	7.9	5.3	6.0	4.8	46.9	37.9	39.8
1968	10.1	11.2	8.9	5.3	6.2	4.9	47.8	44.9	44.3
1969	10.1	11.1	8.8	5.2	6.2	4.9	48.3	43.9	43.9
1970	9.6	9.3	8.5	5.2	6.2	5.4	46.0	33.1	36.1
1971	9.1	7.6	7.0	4.9	4.9	4.4	46.0	35.7	37.4
1972	8.8	8.7	7.4	4.5	5.0	4.4	48.6	42.5	41.3
1973	8.6	9.4	8.0	4.7	5.4	4.9	44.8	42.0	38.8
1974	7.8	7.7	7.3	4.5	4.0	4.4	42.4	47.6	39.7
1975	7.3	7.5	6.4	3.9	4.2	3.7	46.5	44.4	41.7
1976	8.7	10.0	7.9	4.9	5.7	4.8	44.0	42.7	39.9
1977	7.7	9.5	7.2	3.5	4.3	3.5	54.9	54.3	51.2
1978	7.4	9.2	7.5	3.2	4.0	3.7	56.4	56.4	50.5
1979	7.5	9.5	7.9	3.5	3.9	3.8	53.5	58.4	51.2
1980	7.3	8.3	—	3.9	4.0	—	46.9	51.7	—
1981	7.0	8.6	—	4.0	4.5	—	42.8	47.8	—

position to defend their profitability than the smaller corporations in the sample, which includes the medium-sized firms in the whole range of firm sizes in Germany. While the weighted data convey the impression of a rather gradual erosion of profitability, the unweighted figures show more clearly that the environment in which the corporations found themselves in the 1970s was rather different from the environment in the 1960s. It will be shown that the oil price hikes, the currency system of floating exchange rates, and a more aggressive wages policy on the side of the trade unions are the main factors that account for this difference. There is also a remarkable difference concerning the absolute value of profitability when comparing manufacturing corporations with the sector of nonfinancial corporations. The average difference between the two was about 2.5 percentage points between 1961 and 1970. Since then the difference has almost vanished for before tax profits as well as for after tax profits on total capital.

The effective tax rate has varied considerably over time. This is partly the result of changing tax laws, but also partly because of the fact that only some of the taxes vary with business income, while the other taxes are levied on business property and fixed assets but have to be paid from firm income. Taxation on business property has increased. This was partly offset by lower taxes on profits before interest because taxable income was reduced by higher interest payments as firms increased their debt equity ratios. Changes of the corporation tax law in 1977 explain the sharp increase of the effective tax rate in 1977 and subsequent years. Before 1977, corporation income tax was 51 percent of retained earnings. The effective income tax rate for a firm distributing 50 percent was 37 percent. After 1977, the tax rate on retained earnings was raised to 56 percent, and the effective income tax rate for the same company increased to 45 percent. Adding 13 percent franchise tax and 9 percent (on income) for property taxes yields a "theoretical" tax burden of 59 percent for years before 1977 and 67 percent after 1977. The figures in table 7–2 are, of course, not identical with the figures derived above because many firms distribute more than 50 percent of their profits after taxes and thus reduce their effective tax rate.[10] The figures above are intended to make the magnitude of the effective tax rate in Germany, which may seem outrageously high to many a foreigner, plausible. It *is,* in my opinion also, outrageously high.

The Real Rate of Return on Capital. Germany has a remarkable record in fighting inflation. Therefore the effects of inflation are not predominant in the analysis of the erosion of profitability of manufacturing companies, although there should be no question that inflation has a negative influence on the rate of return. In particular, the level of profitability is certainly affected by inflation. While in the 1960s the difference between the real rate and the nominal rate of return was about 1.5 percent on the basis of the overall figures after taxes, the difference rose to 2 percent in the 1970s. The respective differences for the firms in the Bonn Sample are 2.5 percent and 3 percent.

This means that the purchasing prices of the assets held by the firms rose faster than the real profits of the corporations. If the labor unions anticipate the effects of their wage demands on the cost of living and push for wage increases that cover not only the rise in productivity but also the anticipated inflation rate, then clearly the entrepreneurs will try to pass the wage burden on to their customers, and prices on the domestic markets will rise. But when at the same time a revaluation of the currency brings about intensified international competition, then it becomes increasingly difficult to recover all the increase in the wage bill, particularly for export-oriented firms. Real profits are squeezed, while the current cost of the assets owned by the firms still goes up.

Germany witnessed the first significant revaluation in 1969 and introduced floating exchange rates in 1973. Between 1969 and 1975 the trade unions pushed for a significant change in the distribution of income with the backing of the newly established social democratic government. These factors account for the substantial decline in the real rate of profit on capital invested in the 1970s.

Table 7–3 shows the development of the real rate of return on capital and the corresponding effective tax rate for German manufacturing industry. Profitability was somewhat higher in manufacturing than in all nonfinancial corporations in the 1960s while the 1970s witnessed a definitely smaller gap. The larger companies have recovered from the setback caused by the revaluation of the deutschmark somewhat better than the smaller companies. The nonmanufacturing companies, particularly trade and transportation and services in the group of nonfinancial corporations, had significantly higher profits in 1974 than the manufacturing companies. Obviously the oil price increase and the end of the Bretton Woods system affected the manufacturing companies earlier and more severely than the nonproducing corporations. Manufacturing corporations seem most exposed to competition from abroad. The smaller companies were affected by the change in the economic climate after 1973 more severely than were the bigger companies, which resulted in a definitely lower real profitability.

Given the importance of inventories in manufacturing, the difference in the development of the effective tax rates for the nonfinancial and the manufacturing corporations is explained by inflationary gains on inventories.

Table 7-3
Real Rate of Return on Total Capital

	Before Taxes			After Taxes			Effective Tax Rate		
	Manufacturing Corporations		Nonfinancial Corporations	Manufacturing Corporations		Nonfinancial Corporations	Manufacturing Corporations		Nonfinancial Corporations
Year	Unweighted	Weighted		Unweighted	Weighted		Unweighted	Weighted	
1961	10.7	9.8	7.9	3.8	3.9	3.2	64.0	60.3	59.5
1962	9.9	9.4	7.0	3.5	3.7	2.7	64.7	60.9	60.8
1963	9.9	9.7	7.1	3.7	4.2	3.0	62.3	57.3	57.7
1964	9.5	10.2	7.5	3.2	4.0	3.2	66.7	60.3	57.9
1965	8.9	8.8	7.2	3.4	3.9	3.5	61.4	55.9	51.7
1966	8.1	8.1	6.5	3.4	3.8	3.3	57.8	52.4	50.0
1967	8.5	8.3	6.4	4.2	4.8	3.5	50.8	41.7	45.9
1968	9.6	10.1	7.1	5.1	5.4	3.5	46.9	46.9	40.4
1969	7.5	8.8	6.8	3.1	4.2	3.3	59.4	51.9	51.3
1970	6.2	6.1	5.9	2.2	3.2	3.2	65.3	46.7	45.8
1971	5.4	4.3	4.3	1.7	1.8	2.1	70.0	58.0	52.8
1972	5.6	5.5	4.8	1.7	2.2	2.2	68.9	60.9	55.3
1973	3.8	5.1	5.4	0.4	1.6	2.7	88.7	69.7	50.5
1974	0.8	1.7	4.7	-2.0	-1.6	2.1	343.9	193.0	54.5
1975	3.8	4.1	3.8	0.8	1.1	1.5	78.9	72.7	61.3
1976	4.3	6.2	5.3	1.0	2.3	2.5	77.8	62.1	52.6
1977	4.4	6.4	4.7	0.8	1.8	1.5	82.7	72.7	68.0
1978	4.7	6.6	5.0	1.0	1.9	1.7	79.5	71.3	65.7
1979	3.3	5.8	5.3	-0.2	0.6	1.8	104.9	89.7	66.1
1980	1.9	3.5	—	-1.1	-0.3	—	157.9	108.0	—
1981	2.2	4.1	—	-0.2	0.5	—	108.2	87.1	—

The Regression Analyses of the Return on Capital. We now turn to a statistical analysis of the time series presented in the previous sections. In table 7–4 we present the results of single equation regressions for the weighted averages of German industrial corporations.

Obviously several determinants of the rate of return seem theoretically plausible and could therefore be tested. It was decided to use a time factor, real growth of national product, and the inflation rate as explanatory variables. In particular we are interested in the impact of these variables on the different concepts of profitability, that is, before and after tax, real and nominal.[11] Of course, to a certain extent we also test the plausibility of our time series when we explain nominal and real data by inflation.

The simple question of a trend in the time series for nominal and real rates of return could be answered in the affirmative. There is a significant negative trend in the time series of the rates of return on capital invested. The decline in the real rates of return was higher than the decline in the nominal rates of return.

The growth rate of gross national product, which incorporates the influence of the business cycle, has a positive impact on the profitability of manufacturing companies. The impact seems to be strongest for the profitability figures before taxes. Since taxes rise progressively with profitability, this should not be surprising.

The inflation rate has a negligible and insignificant influence on the nominal rate of return but changes when we look at the influence on the real rate of return. Obviously tax payments on inflationary gains cause a stronger negative impact of the inflation rate on the rate of return after than before taxes. The effective tax rate rises with inflation.

Table 7–4
Regression Analysis: Rate of Return for Manufacturing Corporations 1961–81

| | *Explanatory Variables* | | | |
| | | | *Level of Economic*[b] | |
Equation	*Time*	*Inflation*[a]	*Activity*	R^2
(1) Real rate of return before taxes	−0.024 (−3.3)	−0.119 (−4.7)	0.022 (1.6)	0.88
(2) Real rate of return after taxes	−0.058 (−4.0)	−0.233 (−4.3)	0.021 (0.7)	0.85
(3) Nominal rate of return before taxes	−0.002 (−0.2)	−0.016 (−1.1)	0.030 (5.9)	0.87
(4) Nominal rate of return after taxes	−0.019 (−3.6)	−0.005 (−2.0)	0.023 (2.5)	0.78

Note: The Cochrane-Orcutt iterative technique was used. t-statistics appear in parentheses under coefficients.

[a]Annual percentage change in CPI.

[b]Annual percentage change in GNP.

On the other hand higher nominal interest rates in times of inflation reduce tax liabilities. The effect of taxation of inflationary gains obviously dominates.

The Market Valuation of the Rate of Return. When purchasing prices for the real assets of a company rise faster than profits, we have a growing divergence between total current cost of the company and its net present value derived from the stream of future earnings. If we assume that the market prices companies according to their net present value, then we would expect the ratio of its market value to its current cost value to decline. This ratio is called Tobin's Q. Q might therefore provide useful insights into whether the rate of return has declined relative to the cost of capital.

In the previous sections it was stated that real rates of return on corporate investment have declined markedly. If the cost of capital had declined also, then falling rates of return need not necessarily indicate serious problems of the manufacturing companies.

The measurement of the opportunity cost of capital poses serious methodological problems. We define the opportunity cost of capital by

$$\text{cost of capital} = \frac{\text{profits after taxes} + \text{interest paid}}{\text{market valuation of equity} + \text{liability at book value}}$$

If the sum of profit and interest paid is zero because profits are in fact losses, then we have zero opportunity cost of capital. In the numerator we have historical data; in the denominator we have historical data and market expectations. This has to be borne in mind when interpreting the data in table 7–5. We note that the nominal opportunity cost of capital has not decreased significantly during the period 1961 to 1981. Therefore we would expect a decline in Tobin's Q.

The development of Tobin's Q shows a marked decline between 1961 and 1981. This reflects adequately the decline in profitability of the industrial sector, the slump in business investments throughout the 1970s, and the disillusionment of investors on the stock market.[12] It is interesting to note that Tobin's Q is higher for manufacturing companies in the 1960s than for the nonfinancial sector as a whole. This corresponds to the higher rates of return earned in the manufacturing sector than in the rest of the nonfinancial enterprises, noted earlier (see table 7–2). The gap had vanished by the end of the 1970s. The market seems to reflect clearly the overall decline in profitability as well as the erosion of higher profitability in the manufacturing sector. There seems to be a significant difference in the opportunity cost of capital between manufacturing corporations and the rest of the nonfinancial sector. We can only suggest that this is the result of systematic differences in the valuation of the risk of investment in the two classes of the nonfinancial

Table 7-5
The Market Valuation of the Rate of Return and Cost of Capital

Year	Tobin's Q Manufacturing Corporations	Tobin's Q Nonfinancial Corporations	Cost of Capital Nominal Manufacturing Corporations	Cost of Capital Nominal Nonfinancial Corporations	Cost of Capital Real Nonfinancial Corporations	Real User Cost of Capital Manufacturing Corporations	Real Return to Investors Manufacturing Corporations	Real Return to Investors Nonfinancial Corporations
1961	1.99	1.73	2.8	2.4	1.9	—	—	—
1962	1.56	1.39	3.5	2.8	2.0	13.8	—	—
1963	1.59	1.44	3.6	2.8	2.0	17.6	5.6	6.8
1964	1.56	1.44	3.8	3.0	2.2	16.6	5.8	3.7
1965	1.37	1.24	4.2	3.7	2.8	16.2	− 4.0	− 9.6
1966	1.18	1.14	4.8	3.9	2.9	17.6	− 10.3	− 4.0
1967	1.38	1.35	4.1	3.3	2.6	19.5	23.8	20.4
1968	1.41	1.39	4.1	3.3	2.5	20.2	11.3	8.8
1969	1.44	1.43	4.0	3.1	2.3	15.6	16.2	10.0
1970	1.16	1.18	4.9	4.1	2.7	11.1	− 12.1	− 10.1
1971	1.19	1.20	3.7	3.2	1.7	11.7	6.8	5.7
1972	1.24	1.25	3.7	3.1	1.7	16.3	5.4	4.8
1973	1.10	1.12	4.5	3.8	2.4	19.1	− 11.5	− 9.7
1974	1.04	1.06	3.5	3.7	2.0	13.2	− 7.1	− 5.6
1975	1.16	1.16	3.2	2.8	1.3	9.9	13.1	10.1
1976	1.10	1.10	4.7	3.8	2.3	15.6	− 3.1	− 3.8
1977	1.12	1.13	3.6	2.7	1.3	14.9	3.2	3.0
1978	1.14	1.16	3.2	2.8	1.5	16.0	9.6	6.0
1979	1.06	1.06	3.5	3.2	1.7	16.6	− 11.2	− 7.1
1980	1.02	—	3.5	—	—	15.6	1.1	—
1981	0.96	—	4.0	—	—	19.5	− 9.9	—

sector. The capital markets seem to view manufacturing corporations as being in a risk class different from the rest of the nonfinancial enterprises.

In the neoclassical theory of the firm an alternative measure of the cost of capital is used: the user cost of capital. We modify the concept to include also the effects of taxation on business income and business property. The real user cost of capital is defined as

$$c = s \left(r + \delta - \frac{\dot{q}}{q}\right) \tag{7.1}$$

where

c = user cost of capital;
s = tax term (including income tax, franchise tax, property tax, and land tax);
r = interest rate;
δ = depreciation rate;
q = prices per unit of investment goods.

Since the German tax laws are not investment-neutral, s is positive and greater than 1. Since the real depreciation rate is constant, the development of the user cost of capital reflects changes in taxation, the interest rate, and the cost of capital goods. The decline in the user cost of capital after 1968 is the result of a marked increase in the capital goods prices (capital gains), which was not fully offset by increases in the long-term interest rate.

The tax term has changed significantly over time and accounts for a large part of the fluctuations in the user cost of capital. Table 7–6 shows the development of the tax term between 1960 and 1978 and distinguishes between the impact of taxation on the cost of capital for equipment and for plant.[13]

Table 7–5 also lists the real return to investors. This is defined as the difference between the rate of return to investors and the change in the consumer price index. The rate of return to investors is dividends received plus gains in stock prices plus interest paid divided by the market valuation of total capital invested. The wide fluctuations in the real return to investors are due partly to the fact that an increase in the inflation rate is not immediately offset by a corresponding increase in the interest rate. The basic pattern of the real return to investors is easily explained, however. When inflation rates were low, the real return was high. When inflation rates were high, the real return to

Table 7–6
Tax Term in the User Cost of Capital

Year	Machinery and Equipment	Investment in Plant	Total Assets
1960	1.17	1.33	1.23
1961	1.16	1.31	1.23
1962	1.16	1.31	1.22
1963	1.18	1.32	1.22
1964	1.18	1.32	1.24
1965	1.17	1.33	1.24
1966	1.17	1.31	1.22
1967	1.16	1.30	1.19
1968	1.26	1.42	1.30
1969	1.24	1.38	1.29
1970	1.24	1.32	1.26
1971	1.21	1.27	1.21
1972	1.16	1.26	1.19
1973	1.29	1.35	1.31
1974	1.11	1.34	1.20
1975	0.95	1.20	1.02
1976	1.15	1.44	1.20
1977	1.12	1.42	1.15
1978	1.11	1.39	1.16

Source: M. Schleiter "Steuersystem und Unternehmenspolitik," Ph.D. Thesis, Bonn, 1983, with data from the Bonn Sample.

investors became negative. This effect is augmented by the fact that stock prices decline substantially in periods of high inflation rates. This is not surprising in view of our regression results.

The average real return to investors for the period 1963 to 1970[14] was 3.2 percent for the nonfinancial corporations and 4.5 percent for manufacturing corporations. In the 1970s, the real return to investors had dropped to 0.4 percent and 0.6 percent, respectively. This is in line with the development of the real rate of return on capital.

The Return on Equity

The nominal rate of return on equity is computed as the ratio of profits after taxes divided by the book value of equity including reserves. In order to obtain a real rate of return on equity, the nominal profit figures were modified by that part of the inflationary gain only, which arises from equity financed assets (net concept). In assigning equity to assets we assume that equity is first used to finance fixed assets with the longest lifetimes and then covers assets in the order of declining lifetimes. According to the net concept of inflation accounting, inflationary gains from equity financed assets only are deducted from nominal profits. The real value of equity is defined as the value of total assets at replacement cost minus debt or as the book value of equity plus valuation differences, that is, the difference between fixed assets at replacement cost and fixed assets at historical cost.

The Nominal Rate of Return on Equity. From table 7–7 we note that manufacturing corporations have had a higher rate of return on equity than nonfinancial corporations throughout the period. This is not in contrast to the picture gained from the data on the profitability of total capital invested, but while the weighted average of the total return is smaller until the mid-1970s, the return on equity is higher in the case of the weighted averages than in the case of the unweighted averages, with the exception of the early 1970s. The larger companies have used leverage to bring about this result, which is confirmed by the following observation. The thirty largest corporations in the sample increased their debt equity ratio from 2.0 to 2.9 while in the whole sample it increased from 1.5 to 2.2 during the period from 1961 to 1981. In the early 1970s the larger firms obviously had more difficulty in adjusting to a changed and more hostile environment than the smaller companies. They had a higher share of exports in their total sales and were thus exposed to the disadvantageous effects of the revaluation of the deutschmark to a greater extent than the smaller companies.

The Real Rate of Return on Equity. The problem of defining a real rate of return on equity after taxes is well known to financial analysts. We define the real rate of return on equity as real profits before taxes minus actual taxes divided by the real value of equity. Table 7–8 presents the data for the nonfinancial corporations as well as for the manufacturing corporations in the Bonn Sample. It is interesting to note that since 1971 the real rate of return on equity after taxes has been lower than the real rate of return on total capital after taxes for nonfinancial corporations, and that this relation holds true for several years in the 1970s for manufacturing companies as well. Obviously investment in shares has become a proposition with returns that are no longer in keeping with the risks involved; or stated differently: it is very hard to find good economic reasons for holding shares in one's portfolio.

Gearing is defined as the real rate of return on equity divided by the real rate of return on total capital. Table 7–8 shows that while for all non-financial corporations there was a marked drop from the early sixties to the early seventies with a minor recovery in the late seventies only, manufacturing corporations seem on the whole to have been able to keep gearing virtually at the same level throughout the period. Gear-

Table 7–7
Return on Equity

	Nominal Rate of Return after Taxes			Real Rate of Return after Taxes		
	Manufacturing Corporations		Nonfinancial Corporations	Manufacturing Corporations		Nonfinancial Corporations
Year	Unweighted	Weighted		Unweighted	Weighted	
1961	11.1	11.1	8.0	7.5	7.5	5.2
1962	10.8	11.0	7.6	6.5	6.7	4.1
1963	10.6	11.7	7.9	6.6	7.4	4.5
1964	10.3	12.2	8.5	5.8	7.9	4.9
1965	10.9	11.4	9.3	6.4	7.2	5.5
1966	10.2	10.3	8.2	5.8	6.4	4.7
1967	9.2	10.2	7.6	6.2	7.1	4.7
1968	9.8	11.1	8.5	6.6	8.2	5.1
1969	9.8	11.5	8.8	5.3	7.2	4.8
1970	8.3	10.8	9.4	2.8	5.2	4.1
1971	8.3	6.8	6.2	2.4	1.5	1.5
1972	8.2	8.3	7.0	2.8	2.9	2.2
1973	7.1	8.8	7.6	1.6	2.8	2.6
1974	5.9	4.5	5.6	-0.6	-1.3	0.8
1975	5.5	5.6	4.4	0.2	0.3	-0.1
1976	8.5	11.5	9.2	1.9	4.6	3.2
1977	4.9	7.5	4.9	-0.3	1.7	0.5
1978	5.5	6.8	6.1	0.2	1.6	1.2
1979	6.2	6.9	6.8	0.2	0.9	1.5
1980	5.7	6.4	—	-0.8	0.3	—
1981	5.5	7.0	—	-1.0	0.1	—

Table 7–8
Real Rate of Return on Equity

Year	Before Taxes			Gearing		Effective Tax Rate	
	Manufacturing Corporations		Non-Financial Corporations	Manufacturing Corporations	Non-Financial Corporations	Manufacturing Corporations	Non-Financial Corporations
	Unweighted	Weighted		Weighted		Weighted	
1961	24.4	21.6	17.1	2.2	2.2	65.3	69.6
1962	22.3	19.9	14.5	2.1	2.1	66.4	71.6
1963	21.7	20.4	14.5	2.1	2.0	63.8	69.2
1964	20.8	22.1	15.7	2.2	2.1	64.4	68.6
1965	19.6	18.4	14.6	2.1	2.0	60.8	62.4
1966	17.0	16.0	12.3	2.0	1.9	59.9	62.1
1967	16.8	14.9	11.8	1.8	1.8	52.5	60.4
1968	17.2	18.9	13.7	1.9	1.9	56.4	62.8
1969	15.9	17.9	13.4	2.0	2.0	59.6	64.6
1970	12.5	12.1	10.8	2.0	1.8	57.0	61.8
1971	11.4	7.5	7.1	1.8	1.6	79.5	78.8
1972	11.8	10.9	8.8	2.0	1.8	73.8	75.1
1973	10.5	11.5	9.6	2.3	1.8	75.8	72.9
1974	6.7	7.3	7.5	4.2	1.6	117.4	88.9
1975	7.9	7.8	5.9	1.9	1.5	96.5	101.7
1976	10.5	14.3	10.5	2.3	2.0	68.0	69.7
1977	9.0	13.6	8.8	2.1	2.1	87.2	94.5
1978	9.2	13.7	9.7	2.1	1.9	88.4	87.7
1979	8.9	13.8	10.4	2.4	2.0	93.4	86.1
1980	6.1	9.9	—	2.8	—	97.4	—
1981	5.6	9.2	—	2.2	—	98.6	—

ing and the use of leverage also account for the differences between the two groups in the effective tax rates derived from the real rate of return on equity and the real rate of return on total capital.

The Market Valuation of the Return on Equity. While the nominal and the real rates of return reflect current profits on the current valuation of the firms' assets, the stock exchange, of course, reflects the investors' valuation of the company's future earnings power. It seems interesting to compare the nominal and the real rates of return with the market valuation of the return on equity.

This ratio is defined as profits after taxes divided by the market valuation of the total shares outstanding (excluding preferred stock, which is not treated as credit). We interpret this measure as an attempt to estimate the cost of equity to the company.

Figure 7–1 shows the development of the three time series. The decline in the nominal and real rates of return on equity is not reflected in the market valuation. During the 1960s the market held expectations of growth in earnings. The share prices reflected these expectations, and the price earnings ratios were high. The market rate of return on equity was below the real rate of return on equity. This implies that

Figure 7–1. Market Valuation and the Rate of Return on Equity for Manufacturing Corporations

Tobin's Q was greater than the ratio of nominal profits divided by real profits and certainly greater than 1. In 1970 Tobin's Q dropped below nominal profits divided by real profits. Profit expectations and stock prices fell considerably as a consequence of the revaluation of the deutschmark and the political changes in Bonn in 1969.

Figure 7–1 corroborates our previous finding that, relatively speaking, Tobin's Q was larger than 1 during the 1960s and has declined considerably during the 1970s. Furthermore, the gap between the market valuation of the return on equity and the nominal rate of return becomes narrower. This would imply that not only does the market no longer see a profit potential beyond that implied by the current actual profits of the companies but also that investors no longer identify hidden valuation reserves in the book value of equity capital.

Leverage and the Rate of Return on Equity. Table 7–9 shows that the difference between the rate of return on capital invested and the effective interest rate has remained positive throughout and that the debt equity ratio increased over the period. Thus the negative impact that the gradual decrease in the rate of return on total capital had on the rate of return on equity was partly offset by higher leverage. But the difference between the rate of return and the effective interest rate, the so-called leverage factor, became smaller and smaller. In order to keep the difference between the rate of return on equity and the rate of return on total capital constant, the debt equity ratio would have had to rise to 7.1 instead of 2.2 by 1979. This, of course, was certainly not feasible. The risks of using leverage to increase the rate of return on equity become greater as the leverage factor decreases. This is easily seen when we use the well-known leverage equation

$$NRE = NRT + (NRT - EIR) \, DER \qquad (7.2)$$

to derive the first differences

$$\Delta NRE = \Delta NRT + (NRT - EIR) \, \Delta DER$$
$$+ (\Delta NRT - \Delta EIR) \, DER \qquad (7.3)$$

where

$$NRE = \text{nominal rate of return on equity;}$$
$$NRT = \text{nominal rate of return on total capital;}$$
$$EIR = \text{effective interest rate;}$$
$$DER = \text{debt equity ratio;}$$
$$\Delta = \text{indicator of annual change.}$$

Table 7-9
Leverage and the Rate of Return for Manufacturing Corporations

Year	Change in the Rate of Return on Equity	Change in the Rate of Return on Total Capital	Difference between Rate of Return and Effective Interest Rate (Leverage Factor)	Change in the Debt Equity Ratio	Difference between Change of Rate of Return and Change of Effective Interest Rate	Debt Equity Ratio	Computed Change in the Rate of Return on Equity (Unweighted)	Change in the Rate of Return on Equity (Weighted)
1961	—	—	3.34	—	—	1.55	—	—
1962	-0.24	-0.09	3.10	0.02	-0.24	1.56	-0.40	-0.13
1963	-0.26	0.05	3.13	0.01	0.03	1.57	0.12	0.78
1964	-0.33	-0.09	3.14	0.03	0.01	1.61	0.03	0.41
1965	0.64	0.37	3.28	0.04	0.14	1.65	0.73	-0.73
1966	-0.74	0.03	2.82	-0.02	-0.46	1.63	-0.78	-1.12
1967	-0.95	-0.51	2.47	-0.04	-0.35	1.58	-1.18	-0.10
1968	0.55	0.03	2.85	0.03	0.38	1.62	0.74	0.87
1969	0.00	-0.06	2.67	0.12	-0.18	1.74	-0.05	0.40
1970	-1.43	-0.04	1.79	0.16	-0.88	1.91	-1.42	-0.68
1971	0.02	-0.30	1.65	0.05	-0.14	1.95	-0.49	-3.46
1972	-0.12	-0.36	1.77	0.02	0.12	1.97	-0.09	1.42
1973	-1.10	0.20	1.04	0.03	-0.73	2.00	-1.23	0.52
1974	-1.26	-0.23	0.30	0.08	-0.74	2.08	-1.74	-4.26
1975	-0.36	-0.62	0.43	0.00	0.13	2.09	-0.35	1.09
1976	3.00	0.97	2.07	0.03	1.64	2.12	4.5	5.90
1977	-3.61	-1.40	0.74	-0.02	-1.33	2.11	-4.2	-3.99
1978	0.56	-0.23	0.68	-0.01	-0.06	2.10	-0.36	-0.69
1979	0.74	0.26	0.78	0.13	0.10	2.23	0.59	0.11
1980	-0.49	0.37	0.40	0.02	-0.38	2.25	-0.48	-0.53
1981	-0.25	0.13	0.19	-0.01	-0.21	2.24	-0.34	0.61

If the leverage factor in the second summand is small, additional debt financing does not help to stem the tide of decreasing profitability of total capital. On the other hand, if interest rates rise as a result of rising inflation and the profitability of capital decreases, then the change in leverage reduces the rate of return on equity much more severely. The higher the prevailing debt equity ratio, the more important is this negative leverage effect.

Table 7–9 shows actual changes in the rate of return on equity and the changes computed from equation (7.3) using the data in table 7–9. The two columns cannot be identical of course because they are computed from data of the individual companies. The direction of change, however, is computed in the right way if we take the changes in the unweighted and the weighted averages jointly as a basis for comparison. The years of 1966 and 1973 are particularly interesting. While total return on capital invested rises slightly, the rate of return on equity declines sharply because the change in the interest rate far exceeds the change in the rate of total capital invested.

The Determinants of the Rate of Return

Three factors seem to dominate the explanation of the development of the rate of return of German manufacturing companies: (1) the increased intensity of competition due to the revaluation of the deutschmark and the price increase for imported raw materials like oil and mineral ores, (2) the tougher bargaining processes resulting in an effectively higher wage share of firm income, and (3) the successful attempts on the side of creditors to shelter credit from erosion by inflation through higher nominal interest rates (as well as through shorter amortization periods). In this section we will take up these three determinants and look more closely at their impact on profitability.

Rates of Return and Business Risk. In an imperfect market intensified competition will result in a wider spread of rates of return because while some firms gain a competitive edge on their competitors, others lag behind temporarily and have to intensify their efforts to catch up with the market leaders. For the several rates of return the standard deviation of the sample of 222 firms has remained constant on average over the years 1961 to 1981. In connection with the significant decline in profitability one thus concludes that the number of firms operating in a critical region of low profitability has increased. The coefficient of variation of the rates of return among the 222 firms in the sample may therefore be used as an indicator of the risk of the marketplace or of "business risk." It has to be borne in mind, however, that the actual data derived from the financial reports represent the net effect of the market risk on the one hand and of the effects of measures taken by the companies to reduce this risk—by diversification, for example—and shifting the asset structure of the portfolio to less risky assets on the other.

From table 7–10 we infer that while the average rate of return among the manufacturing companies in Germany declined over time, business risk has increased somewhat if we look at the rates of return before taxes. Taxation has had a double effect. On the one hand it has cushioned the decline in the rate of return. On average, the government shared the loss in profitability with the firms. On the other hand, however, taxation increased business risk. The coefficient of variation increased significantly between 1961 and 1981.

The data we have presented so far indicate that the drop in the rate of return of German manufacturing companies reflects a significant structural change in economic climate. Adaptation to the new envi-

Table 7–10
Business Risk and Investment Portfolio of
Manufacturing Corporations

Year	Coefficient of Variation for Nominal Rate of Return on Capital		Tangible and Intangible Fixed Assets to Total Assets		Financial and Liquid Assets to Total Assets	
	Before Tax	After Tax	222 Firms	30 Largest	222 Firms	30 Largest
1961	0.56	0.54	35.2	33.2	14.1	17.7
1962	0.54	0.56	36.5	33.9	14.4	18.3
1963	0.53	0.51	36.8	33.7	14.7	19.6
1964	0.52	0.48	36.5	33.8	14.4	19.5
1965	0.57	0.63	36.0	33.2	13.5	18.4
1966	0.60	0.65	35.9	33.4	12.8	18.2
1967	0.62	0.61	35.9	32.5	14.5	20.4
1968	0.63	0.63	34.6	30.7	16.4	21.8
1969	0.64	0.69	33.0	28.6	16.6	21.2
1970	0.63	0.62	33.0	28.8	15.3	18.9
1971	0.64	0.62	33.5	29.8	15.8	21.1
1972	0.66	0.68	33.7	29.7	16.6	23.0
1973	0.62	0.60	33.0	28.2	16.2	23.4
1974	0.63	0.70	31.5	27.3	15.4	20.6
1975	0.77	0.94	31.2	26.0	16.3	23.3
1976	0.75	1.03	30.7	23.8	17.6	26.4
1977	0.69	0.70	30.2	23.1	17.6	27.9
1978	0.74	0.97	29.8	22.8	17.6	27.8
1979	0.75	0.92	27.8	22.3	18.5	27.0
1980	0.79	0.92	27.2	22.3	18.8	26.3
1981	0.73	0.83	27.7	22.5	18.9	26.8

ronment is a slow process, and obviously some companies, particularly the larger ones, though more seriously affected in the first place, have been able to adapt faster than others. We will now try to point out some indicators of changes in corporate policy that have taken place in order to meet the greater risks of the marketplace in the 1970s.

First, investment in plant and equipment was reduced significantly after 1970. This led to a marked decline of the ratio of fixed assets to total assets. This shift in the composition of the business portfolio may not only be interpreted as a reaction toward less favorable business conditions profitwise but also as an attempt to reduce business risk.

Second, there is a marked increase in the proportion of financial and liquid assets in the investment portfolio of the largest manufacturing corporations since 1970. The smaller companies, on the other hand, could not shift their assets to holding liquid assets because obviously they were under heavier financial constraints. Part of the success of adaptation of the larger companies to the changed economic environment may be attributed to their effective policy of investment in financial assets rather than in plant and equipment located in Germany.

These figures seem to indicate that German corporations have not responded to increased risk in the environment with an increased risk preference but rather with intensified attempts at diversification abroad and at holding a larger share of risk-free assets.

Rate of Return and Financial Risk. The well-known leverage equation clearly shows that firms with equal business risk have a wider spread of their return on equity if they use higher leverage. This risk, which is associated with high debt financing of assets, is called financial risk. Interest payments have to be made regardless of the development of profitability of total capital.

In table 7–11 we present five time series that point out the increased financial risk of German corporations. The ratio of debt to market value of capital has increased by almost 60 percent since 1961. This increase was higher than the increase in the debt ratio calculated from book values. The development of the dynamic debt ratios, which indicate the number of years it would take to pay back net debt (that is, debt-capital minus cash on hand) from the annual cash flows, show the combined effect of higher nominal interest rates and increased leverage. The ratio of interest payments to cash flow and the ratio of net interest to gross receipts again emphasize the heavy burden laid upon the firms by creditors in the 1970s.

Rates of Return and Distribution of Income. Business risk is the joint effect of uncertainty of sales and the uncertainty of expenses. There is

Table 7-11
The Financial Standing of Manufacturing Corporations

Year	Ratio of Debt to Total Capital (Percent)	Ratio of Debt to Market Value of Total Capital (Percent)	Net Debt to Cash Flow	Ratio of Interest to Cash Flow (Percent)	Ratio of Net Interest to Gross Receipts (Percent)
1961	60.8	39.9	5.0	15.2	0.9
1962	61.1	46.1	5.1	16.2	1.1
1963	61.2	45.8	5.0	16.7	1.1
1964	61.7	45.2	4.7	16.0	1.1
1965	62.3	50.1	4.9	17.6	1.3
1966	62.0	54.0	5.1	19.5	1.7
1967	61.3	51.0	5.1	19.9	1.7
1968	61.8	48.6	5.0	19.6	1.4
1969	63.5	45.3	5.1	20.1	1.5
1970	65.6	52.7	6.0	27.4	2.2
1971	66.2	52.6	6.0	27.0	2.3
1972	66.4	48.0	6.0	23.8	1.8
1973	66.7	51.8	6.0	29.8	2.3
1974	67.6	56.9	6.7	31.3	2.8
1975	67.6	55.2	6.3	28.5	2.5
1976	68.0	57.7	5.8	23.3	1.9
1977	67.8	59.7	6.6	25.1	1.9
1978	67.7	53.8	6.4	24.5	1.5
1979	69.1	58.6	6.5	25.1	1.5
1980	69.3	60.4	6.2	27.1	1.9
1981	69.1	62.3	6.0	26.6	1.9

no doubt but that increases in the cost of raw materials have been a major source of risk, particularly since 1974. Wage increases have posed more serious problems, however, particularly in times when wage demands lost touch with developments on the international markets of German manufacturing firms.

We will first look at the results of the bargaining process on the manufacturing firms' distribution of nominal value added.[15] Table 7-12 indicates that the share of value added that workers receive rose from 73 percent in 1961 to 82 percent in 1981. The share that the owners of the companies receive was reduced to less than half of the 1961 share. In the late 1960s high investment and an increasing leverage led to an improvement of the capital share (interest + profit) at the cost of business taxes. When in the early 1970s growth rates declined and excessive wage demands were granted, the stockholders seem to have taken refuge in transferring residual income (profits) into contractual income (interest) in order to limit the risk of their total income stream.

Finally, the improvement of labor's position in the distribution of

Table 7–12
Distribution of Value Added, Real Wage Position
(percent)

	Manufacturing Corporations			Adjusted Wage Share of National Accounts[a]	Real Wage Position,[b] National Accounts
Year	Shareholders' Share	Creditors' Share	Gross Wage Share		
1961	9.3	3.3	72.8	62.1	—
1962	8.8	3.6	74.2	62.8	100.0
1963	8.6	3.5	74.5	63.2	100.2
1964	8.4	3.4	74.5	62.3	99.0
1965	9.0	3.7	75.7	62.6	99.4
1966	8.6	4.4	76.4	63.3	100.2
1967	8.1	4.4	77.1	63.2	98.0
1968	8.7	4.1	76.4	61.3	97.3
1969	8.3	4.4	76.4	61.8	98.1
1970	6.8	5.6	77.5	62.7	103.9
1971	6.1	5.3	79.2	63.6	105.8
1972	6.3	4.6	80.3	63.8	105.6
1973	5.0	5.9	80.6	64.6	107.3
1974	4.0	6.7	81.4	66.3	110.5
1975	4.1	5.4	82.6	66.1	109.0
1976	6.3	4.5	81.4	64.9	106.6
1977	3.6	4.4	82.8	64.7	106.5
1978	3.7	4.3	82.4	64.0	106.3
1979	4.3	4.7	81.8	63.6	105.2
1980	4.0	6.5	80.9	64.5	105.9
1981	3.7	6.8	82.3	65.7	—

[a]See Council of Economic Advisors, *Annual Report 1981/82* (Stuttgart and Mainz, 1981), p. 75.
[b]See Council of Economic Advisors, *Annual Report 1980/81* (Stuttgart and Mainz, 1980), p. 217.

income is demonstrated by the "Real Wage Position." This indicator was developed by the Council of Economic Advisors. The basic idea behind this is that productivity gains and improvements in the terms of trade can be distributed to labor without changing the real cost per unit of output. A rise in the index of the real wage position indicates that the increase in wage exceeds the amount available and vice versa. We conclude this section by stating that trade unions obviously have for much too long a period not been willing to shoulder part of the increased business risk. On the contrary, they have increased their share of value added significantly in the 1970s, thus reducing the margin available to pay risk premia for risk-bearing capital. It is only recently that discussions on profit sharing have been resumed, with the objective of transforming the employment risk into income risk. This would be a way to reduce wage increases without having to give up distribution objectives.

An Econometric Model for the Rate of Return on Equity

An Econometric Explanation of the Rate of Return. The rate of return on capital that a company earns is the final result of the interaction of management decisions with the environment of the company. Management decisions relate to many functional areas of the company's activities and to many product divisions and markets on which the company sells its products. We will therefore try to explain the development of the rates of return of German manufacturing industry by the use of a more complex model, a multi-equation econometric model of the firm based on the assumption of optimizing behavior of the managers in charge of the different functional areas of the company. The twenty-five equations of the model were estimated from the financial data of seventy firms in the Bonn Data Bank for five main branches of industry.[16] If we accept the multi-equation model as a description of rational behavior of the German manufacturing firms in a complex economic environment, then clearly we can try to make a forecast of the rate of return.

Therefore we will first point out the main exogenous variables in the model and their influence on the rate of return. It might not come as a surprise that product prices are a dominant factor for the rate of return. Wage increases and the prices of raw materials in relation to output prices come out as important factors also. Technological progress and productivity gains result in higher profitability of capital and particularly of equity if wages remain the same. In reality, however, wage earners try to internalize technological progress in their wage demands. The effects of the interest rate and of taxation are as one expects in the short run. In the long run their impact on finance and investment affects the firms' possibilities to adapt to a changing environment. Since relative prices of production and goods sold are important, the impact of the rate of real demand on profitability is less important as long as relative prices remain equal.

Figure 7–2 shows actual figures of the nominal rates of return for the seventy firms as well as for the 222 firms. The figure also shows the rate of return on equity estimated from the econometric model of the firm. If one takes into account that the model was not developed in order to explain rates of return but computes profits as a residual (as in reality) from an optimal behavior of the neoclassical firm, then

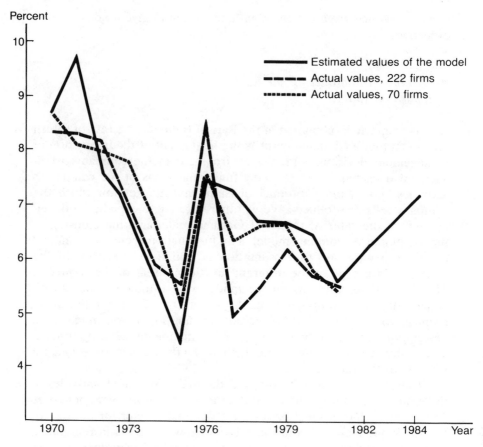

Figure 7–2. Nominal Rate of Return on Equity after Taxes

the fit of the estimated rates of return to the actual rates of return seems remarkably good. The sharp drop in profitability of the 222 firms in 1977 is not reflected in the data of the seventy major companies and is therefore not followed in the development of the estimated figures. In addition, the model does not fully grasp the effect on profitability of the 1977 tax reform.

A Model Forecast of the Rate of Return on Equity. We now use the model to forecast the development of the rate of return on equity for German manufacturing corporations. We base this model forecast on a scenario of exogenous variables. Table 7–13 lists the assumptions. The figures for 1982 are preliminary actual data.

Table 7–13
Forecasts of Exogenous Variables Growth Rate
(percent)

Variable	1982	1983	1984
Price for raw materials	5.5	5.0	5.0
Wages and salaries	4.5	5.0	5.0
Demand (real)	−0.5	0.5	1.0
Price of product	4.5	3.5	3.5
Price of investment goods	5.9	4.5	4.5
Interest rate[a] on long-term debt	9.0	8.0	8.0
Other expenditures and marketing expenditures	5.0	4.5	4.5
Actual interest[a] payment on debt	3.9	3.6	3.3
Other income	4.5	3.5	3.5
Dividends	3.0	10.0	5.0

[a]Absolute Values

Figure 7–2 shows the result of the model forecasts for the rate of return on equity. In the forecast, profitability in 1984 rises to values of the early 1970s. This outcome is mainly the result of the assumed moderate wage increases and the development of interest rates. It should be obvious from the model forecast that it takes only a slight turn in the overall economic conditions under which the firms operate for the rates of return to rise again.

I would like to conclude by saying that the declining rates of return on capital and on equity certainly were a phenomenon of the 1970s. They are, however, by no means a tendency that should be considered as a given for the future. On the contrary, they seem to be a combined effect of structural changes in the world economy brought about by the breakdown of the system of fixed exchange rates and by OPEC on the one hand and by excessive wage demands and lenient government on the other. The 1980s might witness a change toward improved profitability. Whether the favorable conditions required for such a revision of the trend can be brought about in Germany remains doubtful, however.

Notes

1. *Statistisches Jahrbuch für die Bundesrepublik Deutschland*, Annual Editions, 7.14: Financial Reports of Corporations.

2. *Beihefte zu den Monatsberichten der Deutschen Bundesbank*, Reihe 2: Wertpapierstatistik, several volumes.

3. The replacement cost indexes were taken from the *Statistical Yearbook*. They are reported for branches of industry.

4. An extensive description of the method is given in The Real Rate of Return of German Corporations, Schriftenreihe des Instituts für Gesellschafts- und Wirtschaftswissenschaften Nr. 62 (Bonn, 1977); see also the extensive description of the method in W. Koll, *Inflation und Rentabilität. Eine theoretische und empirische Analyse von Preisschwankungen und Unternehmenserfolg in den Jahresabschlüssen deutscher Aktiengesellchaften* (Wiesbaden, 1979).

5. Council of Economic Advisors: *Gegen Pessimismus, Annual Report for 1982/83* (Stuttgart and Mainz, 1982), p. 43.

6. B. Görzig, "Entwicklung von Gewinnen und Renditen im Unternehmensbereich," in *Deutsches Institut für Wirtschaftsforschung: Vierteljahreshefte zur Wirtschaftsforschung* (Berlin, 1981), pp. 321–34.

7. J. Schmidt, Zur Entwicklung der Kapitalrentabilität in den Unternehmensbereichen der Bundesrepublik Deutschland, Mitteilungen des Rheinisch-Westfälischen Instituts für Wirtschaftsforschung, vol. 31 (Essen, 1980), pp. 207–23.

8. D.M. Holland and S.C. Myers, Trends in Corporate Profitability and Capital Costs (Cambridge, Mass.: MIT, WP # 999–78), May 1978.

9. Inflationary gains are also contained in dividends from securities of affiliates. They were subtracted.

10. The effective tax rate in table 7–1 is computed directly from the nominal rates of return before and after taxes. It includes interest paid in the denominator. A more appropriate measure of the effective tax rate is

$$effective\ tax\ rate = \frac{taxes\ on\ income\ and\ property}{taxes\ on\ income\ and\ property\ +\ profit\ after\ tax}$$

This ratio can be computed directly from the data and is given in table 7–14.

11. The time series for the rate of return were normalized to unity.

12. Since we define corporate assets including total assets as reported in the balance sheet, Q seems to be relatively high when one takes the decline of profits into account. On the other hand we might only observe the average Q and not the marginal Q. Therefore it seems more appropriate to interpret changes of Q rather than the levels of Tobin's Q.

13. See M. Schleiter, "Steuersystem und Unternehmenspolitik: Theorie und empirische Ergebnisse zum Einfluß des Steuersystems auf

Table 7–14
Effective Tax Rates

| Year | Manufacturing Corporations | | Nonfinancial Corporations |
	Unweighted	Weighted	
1961	61.8	58.8	63.7
1962	62.0	60.0	63.5
1963	61.8	57.0	61.9
1964	62.0	58.0	61.9
1965	58.4	53.7	55.7
1966	56.5	52.2	54.3
1967	53.3	46.7	53.3
1968	55.1	52.6	55.9
1969	54.5	52.3	56.3
1970	54.5	44.2	49.8
1971	56.2	52.9	56.4
1972	59.5	56.0	57.9
1973	59.3	56.4	56.8
1974	59.5	71.4	63.4
1975	59.4	64.2	66.5
1976	58.7	52.6	53.7
1977	68.6	67.4	71.4
1978	68.6	69.6	67.2
1979	65.8	71.1	66.6
1980	69.1	67.5	—
1981	62.5	65.3	—

die Investitionsentscheidungen deutscher Industrieaktiengesellschaften," Ph.D. diss., Bonn, 1983 (unmimeographed).

14. For the years 1962–73 the average values were 1.9 and 2.1 percent. In the introductory section on methodology we pointed out the influences of the Corporation Act of 1959. As a consequence stock prices peaked in 1961. For this reason we do not give figures for years before 1963. By then stock prices had returned to more rational levels.

15. The computation of value added is based on distribution. The gross wages are computed as the sum of wages and salaries, social security payments, pension fund allowances, and fringe benefits. The creditor's share is interest paid, the shareholders' income is the corporation's net income for the year, and the capital share is the amount distributed among creditors and shareholders. All ratios are related to the total sum of value added.

16. The Bonn Data Bank contains financial data of 222 quoted stock companies. It was impossible, however, to estimate the model from all the firms' data available because of limitations of computer capacity in running large pooled regression analysis. For a more detailed description of the model, see appendix 7A.

Appendix 7A
Definitions and the
Bonn Econometric
Model of the Firm

Definitions

Total Capital   Total Assets − Qualifying Reserves

Equity Capital   Capital Stock + Surplus Reserves + 1/2 Special Items with Reserve Share

Debt Capital (Book Value of Debt)   Total Capital − Equity Capital

Market Value of Equity   Basic Capital × Stock Price

Market Value of Capital   Book Value of Debt + Market Value of Equity

Total Capital at Replacement Cost   Total Capital + Fixed Assets at Replacement Cost − Fixed Assets at Historical Costs

Return on Total Capital before Tax   Net Income + Interest + Taxes on Income and Property

Return on Total Capital after Taxes   Net Income + Interest

Total Inflationary Gain   Inflationary Gain Associated with Fixed Assets + Inflationary Gain from Inventories + Inflationary Gain from Affiliates

Nominal Rate of Return on Total Capital before Taxes   (Return on Total Capital before Taxes) / (Total Capital)

Nominal Rate of Return on Total Capital after Taxes   (Return on Total Capital) / (Total Capital)

Nominal Rate of Return on Equity Capital after Taxes   (Net Income) / (Equity Capital)

Real Rate of Return on Capital before Taxes   (Return on Total Capital before Taxes − Total Inflationary Gain) / (Total Capital at Replacement Cost)

Real Rate of Return on Capital after Taxes   (Return on Total Capital − Total Inflationary Gain) / (Total Capital at Replacement Cost)

Real Rate of Return on Equity before Taxes   (Net Income + Taxes − Inflationary Gain from Equity Financed Assets) / (Total Capital at Replacement Cost − Debt Capital)

Real Rate of Return on Equity after Taxes   (Net Income − Inflationary Gain from Equity-Financed Assets) / (Total Capital at Replacement Cost − Debt Capital)

Cost of Capital (nominal)   (Net Income + Interest) / (Market Value of Capital)

Cost of Capital (real)   (Net Income + Interest − Total Inflationary Gain) / (Market Value of Capital)

Tobin's Q (Market Value of Capital) / (Total Capital at Replacement Cost)

Market Valuation of the Rate of Return on Equity   (Net Income) / (Market Value of Equity Capital)

The Bonn Econometric Model of the Firm

Cash Flow Function before Taxes

$$CFV = p \cdot U - wL - mM - r_T FK_{-1}$$
$$- SA - MA + AOE \tag{7A.1}$$

and the definition of cash flow after taxes

$$CF = CFV - SEEV. \tag{7A.2}$$

Optimal behavior of the submodel of production is described by a three-factor production function that yields the desired levels of factor inputs:

Production Function

Desired labor input:

$$L^* = a_o \left(\frac{\delta' q}{m} \right)^{.066} \left(\frac{m}{w} \right)^{.681} X^{.94} e^{-.012t}. \tag{7A.3}$$

Desired raw materials input:

$$M^* = a_o \left(\frac{\delta' q}{w} \right)^{.066} \left(\frac{w}{m} \right)^{.391} X^{.94} e^{-.012t}. \tag{7A.4}$$

Desired utilization rate of capacity:

$$A^* = a_o \left(\frac{m}{q} \right)^{.615} \left(\frac{w}{q} \right)^{.320} \left(\frac{X^{.94}}{k_{-1}} \right) e^{-.012t}. \tag{7A.5}$$

Of course, the actual values of the input differ from the desired levels because change is not immediate. Therefore we have, taking cost of change into account, actual labor input

$$L = L^{*.46} \cdot L_{-1}^{.54} \cdot M^{*.15} \cdot M_{-1}^{-.15}. \qquad (7A.6)$$

Actual raw materials input:

$$M = M^{*.79} \cdot M_{-1}^{.21} \cdot L^{*.20} \cdot L_{-1}^{-.20}. \qquad (7A.7)$$

Actual capacity utilization:

$$A = A^{*.31} \cdot L^{*.36} \cdot L_{-1}^{-.36}. \qquad (7A.8)$$

Capacity utilization is the result of the effects of capacity expansion and production increase. A capacity expansion is explained by the optimal decisions underlying the investment function.

Investment Function

$$
\begin{aligned}
I = \Bigg[a_o &+ .154 \frac{CF}{q \cdot K} + .1196 \frac{CF_{-1}}{q_{-1} \cdot K_{-1}} \\
&+ .1486 \frac{UB - UB_{-1}}{UB_{-1}} + .1807 \frac{UB_{-1} - UB_{-2}}{UB_{-2}} \\
&+ .0965 \frac{UB_{-2} - UB_{-3}}{UB_{-3}} + .0175 \frac{k - k_{-1}}{k_{-1}} \\
&+ .0248 \frac{k_{-1} - k_{-2}}{k_{-2}} + .0218 \frac{k_{-2} - k_{-3}}{k_{-3}} \\
&+ .0085 \frac{k_{-3} - k_{-4}}{k_{-4}} + .3569 \frac{I_{-1}}{K_{-2}} \Bigg] \\
&\cdot K_{-1} + \delta \cdot K_{-1}.
\end{aligned}
\qquad (7A.9)
$$

Capacity expansion is determined by profitability of capital, by the change in demand in industry, by the change in relative input prices for investment, and by the previous investment rate. Gross investment is determined by capacity expansion plus depreciation. The relative input price for investment goods is given by

$$k = \frac{w^{.36} \cdot m^{.64}}{c} \qquad (7A.10)$$

with c the user cost of capital defined as

$$c = s \cdot q\left(r + \delta - \frac{\dot{q}}{q}\right) \tag{7A.11}$$

where s is the tax factor, q the price for investment goods, r the rate of interest on long-term debt, and δ the real depreciation rate

$$\delta = 0.45 + .045A^3, \tag{7A.12}$$

which has a fixed term for time depreciation and a variable term depending on capacity utilization. Capital stock in real terms is then derived from

$$K = K_{-1}(1 - \delta) + I. \tag{7A.13}$$

Plant and equipment in nominal terms is given by

$$SAV = SAV_{-1}(1 - d) + q \cdot I, \tag{7A.14}$$

with d the book depreciation rate for taxation purposes. Total investment outlay in industry is defined as the sum of the firms' investment expenditures.

$$IB = \sum I. \tag{7A.15}$$

Total sales of the firm depend on the behavior of the firm in the marketplace as well as on the exogenous developments in the market. Assuming that the firm tries to optimize its marketing mix in the light of changes in market demand and behavior of its competitors we get the marketing function.

Marketing Function

$$U = a_o N\left(\frac{MA}{MAB}\right)^{.156}\left(\frac{I}{IB}\right)^{.062}\left(\frac{U_{-1}}{UB_{-1}}\right)^{.63} \tag{7A.16}$$

Total expenses on marketing activities in industry are simply the sum of the firms' marketing expenditures

$$MAB = \sum MA, \tag{7A.17}$$

and total sales in industry are the sum of the firms' sales

$$UB = \sum U. \tag{7A.18}$$

N in (7A.16) is an exogenous parameter describing total demand. The sales of the firm are made from current production and from changes in inventory. Optimal inventory policy is described by the inventory function

Inventory Function

Inventory of finished and semifinished products is the result of an optimization process in the framework of a production smoothing model in which the costs of holding inventory are weighted against the costs of changes in the rate of production. We have inventory of finished and semifinished products

$$VF = a_o U^{.6} \left(\frac{w}{p\left(r + .15 - \frac{\dot{p}}{p}\right)} \right)^{.3} A^{-.3} VF_{-1}^{.4}. \tag{7A.19}$$

It should be noted that the estimated inventory function has sales nearly in the form of the traditional square root formula. The higher the utilization rate of capacity, the less desirable it is to increase inventory because production costs increase more than proportionally. Inventory of raw materials and unfinished products is given by

$$VM = a_o M^{.5} \left(\frac{w}{m\left(r + .25 - \frac{\dot{m}}{m}\right)} \right)^{.3} A^{-.2} VM_{-1}^{.45}. \tag{7A.20}$$

Even though the optimization process follows an approach that differs from that for finished goods, the final equation that describes optimal behavior in industry looks very similar. Optimization is carried out along the lines of the traditional inventory model using the well-known lot size formula but takes into account also adding to inventory for speculative reasons in order to profit from inflationary price increases. Output of the production process is then given by the definition

$$X = U + VF - VF_{-1}. \tag{7A.21}$$

The firm has to provide adequate funds to meet the financial requirements of the different departments. The financing function has to minimize capital cost under the constraint that total demand for funds is met. This requires an optimal management of cash and of the capital structure of the firm.

Financing Function

Cash management in the model takes the form of tax management, as is seen from equation (7A.2), because cash flow before taxes is given once the optimal decisions of the other departments have been made. The taxation function is derived from a careful and detailed study of all the taxes that a firm has to pay according to German tax law.

$$
\begin{aligned}
SEEV = {}& (S51 + S4 - S51S4)(CFV - dSAV_{-1}) \\
& + (S52 - S51 - S52 \cdot S51)DIV \\
& + (S4 - S51 \cdot S4) \cdot r_T FK_{-1} \\
& + (S1 + S3 + S51 \cdot S4 \\
& \quad \cdot S3 - S4 \cdot S3 - S51 \cdot S3)EK_{-1} \\
& + (S3 + S51 \cdot S4 \cdot S3 - S4 \\
& \quad \cdot S3 - S51 \cdot S3)FK_{-1}.
\end{aligned}
\tag{7A.22}
$$

The terms in the brackets denote the various tax rates for different taxes and applicable to different tax bases. Of course, the variables that the firm can vary in order to optimize tax payments are the dividend ratio and the debt equity ratio, if cash flow before taxes, book depreciation rates, and interest rates are given. The optimal debt equity ratio depends, of course, on the relative price of equity. From a portfolio model we derive the optimal level of equity

$$
\begin{aligned}
EK = a_o\left(\frac{CF}{GK}\right)(a_1 + {}& .068GK - 81.7\,\rho + 37.6\,r \\
& - .212\,EK_{-1} - .012\,FK_{-1}) + EK_{-1}.
\end{aligned}
\tag{7A.23}
$$

where GK denotes total capital employed. Debt capital is by definition

$$
FK = GK - EK,
\tag{7A.24}
$$

and total capital is simply the balance-sheet equation

$$
GK = SAV + pVF + mVM + FINLIQ,
\tag{7A.25}
$$

which is determined by investment and production decisions up to the term that gives investment in financial assets and liquidity ($FINLIQ$). Until now we do not have a model that explains optimal holdings of cash and financial paper. Therefore we use the actual figures for the time being. The exogenous variables used in the model are:

d	tax depreciation rate
m	raw materials price
MA	marketing expenditures
N	total demand (real)
p	product price
q	price index for investment goods
r	market rate of interest
r_T	ratio of interest paid to debt capital
ρ	cost of equity
SA	other expenditure
$S1$	federal property tax rate
$S3$	community property tax rate
$S4$	franchise tax rate
$S51$	corporation income tax rate
$S52$	dividend tax factor
s	capital cost tax factor
w	wage rate
AOE	other income
DIV	dividends
$FINLIQ$	investment in financial assets and in cash.

8   Aggregate Rates of Return in Canada

Abraham Tarasofsky

A brief word of explanation is required because the analysis presented below was conceived and conducted quite independently of most of the other contributions to this volume. The rates of return for the period 1947–1976 were originally calculated for a study—of which the present writer was the principal author—prepared as a supplement to the *Sixteenth Annual Review* of the Economic Council of Canada.[1] The following discussion draws heavily upon that study. As to the rates of return on equity reported for the years 1977 and 1978, these derive from a different, but analogous, exercise,[2] which involved a methodology and utilized a data base that resemble closely those applied independently to the preceding thirty years. Hence, it was considered appropriate to report the rates of return for these two years as, in effect, an extension of the basic series.

The analyses of the factors bearing upon fluctuations in various inflation-adjusted rates of return also have their origins in these two studies. The analysis that pertains to the period 1947–1976, and refers to certain inflation-adjusted rates of return on capital employed, derives from the former study. That which pertains to the period 1963–1978, and refers to certain inflation-adjusted rates of return on equity, derives from the latter.

Finally, it should also be mentioned that, in the interests of brevity, only after-tax rates of return are reported below, in figures. For the years 1947–1976, the corresponding before-tax rates of return appear in appendix 8B, all the supporting numerical tables for which are contained in the first of the two above-mentioned studies. The corresponding before-tax rates of return on equity for the years 1977 and 1978 are charted in the second study.

The Operating Capacity Concept of Corporate Income

The various inflation adjustments to reported profits described below derive from the particular concept of corporate income deemed most

313

suitable for the primary purpose at hand—to measure the inflation-adjusted rates of return earned in Canada by the nonfinancial, manufacturing, and nonmanufacturing sectors during the postwar period, as well as certain related indicators. The constituent firms in these sectors are in effect regarded as ongoing entities, expected to continue operating in their established areas of activity. They are thus implicitly regarded as existing independently of their owners of any given moment. The profit measure most appropriate to firms seen in this light is one that defines profit as those operating revenues that remain after deducting all of the costs necessary to maintain the firms' capacities to continue their specific activities—that maintain, in other words, their capital.

The capital maintenance concept of income is, however, amenable to more than one formulation. Three versions of the concept have been developed in the literature: money value, purchasing-power–adjusted money value, and operating capacity.[3] Very briefly, the first version requires that the firm reports a profit only to the extent that its year-end capital value exceeds the *monetary amount* of its capital value at the start of the year. The second version requires that the firm reports a profit only after provision has been made to preserve the purchasing power of its opening capital. The third version—the one that is most pertinent here—requires that the firm report a profit only to the extent that the real value of its operating capacity, as measured by its net productive assets, has increased during the year.

Although the operating capacity version of the capital maintenance concept of income has over the years implicitly characterized Canadian accounting practice, it has done so in modified form. The primary focus has usually been on operating income, profits arising from the sales of the goods that the firm produces or in which it trades. The firm, in other words, is regarded as being in the business of selling certain assets, inventory, but not others, such as capital assets. (Hence, gains in the market value of nontrading assets are not included in profits until realized, and then they are included in distributable, but not operating, income.) In calculating operating income, the guiding principle has been that current costs are to be matched with current revenues. This principle presented few major problems to accounting systems that reported capital assets at acquisition cost and others at the lower of cost or market value—so long as prices remained generally stable. The advent of chronic inflation, however, altered that state of affairs, and the proper calculation of the firm's profit has necessitated the adjustments described below.

The Inflation Adjustments

Depreciation Adjustment

The purpose of the depreciation adjustment is to convert the firms' depreciation expense from the historical-cost basis that was reported to the replacement-cost basis that is required to adjust for inflation. The basic procedure for calculating an individual firm's depreciation expense on a replacement cost basis involves adjusting, at the end of a given current year, the acquisition costs of the stock of depreciable assets held, so as to reflect their current replacement costs. Since these assets were acquired during the current and previous years, the firm must first age them according to the years in which they were acquired. It must then adjust the costs of the assets acquired in each of these years on the basis of the appropriate index representing the cumulative price change from the year of acquisition to the current year. Having thus derived the current replacement costs of the assets, the current year's depreciation expense is calculated for each group of assets by applying to its current replacement cost the appropriate rate of depreciation.

This being an analysis of aggregates, it was impossible to age depreciable assets in the manner described above. Instead, a perpetual inventory method developed at Statistics Canada was adapted. How this was done is described in some detail in appendix 8A.

The inflation-adjusted depreciation expenses calculated for each year along the foregoing lines, being a (negative) component of inflation-adjusted profit, enter into the numerators of each year's rates of return on capital employed and on equity. The assets that have given rise to these expenses are, of course, part of both capital employed and equity. They therefore enter into each year's denominators at values reflecting the undepreciated portions of their current year's replacement cost. In other words, for the purpose of the denominators, accumulated depreciation—the aggregate of the current and previous years' depreciation expense—is calculated entirely on the basis of the current year's replacement values. Of necessity, the accumulated depreciation expenses implicit in these undepreciated asset values exceed the sum of the annual replacement-cost depreciation expenses attributed to the current and preceding years, respectively. These accumulated depreciation components of the denominators are calculated in effect on the basis of "backlog" depreciation; the depreciation expense components of the numerators are not.

Depletion Adjustment: Depletable Assets and Land

Depletion expense is the proportion of the cost of a firm's nonrenewable resources that is used up during the given year. Although it might be thought that the conceptual adjustment would, in principle, have a good deal in common with the depreciation question, it has apparently received very little attention in the literature. In any event, especially severe data problems precluded any attempt to proceed along the same lines as were followed in regard to depreciation. Consequently, the admittedly imperfect adjustment made consisted of adjusting both annual depletion expense and net depletable assets by a measure of inflation based on the index for buildings and equipment. The same index, incidentally, was also used to estimate the replacement values of land.

Cost-of-Sales Adjustment

The basic, traditional accounting principle governing the imputation of a monetary value to a firm's stock of raw material, work in process, and finished goods is that the imputed value should reflect its cost or market value, whichever is lower. While it is never easy to ascertain the market value of an ongoing enterprise's inventory, there is also the further problem in Canada of measuring the cost of that inventory during inflation.

Since Canadian firms are denied the right to use the LIFO method of inventory valuation, or an appropriate equivalent, for tax purposes, their costs of sales have been continually understated, and their taxable incomes continually overstated, during the postwar inflationary eras. For the same reason, reported profits have generally been overstated. Thus, in order to adjust for this overstatement of profits, and on the assumption that firms have been using the first in first out (FIFO) valuation method, reported profits are reduced by the following cost-of-sales adjustment.[4] (The indexes used may be obtained from the present writer upon request.)

$$CSADJ_i = \frac{\Delta p_i}{p_{i-1}} INV_{i-1},$$

where

Δp_i = change in the production cost index during the current year;

p_{i-1} = production cost index of the previous year; and

INV_{i-1} = opening inventory of the current year.

Debt Adjustment

Inflation reduces, by definition, the monetary unit's command over goods and services; hence it necessarily affects the relationship between borrowers and lenders. Since debt is denominated in dollar terms, lenders stand to lose, and borrowers to gain, from inflation. Interest rates therefore rise, as lenders seek to maintain the real yields on loans and to preserve loans' real values. For the borrower the nominal interest payment is recorded as an operating expense, and it is deductible for tax purposes; for the lender it is recorded and taxed as income. No recognition is given in the conventional accounts and in tax policy to the inflation-induced real gain of the borrower or to the real loss of the lender. Consequently, the reported profit of the former is understated and that of the latter overstated.

Because this study is concerned with ex post inflation-adjusted rates of return, it deals with the effects of actual inflation, irrespective of the degree to which it was anticipated. Therefore, instead of reducing the borrower's interest costs by the premium embodied therein for anticipated inflation, his income is increased by his gain on outstanding debt brought on by actual inflation. A corresponding, and opposite, adjustment is made to the income of the lender. The net effects of unanticipated inflation emerge indirectly, however, since the real gains or losses that occur when the actual rate of inflation differs from the anticipated one represent, in effect, transfers between a firm's creditors and its shareholders. They thus enter into the difference between the firm's inflation-adjusted returns on capital employed and those on equity.

The inflation adjustment with respect to short-term debt forms part of the adjustment with respect to other working capital, described below. As to net long-term debt, the adjustment, based on the assumption that the firm's flow of funds is uniform throughout the year, is as follows:

$$\text{Gain/loss on net noncurrent liabilities} = \left(\frac{NCL_i + NCL_{i-1}}{2}\right)\left(\frac{GNE - GNE_{i-1}}{GNE_{i-1}}\right),$$

where

$$NCL_i = \text{net noncurrent liabilities at end}$$
$$\text{of year } i; \text{ and}$$
$$GNE_i = GNE \text{ deflator for year } i.$$

Other-Working-Capital Adjustment

Conventional accounting records most of the firm's current assets, other than inventory, as well as its current liabilities at their cost or nominal values. This means that neither the contraction of the real values of the assets imposed by inflation nor the real gains correspondingly bestowed on the liabilities are captured in the accounts. These effects must be taken into account in determining the firm's inflation-adjusted returns. Assuming that the flows of current assets and liabilities are uniform throughout the year, the adjustment is as follows:

$$\text{Gain/loss on other working capital} = \left[\left(\frac{CL_i + CL_{i-1}}{2}\right)\right]$$
$$- \left[\left(\frac{CA_i + CA_{i-1}}{2}\right)\right]$$
$$\times \left(\frac{GNE_i - GNE_{i-1}}{GNE_{i-1}}\right)\Bigg],$$

where

$$CL_i = \text{current liabilities at end of year } i;$$
$$CA_i = \text{current assets other than inventory}$$
$$\text{at end of year } i; \text{ and}$$
$$GNE_i = GNE \text{ deflator for year } i.$$

Investments in Canadian Affiliates

The acquisition by one corporation of the shares of another appears as an asset in the investing company's books, and the dividends earned on these shares appear as investment income and enter into its profits. Unless these shares were acquired when issued, there is no corresponding entry in the accounts of the corporation whose shares were bought, and the dividends paid on those shares, being charges to retained earnings, are not deducted from its profits. If the two corporations are in different sectors, the asset representing the investment could be considered part of the capital employed in the owning firm's sector; the dividends earned, part of its income. An inflation adjustment might well be necessary, though difficult to calculate, to reflect the changing real value of the asset. If, however, the two corportions are in the same sector, it would be necessary, in order to avoid double counting, to exclude the asset from the capital employed and equity of the owning company and to exclude the related dividends from its income. It was assumed as a practical matter that all affiliated corporations are in the same sector. Although this tends to bias the estimates, the direction of the bias is not readily apparent. In any event, given the relative unimportance of the assets involved, the magnitude of the bias is probably slight.

Other Noncurrent Assets

This category embraces a miscellany of items, ranging from deferred charges to a variety of intangible assets such as goodwill, trademarks, franchises, and the like. The deferred charges usually refer to the various past costs of establishing and maintaining the corporate entity and its financial instruments that have not been written off. It is reasonable to assume that the current equivalent of these costs would be higher because of inflation. The same is true of the intangible assets. There is, however, a practical problem in determining their current dollar value. Many of these items are carried in the accounts at a purely nominal value or at a cost value that has long since gone out of date. Since these items represent, as a group, a negligible proportion of total assets, it was decided, somewhat arbitrarily, to disregard them, both with respect to the inflation-induced changes in their real values and as components of capital employed and equity.

Inflation-Adjusted Rates of Return and Other Inflation-Adjusted Indicators

Capital Employed

Definitions of capital vary in the literature. A number of the writers who recently estimated rates of return have defined capital as the sum of inventory and the depreciated values of fixed assets at replacement cost.[5] This might be regarded as the conventional method, which focuses on the output of the firm and on the assets that produce it directly. Jenkins (1977a) defines capital as the sum of inventory, certain other working capital, and the depreciated values of fixed assets at replacement cost. This is closer to the spirit of the definition used here, since it recognizes that working capital is no less essential to the firm than inventory and fixed assets. Our definition implies a similar view but is somewhat broader. It embraces all current assets (including inventory) less current liabilities plus the depreciated values of fixed assets at replacement cost. (Hence the term "capital employed" is preferred.) This is equivalent to the sum of equity and net noncurrent liabilities, and it represents the net assets employed in the firm's operations.

Rate of Return on Capital Employed after Taxes

The nominal (reported) rate of return on capital employed, after taxes, is defined as follows:

$$NRC_i = \frac{RP_i - DV_i + IN_i - IT_i}{INV_i + OWC_i + BK_i + BL_i},$$

where

RP_i = reported net profit before income taxes in year i;

DV_i = dividends earned in year i;

IN_i = net interest expense on net noncurrent liabilities in year i;

IT_i = income taxes paid in year i;

INV_i = inventory valued at FIFO at mid-year i,[6]

OWC_i = other working capital at mid-year i;

BK_i = depreciable and depletable assets at depreciated book value at mid-year i; and

BL_i = land at book value at mid-year i.

In the light of the foregoing inflation adjustments, the after-tax inflation-adjusted rate of return on capital employed is defined as follows:

$$RRC_i = \frac{RP_i - DV_i + BD_i - RD_i + IN_i - CSADJ_i \pm WC_i - IT_i}{INV_i + OWC_i + RK_i + RL_i},$$

where

BD_i = book depreciation and depletion expense in year i;

RD_i = replacement cost depreciation and depletion expense in year i;

$CASDJ_i$ = cost-of-sales adjustment in year i (also known as inventory-valuation adjustment);

WC_i = real gain or loss on other working capital in year i;

RK_i = depreciable and depletable assets at depreciated replacement cost at mid-year i; and

RL_i = land at replacement cost at mid-year i.

These nominal and inflation-adjusted rates of return, after taxes, are reported graphically in figures 8–1, 8–2, and 8–3.

Since it has a considerable currency in the literature, the inflation-adjusted after-tax rates of return on capital as defined "conventionally" are also presented, in table 8–1. It is defined as follows:

$$RC_i^c = \frac{RP_i - DV_i + BD_i - RD_i + INT_i - CSADJ_i - IT_i}{INV_i + RK_i + RL_i},$$

where

$$INT_i = \text{net interest expense.}$$

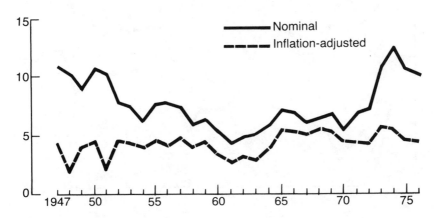

Source: Economic Council of Canada.

Figure 8–1. Nominal and Inflation-Adjusted After-Tax Rates of Return on Capital Employed: Nonfinancial Sector 1947–1976

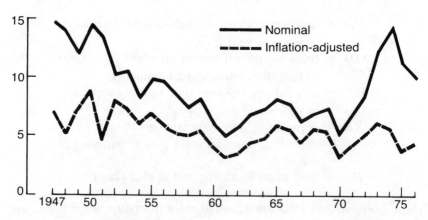

Source: Economic Council of Canada.

Figure 8–2. Nominal and Inflation-Adjusted After-Tax Rates of
Return on Capital Employed: Manufacturing Sector
1947–1976

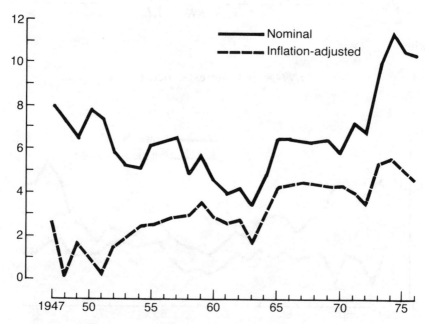

Source: Economic Council of Canada.

Figure 8–3. Nominal and Inflation-Adjusted After-Tax Rates of
Return on Capital Employed: Nonmanufacturing Sector
1947–1976

Table 8–1
Inflation-Adjusted After-Tax Rates of Return on Capital,
"Conventional" Method 1947–76

Year	Nonfinancial Sector	Manufacturing Sector
1947	5.74	8.91
1948	3.63	6.95
1949	5.35	9.50
1950	5.52	11.01
1951	3.45	6.34
1952	5.53	9.55
1953	5.29	8.81
1954	4.99	7.52
1955	5.78	8.81
1956	5.53	7.55
1957	6.13	6.55
1958	5.06	6.56
1959	5.51	7.03
1960	4.33	5.31
1961	3.86	4.33
1962	4.35	5.10
1963	4.02	6.31
1964	4.89	6.61
1965	7.25	7.96
1966	6.91	7.33
1967	6.49	6.19
1968	7.14	7.52
1969	7.02	7.45
1970	6.04	4.95
1971	5.44	5.88
1972	5.12	6.47
1973	6.73	8.05
1974	6.16	6.71
1975	5.22	4.61
1976	5.38	5.28

Source: Economic Council of Canada.

Rate of Return on Equity after Taxes

Equity is simply capital employed less net noncurrent liabilities. It must be recognized, however, that the rate of return on equity is a somewhat ambiguous indicator and not the one that would have been chosen had the exigencies of the data been otherwise. This is because there generally exist various classes of shareholders in the firm, ranging from the common shareholders, who are the most truly residual claimants to its profits, to the several possible types of preferred shareholders. It is the rate of return on the equity held by the common shareholders that is the most meaningful. The data did not, however, permit differentiation between these groups of shareholders. If they had done so, it would have been necessary to take account of the fact that inflation induces real transfers between the holders of the firm's preferred shares and the holders of its common shares, in ways that are analogous to the real transfers induced between creditors and shareholders that were discussed above. Because this was not possible, the rate of return on equity was calculated. Although it must be regarded as a second-best alternative, it remains an indicator of considerable interest, if for no other reason than that it gives, in its inflation-adjusted version, a sense of the transfers between creditors and shareholders. It is defined in nominal after-tax terms as follows:

$$NRNW_i = \frac{RP_i - DV_i - IT_i}{INV_i + OWC_i + BK_i + BL_i - NCL_i},$$

where

NCL_i = net noncurrent liabilities at mid-year i.

The inflation-adjusted rate of return on equity after taxes is defined as follows:

$$RRNW_i = \frac{RP_i - DV_i + BD_i - RD_i}{INV_i + OWC_i + RK_i + RL_i - NCL_i} - \frac{CSADJ_i \pm WC_i + GL_i - IT_i}{INV_i + OWC_i + RK_i + RL_i - NCL_i},$$

where

GL_i = gain on net noncurrent liabilities in year i.

These nominal and inflation-adjusted rates of return, after taxes, are presented graphically in figures 8–4, 8–5, and 8–6. In general, and given stable prices, the difference between the rate of return on capital employed by a firm and the rate of return on its equity will be determined largely by the relationship between the former and the average annual rate of interest that the firm paid on its net noncurrent debt. The advent of unanticipated inflation (or deflation), however, causes, as has been shown, real transfers to take place between the firm's creditors and its shareholders. It is thus reasonable to attribute to two basic factors the fact that inflation-adjusted after-tax rates of return on equity in each of the aggregate sectors reported were invariably greater

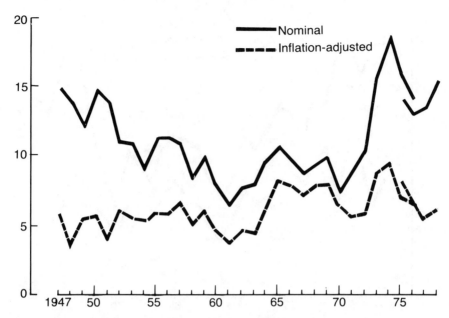

Sources: Economic Council of Canada, Department of Finance.

Figure 8–4. Nominal and Inflation-Adjusted After-Tax Rates of
Return on Equity: Nonfinancial Sector 1947–1978

than corresponding real after-tax rates of return on capital employed.
We cannot, however, easily differentiate between them. One factor is
the net return that firms earned on borrowed resources; the other is
the gains that shareholders earned at the expense of creditors, as actual
inflation consistently turned out, apparently, to be higher than had
been anticipated and reflected in interest rates. Since the effects of
unanticipated inflation are reflected in the inflation-adjusted, but not
in the nominal, rates of return on equity, it is not surprising that these
two rates of return have not varied together as closely as did the corresponding rates of return on capital employed.

Factors Influencing the Variation in the Inflation-Adjusted Rates of Return

Two separate collections of empirical evidence are available, one referring to the thirty-year series 1947–1976 of inflation-adjusted rates
of return on capital employed and the other referring to a different

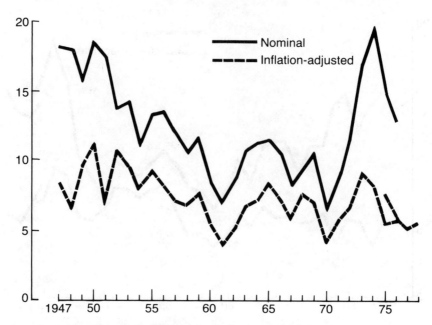

Sources: Economic Council of Canada, Department of Finance.
[a] Nominal values available only for 1947–1976.

Figure 8–5. Nominal[a] and Inflation-Adjusted After-Tax Rates of
Return on Equity: Manufacturing Sector 1947–1978

fifteen-year series, 1963–1978, of inflation-adjusted rates of return on
equity.

With respect to the longer series, the main result is straightforward:
there is a fairly strong and robust downward trend in the inflation-
adjusted aggregate rate of return on capital employed in the manufacturing sector. Otherwise, only business cycle indicators had a significant
and robust effect, both for manufacturing and for all nonfinancial firms.
As table 8–2 shows, all other variables tested for proved to be either
insignificant or far from robust, and it may be concluded that they had
no direct influence on the inflation-adjusted rate of return on capital
employed.

To repeat, one of the most unambiguous findings is a significant
downward trend in the inflation-adjusted rate of return on capital employed in manufacturing. No other variable seems to describe nearly
so well the secular pattern of historically high inflation-adjusted rates
of return during the 1950s. Judging from the pattern of residuals, a
nonlinear trend, close to zero in later years, would give a better fit.
Perhaps this reflects specific circumstances in the 1950s and 1970s—

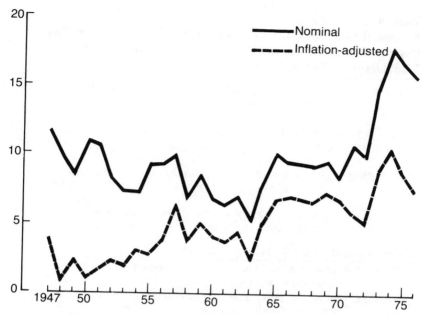

Source: Economic Council of Canada.

Figure 8–6. Nominal and Inflation-Adjusted After-Tax Rates of Return on Equity: Nonmanufacturing Sector 1947–1976

the former being unusually favorable, the latter unusually unfavorable—that are not reflected in the explanatory variables. No such trend is present in the inflation-adjusted rate of return on the capital employed in nonfinancial firms, of which manufacturing accounts for a substantial share. This indicates that a rising trend occurred in the inflation-adjusted rates of return on capital employed of nonmanufacturing firms. It is a plausible assumption that changes in the relative price of energy during the 1970s had a distinct influence.

The second finding is that cyclical variables have substantial explanatory power. Various output-gap measures performed well, but a second indicator—the difference between the actual and the equilibrium unemployment rate—consistently performed better. This was unexpected, since an output-based indicator should, in principle, be a better proxy for the degree of utilization of a firm's resources and hence for its inflation-adjusted return on capital employed. Allowing for a lagged effect of the cyclical variables improved the goodness of fit—also a somewhat surprising result. The coefficients of the cyclical variables were consistently larger for before-tax inflation-adjusted rates of

Table 8–2
Estimated Equations, Inflation-Adjusted Before- and After-Tax
Rates of Return on Capital Employed, Nonfinancial, and
Manufacturing Sectors

$$BUT = 8.38 + .028TIME - 0.70UGAP - 0.28UGAP_{-1} - 1.42D51 \quad \overline{R}^2 = .75$$
$$\quad\quad (28.5) \quad (1.6) \quad\quad (4.8) \quad\quad (2.1) \quad\quad (1.9) \quad DW = 1.59$$

$$RAT = 4.33 + 0.041TIME - 0.34UGAP - 0.17UGAP_{-1} - 2.58D51 \quad \overline{R}^2 = .68$$
$$\quad\quad (18.6) \quad (3.0) \quad\quad (3.0) \quad\quad (1.6) \quad\quad (4.3) \quad DW = 1.37$$

$$BUM = 13.22 - 0.143TIME - 1.36UGAP - 1.94D51 \quad \overline{R}^2 = .76$$
$$\quad\quad (26.3) \quad (4.8) \quad\quad (7.6) \quad\quad (1.5) \quad DW = 1.55$$

$$RAM = 7.55 - 0.099TIME - 0.76UGAP - 3.53D51 \quad \overline{R}^2 = .69$$
$$\quad\quad (21.5) \quad (4.8) \quad\quad (6.1) \quad\quad (4.0) \quad DW = 1.50$$

Estimation period: 1950–76; t statistics in parentheses

BUT = inflation-adjusted before-tax rate of return on capital employed: nonfinancial sector

RAT = inflation-adjusted after-tax rate of return on capital employed: nonfinancial sector

BUM = inflation-adjusted before-tax rate of return on capital employed: manufacturing sector

RAM = inflation-adjusted after-tax rate of return on capital employed: manufacturing sector

$TIME$ = linear trend 1950 = 1

$UGAP$ = difference between actual and equilibrium unemployment rate

$D51$ = dummy for 1951 (Korean crisis)

Source: Economic Council of Canada.

return than for after-tax rates, reflecting the smoothening effect of corporate taxes. The inflation-adjusted rate of return on capital employed in manufacturing was found to have a larger cyclical amplitude than the inflation-adjusted corresponding rate of return in the nonfinancial sector.

The rate of growth of output and the rate of growth of output per employed person proved to be very poor substitutes for these cyclical indicators. They obviously have a cyclical content, and they also reflect medium-term or structural changes in the rate of growth of the economy, but they were consistently insignificant in the regressions.

A third group of variables, representing Canadian prices or costs relative to those of her trading partners, also proved insignificant. For the nonfinancial sector as a whole, the ratios of export and import prices to domestic prices were expected to have a positive influence on inflation-adjusted profits, on the grounds that firms may respond to changes in the trading environment by making price adjustments, in addition to making quantity adjustments that are reflected in the cyclical variables. The same reasoning underlay testing for an independent effect of the relative unit labor cost (United States versus Canada) upon manufacturing. Neither hypothesis proved tenable.

Changes in the terms of trade have a direct impact on the amount of real income available in the economy; and a direct effect upon the inflation-adjusted rate of return may therefore be hypothesized. The regressions showed a small effect upon the nonfinancial sector as a whole but not upon the manufacturing sector. The explanation may lie in the structure of Canada's foreign trade. Manufacturing firms experience competition from imports but account for only a moderate share of exports. They are therefore unlikely to be the initial beneficiaries of an improvement in the terms of trade. Canadian producers of resource products are in a better position, especially when terms-of-trade improvement involves a rise in export prices.

No convincing evidence emerged of a direct effect of inflation upon inflation-adjusted rates of return on capital employed in either sector, whether positive or negative. The change in the rate of inflation showed a negative effect; this, however, was small and generally insignificant.

The evidence pertaining to the inflation-adjusted before-tax rate of return on equity refers to the much shorter period, 1963–1978, and to the manufacturing, energy, and nonenergy, nonmanufacturing sectors. The regression results are presented in table 8–3. The first sector is the most relevant one for present purposes; and the most striking finding is that, in contrast to its lack of impact upon the inflation-adjusted rate of return on capital employed over the longer period, the rate of inflation had a significant negative impact upon this inflation-adjusted rate of return over the shorter period. (As before, various cyclical factors were also significant.)

Intervals of very different duration are involved in these two estimates—one of thirty years and the other of fifteen—and the ability of Canada's manufacturing sector to protect its profits against inflation may well have been greater over the longer interval than over the shorter. It is also true that the analysis over the longer interval refers to returns on capital employed while that over the shorter interval refers to returns on equity. This consideration, however, could conceivably imply an even stronger negative impact on the part of inflation upon returns to capital employed during this period, when, apparently, actual inflation generally outstripped anticipated inflation, and shareholders gained at the expense of creditors. Perhaps the most important differentiating factor is the fact that the inflation of the later interval

Table 8–3
Estimated Equations, Inflation-Adjusted Before-Tax Rates of Return on Equity, Energy, Manufacturing, and Nonenergy, Nonmanufacturing Sectors[a]

Energy[b]

$$BTRR_{ENG} = 10.74 + 0.17\ CAPU_{ENG} + 0.08\ \frac{PE_{ENG}}{PL_{ENG}}\quad \overline{R}^2 = 0.60$$
$$\quad\quad\quad (29.0)\quad (2.9)\quad\quad\quad\quad (5.0)\quad\quad\quad\ DW = 1.09$$

Manufacturing

$$BTRR_{MAN} = 17.78 - 0.64\ \frac{ULC_{MAN}}{ISPI_{MAN}} - 0.12\ \frac{PE_{MAN}}{ISPI_{MAN}}$$
$$\quad\quad\quad (11.0)\quad (4.6)\quad\quad\quad\ (5.9)$$
$$\quad\quad + 0.36\ \frac{PX}{PM} - 0.81\ P\quad \overline{R}^2 = 0.78$$
$$\quad\quad\quad (2.2)\quad\quad (3.0)\quad\quad DW = 1.94$$

Nonenergy, nonmanufacturing

$$BTRR_{ONE} = 13.18 - 0.90\ \frac{ULC_{ONE}}{OPI_{ONE}} - 0.12\ \frac{PE_{ONE}}{OPI_{ONE}} + 0.20\ \frac{PX}{PM}\quad \overline{R}^2 = 0.87$$
$$\quad\quad\quad (46.9)\quad (4.3)\quad\quad\quad\ (6.7)\quad\quad\quad (2.7)\quad\quad DW = 1.92$$

Source: Department of Finance.

[a]Estimation period 1963–78; t statistics in parentheses. Except for the rate of inflation, all independent variables were measured as percentage differences from their 1963–1978 average.

[b]This equation was also estimated with a correction for autocorrelation. The resulting coefficients were only marginally different from those shown above.

$BTRR$ = inflation-adjusting before-tax rates of return;

$CAPU$ = index of capacity utilization;

PE = index of energy prices;

PL = index of compensation per man-hour;

ULC = index of unit labor cost (labor compensation per unit of output);

$ISPI$ = index of industry selling prices for manufactures (excluding petroleum and coal products);

PM = index of import prices (all products);

P = rate of change of domestic demand deflator;

OPI = price deflator for industrial value added, equal to the ratio of GDP at current and constant 1971 dollars in the relevant industries.

The subscripts *ENG, MAN,* and *ONE* indicate that the subscripted variable pertains to, respectively, the energy, manufacturing and other nonenergy, nonmanufacturing sectors. Unsubscripted variables pertain to all sectors.

was rooted in sharp increases in the relative prices of energy whereas that of the previous interval had far more generalized origins, namely the overall conditions of the immediate postwar years. Given manufacturing's relatively heavy dependence upon energy inputs, together with its relatively weak competitive position as far as imports are concerned, its earnings would presumably be especially vulnerable to energy-provoked inflationary pressures.

Notes

1. A. Tarasofsky, T.G. Roseman, and H.E. Waslander, *Ex Post Aggregate Real Rates of Return in Canada: 1947–76* (a study prepared for the Economic Council of Canada, Ottawa, Supply and Services Canada, 1981). Cited hereafter as ECC.

2. Gerard Belanger and Neil McIlveen, *Rates of Return and Investment Profitability* (Ottawa, Department of Finance, 1980). Cited hereafter as Finance.

3. These are discussed more fully in Scapens (1977), pp. 64–66.

4. This adjustment methodology is derived from Bossons (1977), and involves, among other things, the assumption that the closing inventories of all firms are valued on a FIFO basis at year-end replacement cost.

5. See, for example, Kopcke (1978); Lovell (1978), though it is not obvious that he includes inventory in capital; and Feldstein and Summers (1977).

6. Strictly speaking, capital employed should be measured at the start of the year. But because the crucial data on fixed assets were available only in mid-year terms, the other capital elements were also measured in mid-year terms.

References

Bossons, John. *The Impact of Inflation on Income and Financing of Large Non-Financial Corporations.* Toronto: Government of Ontario, 1977.

Feldstein, M., and Summers, L. "Is the Rate of Profit Falling?" *Brookings Papers on Economic Activity,* 1:1977.

Jenkins, Glenn P. *Capital in Canada: Its Social and Private Performance, 1965–74.* Ottawa: Economic Council of Canada, 1977.

Kopcke, Richard W. "The Decline in Corporate Profitability." *New England Economic Review,* May-June 1978.

Lovell, Michael C. "The Profit Picture: Trends and Cycles." *Brookings Papers on Economic Activity,* 3:1978.

Scapens, Robert W. *Accounting in an Inflationary Enviroment.* London: Macmillan, 1977.

Appendix 8A
Notes on Data and
Adjustment
Methodology[1]

Primary Data Sources

1. Department of National Revenue, *Taxation Statistics*, 1947–64; Statistics Canada, *Corporation Financial Statistics* (Cat. 61–207).

   The structures of the samples that underpin the contents of the foregoing statistical publications have, of course, evolved over the years, as have those of the samples pertaining to the contents of the following publications. The above samples consist of taxpaying corporations such that most large corporations are included together with stratified samples of smaller ones. The data are derived from the tax returns of the firms included in the samples.

2. Statistics Canada, *Fixed Capital Stocks and Flows* (Cat. 13–211).

   The estimates presented in this publication are derived from a stratified sample of business *establishments* rather than of taxpaying corporations.

3. Statistics Canada, *Industrial Corporations: Financial Statistics* (Cat. 61–003).

   The samples underlying the estimates presented in this publication consist, as do the samples referred to in source 1, of most large corporations plus random samples of smaller ones. Unlike the data involved in source 1, however, the data presented here are derived from quarterly, rather than annual, surveys. Full details of the contents of all of the above publications are, of course, contained therein.

The income and balance sheet data provided by the sources in 1 and 3 above are in terms of fiscal year-end. The fiscal years of some corporations do not correspond to the calendar year. Since the various deflators used in the inflation adjustments are annual ones, this may impart a slight downward bias to the inflation-adjusted rates of return for the years during which inflation was relatively high.

Crown Corporations

Prior to 1965, the Department of National Revenue excluded Crown corporations from the taxation statistics. From 1965 to 1970, however, Statistics Canada included federal proprietary Crown corporations in the financial statistics; thereafter, agency Crown corporations and provincial and municipal Crown corporations were also included.

333

Very little information is available regarding the proprietary Crown corporations for the years 1965 to 1969, inclusive. The data for 1970 are much more complete, but the sectoral breakdown does not permit separating the financial Crown corporations from the nonfinancial. In order to deal with this situation with respect to these six years, reference was made to Finance, whose data did not present this problem, and an admittedly rough scaling adjustment was made to our results. While the adjusted rates of return are plausible for the nonfinancial sector, there is some uncertainty about those for the manufacturing sector. The possibility cannot be excluded that these adjusted rates of return are slightly too high. It is doubtful, however, whether the upward bias during these six years is sufficient to affect the long-term trends.

Statistics Canada was able to provide additional information for the years 1971 and 1976, inclusive, which made it possible to remove Crown corporations from the sample for those years.

Income Taxes: Payable and Deferred

Income taxes paid in each year are the provision for current taxes payable for that year. Each year's closing balance of deferred income taxes was regarded as part of that year's equity. This item generally derives from the difference between book depreciation expense and the capital cost allowances used for income tax purposes. Consequently, as long as the firm engages in capital formation at a steady or increasing rate, this amount will probably never be paid. A problem arose, however, with respect to the years 1965 to 1970, inclusive, because the data did not permit distinguishing between current taxes payable and deferred taxes. Since no satisfactory way could be found to estimate the deferred taxes for these years, no adjustment was made. Hence taxes paid during those years are overstated. But, given the above adjustment with respect to Crown corporations, which had the effect of scaling the results on the basis of data that are free of this problem, it is likely that the estimates of after-tax rates of return were not adversely affected to a significant extent.

The same, however, could not be said of the ECC estimates of inflation-adjusted effective tax rates. They were therefore considered too unreliable to be presented here.

1965 Data

The data for the year 1965 constitute a problem. This is the first year of the *Corporation Financial Statistics* series, and Statistics Canada reports that it is not fully compatible with the preceding series. It appears, however, that although the 1965 data have never been revised, the problems that occurred in relation to that year were largely resolved during the following years.

The Depreciation Adjustment

In order to estimate accurately the replacement cost of depreciable assets as well as replacement cost depreciation, it is necessary to know when investments were made and when old assets were written off. Also, for the starting year of the analysis (1947), it is necessary to know the age distribution of the depreciable assets held at that time so that the replacement cost for that year can be accurately estimated.

While *Taxation Statistics* and *Corporation Financial Statistics* provide some of this information, they are by no means complete for the following reasons: (1) *Taxation Statistics* start in 1947; thus we do not know the age distribution of depreciable assets held in that year. (2) More generally, *Taxation Statistics* and *Corporation Financial Statistics* do not deal with write-offs (and write-ups) in a systematic manner.

For these reasons it was decided to make use of the so-called perpetual inventory technique to build up gross and net capital stocks. It is this computational technique that is used in the estimates reported in *Fixed Capital Stocks and Flows*. This approach has the added advantage that the computational technique makes it relatively simple to compute replacement cost figures with and without backlog depreciation. The method involves the accumulation of gross investment over a period of years in order to obtain the gross depreciable assets in a given year. The technique also generates estimates of the depreciation expense for each year. In order to compute the replacement values of gross fixed assets, net fixed assets, and depreciation expense, price indexes are needed for each sector. These indexes are contained in *Fixed Capital Stocks and Flows*.

Estimation of Average Asset Life

As a first step, it was necessary to estimate average asset life (the asset lives given in *Fixed Capital Stocks and Flows* seemed too long). Average asset life is defined as follows:

$$L_i = \frac{GDA_i}{BD_i},$$

where

L_i = average asset life of total depreciable assets in year i;
GDA_i = gross depreciable assets at the end of year i;
BD_i = book depreciation expense in year i.

A problem arose with regard to the years 1947–1964. The data source for those years, *Taxation Statistics*, does not report book depreciation expense. Instead, capital cost allowances used for income tax purposes are reported. These were probably always substantially greater than book depreciation expense and therefore could not be used for the above purpose. (When capital cost allowances were used to estimate average asset life, the results were implausibly low.) Since *Corporation Financial Statistics* reported book depreciaton expense for the years 1965–1976, these twelve observations were used to calculate L^* as an unvarying estimate of L_i. L^* turned out to be nineteen years for both sectors. Since there is some evidence that asset lives have been getting shorter in recent decades, nineteen years may be an underestimate. This figure was used, however, because no better estimate was readily available.

In developing the investment series, it was necessary to distinguish between the pre-1947 period and the post-1947 period. It was not possible to obtain from *Fixed Capital Stocks and Flows* an investment series that was consistent with *Corporation Financial Statistics*. Two of the reasons for this are: (1) the data in *Fixed Capital Stocks and Flows* are collected on an establishment rather than on a corporate basis and (2) *Corporation Financial Statistics* refer in certain years to non-Crown corporations while *Fixed Capital Stocks and Flows* include both Crown corporations and unincorporated firms.

The investment series for the 1947–1976 period was therefore calculated from *Taxation Statistics* and *Corporation Financial Statistics* as follows:

$$X_i = NDA_i - NDA_{i-1} + BD_i,$$

where

X_i = gross investment in year i; and
NDA_i = net depreciated assets in year i.

Book depreciation expense had to be estimated for the years 1947–1964. This was done by dividing gross depreciable assets at the end of each year by 19, the estimated average useful life of these assets.

In order to calculate the replacement value of the stock of depreciable assets held at the start of 1947, it was necessary to have an annual investment series, which begins in 1927. Since the *Taxation Statistics* series does not go back that far, it was necessary to adapt the pre-1947 data provided in *Fixed Capital Stocks and Flows*. This was done by scaling the annual investment figures in the latter publication on the basis of the average ratio of the two investment series for the years for which both are available.

Estimation of Replacement-Cost Gross and Net Depreciated Assets and Depreciation Expense

This was done using the methodology described in the *Fixed Capital Stocks and Flows*. But the capital stock series, based on the perpetual inventory data contained in *Fixed Capital Stocks and Flows,* are mid-year estimates; the data contained in *Taxation Statistics* and *Corporation Financial Statistics* represent year-end figures. Since annual investment, X_i, tended to rise consistently over the long interval, reliance upon the perpetual inventory methods results in the underestimation of annual depreciation expense and, therefore, of accumulated depreciation. Consequently, net depreciated assets are overestimated. In order to correct for these biases, the estimates of annual depreciation expense and annual net depreciated assets were both scaled on the basis of the annual ratios of the figures in *Corporation Financial Statistics* to the corresponding figures in *Fixed Capital Stocks and Flows*.

Note

1. ECC was based on data sources (1) and (2); Finance was based on data source (3). Except for the note regarding the methodology for the depreciation adjustment, which is basically applicable to both ECC and Finance, the other two notes refer only to ECC. Analogous, specific notes pertaining to Finance can be found therein.

Appendix 8B
Basic Tables

Table 8B1
Nominal and Inflation-Adjusted Rates of Return on Capital Employed 1947–76
(percent)

| | Before Tax | | | | | | After Tax | | | | | |
| | NFC^a | | MC^b | | NMC^c | | NFC | | MC | | NMC | |
Year	N^d	$I\text{-}A^e$	N	I-A	N	I-A	N	I-A	N	I-A	N	I-A
1947	15.7	8.1	21.0	12.5	11.3	5.1	11.2	4.5	15.0	7.1	8.1	2.7
1948	15.1	5.8	20.1	10.3	10.7	2.4	10.5	2.2	14.1	5.1	7.3	0.1
1949	13.1	7.6	17.8	12.4	9.3	3.8	9.2	4.3	12.3	8.0	6.4	1.6
1950	16.1	8.7	21.5	14.9	11.3	3.7	11.0	4.6	14.6	9.1	7.8	1.0
1951	17.4	8.0	23.0	12.9	12.5	4.1	10.3	2.3	13.5	4.9	7.5	0.3
1952	14.7	10.0	18.7	15.3	11.1	5.7	8.0	4.6	10.4	8.3	5.9	1.6
1953	13.3	9.2	17.6	13.7	9.5	5.4	7.7	4.5	10.6	7.6	5.2	2.0
1954	10.8	7.7	13.8	11.1	8.1	4.9	6.6	4.2	8.3	6.2	5.2	2.4
1955	12.5	8.6	16.2	12.7	9.4	5.2	7.9	4.6	10.0	7.2	6.2	2.5
1956	12.5	8.3	16.0	11.4	9.7	5.8	8.0	4.2	10.0	6.0	6.3	2.8
1957	11.1	8.0	13.3	9.4	9.3	6.9	7.6	4.9	8.8	5.4	6.6	4.5
1958	9.0	6.5	11.4	8.6	7.1	4.9	6.1	4.0	7.7	5.1	4.9	3.0
1959	10.3	7.5	12.9	9.7	8.3	5.8	6.9	4.5	8.4	5.6	5.7	3.6
1960	8.4	6.3	10.2	7.7	7.0	5.1	5.3	3.4	6.2	4.1	4.6	2.9
1961	7.4	5.6	8.8	6.6	6.3	4.8	4.5	2.9	5.1	3.2	4.0	2.7
1962	8.0	5.9	9.8	7.3	6.5	4.8	5.0	3.2	5.9	3.7	4.3	2.8
1963	8.2	5.8	11.2	8.3	5.8	3.8	5.2	3.1	7.2	4.7	3.5	1.8
1964	9.2	6.8	11.5	8.5	7.4	5.4	6.0	3.9	7.5	4.9	4.8	3.1
1965	11.6	8.7	14.4	10.8	9.5	7.0	7.3	5.7	8.3	6.2	6.5	4.3
1966	11.3	8.4	13.7	10.1	9.6	7.2	7.2	5.7	8.1	5.9	6.6	4.5
1967	10.2	7.6	11.1	8.2	9.5	7.2	6.5	5.2	6.4	4.7	6.5	4.5
1968	10.7	8.4	12.4	9.9	9.6	7.4	6.7	5.7	7.2	5.9	6.4	4.5

1969	11.0	8.2	13.2	10.1	9.5	7.0	7.0	5.5	7.8	5.8	6.5	4.4
1970	9.2	7.0	9.4	6.8	9.2	7.2	5.7	4.6	5.3	3.4	5.9	4.3
1971	10.5	7.2	11.3	8.4	9.9	6.4	7.1	4.3	7.0	4.5	7.3	4.1
1972	11.1	7.3	13.2	9.4	9.7	6.0	7.6	4.2	8.6	5.2	6.9	3.5
1973	15.4	9.7	18.0	11.6	13.7	8.5	11.0	5.9	12.5	6.6	10.1	5.4
1974	18.2	10.4	21.2	11.5	16.3	9.7	12.8	5.8	14.8	6.0	11.5	5.7
1975	15.8	8.5	16.7	8.3	15.1	8.7	11.0	4.7	11.5	4.0	10.6	5.1
1976	14.6	8.0	14.7	8.1	14.5	7.9	10.2	4.5	10.1	4.4	10.3	4.6

Source: Economic Council of Canada.

[a] Nonfinancial sector.
[b] Manufacturing sector.
[c] Nonmanufacturing sector.
[d] Nominal.
[e] Inflation-adjusted.

Table 8B2
Nominal and Inflation-Adjusted Rates of Return on Equity 1947–76
(*percent*)

| | Before Tax | | | | | | After Tax | | | | | |
| | NFC^a | | MC^b | | NMC^c | | NFC | | MC | | NMC | |
Year	N^d	$I\text{-}A^e$	N	$I\text{-}A$	N	$I\text{-}A$	N	$I\text{-}A$	N	$I\text{-}A$	N	$I\text{-}A$
1947	21.4	15.0	10.6	5.8	16.7	7.1	25.8	18.2	15.0	8.4	11.6	3.8
1948	20.6	14.0	8.4	3.6	15.0	4.4	26.1	18.1	13.4	6.8	9.8	1.0
1949	18.1	12.3	9.9	5.6	13.2	5.2	22.9	15.7	15.6	9.7	8.7	2.1
1950	22.1	14.9	11.2	5.8	16.3	4.8	27.7	18.7	18.6	11.2	10.9	1.0
1951	24.5	14.2	11.7	4.1	18.4	6.9	30.3	17.6	17.2	6.9	10.6	1.6
1952	20.9	11.0	13.7	6.3	16.6	8.1	25.1	13.7	20.0	10.8	8.3	2.2
1953	19.3	10.8	12.1	5.6	14.3	7.4	24.2	14.3	17.8	9.6	7.0	2.0
1954	17.7	9.2	10.5	5.4	12.3	6.7	19.0	11.1	14.7	8.0	7.3	3.0
1955	18.4	11.3	11.7	6.0	14.9	7.1	22.3	13.5	16.7	9.2	9.2	2.9
1956	18.6	11.3	11.8	6.0	15.1	8.5	22.1	13.5	15.5	8.2	9.3	3.9
1957	16.5	10.9	11.3	6.8	14.4	10.1	18.7	12.1	12.7	7.1	9.9	6.5
1958	13.3	8.6	9.2	5.3	10.7	7.0	16.2	10.5	11.6	6.8	6.6	3.9
1959	15.8	10.0	11.0	6.2	13.3	8.8	18.4	11.6	13.4	7.6	8.5	5.0
1960	13.2	7.7	9.3	4.7	11.7	7.9	14.6	8.5	10.6	5.4	6.9	4.1
1961	12.1	6.7	8.4	3.9	11.3	7.8	12.8	6.9	9.1	4.0	6.5	3.8
1962	13.2	7.7	9.3	4.7	11.7	8.2	14.8	8.4	10.5	5.1	7.0	4.4
1963	13.6	8.0	9.3	4.6	10.0	6.4	17.1	10.7	12.2	6.6	5.3	2.5
1964	15.7	9.7	11.1	6.2	13.4	9.6	17.7	11.3	12.7	7.2	8.1	5.3
1965	18.1	10.8	16.4	8.4	15.8	12.3	20.5	11.4	17.3	8.3	10.1	6.9
1966	16.4	10.0	14.6	8.1	14.8	11.4	18.2	10.3	15.1	7.3	9.5	7.1
1967	14.8	8.9	13.4	7.4	14.7	11.3	14.9	8.2	12.7	6.0	9.4	7.0
1968	15.9	9.4	14.7	8.1	15.0	11.6	17.0	9.5	15.7	7.7	9.3	6.8

Year												
1969	16.4	10.0	14.9	8.2	14.9	11.7	18.4	10.3	15.4	7.0	9.5	7.4
1970	13.6	7.6	12.6	6.6	14.3	11.6	12.7	6.6	10.4	4.3	8.5	6.9
1971	15.5	10.0	10.2	5.7	15.6	9.5	15.4	9.1	11.1	5.6	10.8	5.8
1972	16.5	10.5	10.7	5.9	15.1	9.2	18.1	11.3	12.7	6.8	9.9	5.2
1973	22.6	15.9	14.8	9.0	20.7	13.9	24.9	16.9	16.0	9.2	15.2	8.9
1974	27.6	18.7	16.5	9.7	26.5	16.9	29.0	19.8	15.9	8.5	17.9	10.6
1975	23.7	15.8	12.8	7.2	24.7	14.2	22.4	15.0	11.0	5.3	16.5	8.6
1976	21.5	14.4	11.9	6.7	23.2	12.8	19.5	12.9	10.7	5.7	15.7	7.6

Source: Economic Council of Canada.

[a]Nonfinancial sector.
[b]Manufacturing sector.
[c]Nonmanufacturing sector.
[d]Nominal.
[e]Inflation-adjusted.

Table 8B3
Inflation-Adjusted Rates of Return on Capital,
"Conventional Method"

Year	Before Tax		After Tax	
	NFC[a]	MC[b]	NFC	MC
1947	10.05	15.39	5.74	8.91
48	8.01	13.12	3.63	6.95
49	9.37	15.16	5.35	9.50
1950	10.50	18.10	5.52	11.01
51	10.18	15.69	3.45	6.34
52	11.88	17.49	5.53	9.55
53	10.79	15.74	5.29	8.81
54	9.25	13.13	4.99	7.52
55	10.56	15.19	5.78	8.81
56	10.36	13.74	5.53	7.55
57	9.78	11.15	6.13	6.55
58	8.12	10.49	5.06	6.56
59	9.16	11.87	5.51	7.03
1960	7.66	9.61	4.33	5.31
61	7.06	8.41	3.86	4.33
62	7.59	9.45	4.35	5.10
63	7.33	10.77	4.02	6.31
64	8.36	10.99	4.89	6.61
65[c]	12.72	15.38	7.25	7.96
66[c]	11.76	13.86	6.91	7.33
67[c]	10.84	11.55	6.49	6.19
68[c]	11.98	13.63	7.14	7.52
69[c]	11.75	13.79	7.02	7.45
1970[c]	10.25	9.66	6.04	4.95
71	8.62	10.12	5.44	5.88
72	8.54	11.06	5.12	6.47
73	10.87	13.38	6.73	8.05
74	10.99	12.44	6.16	6.71
75	9.17	8.94	5.22	4.61
76	8.95	9.09	5.38	5.28

Source: Economic Council of Canada.

[a]Nonfinancial sector.

[b]Manufacturing sector.

[c]The rates of return for the years 1965 to 1970 inclusive should be viewed with caution. They are subject to the problem of Crown corporations described in appendix 8A and were estimated, as indicated there, by reference to the more reliable series reported in Finance.

9

Measuring the Profitability of the Nonfinancial Corporate Sector in Japan

Takaaki Wakasugi,
Kazuhiko Nishina,
Fumiko Kon-ya, and
Moriaki Tsuchiya

Almost everyone accepts the fact that Japan achieved a high rate of economic growth between the end of World War II and the first oil crisis. The reasons for this growth have caused a great deal of discussion. Among many possible factors, the most important and critical contribution has been made by the return on capital investment. Other essential factors have also been identified, such as entrepreneurial ambitions for a firm's growth, technical innovations that stimulated entrepreneurship, and public cooperation in both moderate consumption and positive saving. In addition, the serious competition between firms is cited as a factor—often between groups of firms in every economic field. Nor can the unique financial system in Japan be neglected. Yet returns on capital investment remains the most important and critical factor. Investments would never have been made without confidence in future profits, and expectations of high profitability motivate investment. The purpose of this chapter is to measure the past performance of capital investment by using the concept of "real" rates of return on capital.

Two kinds of data are available for measurement. One is macro statistical data on an aggregated level, which is represented by the System of National Accounts (SNA) statistics. The other is data on individual corporations, such as the financial statements of listed companies as reported to the stock exchange. On one hand, if the profitability of the total corporate capital is stressed, the former type of data is much better for the measurement than the latter. On the other hand, the latter data has the merit of containing much more detailed infor-

Our research depends on the kind assistance of too many people to name individually, but we wish to thank particularly Daniel M. Holland and Stewart C. Myers for their helpful comments on the early versions of this chapter. We are grateful to the Japan Securities Research Institute for financial aid.

mation. Employing the latter data, rather specialized and detailed items can be obtained, and the market values of the companies can be directly estimated from stock prices. Finally, we can measure the profitability of the listed companies based on their accounting information. The direct estimate of the total nonfinancial corporate sector using the SNA data is made additionally, since the listed companies comprise only a part of the total corporate sector—however large it may be in Japan.

Our measurements essentially conform to those listed in the common glossary in Appendix 1A. But our measurements are so concerned with the adjustment for difference in the time of valuing variables that our method of calculation is a little more complicated than that defined in the glossary. The following descriptions are mainly explanations of our basic concepts and our computational procedures.

In the next section, our sample and data sources are explained, and then the basic concepts are discussed. The notations and all the estimated variables are also defined. In the following section, we clarify the methods of estimating the basic variables from which other variables are calculated. In the final section, our findings are examined briefly, with tables. The basic estimates for the total corporate sector are reported in Appendix 9A.

Sample and Basic Data for Estimation

Sample and Data

The main data we employed were the Data Base Nikkei Financials, or the so-called NEEDS data.[1] We used the aggregate financial data on the nonfinancial companies listed on the First Section of the Tokyo Stock Exchange (TSE). These financial data comprise the financial statements (balance sheets, profit and loss statements, and their supplements) reported to the TSE and additional data derived from NEEDS's regular questionnaire survey. The data covers seventeen fiscal years, from 1965 to 1981 (the fiscal year runs from April to the following March). Stock prices and numbers of outstanding stocks were also selected from NEEDS.

Our sample consisted of 848 companies, which accounted for about one-third of the assets, one-quarter of the sales, and one-third of the operating income of all corporations in 1982.[2] The corporate accounting system in Japan is considered to be very similar to that of the United States.

The accounting system and practices of Japanese companies relevant to our concern are:

1. In principle every transaction must be recorded on a historical basis, or on an acquisition basis. Therefore the cost of sales is calculated based on historical costs, and the amount of depreciation is determined by the acquisition costs of depreciable assets.
2. Almost all companies employ the declining balance method in their depreciation policy, even if other methods are adopted for some assets.
3. Almost all companies practice the FIFO method, partially or wholly, in inventory valuation. No company in Japan practices inflation accounting.

Additional data sources were:

Economic Planning Agency, *Annual Reports on National Accounts*. Lists the current value of lands held by the corporate sector.

Ministry of Home Affairs, *Survey of Fixed Assets*. Lists the areas of land held by the corporate sector.

National Land Agency, *Public Announcement of Land Prices*. Provides land prices.

Bank of Japan, *Price Indices Annual,* and *Economic Statistics Annual*. WPI, CPI, and prices for individual capital goods are given.

Japan Securities Research Institute, *The Rates of Return on the Listed Stocks*. Lists the rates of return on listed stocks.

Estimation Procedures

Our estimation procedures were:

1: Revaluating the current value of capital stocks at the end of a fiscal year.

2: Estimating inflation-adjusted return on capital by excluding surpluses or deficits of both cost of sales and depreciation from accounting income.

3: Calculating the holding gains on existing capital stocks arising from inflation, including both realized and unrealized gains.

4: Adding the inflation-adjusted return and the holding gains to get the nominal return on capital.

5: Deriving the nominal rate of return on capital, by dividing the nominal return on capital by the revaluated capital stock at the beginning of a period.

6: Deflating the nominal rate of return by CPI to get the real rate of return on capital (it is assumed that the return on capital is valued at end-of-period prices).

We also estimate the return to investors from the rate of return on stocks and the average interest rate of interest-bearing debt, and calculate derivative ratios such as leverage ratios, effective tax rates, distribution ratios, and Tobin's q ratio.

Discussion of Basic Concepts

Capital Stock. The main purpose of our measurement is to estimate the profitability of the capital owned by the corporations. The definition of a company's capital (capital stocks or assets) varies according to the purpose of the measurement. The most inclusive definition is all the assets that a company holds, both physical assets and financial assets. By this definition the amount of capital corresponds to the total amount of money necessary to invest in a company.

At the opposite extreme capital can be defined as only plant and equipment, for example. In order to adapt to various purposes, we do not confine ourselves to one particular concept of capital. Four definitions of capital and their relevant returns on capital are estimated in this study. Since our space is limited, however, the descriptions are often based on the most inclusive concept of capital.

Values of capital stocks are recorded in financial statements at the historical cost, and are called book values. Any meaningful concept of the value of capital stocks must involve, needless to say, their market values from the standpoint of economics. Debt holders and stockholders have claims to capital stock. Thus, the remaining capital, once the debt has been subtracted, is defined as the equity of a company.

Return on Capital. Economic return on capital investment is defined as the difference between the total value at the end of the investment and the the value of the initial investment. This definition of income is based on the presumption of a "going concern," which implies that the invested capital should be maintained. For simplicity we suppose a one-period model, and assume there is no additional finance or investment in fixed assets.

The following notations are used: W_{-1} and W = the value of capital stocks at the beginning and at the end of a period, respectively; $SL =$ total cash inflow during a period; $C =$ total cash outflow during a period; and $E =$ return on capital. Suppose that capital stock consists of monetary assets and fixed assets, and that the fixed assets are inventory, plant and equipment, and land. Let the following notations be added: $M =$ monetary assets; $F =$ fixed assets; $G =$ inventory; $E + B =$ plant and equipment; and $L =$ land. Thus, $W = M + F = M + L + G + E + B$. Stock variables, with the subscript -1 mean beginning-of-period amounts and those without the subscript, end-of-period amounts. Based on the assumption that there is no additional investment in fixed assets, we can derive the following relations: $E + B - E + B_{-1}$ is equal to the amount of depreciation in plant and equipment; M is the sum of M_{-1} plus the difference between SL and C, that is, $SL - C$ is assumed to be held in the form of monetary assets; and L is equal to L_{-1} because land does not depreciate.

First, assume that there is no change in prices. In this case the return on capital, E, is expressed as follows:

$$E = W - W_{-1}$$
$$= SL - C - (G_{-1} - G) - (E + B_{-1} - E + B).$$

$C + G_{-1} - G$ is equal to cost of sales in accounting terms and $E + B_{-1} - E + B$ is assumed to be equal to depreciation. Thus, return on capital is sales, SL, minus the cost of sales, CS, minus depreciation, D.

$$E = SL - CS - D.$$

In the case of no price change, the economic return on capital, as defined above, is the same as the return computed by the present accounting system. But when prices change, economic and accounting returns are not identical.

Next we discuss the case in which prices change over time. Denote the value of an asset at the beginning-of-period price by $\underline{X}$ and at the end-of-period price by $\overline{X}$. Generally,

$$\overline{X} = (1 + PX)\,\underline{X},$$

where PX denotes the rate of price change of the asset. In the case of monetary assets, $\overline{X} = \underline{X}$. Monetary assets are therefore expressed by X.

As the first step toward calculating the real return on capital, we revaluate capital stock W at the current price at both the beginning and the end of the time period. Next we define nominal return on capital, E^n, as the difference between the end-of-period capital value at the end-of-period price, $\overline{W}$, and the beginning-of-period capital value at the beginning-of-period price, $\underline{W}_{-1}$.

$$E^n = \overline{W} - \underline{W}_{-1}$$
$$= (\overline{W} - \overline{W}_{-1}) + (\overline{W}_{-1} - \underline{W}_{-1}).$$

The nominal return proves to be divided into two parts. One is the difference between the end-of-period capital assets, $\overline{W}$, and the beginning-of-period capital assets, $\overline{W}_{-1}$, both of which are valued at the end-of-period price. The difference, $\overline{W} - \overline{W}_{-1}$, is the real return expressed at the end-of-period price. We call it the inflation-adjusted operating income and denote it by Y^r.

$$Y^r = \overline{W} - \overline{W}_{-1}$$
$$= SL - C - (\overline{G}_{-1} - \overline{G}) - (\overline{E + B}_{-1} - \overline{E + B})$$
$$= SL - \overline{CS} - \overline{D}.$$

Thus, the inflation-adjusted operating income proves to be the remainder of the sales, SL, after the subtraction of the total cost of sales and the depreciation, $\overline{CS} + \overline{D}$, revaluated by the replacement cost at current prices. Let us call $\overline{CS}$ and $\overline{D}$ economic cost of sales and economic depreciation, respectively.

In the present corporate accounting system, however, capital assets are valued at the acquisition price, so the accounting return on capital is defined as follows.

$$Y^b = SL - C - (\underline{G}_{-1} - \underline{G}) - (\underline{E + B}_{-1} - \underline{E + B})$$
$$= SL - \underline{CS} - \underline{D},$$

where $\underline{CS}$ and $\underline{D}$ are cost of sales and depreciation at the acquisition price, respectively. Thus,

$$Y^r = Y^b - (\overline{CS} - \underline{CS}) - (\overline{D} - \underline{D}).$$

To estimate the inflation-adjusted operating income, Y^r, from the accounting income, Y^b, we must get two differences, that is, the deficit of cost of sales, $\overline{CS} - \underline{CS}$, and the deficit of depreciation, $\overline{D} - \underline{D}$.

On the other hand, the latter part of the equation is the difference between the end-of-period and beginning-of-period values of the capital assets held at the beginning of a period, $\overline{W}_{-1} - \underline{W}_{-1}$. Let us call it the nominal holding gain and denote it by H^n. The nominal holding gain, H^n, is equal to the total amount of appreciation in the capital assets held at the beginning of a period.

$$
\begin{aligned}
H^n &= \overline{W}_{-1} - \underline{W}_{-1} \\
&= WPI \cdot \underline{G}_{-1} + PL \cdot \underline{L}_{-1} + PD \cdot \underline{E + B}_{-1},
\end{aligned}
$$

where WPI, PL, and PD, are the rates of price rises in inventory, land, and plant and equipment, respectively. So the rate of nominal holding gain on total capital assets, RH^n, is the weighted average of the price changes of each asset, where the weight applied to a price change is the proportion of each asset's value to the total capital at the beginning of a period.

$$
RH^n = WPI \cdot \frac{\underline{G}_{-1}}{\underline{W}_{-1}} + PD \cdot \frac{\underline{E + B}_{-1}}{\underline{W}_{-1}} + PL \cdot \frac{\underline{L}_{-1}}{\underline{W}_{-1}}
$$

Now we will define the real return on capital. Our definition of real return on capital is the difference between the end-of-period capital assets and the beginning-of-period capital assets, both of which are valued at the end of a period. If we presume "real (or physical) capital maintenance," then the real economic return, E^r, should be defined as follows.

$$
\begin{aligned}
E^r &= \overline{W} - \overline{W}_{-1} \\
&= \overline{W} - (1 + RH^n) \underline{W}_{-1}.
\end{aligned}
$$

But remembering that, ultimately, investors in capital stocks are individuals whose final purpose is consumption, it is not real capital but purchasing power at the beginning of a period that should be maintained. Purchasing power can be measured by the consumer price index. The definition of real economic return, presuming "purchasing power maintenance," E^r, is:

$$
\begin{aligned}
E^r &= \overline{W} - (1 + CPI) \underline{W}_{-1} \\
&= \overline{W} - \overline{W}_{-1} - (1 + CPI) \underline{W}_{-1} \\
&= Y^r + H^r;
\end{aligned}
$$

where CPI shows the rate of change in the consumer price index.

The real economic return is the sum of the inflation-adjusted operating income, Y^r, and the real holding gain, H^r. The real holding gain arises from the difference between the change in capital stock price and the change in consumer goods prices.

$$
\begin{aligned}
H^r &= \overline{W}_{-1} - (1 + CPI)\, \underline{W}_{-1} \\
&= (RH^n - CPI)\, \underline{W}_{-1} \\
&= (WPI - CPI)\, \underline{G}_{-1} + (PD - CPI)\, \underline{E + B}_{-1} \\
&\quad + (PL - CPI)\, \underline{L}_{-1} - CPI \cdot M_{-1}.
\end{aligned}
$$

If we presume "real capital maintenance," CPI in the second line of the above equation would be replaced by RH^n, and the real holding gain would reduce to zero, that is, $H^r = 0$.

According to our definition of real economic return, however, the real (= net) holding gain is composed of both the gains from the increases in the price of fixed assets above the consumer price and the loss from deterioration of monetary assets caused by inflation.

The real return on equity under inflationary conditions is defined similarly. Let the following notations be added: EQ^r = real economic return on equity, DB = debt, and $I(P)$ = interest payments. Then EQ^r is expressed as follows, assuming that there is no additional finance or dividend payments during a period.

$$
EQ^r = (\overline{W} - DB) - (1 + CPI)(\underline{W}_{-1} - DB_{-1}).
$$

Note that $W - DB$ is equity value and that debt is negative holding of monetary assets. Thus $DB = DB_{-1} + I(P)$. Taking this into account, the above equation can be rewritten:

$$
\begin{aligned}
EQ^r &= (Y^r - I(P)) + (H^r + CPI \cdot DB_{-1}) \\
&= E^r - I(P) + CPI \cdot DB_{-1}.
\end{aligned}
$$

Put in words, the real return on equity, presuming "purchasing power maintenance," is the remainder of the real return on total capital including debt, E^r, minus interest payments, $I(P)$, and borrowers' gains from dilution of debt caused by inflation, $CPI \cdot DB_{-1}$.

Rate of Return on Capital. To define the real rate of return on capital, the time must be considered, because the real return on capital and capital at the beginning of a period are compared with each other. Either by transforming the capital stock value at beginning-of-period into the value at the end-of-period, or conversely, by transforming the

real return on capital, the real rate of return on capital, ROC^r, is defined operationally as follows.

$$ROC^r = \frac{\overline{W} - (1 + CPI)\,\underline{W}_{-1}}{(1 + CPI)\,\underline{W}_{-1}} = \frac{E^r}{(1 + CPI)\,\underline{W}_{-1}}$$

$$= \frac{Y^r}{(1 + CPI)\,\underline{W}_{-1}} + RH^r,$$

where RH^r expresses the rate of real holding gain.

The nominal rate of return on capital, ROC^n, can be also defined and expressed:

$$ROC^n = \frac{\overline{W} - \underline{W}_{-1}}{\underline{W}_{-1}} = \frac{E^n}{\underline{W}_{-1}} = \frac{Y^r}{\underline{W}_{-1}} + RH^n.$$

It can be easily proved that it is transformed into a real rate of return by the deflator CPI.[3]

Glossary of Notations and Definitions

In the notations, superscripts b, n, and r are used to differentiate among accounting, nominal, and real variables (for example, Y^b, Y^n, and Y^r). Stock variables with subscript -1 signify the beginning-of-period amount valued at the beginning-of-period price, and without subscript -1, the end-of-period amount valued at the end-of-period price. Flow variables are valued at the end of period.

Revaluated Capital Stock Variables

G	= Inventory
L	= Land
$E + B$	= Plant and Equipment
M	= Cash + Accounts Receivable − Accounts Payable + Other Monetary Assets
DB	= Debt
W	= $G + L + E + B + M$
F	= $G + L + E + B$
A	= $F - L$
O	= $W - L$
S	= $W - DB$

Market Value Variables

MV = Total Market Value
MS = Market Value of Stocks

Prices

WPI = Rate of Price Change in Inventory, Wholesale Price Index
PD = Rate of Price Change in Plant and Equipment
PL = Rate of Price Change in Land
CPI = Rate of Change in Consumer Price Index

Income Variables

Operating Income

Y^b = Accounting Operating Income Including Interest Received
Y^r = Inflation Adjusted Operating Income Including Interest Received
$I(R)$ = Interest Received
$I(P)$ = Interest Payments
P^r = Inflation Adjusted Operating Income After Interest Payment = $Y^r - I(P)$
T = Income Tax

Holding Gain

$H_F{}^n$ = Holding Gain of Fixed Assets
$\qquad = (WPI \cdot G_{-1} + PD \cdot E + B_{-1} + PL \cdot L_{-1})$
$H_A{}^n$ = Holding Gain of Fixed Assets Except Land
$\qquad = (WPI \cdot G_{-1} + PD \cdot E + B_{-1})$
g = Dilution of Debt = $CPI \cdot DB_{-1}$
m = Dilution of Monetary Assets = $CPI \cdot M_{-1}$
$H_F{}^r$ = Net Holding Gain of Fixed Assets = $H_F{}^n - CPI \cdot F_{-1}$
$H_W{}^r$ = Net Holding Gain of Total Assets = $H_F{}^r - m$
$H_A{}^r$ = Net Holding Gain of Fixed Assets Except Land
$\qquad = H_A{}^n - CPI \cdot A_{-1}$

H_o^r = Net Holding Gain of Total Assets Except Land
$$= H_A^r - m$$
H_S^r = Net Holding Gain of Equity = $H_F^r - m + g$

Real Return on Capital with Net Holding Gain

E_W^r = Real Return on Total Assets = $Y^r + H_w^r$
E_F^r = Real Return on Fixed Assets = $Y^r - I(R) + H_F^r$
E_A^r = Real Return on Fixed Assets Except Land
$$= Y^r - I(R) + H_A^r$$
E_o^r = Real Return on Total Assets Except Land
$$= Y^r + H_o^r$$
EQ^r = Real Return on Equity = $P^r + H_s^r$

Rates of Return on Capital

Nominal Rates of Holding Gain

$$RH_w^n = H_F^n / W_{-1}$$
$$RH_f^n = H_F^n / F_{-1}$$
$$RH_A^n = H_A^n / A_{-1}$$
$$RH_o^n = H_A^n / O_{-1}$$
$$RH_s^n = H_F^n / S_{-1}$$

Nominal Rates of Return on Capital Before Tax

$$ROC_W^n(BT) = Y^r / W_{-1} + RH_w^n$$
$$ROC_F^n(BT) = (Y^r - I(R)) / F_{-1} + RH_f^n$$
$$ROC_A^n(BT) = (Y^r - I(R)) / A_{-1} + RH_A^n$$
$$ROC_O^n(BT) = Y^r / O_{-1} + RH_o^n$$
$$REQ^n(BT) = P^r / S_{-1} + RH_S^n$$

After Tax

$$ROC_W^n(AT) = (Y^r - T) / W_{-1} + RH_w^n$$
$$ROC_F^n(AT) = (Y^r - I(R) / F_{-1} + RH_F^n$$
$$ROC_A^n(AT) = (Y^r - I(R) / A_{-1} + RH_A^n$$
$$ROC_O^n(AT) = (Y^r - T) / O_{-1} + RH_o^n$$
$$REQ^n(AT) = (P^r - T) / S_{-1} + RH_S^n$$

Nominal Rates of Return on Capital without Holding Gain Before Tax

$$'ROC'_w(BT) = Y^r / W_{-1}$$
$$'ROC'_F(BT) = (Y^r - I(R)) / F_{-1}$$
$$'ROC'_A(BT) = (Y^r - I(R)) / A_{-1}$$
$$'ROC'_o(BT) = Y^r / O_{-1}$$
$$'REQ'(BT) = P^r / S_{-1}$$

After Tax

$$'ROC'_w(AT) = (Y^r - T) / W_{-1}$$
$$'ROC'_F(AT) = (Y^r - I(R) - T) / F_{-1}$$
$$'ROC'_A(AT) = (Y^r - I(R) - T) / A_{-1}$$
$$'ROC'_o(AT) = (Y^r - T) / O_{-1}$$
$$'REQ'(AT) = (P^r - T) / S_{-1}$$

Real Rates of Return on Capital Before Tax

$$ROC_W^r(BT) = (1 + ROC_W^n(BT)) / (1 + CPI) - 1$$
$$ROC_F^r(BT) = (1 + ROC_F^n(BT)) / (1 + CPI) - 1$$
$$ROC_A^r(BT) = (1 + ROC_A^n(BT)) / (1 + CPI) - 1$$
$$ROC_o^r(BT) = (1 + ROC_o^n(BT))(1 + CPI) - 1$$
$$REQ^r(BT) = (1 + ROC_S^n(BT)) / (1 + CPI) - 1$$

After Tax

$$ROC_W^r(AT) = (1 + ROC_W^n(AT)) / (1 + CPI) - 1$$
$$ROC_F^r(AT) = (1 + ROC_F^n(AT)) / (1 + CPI) - 1$$
$$ROC_A^r(AT) = (1 + ROC_A^n(AT)) / (1 + CPI) - 1$$
$$ROC_o^n(AT) = (1 + ROC_o^r(AT)) / (1 + CPI) - 1$$
$$REQ^r(AT) = (1 + ROC_S^n(AT)) / (1 + CPI) - 1$$

Tax Rates and Distribution Ratios

Accounting Rate

tY^b = Tax Rate on Accounting Return = T / Y^b
iY^b = Share to Debt = $I(P) / Y^b$
eqY^b = Share to Equity = $(P^b - T) / Y^b$
tP^b = Tax Rate on Return on Equity = T / P^b

Effective Rate on Real Return without Holding Gain

$$tY^r = T / Y^r$$
$$iY^r = I(P) / Y^r$$
$$egY^r = P^r / Y^r$$
$$tP^r = T / P^r$$

Effective Rate on Real Return

$$tE_w^r = \text{Tax Rate on Total Capital} = T / E_w^r$$
$$iE_w^r = \text{Share to Debt} = (I(P) - g) / E_w^r$$
$$eqE_w^r = \text{Share to Equity} = (EQ^r - T) / E_w^r$$
$$tEQ^r = \text{Tax Rate on Equity} = T / EQ^r$$

Ratio of Debt to Total Capital

$$L_b = DB / W^b$$
$$L_M = DB / MV$$

Return to Investors

$$RS^n = \text{Rates of Return on Common Stock}$$
$$RB^n = \text{Interest Rates} = I(P) \cdot 2 / (DB'_{-1} + DB')$$
$$(DB' = \text{Interest Bearing Debt})$$
$$RCC^n = \text{Nominal Rates of Return to Investors}$$
$$= RS \cdot (1 - L_M) + RB \cdot L_M$$
$$RCC^r = \text{Real Rates of Return to Investors}$$
$$(1 + RCC^n) / (1 + CPI)^{-1}$$

Cost of Capital

$$\rho^n = \text{Nominal Cost of Capital} = (Y^r - T) / MV$$
$$\rho^r = \text{Real Cost of Capital} = (1 + \rho^n) / (1 + CPI)$$

Tobin's q Ratio

$$q(W) = MV / W$$
$$q(F) = MV / F$$
$$q(A) = MV / A$$
$$q(O) = MV / O$$

Methods of Revaluation and Inflation Adjustment

Revaluation of Capital Stocks

We revaluated inventory, plant and equipment (referred to below as depreciable assets according to accounting terminology), and land at current prices. As for other assets, we regarded book values as being equal to current prices. Current prices of marketable securities and other financial assets are often significantly different from book values. Since their weight in total assets is negligible, and since their revaluation has many attendant difficulties, we did not revaluate them.

Inventories. Book values (BV) of inventory assets at the end of a period are derived from the aggregated balance sheets of the entire industry and transformed into current values by use of both the estimated average turnover ratios of inventories for the industry and the wholesale price index (WPI). Assuming FIFO, the current values of inventories are estimated as follows.

$$G = G^{\mathrm{B}}\left(1 + \frac{1}{2}A\cdot\mathrm{WPI}\right)$$

G = current value of inventory

G^{B} = book value of inventory

A = average inventory period

WPI = rate of change in wholesale price index

Under FIFO and the assumption that production rate and sales rate are equal and constant, the ratio of average inventories to the cost of sales, A, which is the inverse of the turnover ratio of inventories, expresses an average holding period during the accounting period. Then $A / 2$ equals the average lapsed time for outstanding inventories at the end of the period.

Depreciable Assets. Depreciable assets were collectively revalued in almost the same way as inventories.

$$E + B = E + B^b \prod_{t=-z}^{0} (1 + PD_t)$$

$E + B$ = current value of depreciable asset

$E + B^b$ = book value of depreciable asset
Z = average age of depreciable asset
PD = rate of change in price for depreciable asset

The weighted average of the price indexes of individual depreciable assets was used as the price index for investment goods. The average age (Z) in the above equation was estimated as follows.

$$Z = \frac{\log\left(1 - \dfrac{E + B^b}{AD^b + E + B^b}\right)}{\log\left(1 - \dfrac{D^b}{E + B^b + D^b}\right)}$$

AD^b = accounting accumulated depreciation
D^b = accounting depreciation

It was assumed that depreciation was calculated according to the declining balance method. This assumption seems to be plausible since more than 90 percent of the listed companies employed this method.

NEEDS provides the total depreciation and the total accumulated depreciation for all kinds of depreciable assets, but it does not provide individual data on each category of depreciable asset. Therefore we cannot estimate the average age of each depreciable asset: we can only assume that every depreciable asset has the same age.

Land. The current value of land was estimated by employing the following equation.

$$L = L_P \times Q$$

L = current value of land
L_P = land price per square kilometers
Q = area measured in square kilometers

First, for the land held by the whole corporate sector, areas and current values by use are taken from the *Survey of Fixed Assets* (annual) and *Annual Reports on National Accounts* respectively. Average prices per unit are then calculated, according to the use of the land, by weighing the areas of different use. Recent data on areas were drawn from NEEDS, and the other data was taken directly from the annual reports of the companies.

Estimation of Economic Return on
Capital from Accounting Income

The computational definition of operating income on capital is the sum
of the operating income plus interest and dividends received.[4] In cases
where capital is defined as the total of physical assets, interest and
dividends received are not included in the return on capital. As stated
before, real or economic return on capital is the accounting return minus
adjustment for cost of sales and depreciation.

We added the estimated value of deficits in both cost of sales and
depreciation to the accounting income to obtain inflation-adjusted
income.

Adjustment for Cost of Sales. The adjustment for cost of sales is made
for an inventory period, because it is assumed that the money obtained
from sales is held in the form of monetary assets until the end of a
period.

$$\Delta CS = [CS^b - D(CS)^b] \times A \times WPI$$

ΔCS = adjustment of cost of sales
CS^b = accounting cost of sales
$D(CS)^b$ = accounting depreciation included in CS^b

The average inventory period was previously defined as the ratio of
average inventory to the cost of sales, A. The depreciation in cost of
sales, which is assumed to be equal to the depreciation in cost of products in NEEDS, is deducted to avoid double counting, since depreciation is also independently adjusted for.

**Economic Depreciation and Valuation Adjustment for Deprecia-
tion.** Excess or deficit depreciation results from the accounting rule
that depreciation is reported according to the historical value of the
asset. To maintain capital, economic depreciation must be calculated
by the current value of capital, not by the book value of capital as is
accounting depreciation. We calculated the balance of accounting minus
economic depreciation to equal the estimated excess or deficit depreciation. Economic depreciation for depreciable assets can be calculated
using revalued depreciable assets.

$$D = D^b \times \frac{E + B}{E + B^b}$$
$$\Delta D = D - D^b$$

$$D = \text{economic depreciation}$$
$$\Delta D = \text{adjustment of depreciation}$$

Accounting data such as depreciation and depreciable assets are provided by NEEDS. The price indexes and the age of depreciable assets are those used in the revaluation of depreciable assets. It is assumed that depreciation is determined according to the asset value at the beginning of an accounting period.

Measurement of a Firm's Value and
Rate of Return to Investors

Japanese corporations substantially finance their equity by common stock issues and earnings retention. So the market value of equity is equal to the market value of common stocks. On the other hand, it is difficult to estimate the market value of debt, because most debt is financed by banks loans or loans from other financial institutions. We regarded the market value of debt to be equal to the book value. Thus the firm's value is calculated as follows:

$$MS = S_P \times N$$
$$MV = MS + DB^b$$

$$MS = \text{market value of equity}$$
$$S_P = \text{stock price at the end of period}$$
$$N = \text{number of outstanding shares}$$
$$DB^b = \text{book value of debt}$$

The nominal rate of return on common stock is calculated as follows:

$$RS = \frac{DIV + S_P - S_{P-1}}{S_{P-1}}$$

$$RS = \text{rate of return on common stock}$$
$$DIV = \text{dividend per share}$$

Ex-rights of newly issued shares, as well as ex-dividends, are taken into consideration as necessary. The rate of return on debt is estimated by using the interest rate of interest-bearing debt. The nominal rate of return to investors is the average of the two rates of return, weighted by the market value of equity and the book value of debt.

Findings

Some measures and findings based on them are introduced in this section. The other measures can be easily derived from the basic estimates given in Appendix 9A.

Rate of Return on Capital

Rates of return, according to the various definitions of capital before and after tax, are shown in tables 9–1 to 9–4. Real rates of return on total capital (*ROCW*) and return on inventory plus plant and equipment are given in table 9–4. These two rates of return include the holding gains from assets, corresponding to the difference between the rate of holding gains and the CPI as a part of economic return on capital.

The *ROCW,* our main measure, dropped dramatically in 1974 (immediately after the first oil crisis) but after three years of deficits, it recovered rapidly to reach the levels of the later half of the 1960s. Because accounting rates of return on total capital did not show such a drop, we can assume that business activity was greatly disturbed by the unexpected inflation before and after the crisis. The second oil crisis, however, did not seem to produce serious damage to the *ROCW,* and the effects of the second crisis on the Japanese economy are not considered to have been so serious.

ROCW measures before and after tax run almost parallel to each other, but the tax burden on returns on capital gradually increases during the measurement period.

The *ROCA* in table 9–4 shows similar short-term fluctuations, but a falling trend can be clearly seen. Given that the *ROCW* remains steady, this downward slope is explained by the increasing weight of inventories plus depreciable assets on the total assets. These shares, in book values, show a slight downward trend, while, conversely, market values move upward. (These weights can be calculated from table 9A-1 in Appendix 9A.)

Although the growth rate of land prices is much higher than the average CPI rate, the rates of return on capital (including land) with holding gain are not always higher than those without holding gains. Buying and selling firms is not a popular business custom in Japan, so it is not possible for companies to realize holding gains on land by selling the firms. Thus investment in land apparently pulls down the rate of return on capital, but this factor does not seem to have prevented firms from making investments that include investment in land.

Table 9-1
Nominal[a] Rates of Return on Capital with Holding Gain
(percent)

| | Before Tax | | | | After Tax | | | |
	(1)	(2)	(3)	(4)	(5)	(6)	(7)	(8)
1966	13.4	15.5	14.8	19.8	12.1	13.0	13.2	16.1
1967	15.6	15.4	17.4	19.6	14.1	12.7	15.6	15.4
1968	16.8	14.6	18.7	18.0	15.3	11.8	16.9	13.7
1969	19.1	16.8	21.3	21.1	17.5	13.7	19.4	16.4
1970	13.7	15.3	14.6	18.5	12.2	12.5	12.9	14.3
1971	13.6	11.4	14.6	12.7	12.5	9.3	13.3	9.5
1972	20.3	13.8	23.5	17.9	19.1	11.5	22.0	14.1
1973	23.0	20.3	26.9	29.3	21.6	17.4	25.1	24.5
1974	4.3	15.9	3.4	19.8	3.1	13.5	2.0	16.0
1975	3.6	6.4	2.5	5.4	2.6	4.7	1.3	2.8
1976	7.7	10.1	7.6	11.2	6.4	7.8	6.0	7.7
1977	5.8	7.6	5.5	7.9	4.6	5.5	4.0	4.6
1978	8.6	7.9	9.2	8.9	7.2	5.6	7.5	5.4
1979	14.8	12.5	16.9	16.0	13.2	9.7	15.0	11.6
1980	14.1	13.7	15.6	17.0	12.3	10.3	13.4	11.7
1981	12.5	9.9	13.5	11.1	10.9	6.8	11.6	6.1

Before Tax:
  (1) = Nominal Rates of Return on Total Assets $[ROC_W^n(BT)]$
  (2) = Nominal Rates of Return on Total Assets except Land $[ROC_O^n(BT)]$
  (3) = Nominal Rates of Return on Fixed Assets $[ROC_F^n(BT)]$
  (4) = Nominal Rates of Return on Fixed Assets except Land $[ROC_A^n(BT)]$
After Tax:
  (5) = Nominal Rates of Return on Total Assets $[ROC_W^n(AT)]$
  (6) = Nominal Rates of Return on Total Assets except Land $[ROC_O^n(AT)]$
  (7) = Nominal Rates of Return on Fixed Assets $[ROC_F^n(AT)]$
  (8) = Nominal Rates of Return on Fixed Assets except Land $[ROC_A^n(AT)]$

[a]"Nominal" means that assets are measured at the beginning-of-period prices and returns are measured at the end-of-period value of money, that is, that they are valuated at different values of money. Returns, here, include holding gains on fixed assets.

Tables 9-1 and 9-2 show nominal rates of return with and without holding gain; these rates correspond to the rates of return on capital, ROC (BT), and ROC (AT), in the common glossary in Appendix 1A. Both rates of return show a decreasing trend, but the rate of return without holding gain is more stable than the rate with holding gain.

Table 9–2
Nominal[a] Rates of Return on Capital without Holding Gain
(percent)

	Before Tax				After Tax			
	(1)	(2)	(3)	(4)	(5)	(6)	(7)	(8)
1966	6.8	12.4	6.7	15.2	5.5	10.0	5.1	11.5
1967	7.3	13.6	7.3	16.8	5.8	10.8	5.5	12.6
1968	7.2	13.6	7.1	16.5	5.7	10.8	5.2	12.3
1969	7.2	14.0	7.0	17.0	5.6	11.0	5.0	12.3
1970	6.7	13.2	6.2	15.4	5.2	10.4	4.5	11.1
1971	6.0	11.6	5.4	13.0	4.9	9.5	4.0	9.8
1972	5.3	10.4	4.8	12.3	4.1	8.0	3.3	8.4
1973	3.0	6.2	2.0	5.6	1.6	3.4	0.3	0.8
1974	1.6	3.3	0.1	0.3	0.4	0.8	-1.3	-3.5
1975	3.3	6.1	2.2	4.9	2.4	4.3	1.0	2.3
1976	3.6	6.4	2.5	5.5	2.3	4.1	0.9	2.0
1977	3.5	6.2	2.6	5.6	2.3	4.0	1.1	2.3
1978	3.9	6.7	3.3	7.1	2.5	4.4	1.6	3.5
1979	3.3	6.0	2.6	5.8	1.8	3.1	0.6	1.4
1980	4.2	7.9	3.3	8.0	2.4	4.5	1.1	2.6
1981	5.0	9.9	4.3	11.0	3.4	6.7	2.4	6.1

Before Tax:
  (1) = Nominal Rates of Return on Total Assets ['ROC$_W$'(BT)]
  (2) = Nominal Rates of Return on Total Assets except Land ['ROC$_O$'(BT)]
  (3) = Nominal Rates of Return on Fixed Assets ['ROC$_F$'(BT)]
  (4) = Nominal Rates of Return on Fixed Assets except Land ['ROC$_A$'(BT)]
After Tax:
  (5) = Nominal Rates of Return on Total Assets ['ROC$_W$'(AT)]
  (6) = Nominal Rates of Return on Total Assets except Land ['ROC$_O$'(AT)]
  (7) = Nominal Rates of Return on Fixed Assets ['ROC$_F$'(AT)]
  (8) = Nominal Rates of Return on Fixed Assets except Land ['ROC$_A$'(AT)]

[a]"Nominal" means that assets are measured at the beginning-of-period prices and returns are measured at the end-of-period value of money, that is, that they are valuated at different values of money. Returns, here, exclude holding gains on fixed assets.

Rate of Return on Equity

Table 9–5 shows the nominal (with and without holding gains) and real rates of return on equity both before and after tax. The equity corresponds to the total capital. These rates are adjusted for gearing effects, according to our definition of the economic rates of return on equity. The rates exhibit fluctuations very similar to the *ROCW,* but are at

Table 9–3
Rates of Holding Gain
(percent)

	(1)	(2)	(3)	(4)	(5)	(6)	(7)	(8)
1965	6.4	1.1	5.2	1.6	0.0	0.0	0.0	0.0
1966	4.7	2.8	10.9	5.4	6.6	3.0	8.1	4.6
1967	4.2	1.4	15.8	3.4	8.3	1.8	10.2	2.8
1968	4.9	0.7	19.2	1.8	9.6	1.0	11.6	1.5
1969	6.4	3.3	21.5	4.5	11.9	2.7	14.4	4.1
1970	7.3	2.2	12.0	3.6	7.0	2.1	8.4	3.1
1971	5.7	-0.8	15.9	-0.1	7.6	-0.2	9.2	-0.3
1972	5.2	3.2	27.0	6.9	15.0	3.5	18.7	5.6
1973	16.1	22.7	25.5	24.2	20.0	14.1	24.9	23.7
1974	21.8	23.5	-6.6	17.2	2.7	12.7	3.3	19.5
1975	10.4	1.9	0.1	-0.4	0.2	0.3	0.3	0.5
1976	9.4	5.5	4.7	5.8	4.1	3.7	5.1	5.7
1977	6.7	0.4	3.4	3.2	2.3	1.5	2.9	2.3
1978	3.4	-2.3	9.4	3.7	4.7	1.2	5.9	1.8
1979	4.8	12.9	17.7	9.0	11.5	6.6	14.3	10.2
1980	7.8	13.3	14.6	6.7	10.0	5.8	12.3	9.1
1981	4.0	1.4	15.1	-0.9	7.5	0.0	9.2	0.0

(1) = Rates of Change in Consumer Price Index [CPI]
(2) = Rates of Change in Wholesale Price Index [WPI]
(3) = Rates of Change in Land Price [PL]
(4) = Rates of Change in Price of Equipment and Plant [PD]
(5) = Rates of Holding Gain on Total Assets [RH_W^n]
(6) = Rates of Holding Gain on Total Assets except Land [RH_O^n]
(7) = Rates of Holding Gain on Fixed Assets [RH_F^n]
(8) = Rates of Holding Gain on Fixed Assets except Land [RH_A^n]

much higher levels because of the effects of financial leverage on the rates of return on equity. As seen later, the debt to total capital ratio has an upward trend. If the level of the *ROCW* stays constant, a decrease in leverage lowers the *REQW*. But the recovery from the sharp drop in 1974 was so rapid that the falling trend cannot be clearly perceived.

Distribution of Returns on Capital and
Effective Tax Rate

Returns on capital are distributed among equity (stockholders), debt (creditors), and tax (the government). Whether rules for distribution

Table 9–4
Real[a] Rates of Return on Capital
(percent)

	Before Tax				After Tax			
	(1)	(2)	(3)	(4)	(5)	(6)	(7)	(8)
1966	8.3	10.3	9.7	14.5	7.0	7.9	8.1	10.9
1967	10.9	10.8	12.7	14.8	9.5	8.1	11.0	10.8
1968	11.3	9.2	13.1	12.4	9.9	6.6	11.4	8.4
1969	11.9	9.7	14.0	13.8	10.4	6.9	12.2	9.4
1970	5.9	7.5	6.8	10.5	4.6	4.8	5.2	6.5
1971	7.4	5.4	8.4	6.6	6.4	3.4	7.2	3.6
1972	14.3	8.2	17.4	12.1	13.2	6.0	16.0	8.4
1973	5.9	3.6	9.3	11.4	4.7	1.2	7.8	7.2
1974	-14.4	-4.8	-15.1	-1.6	-15.4	-6.9	-16.3	-4.8
1975	-6.2	-3.6	-7.2	-4.6	-7.1	-5.2	-8.2	-6.9
1976	-1.6	0.6	-1.6	1.7	-2.7	-1.5	-3.1	-1.6
1977	-0.8	0.9	-1.2	1.1	-2.0	-1.1	-2.6	-2.0
1978	5.0	4.4	5.6	5.3	3.7	2.1	4.0	1.9
1979	9.6	7.4	11.6	10.7	8.0	4.7	9.7	6.5
1980	5.9	5.5	7.2	8.6	4.2	2.3	5.2	3.6
1981	8.1	5.6	9.1	6.8	6.6	2.6	7.3	2.1

Before Tax:
  (1) = Real Rates of Return on Total Assets [$ROC_W^r(BT)$]
  (2) = Real Rates of Return on Total Assets except Land [$ROC_O^r(BT)$]
  (3) = Real Rates of Return on Fixed Assets [$ROC_F^r(BT)$]
  (4) = Real Rates of Return on Fixed Assets except Land [$ROC_A^r(BT)$]
After Tax:
  (5) = Real Rates of Return on Total Assets [$ROC_W^r(AT)$]
  (6) = Real Rates of Return on Total Assets except Land [$ROC_O^r(AT)$]
  (7) = Real Rates of Return on Fixed Assets [$ROC_F^r(AT)$]
  (8) = Real Rates of Return on Fixed Assets except Land [$ROC_A^r(AT)$]

[a]"Real" means that values of at the beginning-of-period assets at the beginning-of-period prices are transformed to those at end-of-period prices because returns are measured at the end-of-period values of money. This computation process makes this rate of return reflect both "Net Holding Gain" of fixed assets caused by the difference between the rate of holding gain and the rate of change in CPI, and deterioration of monetary assets.

of the return on capital have changed because of inflation (especially the taxes) is a matter of concern.

Table 9–6 shows the distribution ratios of the real return on capital to equity, debt and tax, and; for reference, the table also gives the distribution ratios of accounting return and inflation-adjusted operating income. Effective tax rates on real returns, both on capital and equity,

Table 9–5
Rates of Return on Equity with and without Holding Gain
(percent)

	Before Tax				After Tax			
(1)	(2)	(3)	(4)	(5)	(6)	(7)	(8)	(9)
1966	15.6	5.3	8.0	10.4	13.5	3.2	5.9	8.4	10.3
1967	18.8	6.1	8.3	14.0	16.5	3.8	6.1	11.8	12.7
1968	20.6	6.0	8.6	15.0	18.3	3.7	6.3	12.8	14.6
1969	23.9	5.9	9.2	16.4	21.5	3.5	6.8	14.2	18.0
1970	15.5	5.0	8.6	7.6	13.4	2.8	6.5	5.6	10.5
1971	15.6	4.0	7.0	9.4	13.9	2.4	5.3	7.8	11.6
1972	27.0	3.5	6.4	20.7	25.1	1.6	4.6	18.9	23.4
1973	30.2	0.0	8.3	12.2	28.1	-2.1	6.2	10.4	30.2
1974	1.4	-2.6	7.5	-16.8	-0.4	-4.4	5.8	-18.2	4.0
1975	0.1	-0.2	5.4	-9.3	-1.4	-1.7	3.9	-10.7	0.3
1976	6.8	0.2	5.9	-2.4	4.8	-1.9	3.8	-4.2	6.6
1977	4.4	0.8	4.8	-2.1	2.5	-1.2	2.8	-3.9	3.7
1978	9.4	2.0	4.0	5.8	7.3	-0.1	1.9	3.8	7.4
1979	18.7	0.9	3.6	13.3	16.3	-1.5	1.1	10.9	17.8
1980	16.8	1.4	5.7	8.4	14.0	-1.4	2.9	5.8	15.4
1981	14.5	3.0	5.1	10.0	12.0	0.6	2.7	7.7	11.4

Before Tax:

  (1) = Nominal Rates of Return on Equity with Holding Gain [$REQ^n(BT)$]
  (2) = Nominal Rates of Return on Equity without Holding Gain ['REQ'(BT)]
  (3) = Nominal Rates of Return on Equity with Gearing Effect and no Holding Gain ['REG'(BT)]
  (4) = Real Rates of Return on Equity with Net Holding Gain [$REQ^r(BT)$]
After Tax:
  (5) = Nominal Rates of Return on Equity with Holding Gain [$REQ^n(AT)$]
  (6) = Nominal Rates of Return on Equity without Holding Gain ['REQ'(AT)]
  (7) = Nominal Rates of Return on Equity with Gearing Effect and no Holding Gain ['REG'(AT)]
  (8) = Real Rates of Return on Equity with Net Holding Gain [$REQ^r(AT)$]
  (9) = Rates of Holding Gain on Equity [RH_s^n]

are also provided. It is remarkable that both of the effective tax rates increased dramatically after the first oil crisis, although large fluctuations resulted from the net holding gains. The increase in the tax burden can be understood in an accounting context, but it seems certain that the tax burden is increasing partly because more than net holding gains are taxed and partly because the taxes on corporate income are increasing.

Under special tax treatment legislation, the government had, for a long time, permitted corporations to retain tax-free earnings in order

Table 9–6

Accounting and Effective Tax Rates and Distribution Ratios on Return on Capital

(percent)

	on Accounting Return				on Inflation-adjusted Return				on Real Return on Capital			
	(1)	(2)	(3)	(4)	(5)	(6)	(7)	(8)	(9)	(10)	(11)	(12)
1966	18.0	46.0	36.0	33.3	19.7	50.3	30.1	39.5	15.4	19.9	64.7	19.3
1967	18.6	41.8	39.6	31.9	20.2	45.5	34.3	37.1	12.9	16.3	70.7	15.5
1968	19.1	42.4	38.5	33.2	20.6	45.8	33.7	38.0	12.5	13.5	74.0	14.4
1969	19.3	40.3	40.5	32.3	21.9	45.7	32.4	40.3	12.4	8.8	78.8	13.6
1970	18.9	44.2	36.9	33.9	21.4	50.1	28.4	43.0	22.4	14.2	63.3	26.1
1971	17.3	52.9	29.8	36.7	18.2	55.8	26.0	41.2	13.8	17.4	68.7	16.7
1972	19.6	49.3	31.1	38.7	22.8	57.2	20.0	53.2	8.0	7.6	84.4	8.6
1973	20.5	44.7	34.8	37.0	45.8	99.9	-45.7	90955.8	20.1	-35.5	115.4	14.9
1974	20.6	57.6	21.8	48.5	76.1	213.2	-189.3	-67.2	-6.9	20.3	86.6	-8.7
1975	20.4	73.3	6.3	76.5	29.0	104.2	-33.2	-692.3	-14.2	2.6	111.6	-14.5
1976	22.8	61.2	16.0	58.8	36.1	96.8	-32.9	1123.0	-75.3	5.3	170.0	-79.6
1977	24.4	61.0	14.6	62.5	34.4	86.1	-20.5	247.6	-137.2	-59.9	297.1	-85.8
1978	27.1	52.1	20.8	56.6	34.5	66.5	-1.1	103.2	25.9	25.8	48.3	34.9
1979	27.1	47.3	25.6	51.5	47.3	82.5	-29.8	270.2	15.8	10.5	73.8	17.6
1980	27.5	49.8	22.7	54.8	43.2	78.1	-21.2	196.9	28.5	7.8	63.7	30.9
1981	26.9	51.4	21.8	55.2	31.6	60.4	8.0	79.7	18.6	19.2	62.2	23.1

on Accounting Return:

(1) = Accounting Tax Rates on Return on Total Capital [tY^b]

(2) = Ratios of Return on Total Capital Shared to Debt [iY^b]

(3) = Ratios of Return on Total Capital Shared to Equity [pY^b]

(4) = Accounting Tax Rates on Return on Equity [tP]

on Inflation-adjusted Return:

(5) = Effective Tax Rates on Return on Total Capital ['tY']

(6) = Ratios of Return on Total Capital Shared to Debt ['iY']

(7) = Ratios of Return on Total Capital Shared to Equity ['pY']

(8) = Effective Tax Rates on Return on Equity [tP]

on Real Return on Capital:

(9) = Effective Tax Rates on Return on Total Capital [tE^r]

(10) = Ratios of Return on Total Capital Shared to Debt [iE^r]

(11) = Ratios of Return on Total Capital Shared to Equity [eqE^r]

(12) = Effective Tax Rates on Return on Equity [tEQ^r]

---

a Inflation-adjusted return expresses accounting operating income less adjustment of both cost of sales and depreciation.

b Real return on capital is inflation-adjusted operating income plus net holding gain on fixed assets less dilution of monetary assets, and real return on equity is real return on capital less interest payments on debt plus dilution of debt.

to encourage capital accumulation within corporations. After the oil crises, slow economic activity has resulted in decreased fiscal revenue. The government, therefore, began to apply taxation more strictly, in order to increase revenues. But the tax authorities did not make major changes in the tax system, including changes in tax rates.

Rate of Return to Investors

The rate of return to investors, realized through the capital markets, corresponds to the rate of return on capital to the companies. They appear in table 9–7 as the nominal rate and the real rate of return.

Table 9–7
Rates of Return to Investors and Capital Cost
(percent)

	(1)	(2)	(3)	(4)	(5)	(6)
1966	19.7	7.9	12.7	7.6	9.1	4.2
1967	2.0	7.7	5.4	1.2	9.9	5.5
1968	25.8	7.8	14.5	9.1	10.4	5.3
1969	31.6	7.9	17.6	10.5	9.8	3.2
1970	0.5	8.3	4.9	-2.2	8.9	1.5
1971	29.5	8.2	15.9	9.7	9.0	3.1
1972	76.0	7.4	33.4	26.8	7.0	1.8
1973	3.7	8.1	6.0	-8.7	2.5	-11.7
1974	-9.1	9.8	2.2	-16.1	0.7	-17.3
1975	8.5	9.4	9.1	-1.2	4.3	-5.5
1976	14.0	8.8	10.7	1.2	3.8	-5.1
1977	8.0	7.9	8.0	1.2	3.8	-2.7
1978	16.1	7.0	10.6	6.9	4.2	0.8
1979	6.8	7.6	7.3	2.4	2.9	-1.9
1980	9.6	9.3	9.4	1.5	3.9	-3.6
1981	17.5	8.9	12.6	8.3	5.6	1.5

(1) = Nominal Rates of Return on Common Stock [RS^n]
(2) = Nominal Interest Rates on Debt [RB^n]
(3) = Nominal Rates of Return to Investors [RCC^n]
(4) = Real Rates of Return to Investors [RCC^r]
(5) = Nominal Cost of Capital [$'\rho^n$]
(6) = Real Cost of Capital [$'\rho^r$]

This table also gives their components, rates of return on stocks, and estimated interest rates, as well as estimates of the cost of capital. Both nominal and real rates of return to investors do not have any trend, though they are subject to large fluctuations. The rates peaked in 1968–72 as a result of the boom caused by the so-called excess liquidity phenomena in the economy. But both rates also suffered a sharp drop, together, immediately after the first oil crisis. For several years after the first crisis, however, their movements are different, particularly in that real rates hovered around values under zero and recovered the old level rapidly. If the rates of return to investors reflect investors' expectations of the future, we can assume that investors have been optimistic recently, in spite of bitter experience.

Comparing the rate of return to investors with the rate of return on capital, the correlation coefficients—even those with lags—do not seem to be large enough. It may be necessary for us to compare these rates with each other through the use of another index.

Tobin's q Ratio

The valuation ratios, the so-called Tobin's q ratios, as calculated, are shown in table 9–8. Although our preferred concept of capital is the most inclusive one and therefore the ratio $q(W)$ is important for us, three other variants are shown as well.

The numerator of the q ratio is the total market value of the companies, estimated mainly by using data on the capital markets. On the other hand, the denominator is the total value of the revalued assets of the companies, calculated from financial data and data on the asset markets. Despite the fact that both the estimations are undertaken quite independently, the q ratios, especially $q(W)$, are marvelously stable. The peak in 1972 was caused by a boom in the stock market. In a simplified model, the q ratios in the equilibria of the capital markets and the asset markets can easily be proved to be unique. In reality, however, we cannot definitely determine the level because of differences in the market value of a company's assets and the company itself. As stated before, the practice of buying and selling firms is not popular in Japan, which means that assets cannot be sold as a whole, but only separately. Since the transaction costs of selling a company's existing assets are omitted, the possibility remains that the asset values might be overestimated. This means that the q ratios might be higher than in the present estimates.

Table 9–8
Tobin's _q_ Ratios

	(1)	(2)	(3)	(4)
1965	0.604	1.101	0.747	1.690
1966	0.587	1.092	0.720	1.666
1967	0.548	1.036	0.665	1.556
1968	0.573	1.118	0.693	1.691
1969	0.587	1.167	0.707	1.756
1970	0.541	1.050	0.657	1.597
1971	0.578	1.135	0.720	1.853
1972	0.656	1.353	0.817	2.279
1973	0.532	1.099	0.640	1.690
1974	0.547	1.002	0.662	1.471
1975	0.591	1.056	0.736	1.628
1976	0.602	1.055	0.753	1.629
1977	0.605	1.055	0.756	1.621
1978	0.617	1.102	0.770	1.710
1979	0.604	1.144	0.746	1.789
1980	0.610	1.207	0.750	1.907
1981	0.591	1.202	0.723	1.913

(1) = _q_ Ratio of Firm's Value to Total Assets [q(W)]
(2) = _q_ Ratio of Firm's Value to Total Assets except Land [q(O)]
(3) = _q_ Ratio of Firm's Value to Fixed Assets [q(F)]
(4) = _q_ Ratio of Firm's Value to Fixed Assets except Land [q(A)]

Ratio of Debt to Company Value

The level of financial leverage of a company is an important measure to determine how the business risk is borne by the equity. In Japanese companies, until recently, the equity-to-total capital ratios were very low and consistently decreased, which aroused much discussion among academics and business people.

Table 9–9 provides ratios of the book value of debt to the total book value of debt plus the market value of stock, and ratios of debt to total capitalization as derived from company records.

The latter ratio in terms of book value has been decreasing for a long time, but has increased recently, while the theoretically meaningful measure of financial leverage ratio in terms of market value remained at almost the same level, despite rather big fluctuations. Analysis of this behavior is left as a future problem.

Table 9–9
Ratio of Debt to Total Capital
(percent)

	(1)	(2)
1965	0.640	0.598
1966	0.640	0.592
1967	0.655	0.631
1968	0.664	0.592
1969	0.670	0.567
1970	0.681	0.635
1971	0.702	0.622
1972	0.704	0.518
1973	0.714	0.598
1974	0.733	0.643
1975	0.746	0.637
1976	0.746	0.621
1977	0.738	0.604
1978	0.728	0.576
1979	0.729	0.587
1980	0.716	0.568
1981	0.707	0.564

(1) = Ratio of Book Value of Debt to Total Book Value of Assets $[K_B]$
(2) = Ratio of Book Value of Debt to Market Value of Firm $[K_K]$

Notes

1. This data is commercially provided by Nihon Keizai Shimbun, Inc. (Japan Economic Journal, Inc.).

2. The shares of sample companies in the whole corporate sector have, however, been gradually decreasing on an accounting base.

	1965	1973	1982
Total assets	46%	38%	32%
Fixed assets	48%	36%	31%
Sales	34%	31%	28%
Operating income	47%	32%	37%

3. It can be proved as follows.

$$\frac{1 + ROC^n}{1 + CPI} - 1 = \frac{ROC^n - CPI}{1 + CPI}$$

$$= \frac{\dfrac{Y^r + \overline{W}_{-1} - \underline{W}_{-1}}{\underline{W}_{-1}} - CPI}{1 + CPI}$$

$$= \frac{Y^r + \overline{W} - \underline{W}_{-1} - \underline{W}_{-1} \cdot CPI}{\underline{W}_{-1}(1 + CPI)}$$

$$= \frac{Y^r + \underline{W}_{-1}\dfrac{\overline{W} - \underline{W}_{-1}}{\underline{W}_{-1}} - \underline{W}_{-1} \cdot CPI}{\underline{W}_{-1}(1 + CPI)}$$

$$= \frac{Y^r + \underline{W}_{-1}(RH_W - CPI)}{\underline{W}_{-1}(1 + CPI)}$$

$$= ROC^R.$$

4. In the estimation process, accounting profits from business operations (A) were not calculated as the sum (B) of ordinary profits plus interest payments, but as net operating income. (A) and (B) do not coincide because there are other kinds of nonoperating income and expenses in addition to interest payments and interest received. The reason for using the net operating income is that in the Japanese accounting system, ordinary income may often contain profits or losses arising from revaluation of assets. Such profits and losses should be omitted in order to avoid the danger of double counting.

5. The rate of investment is calculated as the ratio of gross amount of investment to total capital at current value ($W^b - W_{-1}^b + D / W_{-1}^n$).

References

Bank of Japan, *Economic Statistics Annual*.
———, *Price Indices Annual*.
Economic Planning Agency, *Annual Reports on National Accounts*.
Holland, Daniel M., and Stewart C. Myers, "Profitability and Capital Costs for Manufacturing Corporations and All Nonfinancial Corporations," *American Economic Review*, 70, no. 2 (1980).
Japan Securities Research Institute, *The Rates of Return on the Listed Stocks* (Annual).
Ministry of Finance, *Incorporated Enterprise Statistics* (Annual).
Ministry of Home Affairs, *Survey of Fixed Assets* (Annual).

National Land Agency, *Public Announcement of Land Prices* (Annual).

Takaaki Wakasugi and Fumiko Kon-ya, "Rate of Return on Capital and Tobin's 'q'," *Keisokushitsu Technical Paper,* no. 52 (December 1980), no. 56 (August 1982) (in Japanese).

Takaaki Wakasugi, Kazuhiko Nishina, and Moriaki Tsuchiya, "Trends in Returns on Capital in Postwar Japan," *The Journal of Economics* (Tokyo), 42, no. 2 (1976), 42, no. 3 (1976) (in Japanese).

Appendix 9A
Data

Table 9A1
Assets
(billion yen)

	Inventory		Equipment & Plant		Land		Monetary[b]	Total Assets	
	B.V.[a]	M.V.[a]	B.V.	M.V.	B.V.	M.V.	B.V.	B.V.	M.V.
1965	3,609	3,612	8,228	8,565	870	15,389	6,513	19,220	34,080
1966	3,969	3,977	8,601	9,435	1,028	17,630	7,046	20,644	38,088
1967	4,934	4,938	9,495	10,777	1,265	21,052	7,885	23,578	44,651
1968	5,680	5,683	10,729	12,285	1,504	25,861	9,211	27,124	53,040
1969	7,045	7,061	12,516	14,744	1,826	32,361	11,001	32,388	65,166
1970	8,707	8,720	14,441	17,343	2,112	37,285	13,567	38,826	76,916
1971	9,444	9,438	16,253	18,496	2,460	43,948	17,664	45,821	89,546
1972	10,734	10,759	17,777	20,924	2,869	56,707	21,685	53,066	110,075
1973	15,740	15,993	19,539	28,058	3,385	72,295	23,712	62,376	140,059
1974	20,449	20,819	21,836	35,156	3,791	68,340	26,161	72,237	150,476
1975	20,691	20,725	23,484	36,353	4,153	69,231	30,926	79,254	157,235
1976	21,220	21,312	25,364	41,547	4,455	73,078	34,175	85,215	170,112
1977	20,937	20,944	27,290	46,175	4,785	76,693	35,972	88,985	179,784
1978	21,222	21,185	29,107	47,793	5,050	84,127	38,025	93,403	191,130
1979	25,250	25,473	31,607	45,545	5,449	99,376	40,104	102,411	210,499
1980	29,230	29,497	34,011	44,623	5,863	114,415	43,021	112,125	231,555
1981	31,058	31,089	36,855	48,096	6,235	130,233	46,834	120,982	256,250

[a]B.V. = book value, M.V. = market value.
[b]Monetary = net monetary assets [M].

Table 9A2
Equity and Debt
(billion yen)

	Equity		Debt	Firm's Value	
	B.V.[a]	M.V.[b]	B.V.	B.V.	M.V.
1965	6,915	8,275	12,306	19,220	20,581
1966	7,424	9,129	13,220	20,644	22,349
1967	8,136	9,013	15,442	23,578	24,455
1968	9,119	12,386	18,006	27,124	30,392
1969	10,693	16,586	21,695	32,388	38,281
1970	12,385	15,170	26,442	38,826	41,612
1971	13,633	19,565	32,187	45,821	51,752
1972	15,687	34,830	37,379	53,066	72,209
1973	17,851	29,926	44,525	62,376	74,451
1974	19,321	29,416	52,916	72,237	82,332
1975	20,114	33,763	59,140	79,254	92,903
1976	21,643	38,822	63,572	85,215	102,394
1977	23,289	43,081	65,696	88,985	108,777
1978	25,430	49,950	67,973	93,403	117,923
1979	27,778	52,436	74,633	102,411	127,069
1980	31,853	61,089	80,273	112,125	141,362
1981	35,486	65,959	85,496	120,982	151,455

[a]B.V. = book value
[b]M.V. = market value

Table 9A3
Return on Capital
(billion yen)

	(1)	(2)	(3)	(4)	(5)	(6)	(7)	(8)	(9)	(10)	(11)
1965	1,673	443	38	44	2,034	0	0	0	0	389	0
1966	2,068	474	102	114	2,326	306	945	639	2,965	457	2,508
1967	2,500	522	60	186	2,778	296	1,858	1,562	4,339	561	3,778
1968	2,844	625	36	216	3,217	386	2,469	2,083	5,300	662	4,637
1969	3,562	769	204	311	3,817	590	3,495	2,906	6,723	834	5,888
1970	3,938	985	168	414	4,341	803	615	-188	4,153	931	3,222
1971	3,651	1,189	-70	321	4,590	773	2,230	1,457	6,047	836	5,211
1972	4,193	1,291	313	446	4,725	919	9,706	8,788	13,513	1,077	12,436
1973	5,896	1,553	2,935	1,184	3,331	3,491	7,735	4,244	7,575	1,525	6,050
1974	6,156	2,070	4,165	1,838	2,223	5,169	-21,550	-26,720	-24,497	1,691	-26,188
1975	4,871	2,272	382	1,735	5,026	2,721	-12,606	-15,326	-10,300	1,459	-11,759
1976	6,410	2,441	1,127	2,127	5,596	2,907	-5,371	-8,278	-2,681	2,020	-4,701
1977	6,002	2,460	82	2,385	5,994	2,290	-5,208	-7,498	-1,504	2,064	-3,568
1978	6,682	2,187	-473	2,391	6,952	1,223	3,546	2,323	9,275	2,401	6,874
1979	8,744	2,385	2,934	1,812	6,383	1,825	14,576	12,751	19,134	3,018	16,116
1980	10,654	3,134	3,548	1,449	8,791	3,128	7,658	4,529	13,321	3,775	9,526
1981	10,210	3,361	413	1,615	11,543	1,721	9,747	8,026	19,569	3,645	15,924

(1) = Accounting Operating Income excluding Revenues from Monetary Assets
(2) = Revenues from Monetary Assets (Interest and Dividends Received)
(3) = Adjustment of Cost of Sales
(4) = Adjustment of Depreciation
(5) = Inflation Adjusted Operating Income (Real Return on Total Capital without Holding Gain) = (1) + (2) − (3) − (4) [γ^r]
(6) = Dilution of Monetary Assets [m]
(7) = Net Holding Gain of Fixed Assets [H_F]
(8) = Net Holding Gain of Total Capital = (7) − (6) [H_W]
(9) = Real Return on Capital = (5) + (8) [E^r]
(10) = Corporate Income Tax [T]
(11) = After-tax Real Return on Capital with Net Holding Gain = (9) − (10)

Table 9A4
Return on Equity
(billion yen)

	(1)	(2)	(3)	(4)	(Billion Yen) (5)	(6)
1965	1,109	925	0	0	0	0
1966	1,169	1,157	578	1,218	2,375	1,917
1967	1,264	1,512	555	2,118	3,629	3,068
1968	1,472	1,745	757	2,839	4,584	3,922
1969	1,745	2,072	1,152	4,058	6,130	5,296
1970	2,175	2,166	1,584	1,396	3,562	2,631
1971	2,561	2,029	1,507	2,964	4,993	4,157
1972	2,702	2,023	1,674	10,462	12,484	11,408
1973	3,329	2	6,018	10,262	10,264	8,739
1974	4,740	-2,517	9,706	-17,013	-19,530	-21,222
1975	5,237	-211	5,503	-9,823	-10,034	-11,493
1976	5,417	180	5,559	-2,719	-2,539	-4,559
1977	5,160	834	4,259	-3,239	-2,405	-4,469
1978	4,625	2,327	2,234	4,557	6,884	4,483
1979	5,266	1,117	3,263	16,013	17,130	14,112
1980	6,864	1,928	5,821	10,351	12,278	8,484
1981	6,969	4,574	3,211	11,237	15,811	12,166

(1) = Interest Payment [I(P)]
(2) = Inflation Adjusted Net Income (Real Return on Equity without Holding Gain) [P^r]
(3) = Dilution of Debt [g]
(4) = Net Holding Gain of Equity [H$_s^r$]
(5) = Real Return on Equity with Net Holding Gain [EQ^r]
(6) = After-tax Real Return on Equity with Net Holding Gain

Appendix 9B
Rate of Return on Capital in the Nonfinancial Sector Based on SNA

The Old and the New SNA in Japan

Before going into an explanation of the measurement procedure, we have to make clear the essential difference between the old and the new SNA in Japan. For stock variables, the new SNA, which provides data for the years after 1969, offers the current values of every asset in the annual balance sheet of the corporate sector as a whole, whereas the old SNA reports the balance sheet data at current value for every five years until 1970. As for the flow values, both systems provide essentially the same data for identical time intervals, that is, annually and quarterly.

Although it could be possible to estimate the stock values in the years neglected in the old SNA, we did not attempt it here because no reliable data other than the old SNA were available to support the estimation. Since one of the purposes of our estimation is to prepare rate of return statistics for future research, we decided to restrict our estimates to the published data. Therefore, we measured the rate of return only from 1970 to 1980.

The Assumptions and the Outline of Measurement

The purpose of this section is to measure the rate of return on capital (ROC) for the nonfinancial corporate sector in Japan. It is usual that a specified objective, which necessarily defines the variables in the measurement procedure, is established in research like this. But our primary concern is simply to develop estimates of profitability during the period of recent inflation. Without a concrete objective for estimation, it is apparently difficult to examine the adequacy of the measurement method as well as the desirability of the data employed. In that case we must begin by explaining the theoretical assumptions upon which the measurement is based.

We intended to measure the profitability of the nonfinancial corporate sector as a whole. The reason we exclude the financial corporations is as follows. When we focus on the efficiency of capital employed in the production process, the activities of financial intermediaries are essentially different from those of nonfinancial firms. And more important is the fact that, if we aggregate the profits of all industries, we would be double counting a large portion of the financial industries' profits.

Here we do not include as profit any holding gains that might occur in reported corporate profit during a period of inflation. In other words, profit by our definition is brought about only by production activities of goods and services, not by price fluctuation. And this corresponds to the inflation-adjusted operating income, Y^r, in the text.

The Measurement Procedure

Following the assumptions stated in the previous section, we take the operating surplus as the return on capital. The operating surplus for the nonfinancial corporate sector is reported in Income and Outlay Accounts by Institutional Sectors. All statistical materials underlined are contained in the new SNA hereafter.[1]

In these accounts, the operation surplus is calculated after subtracting the holding gain in inventories, whereas the depreciation is taken to be a value on book base. Therefore, the only problem we must solve in deriving the return on capital is estimating depreciation based on replacement cost.

Depreciation at Replacement Cost

While, in Income and Outlay Accounts by Institutional Sectors, depreciation appears to be a book value, in the Closing Balance Sheet Accounts the depreciable asset is measured at replacement cost. If the difference between the depreciation at replacement cost and at book value is available, we can measure the necessary figures easily. This is the case only for Consolidated Accounts for the Nation, and not for Nonfinancial Incorporated Enterprise.

On Capital Finance Account in Consolidated Accounts for the Nation, the item of statistical discrepancies signifies the difference between replacement cost and book value depreciation. Then, by adding this amount to the depreciation in Gross Domestic Product and Expenditure, where depreciation is on book base, we obtain the depreciation consistent with the current value of depreciable assets for the nation as a whole.

If we can assume that the statistical discrepancies of the nation and nonfinancial corporate sector occurred in proportion to their depreciation at book value, we can get an estimate of the depreciation for the nonfinancial corporate sector.[2]

We regard the difference between this estimated amount and the reported depreciation to be the deficiency in depreciation needed to maintain the real value of capital. If the former is larger than the latter, the profit reported in the nonfinancial corporate sector contains a holding gain that should not have been consumed.

Inflation-Adjusted Return on Capital

Following our assumptions, we corrected the reported operating surplus by adding the amount we calculated previously. We call in inflation-adjusted return on capital, which does not contain any holding gains related to either the depreciable assets or inventories.

We have inflation-adjusted return for after and before corporate tax payment.

Current Values of Productive Assets

The assets in the Closing Balance-sheet Accounts of Nonfinancial Incorporated Enterprises consist of such items as

1. Inventories
2. Net Fixed Assets (Depreciable Assets)
3. Nonreproducible Fixed Assets
   Land
   Forests
   Underground resources
4. Financial Assets

All of these items are measured in current prices.

Since we are to observe the profitability of capital utilized in a production process, the denominator of the rate of return on capital should be the total capital employed in the nonfinancial corporate sector.

For an individual firm, it is impossible to get rid of any asset on the balance sheet to isolate the productive assets. But we should exclude at least some of the financial assets in order to avoid double counting of capital when we aggregate the assets of all nonfinancial corporations. It is obscure and often meaningless, however, to distinguish one financial asset from another. Therefore, we aggregate the three items inventories, net fixed assets and nonreproducible assets to be the capital employed.

Table 9B1
SNA
(billion yen)

			—Nation—		
	Total Assets	Net Fixed Assets	Financial Assets	Depreciation	Statistical Discrepancy
1970	545,861	88,240	248,690	9,848	−65.5
1971	644,509	107,257	294,193	11,063	250.8
1972	788,975	132,501	357,168	12,997	−472.8
1973	998,684	178,068	439,603	15,495	−1,285.5
1974	1,182,830	233,737	519,184	18,006	80.0
1975	1,320,460	272,808	595,354	19,313	670.0
1976	1,477,780	307,014	686,314	21,288	−52.5
1977	1,642,430	344,869	780,351	24,034	1,415.3
1978	1,830,870	381,460	880,862	26,379	1,571.3
1979	2,090,570	435,601	994,595	28,939	1,011.9
1980	2,385,120	498,321	1,111,720	31,516	190.3

Inflation-Adjusted Rate of Return on Capital

Our primary purpose is to observe profitability, not to analyze the measured result. If we wish to explore an underlying feature of the trend or the level of profitability, obviously far more data and measurements would be necessary. Observing the results in tables 9B1 and 9B2, we should, however, take into account the assumptions for the measurement.

During the measurement period, the *ROC* was declining. For reference, we show a figure of rate of return on capital reported in Incorporated Enterprise Statistics, which is published annually by the Ministry of Finance.[3] The figures in it are made up of the aggregated data in financial statements of all nonfinancial corporations. In figure 9B1 we see a clear difference in the rate of return based on current

Table 9B2
Rates of Return on Capital for Nonfinancial Corporate Sector

1970	12.9%
1971	10.2
1972	9.6
1973	8.7
1974	6.9
1975	6.2
1976	7.0
1977	6.9
1978	7.6
1979	7.0
1980	7.0

Table 9B1 *(continued)*

					Economic Return	
	Net Fixed	*Financial*		*Operating Surplus*		
Total Assets	*Assets*	*Assets*	*Depreciation*	*(Return)*	*Before Tax*	*After Tax*
188,402	43,425	80,103	6,980	13,882.3	13,928.7	11,301.1
221,640	53,481	92,497	7,769	13,290.2	13,114.1	10,243.9
265,221	64,939	108,333	9,158	14,779.4	15,112.6	12,226.1
336,519	85,940	132,896	10,884	16,852.8	17,755.8	13,680.8
404,076	113,129	154,446	12,321	17,250.8	17,196.1	10,977.5
445,906	130,866	169,092	12,448	17,654.6	17,222.8	11,892.5
485,872	143,372	188,861	13,158	20,722.9	20,755.4	15,554.8
521,442	156,741	205,556	14,668	22,530.8	21.767.0	15,812.9
559,352	168,906	220,690	15,707	26,671.3	25,735.7	18,811.3
627,308	187,726	224,764	16,993	27,381.9	26,787.7	19,084.2
710,600	212,194	269,099	18,175	30,848.7	30,739.0	21,576.0

—Nonfinancial Corporation—

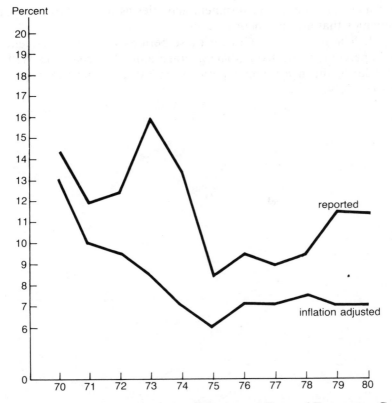

Figure 9B1. Inflation-Adjusted and Reported Rate of Return on Capital *(ROC)* for Nonfinancial Corporate Sector

value and on book value. There are distinctively opposite movements from 1971 to 1973 and from 1978 to 1979. The rates of increase of WPI for these two periods were 12.5 percent and 12.9 percent per year, respectively, and they have been the highest in this decade.[4] Many important factors characterize those two periods, represented by the oil crises, drastic change in international money market conditions, and so on.

Notes

1. The System of National Accounting (SNA) is published by the Economic Planning Agency as *Annual Report of National Accounts*. All accounts cited in appendix 9B are found in this publication.

2. These data are shown in the Table 9B1.

3. The number of nonfinancial corporations contained in Incorporated Enterprise Statistics is smaller than that of SNA. The latter contains some part of government activities as well as large corporate activities that are not incorporated.

4. The increases in CPI for those periods were 10.59 percent and 4.78 percent, respectively. The average annual increases in WPI and CPI during the measurement period were 7.07 percent and 8.54 percent, respectively.

10

Rates of Return, Cost of Capital, and Valuation Rates in Finnish Manufacturing 1960–1980

Heikki Koskenkylä

The international background to this investigation is the ongoing debate and argument that started in the mid-1970s about the development and possible decline in the rate of return on corporate capital in most Western countries. The potential significance of the behavior of corporate profitability is clear, but its actual development over time has raised many theoretical and empirical issues.

W. Nordhaus laid the ground for this discussion by concluding that in the postwar period (1948–1970) the rate of return revealed a downtrend in corporate profitability in the United States.[1] Feldstein and Summers (1977), on the other hand, disputed this finding, their conclusion being that "our analysis of these rates of return provides no support for the view that there has been a gradual decline in the rate of return over the post-war period." Von Furstenberg and Malkiel (1977) also doubt the argument for the overall decline in profitability. Instead they emphasize the importance of the reduction in real indebtedness for developments in profits and retained earnings.

Holland and Myers (1978, 1980) have carefully analyzed the performance of U.S. nonfinancial corporations since the war by using both rates of return to investors and return on capital. They conclude that these corporations have fared poorly since the mid-1960s, but they, too, were unable to find evidence of a clear long-term downtrend.

In many other countries studies in this field have found evidence of a significant downtrend in corporate profitability over the last decade and especially following the first oil crisis in 1973. Reference can be made here to the studies carried out in the United Kingdom and Sweden.[2] International organizations have also devoted attention to changes in and measurement of company profitability in the latter half of the 1970s (the Organisation for Economic Cooperation and Development, etc.).

The collection of statistical data and the calculations used in this chapter were carried out by Sirpa Wallius. Seija Leino typed the manuscript for this chapter, and the language was checked by Malcolm Waters.

387

Given this background the principal objective of the present study is the analysis of the performance of the Finnish manufacturing sector in the period 1960–1980. The analysis is restricted to manufacturing companies because of data limitations. The performance of these companies is examined by means of various indicators. The main emphasis is on the movements in and measurement of rates of return on capital, although some calculations of Tobin's q variable are also made. The second purpose is to analyze the behavior of capital costs in the manufacturing sector. Finally, we attempt to discover statistically whether there has been a trend in profitability.

The basic data used in the calculations of this report are taken from official national income accounts, but use is also made of firms' balance sheet data (book accounts), industrial statistics, and capital market data.

The chapter is organized as follows: in the next section various estimates of total capital, physical capital, own capital, and debt equity ratios are presented. We also discuss the basic formulas for calculating the economic rate of profit, or operating income, and the official (statutory) and effective tax rates for manufacturing industries. The following section attempts to trace the development of real profitability in manufacturing by developing various estimates of the real rate of return on total and own capital. The section entitled "The Valuation Ratio and the Cost of Capital" provides an analysis of developments in the cost of capital and the valuation ratio (Tobin's q) in relation to the real rate of return. In the section entitled "Determinants of the Rate of Return and the Effective Tax Rate" we perform some simple regression analysis of the determinants of the rate of return and try to discover whether or not there has been a trend in profitability. A similar test is also carried out for effective tax rates. Finally, in "Conclusions" we present the conclusions of this investigation.

Total Capital, Own Capital, and the Rate of Profit

Total Capital and Its Components

The concept and measurement of capital is a complicated task both from the theoretical and the empirical point of view. The main problems usually arise in connection with the stock of physical assets, that is, plant, equipment, land, and inventories. It is generally assumed that fairly reliable estimates of financial assets can be derived from official statistics.

In this study estimates of total capital in manufacturing have had to be drawn from a variety of statistical sources and earlier Finnish studies. Both national income accounts and balance sheet data have been used in these calculations. The time series for fixed capital stock, K, was constructed by means of the perpetual inventory method,

$$K_t = I_t^g + (1-\delta)K_{t-1}, \tag{10.1}$$

where the average depreciation coefficient δ is 7.8 percent per annum. Variable K includes equipment and plant, that is, $K = E + B$ (see the Common Glossary). Variable I^g stands for manufacturing gross investment (in 1975 prices) and is obtained from national income statistics. The current value of this net capital stock is obtained by multiplying by the price index of investment goods.

In earlier calculations of fixed capital stock we used a somewhat lower estimate of the depreciation coefficient (5.4 percent) than in the present calculations (7.8 percent). The estimates of fixed capital stock used here were constructed by the Central Statistical Office of Finland. Figure 10–1 shows the development of the current value (net replacement cost value) of fixed capital stock in the Finnish manufacturing sector as well as the other components of total capital.

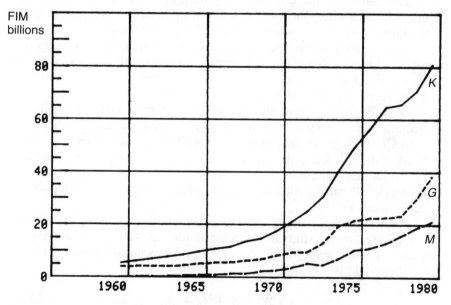

Figure 10–1. Current Value of Fixed Capital Stock *(K)*, Inventories *(G)*, and Net Financial Assets *(M)* in Finnish Manufacturing, 1960–1980

The use of Finnish data for the estimation of the current value of inventories raises various problems, which have been analyzed in some other Finnish studies (Salo, 1977; Ylä-Anttila and Heikkilä, 1980). In Finland, the practice of revaluing inventories according to the first-in-first-out (FIFO) principle is applied in taxation. It is, however, permissible to enter into the accounts certain future inventory expenses, that is, inventories can be undervalued. Since 1969, the maximum rate of undervaluation has been 50 percent of the acquisition cost of inventories. Earlier the maximum rate was 100 percent. In effect this undervaluation means that nowadays 50 percent of the value of inventories (at historic cost) can be regarded as expenses when calculating the taxable income.

In this way, companies can create "hidden reserves," or tax credits, which can at least to some extent be regarded as comparable to other components of own capital. This question will be discussed in the next section when estimating the own capital of Finnish manufacturing companies. The rationale behind this undervaluation lies partly in the fact that during inflationary periods the FIFO principle operates so that the increase in the value of inventories is transferred to sales income and hence becomes taxable income. Undervaluation is designed to exempt, at least partially, these nominal capital gains from corporate income taxation. It is worth mentioning that during the 1970s companies' profitability levels did not allow full use of undervaluation.

Figure 10–1 shows the estimated current value of inventories (G) for the Finnish manufacturing sector. To obtain this series both the undervaluation correction and inflation adjustment were made on the book value of inventories.[3]

Finally, figure 10–1 also shows the net monetary assets (M) of manufacturing companies. Variable M is defined according to the Common Glossary (financial assets minus accounts payable) and this series is taken directly from the enterprise data. It can, however, be regarded as a reliable estimate of the current value of net financial assets since no major valuation problems arise in connection with the various items of financial assets.

From the foregoing it can be seen that the basic concept of total capital used in this study includes the following assets: plant and equipment (K) plus inventories (G) plus net financial assets (M).[4] Hence total capital (W) is equal to

$$W = K + G + M, \qquad (10.2)$$

where $K = B + E$. In calculating the value of own capital, however, we use the following concept of total capital:

$$\overline{W} = K + G + M^g, \tag{10.3}$$

where M^g = gross financial assets. Total physical capital (F) is defined as

$$F = K + G. \tag{10.4}$$

Figure 10–2 shows various estimates of total capital in Finnish manufacturing. In addition to the standard estimates of the current values of total assets and total physical (fixed) assets the book value of all assets $(\overline{W}_B)$ is also shown.

Own Capital and Debt Ratios

The analysis of the preceding section provides the basis for estimating the "true" value of own capital of the Finnish manufacturing sector. The basic estimate of own capital (OC) is obtained by subtracting the

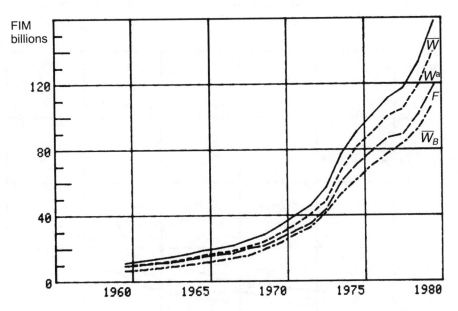

ᵃ Calculated using M.

Figure 10–2. Current Values of Total Assets $(\overline{W}$ and $W^a)$ and Total Fixed Assets (F) and Book Value (Historic Cost) of Total Assets $(\overline{W}_B)$ in Finnish Manufacturing 1960–1980

book value of debt capital (D_B) from the current value of total assets, that is,

$$OC = \overline{W} - D_B,\tag{10.5}$$

where the book value of debt is obtained from the official enterprise statistics. This method of estimating the value of own capital produces a maximum value, since the total amount of various "hidden reserves" is included in the concept of own capital. These "hidden reserves" are largely created as a result of accelerated depreciation rules and under-valuation of inventories. An estimate of the total value of these "hidden reserves" is obtained by subtracting the book value of all assets ($\overline{W}_B$) from the current value of all assets.

If it is assumed that a certain portion of these reserves, given by the proportional statutory tax rate (u) belongs to the debt capital (in the form of interest-free tax credits), another measure of own capital is obtained (OC_u). The portion $(1 - u)$ of the "hidden reserves" hence belongs to own capital.[5] Figure 10–3 shows the two different estimates of own capital (OC and OC_u) as well as the book value of own capital. Table 10–1 shows three different measures of the ratio of debt to own

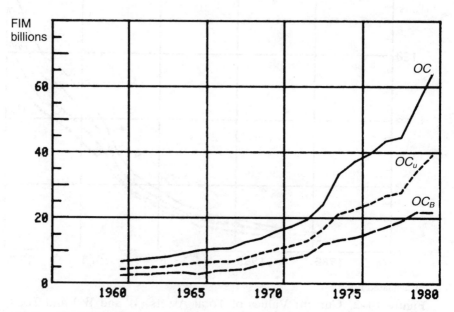

Figure 10–3. Estimates of Own Capital in Finnish Manufacturing 1960–1980

Table 10-1
The Ratio of Debt to Own Capital in Finnish
Manufacturing 1960-80

Year	e_1	e_2	e_3
1960	0.69	1.58	1.84
1961	0.72	1.61	1.88
1962	0.78	1.71	2.05
1963	0.82	1.77	2.11
1964	0.83	1.83	2.26
1965	0.87	1.91	2.94
1966	0.92	1.98	2.50
1967	1.07	2.23	2.72
1968	1.01	2.19	2.81
1969	1.08	2.08	2.46
1970	1.15	2.24	2.73
1971	1.30	2.42	2.93
1972	1.35	2.51	2.99
1973	1.36	2.44	2.70
1974	1.32	2.63	3.28
1975	1.43	3.00	3.80
1976	1.54	3.11	3.91
1977	1.55	3.15	3.92
1978	1.63	3.20	3.82
1979	1.45	2.89	3.57
1980	1.47	3.02	4.30
Average	1.16	2.36	2.93

capital (e). The first ratio (e_1) is defined as the ratio of the book value of debt to the maximum value of own capital, that is, $e_1 = D_B/OC$. The second ratio (e_2) is defined as the ratio of the book value of debt plus "tax credits" to the OC_u measure of own capital. The third ratio (e_3) is defined as the ratio of the book value of debt to the book value of own capital. From table 10-1 it can be seen that all these debt-own capital ratios have increased in a trendwise manner. There remains, however, a significant difference between the levels of various debt ratios.

Profit, Taxes, and Effective Tax Rate

In this section the formulas for determining "economic" profits and taxes are derived, together with their estimates, using both national income accounts and balance sheet statistics. Estimates of tax rates and holding gains on fixed capital are also presented. The standard national income accounts definition of the current value added (Q) in manufacturing production is as follows

$$Q = N + D + I + P^b, \tag{10.6}$$

where

Q = value-added in production (current price)
N = total labor costs
D = Depreciation charges (economic rate of depreciation)
I = net interest payments ($= rD_B$)
P^b = gross profits, that is, profits before taxes.

The values of variables Q and N are taken directly from the national income accounts data. An estimate of the economic depreciation charges ($\delta q K$) is calculated in conjunction with the estimates of fixed capital stock. The series for net interest payments (interest expenses minus interest revenues) originates from enterprise statistics. From this basic formula for value-added production, profits before taxes are determined as

$$P^b = Q - N - D - I. \tag{10.7}$$

Income from operations (operating income) is defined as

$$Y = P^b + I = P^a + T + I, \tag{10.8}$$

where

P^a = profits after taxes
T = direct corporate income taxes (paid in)

and hence $P^b = P^a + T$.

Table 10–2 shows the percentage distribution of operating income in its three components. It can be seen that the relative proportion of interest payments has risen in a trendwise manner reflecting both the continuous increase in the debt-equity ratio and in the interest rate level. Table 10–2 also indicates a declining trend in the share of income taxes. This is also reflected in the declining effective tax rates for the manufacturing sector, as can be seen in table 10–3. The effective tax rate on operating income is defined as

$$t_y = \frac{T}{Y} \tag{10.9}$$

Table 10–2
The Distribution of Operating Income into Its Components
(percent)

Year	Net Profit	Taxes	Interest
1960	70.40	19.10	10.50
1961	69.30	18.86	11.85
1962	59.45	22.94	17.61
1963	62.11	19.82	18.07
1964	61.52	18.99	19.49
1965	55.60	20.58	23.82
1966	48.36	23.65	27.99
1967	47.78	20.32	31.90
1968	59.68	14.35	25.97
1969	71.20	10.21	18.59
1970	71.94	8.84	19.22
1971	57.06	11.52	31.42
1972	58.76	9.56	31.68
1973	62.87	8.74	28.39
1974	69.93	6.43	23.64
1975	44.02	11.93	44.05
1976	27.29	16.13	56.57
1977	16.42	15.05	68.53
1978	40.97	9.50	49.52
1979	58.38	8.04	33.58
1980	54.19	8.32	37.49
Average	55.58	14.42	29.99

and is hence the share of paid corporate income tax in total operating income.

Table 10–3 shows that the statutory tax rate, consisting of both state and local taxes, was virtually constant in the 1970s.[6] The decline of the effective rate largely stems from accelerated depreciation charges and the undervaluation of inventories.[7] Finnish manufacturing companies have been able to manipulate their taxable income with these two methods in order to avoid paying higher income tax in times of rising inflation rates.[8]

In measuring the value of true economic profits in this section we have not taken into account the effect of holding gains on existing fixed capital stock. This is done separately here since the role of holding gains on physical assets is a matter of some dispute. It can be argued that firms seldom sell their physical assets (investment goods) and hence do not realize these holding gains except in the case of inventories. The nominal relative holding gains on total physical assets (F) are defined as

$$1 + p_F = \frac{1 + p^*}{1 + p^{**}}, \tag{10.10}$$

Table 10–3
Statutory and Effective Income Tax Rates in Finnish
Manufacturing 1960–80

Year	u^c	t_y [a]	t_p [b]
1960	0.50	0.19	0.21
1961	0.50	0.19	0.21
1962	0.55	0.23	0.28
1963	0.50	0.20	0.24
1964	0.57	0.19	0.24
1965	0.61	0.21	0.27
1966	0.61	0.24	0.33
1967	0.62	0.20	0.30
1968	0.72	0.14	0.19
1969	0.63	0.10	0.13
1970	0.61	0.09	0.11
1971	0.58	0.12	0.17
1972	0.58	0.10	0.14
1973	0.58	0.09	0.12
1974	0.58	0.06	0.08
1975	0.59	0.12	0.21
1976	0.59	0.16	0.37
1977	0.59	0.15	0.48
1978	0.59	0.10	0.19
1979	0.59	0.08	0.12
1980	0.59	0.08	0.13
Average	0.58	0.14	0.22

[a] $t_y = T/Y$.
[b] $t_p = T/P^b$.
[c] u = statutory rate.

where

p^* = annual rate of change of the current value of total
fixed assets (F)

p^{**} = annual rate of change of the volume (at 1975 prices)
of F.

Thus the variable p_F measures the annual rate of change of the implicit
price index for total physical assets.

The relative real holding gains are measured by the formula

$$p_{F,r} = \frac{(1 + p_F)}{(1 + p_{CP})} - 1, \tag{10.11}$$

where real holding gains are measured relative to the development of
the general price level (p_{CP} = rate of change in the CPI).

Table 10–4 shows the percentage nominal and real holding gains

Table 10–4
Nominal and Real Holding Gains on Total Fixed Assets in Finnish Manufacturing 1961–80
(percent)

Year	Nominal P_F	Real $P_{F,r}$
1961	1.81	0.01
1962	3.73	−0.70
1963	4.81	−0.06
1964	5.59	−4.32
1965	5.62	0.76
1966	2.14	−1.73
1967	6.34	1.71
1968	10.33	0.70
1969	4.78	2.51
1970	8.06	5.19
1971	10.14	3.42
1972	11.66	4.68
1973	20.03	8.40
1974	24.72	6.65
1975	13.38	−3.78
1976	10.27	−3.56
1977	10.35	−2.05
1978	3.98	−3.34
1979	7.86	0.53
1980	9.36	−1.98
Average	8.75	0.65

on total fixed assets. From table 10–4 it can be noted that percentage nominal holding gains increased very rapidly in the 1970s as compared to their development in the 1960s. This was the result of the rapid increase in the prices of investment goods. By contrast, percentage real holding gains were, on average, close to zero although the year-to-year variations were large. The annual variations of holding gains should, however, be viewed with caution because of difficulties in the estimation of the implicit price index of total physical assets.

The Rate of Return on Total Capital and Own Capital

Rate of Return on Total Capital

In this section we first present the estimates of the real rate of return on total capital for Finnish manufacturing industries in the period 1960–1980. The main results are shown in tables 10–5 and 10–6 and in figure 10–4, while the averages of some alternative estimates are given in table 10–7. The basic formula for the real rate of return on total fixed assets (before tax) is defined as

$$ROC_F(BT) = \frac{Y}{F}, \tag{10.12}$$

where Y = operating income ($= P^a + I + T$) and F = total fixed assets (replacement cost value). The equivalent formula for the rate of return after tax is

$$ROC_F(AT) = \frac{Y - T}{F}. \tag{10.13}$$

Replacing the variable F by the variables W or $\overline{W}$ in formulas (10.12) and (10.13) gives the equivalent rates of return on total assets.[9] It should be noted that real holding gains are not taken into account in these definitions of the rate of return. The nominal rate of return on total fixed assets (before taxes) is given by the expression

$$ROC_{F,N}(BT) = \frac{Y + NHG}{F}, \tag{10.14}$$

where[10]

$$NHG = \left(\frac{P_F}{100}\right)F,$$

that is, the absolute value of nominal holding gains on total fixed assets (F) is obtained by multiplying the current value of F by the relative nominal holding gains ($p_F/100$). Strictly speaking in formulas (10.12) and (10.13) operating income (Y) equals real total income only if real holding gains are zero. This means that the implicit price index of fixed assets rises by exactly the same rate as prices generally. Including real holding gains (or losses) in the measure of real income gives the second basic formula for the real rate of return (before taxes)

$$ROC_F^*(BT) = \frac{Y + RHG}{F}, \tag{10.15}$$

where

$$RHG = \left(\frac{p_{F,r}}{100}\right)F$$

(see equation 10.11) and $p_{F,r}$ is the percentage annual real holding gain (see table 10–4). Equivalent formulas for the real rate of return on total assets are defined by replacing F with W (total assets).[11]

These general principles were used to calculate the real rate of return on total fixed assets in the Finnish manufacturing sector in 1961–1980. Table 10–5 shows the rate of return estimates (before and after taxes) excluding real holding gains (equations 10.12 and 10.13). Table 10–5 indicates that the average profitability of Finnish manufacturing firms was quite high as measured by the real rate of return, but the variations in profitability have also tended to be large, reflecting the general sensitivity of the Finnish economy to business fluctuations. We shall return in the section entitled "Determinants of the Rate of Return and the Effective Tax Rate" to the general features of profitability and output (or export) behavior of the manufacturing sector when testing for the existence of a trend in the rates of return of this sector. It can also be seen from table 10–5 that the difference between before- and after-tax estimates of real rate of return is very small. This is mainly the result of the low level of the effective tax rate on operating income, as was seen earlier (see table 10–3). Table 10–6 shows developments in real rate of return (before and after tax) including real holding gains (equation 10.15 and the equivalent measure for the after-tax variable).

Table 10–5
Real Rate of Return on Total Fixed Assets in Finnish Manufacturing 1961–80
(percent, excluding real holding gains)

Year	$ROC_F(BT)$	$ROC_F(AT)$
1961	13.92	11.30
1962	11.06	8.53
1963	11.31	9.07
1964	11.08	8.97
1965	9.68	7.68
1966	8.40	6.41
1967	8.27	6.59
1968	10.85	9.29
1969	14.97	13.44
1970	14.76	13.46
1971	10.02	8.86
1972	10.34	9.35
1973	11.58	10.57
1974	14.83	13.88
1975	7.96	7.01
1976	6.43	5.39
1977	5.77	4.90
1978	8.36	7.57
1979	11.73	10.79
1980	11.13	10.21
Average	10.62	9.16
Standard deviation	2.65	2.57

Table 10–6
Real Rate of Return on Total Fixed Assets in Finnish
Manufacturing 1961–80
(percent, including real holding gains)

Year	$ROC_F^x(BT)$	$ROC_F^x(AT)$
1961	13.93	11.30
1962	10.34	7.80
1963	11.25	9.01
1964	6.54	4.43
1965	10.49	8.50
1966	6.60	4.62
1967	10.03	8.35
1968	11.60	10.04
1969	17.60	16.07
1970	20.40	19.10
1971	13.72	12.56
1972	15.33	14.34
1973	20.93	19.91
1974	22.51	21.56
1975	3.87	2.92
1976	2.68	1.64
1977	3.63	2.76
1978	4.99	4.20
1979	12.30	11.36
1980	8.99	8.07
Average	11.38	9.92
Standard deviation	5.86	5.90

From tables 10–5 and 10–6 it can be seen that the average effect of real holding gains on the estimates of the real rate of return on total fixed assets is quite small (less than 1 percent; see also table 10–4), but that the year-to-year effects are much greater. Variations in the profitability of the manufacturing sector are much larger if measured by the rate of return including, rather than excluding, holding gains.

Figure 10–4 shows the real rate of return on both total assets and total fixed assets (after taxes and excluding real holding gains) over the period 1961–1980. The corresponding before-taxes measures are not shown here since the small difference between before- and after-tax estimates of rates of return can be ascertained from table 10–5. It can be seen from figure 10–4 that the fluctuations in the real rate of return were large and very similar for both measures of total capital. Table 10–7 gives means and standard deviations for selected measures of the rate of return on capital in Finnish manufacturing industries in the period 1961–1980. From table 10–7 can be seen that in general the profitability of Finnish manufacturing is fairly insensitive to the choice of the real rate of return as long as the measure of capital is some form of the replacement cost values. The inclusion or exclusion of holding

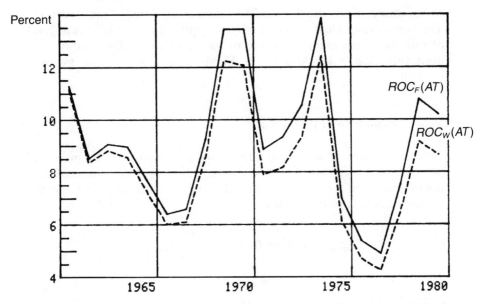

Figure 10–4. Real Rate of Return on Total Assets *(W)* and Total Fixed
Assets *(F)* after Taxes in Finnish Manufacturing 1961–
1980, Percent (Excluding Real Holding Gains)

Table 10–7
**Mean Values and Standard Deviations for Various Measures of the
Rate of Return on Capital in Finnish Manufacturing 1961–80**
(percent)

	Rate of Return	
Concept of Capital[a]	*Mean*	*Standard Deviation*
Total assets *(AT[b], RHG[c])*	9.0	5.3
Total assets *(BT[d], RHG)*	10.4	5.3
Total assets *(AT)*	8.3	2.4
Total assets *(BT)*	9.7	2.5
Total fixed assets *(AT, RHG)*	9.9	5.9
Total fixed assets *(AT)*	9.2	2.6
Book value of total assets *(AT)*	6.2	0.6
Book value of total assets *(BT)*	8.5	1.7

[a]Corresponding concepts of profits and operating income have been used.

[b]*AT* = after taxes.

[c]*BT* = before taxes.

[d]*RHG* = including real holding gains; otherwise excluding *RHG*.

gains mainly affects the standard deviation (variations) of rate of return. The book values (historic cost) of total capital give a much lower level of rate of return mainly because of the accelerated depreciation and undervaluation rules applied in Finnish business income taxation legislation.

Rate of Return on Own Capital

The rate of return on own (equity) capital is estimated by means of two different methods. The first is based directly on the ratio of economic profits to total own capital (defined by equation 10.5) and the corresponding formula is thus

$$REQ_{\overline{W}}(BT) = \frac{P^b}{\overline{\overline{W}} - D_B}, \qquad (10.16)$$

where

$$P^b = \text{profits before taxes (equation 10.7)}$$
$$\overline{W} = \text{total assets (current value);}$$
$$\quad \text{see equation 10.3}$$
$$D_B = \text{total debt (book value).}$$

The equivalent after-tax real rate of return on own capital is defined by

$$REQ_{\overline{W}}(AT) = \frac{P^a}{\overline{\overline{W}} - D_B}, \qquad (10.17)$$

where $P^a = P^b - T$. In these two concepts of rate of return on own capital no adjustment is made to take account of the impact of the rate of inflation through the real value of debt capital.

The rate of return on own capital with "gearing adjustment" is the approach used to account for the decrease in the real value of debt due to rising rates of inflation. The decrease in the real indebtedness of firms results in capital gains for equity owners of a firm and, conversely, losses for creditors.[12]

Real rate of return on own capital with gearing adjustment (before taxes) is defined as

$$REG_{\overline{W}}(BT) = \frac{P^b + g}{\overline{\overline{W}} - D_B}, \qquad (10.18)$$

where $g = p_{CP}D_B$, p_{CP} is the relative (proportional) rate of change of the consumer price index. The corresponding after-tax rate of return is defined as

$$REG_{\overline{W}}(AT) = \frac{P^b + g - T}{\overline{W} - D_B}.$$ (10.19)

If account is also taken of the effect of the rate of inflation on the value of net financial assets (M), the rate of return on own capital (before tax) is

$$REGM_{\overline{W}}(BT) = \frac{P^b + g - m}{\overline{W} - D_B},$$ (10.20)

where $m = p_{CP}M$ is the change in the real value of net monetary assets. The corresponding after-taxes measure is defined analogously to equation (10.19).

Tables 10–8 and 10–9 and figure 10–5 present the main results of

Table 10–8
Real Rate of Return on Own Capital in Finnish Manufacturing 1960–80
(percent)

Year	$REQ_{\overline{W}}(BT)$	$REQ_{\overline{W}}(AT)$
1960	16.35	12.86
1961	16.86	13.26
1962	12.86	9.28
1963	13.22	10.02
1964	12.47	9.53
1965	10.46	7.63
1966	8.99	6.03
1967	8.93	6.27
1968	11.98	9.66
1969	18.61	16.28
1970	18.13	16.15
1971	11.23	9.35
1972	11.88	10.22
1973	13.60	11.94
1974	17.69	16.20
1975	7.83	6.16
1976	5.29	3.32
1977	3.47	1.81
1978	8.35	6.78
1979	13.66	12.01
1980	12.00	10.40
Average	12.09	9.76
Standard deviation	4.08	3.97

Table 10–9
Real Rate of Return on Own Capital with Inflation Adjustments in Finnish Manufacturing 1960–80
(percent)

Year	$REG_{\overline{w}}(AT)^a$	$REGM_{\overline{w}}(AT)^b$
1960	15.10	14.88
1961	14.56	14.44
1962	12.74	12.46
1963	14.03	13.62
1964	18.16	17.18
1965	11.82	11.39
1966	9.65	9.33
1967	11.14	10.52
1968	19.30	18.07
1969	18.66	18.29
1970	19.30	18.78
1971	17.80	16.31
1972	19.21	17.54
1973	26.56	24.15
1974	38.53	34.47
1975	31.73	27.22
1976	25.43	21.91
1977	21.46	18.36
1978	19.11	16.50
1979	22.57	20.60
1980	27.37	24.18
Average	19.73	18.11
Standard deviation	7.15	5.95

[a]With gearing adjustment (after taxes).
[b]With gearing adjustment and adjustment for change in the real value of net financial assets (after taxes).

the calculations of the real rate of return on own capital. It can be seen that the fluctuations in the rate of return on own capital were very large, as was also the case with the rate of return on total capital. Furthermore, it can be noted that the effect of the rate of inflation involving the decrease in the real value of debt capital has been quite high. This effect is most clearly evident in figure 10–5 (the difference between $REGM_{\overline{w}}(AT)$ and $REQ_{\overline{w}}(AT)$). In the previous section it was shown that the average real rate of return on total capital (after taxes) was about 8 percent. The next section shows that the average real rate of interest was about 1 percent (table 10–11). Table 10–9 shows that the average real rate of return on own capital with inflation adjustments was about 18 percent. Since the shares of debt and own capital in total capital are roughly equal (see table 10–1, e_1), these results agree by and large with the hypothesis that average real profitability has been approximately equal to the average real cost of financial capital (in the long-run sense).[13]

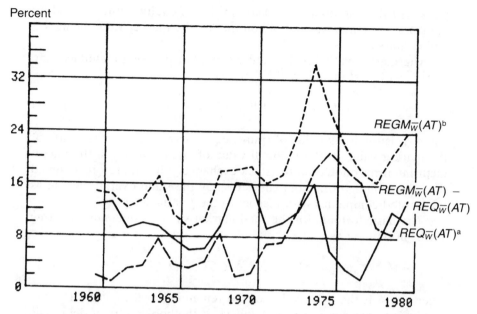

Percent

^a Rate of return on own capital (basic formula).
^b Rate of return on own capital with gearing and financial assets adjustment.

Figure 10–5. The Effect of Real Indebtedness on the Rate of Return on Own Capital in Finnish Manufacturing 1960–1980, Percent

The Valuation Ratio and the Cost of Capital

In the previous section we based the analysis of movements in real profitability on the real rate of return on total and own capital. The calculations of these rates were based on the joint use of national income accounts and enterprise (balance sheet) data. The rate of return measures can be interpreted as reflecting the attitudes and interests of the companies themselves. In this section, we turn to the use of capital market data. The behavior of the stock market can in principle be assumed to reflect the attitudes of the owners of the companies.

It is, however, important to emphasize that the capital market does not play a very important role in the financing of operations (investment) by Finnish manufacturing companies. The share of equity capital in total capital (at book value) was about 10 percent in the 1970s, but only part of the total equity capital owned by manufacturing companies was quoted on the stock exchange. In 1978, for example, the nominal value of total equity capital in the manufacturing sector was 8.3 billion marks (FIM). The nominal (taxable) value of equity capital quoted on the stock exchange was 3.0 billion marks, the market value being 4.3 billion marks.

The market value of the equity capital of the total manufacturing sector can be estimated by the formula

$$E^M = fE, \tag{10.21}$$

where E is the book value of (pure) equity capital and f is the ratio of the market value to the nominal value of equity capital in the manufacturing firms quoted on the stock exchange.[14] It is therefore assumed that all manufacturing companies display the same overall pattern as the quoted companies with respect to the f variable.

The basic formula for the total market value of the manufacturing sector in defined as

$$MV_1 = E^M + OC^* + D_B, \tag{10.22}$$

where OC^* is the book value of the remaining own capital (after deduction of pure equity capital) and D_B is the book value of debt. The inclusion of the book value of debt in the definition of total market value can be defended on the grounds of the credit rationing situation prevailing almost continuously in Finnish financial markets. The interest rate has not fluctuated in Finland so as to even out the demand for and supply of credit. The interest rates on lending have been institutionally controlled by the central bank (Bank of Finland). A negligible fraction of firms' bonds are also traded on the stock exchange.

The second approach calculating the market value is based on the assumption that total own capital (OC_u), corrected for tax credits (see section entitled "Own Capital and Debt Ratios"), has a market value determined by the f variable. This gives the following formula:

$$MV_2 = OC_u^M + D_B^*, \tag{10.23}$$

where D_B^* is book value of debt plus tax credits. The valuation ratio (Tobin's q) is defined as

$$q = \frac{MV}{W}, \tag{10.24}$$

where

> MV = market value of total capital of manufacturing sector
> W = replacement cost value of total capital of manufacturing sector.

Table 10–10 shows developments in q variables in Finnish manufacturing. From table 10–10 it can be seen that the fluctuations in q_1 have been very small since changes in market value are only reflected in the pure equity capital. Variable q_2 displays much larger variations because of the wider coverage of the market value concept. The q_2 measure of Tobin's q also reflects fairly well the general development of profitability in Finnish manufacturing firms. The marked decline in the performance of the manufacturing sector (and the whole economy) is very clearly evident in the movements of the q_2 variable over the period 1975–1979. It should, however, be noticed that the level of the valuation ratio is quite sensitive to the choice of the measure for total market value.

We next turn to the analysis of the behavior of the cost of capital in Finnish manufacturing in the period 1961–1980. The approach used here follows directly the methodology suggested by Holland and Myers (1978). The real cost of capital is defined as

$$\rho = \frac{ROC}{q},\qquad\qquad(10.25)$$

where

Table 10–10
Valuation Ratio in Finnish Manufacturing 1961–80

Year	$q_1 = \dfrac{MV_1}{W}$	$q_2 = \dfrac{MV_2}{W}$
1961	1.34	1.65
1962	1.36	1.67
1963	1.37	1.64
1964	1.34	1.60
1965	1.25	1.45
1966	1.25	1.30
1967	1.24	1.21
1968	1.28	1.34
1969	1.29	1.41
1970	1.32	1.51
1971	1.31	1.49
1972	1.35	1.68
1973	1.45	1.98
1974	1.32	1.61
1975	1.26	1.41
1976	1.23	1.27
1977	1.21	1.20
1978	1.23	1.24
1979	1.23	1.29
1980	1.21	1.25
Average	1.29	1.46
Standard deviation	0.06	0.21

$$ROC = \text{real rate of return on total capital}$$
$$q = \text{Tobin's } q.$$

This expression is valid for the estimation of cost of capital if the present value of the future growth opportunities term is excluded from the definition of market value.[15]

    Table 10–11 shows the estimates of real cost of capital with the two variants of the q variable and also the real rate of interest on debt capital. Since the q variables behaved fairly smoothly, the variations in cost of capital follow closely the development of real profitability (rate of return). As was noted in the previous section the real interest rate receives a very low value as compared to real rates of return on total and on own capital (see also note 13). It was noted that this difference is due mainly to the high level of real rate of return on own capital, which explains the quite high (average) values of the real cost of capital. It should, however, be emphasized that owing to the rather

Table 10–11
Real Cost of Capital and Real Rate of Interest in Finnish Manufacturing 1961–80
(percent, after taxes figures)

Year	$\rho_1{}^a$	$\rho_2{}^b$	r
1961	8.36	6.80	5.09
1962	6.16	4.99	2.46
1963	6.44	5.39	2.17
1964	6.40	5.35	-2.81
1965	5.79	5.00	2.53
1966	4.83	4.63	3.46
1967	4.93	5.04	2.87
1968	6.72	6.42	-1.70
1969	9.51	8.68	5.38
1970	9.14	8.00	4.90
1971	6.06	5.30	2.11
1972	6.05	4.88	1.41
1973	6.46	4.71	-1.60
1974	9.41	7.70	-6.07
1975	4.88	4.38	-6.62
1976	3.84	3.71	-3.67
1977	3.54	3.56	-2.36
1978	5.29	5.23	0.88
1979	7.46	7.10	1.14
1980	7.18	6.95	-1.40
Average	6.42	5.69	0.41
Standard deviation	1.71	1.42	3.52

^{a}Calculated with q_1.
^{b}Calculated with q_2.

rough approximations made in the calculations of market values, these estimates of cost of capital should be regarded as highly tentative.

Determinants of the Rate of Return and the Effective Tax Rate

In this section we perform some statistical tests in order to discover whether there has been trendwise behavior in the real rate of return on total capital and in the effective tax rate. This is done by means of standard regression analysis of the determinants of the rate of return and the effective tax rate.

The aim is not a thoroughgoing analysis of the factors affecting the behavior of these explanatory variables since this would be rather difficult using only the single equation method. It can be assumed that both the rate of return and the effective tax rate depend upon the development of various price and cost factors as well as economic policy variables. We try to capture the effect of the general business fluctuations in the manufacturing sector by three variables: the percentage change in the production of this sector, the level of capacity utilization in the whole economy, and the trend deviation of total Finnish exports.

In addition to a trend variable (time), we also use the rate of price changes, which can take the form of different price indexes. Our hypothesis is that a price variable might reflect to a large extent the impact of inflation on effective corporation income tax rates. It could also be argued that the rate of inflation takes into account the impact of holding gains or decrease in the real value of debt. We also experimented directly with the tax rate variable as an independent variable, however. Finally, similar econometric tests were tried with the effective tax rate (t_y) as the dependent variable. All models are estimated by the OLS method.

Table 10–12 shows the main results of our econometric experiments. As a general conclusion it can be said that these simple models explain the behavior of rate of return quite well in terms of R^2, t statistics, and the Durbin-Watson (DW) statistics. All the accelerator variables seem to capture the basic features of demand (or income) fluctuations although the export variable (trend deviation) receives the highest t statistic. The two variables measuring the rate of inflation are significant (especially p_i), but they add very little to the total explanation of the models (5 to 10 percent).

In most Western economies there has been a declining trend in profitability during the postwar period, as the other chapters in this publication demonstrate. Hence, it is interesting to observe that the

Table 10–12
Determinants of the Real Rate of Return on Total Fixed Assets in Finnish Manufacturing 1961–80

Equation	Dependent Variable	Trend	Accelerator[a]	Inflation[b] P_{CP}	Inflation[c] P_I	R^2	DW
1	$ROC_F (AT)$	0.06	0.63[1]			0.57	1.48
		(0.90)	(5.05)				
2	"	−0.08	0.53[2]	0.22		0.48	1.53
		(0.88)	(4.29)	(1.56)			
3	"	−0.14	0.47[2]		0.29	0.69	1.70
		(2.01)	(6.00)		(3.84)		
4	"	−0.22	0.76[3]	0.36		0.73	2.33
		(1.45)	(7.17)	(1.75)			
5	"	−0.12	0.32[3]		1.32[d]	0.82	1.93
		(1.23)	(2.49)		(3.41)		
6	$ROC_F(BT)$	−0.17	0.53[2]	0.21		0.53	1.58
		(1.89)	(4.37)	(1.55)			

Notes: t-statistics appear in parentheses under the coefficient estimates.

All dependent variables are excluding real holding gains.

$ROC_F(AT)$ is after taxes and $ROC_F(BT)$ is before taxes variable.

[a]Accelerator variables are: [1]rate of capacity utilization in the whole economy; [2]rate of change of manufacturing production; [3]trend deviation of total Finnish exports.

[b]P_{CP} = rate of change of consumer price index.

[c]P_I = rate of change of investment goods price index.

[d]Rate of change of P_I/P_{CP}.

results presented in table 10–12 suggest that there does not seem to be any clear trend in profitability of the Finnish manufacturing sector. This can also be seen from figure 10–4. Only when the rate of change of production is used as the accelerator variable is there some slight evidence of a downward trend in the real rate of return (both before and after tax).

The results of these econometric experiments conform very well with the general tendency of the Finnish economy (a small open economy) to display large cyclical fluctuations. One of the basic reasons for this behavior is the one-sidedness of Finnish exports, 50 percent of which are still accounted for by the forest industry. In the conclusions below we shall point out some reasons why the general performance of profitability in the manufacturing sector has been quite good as compared to most other OECD countries.

We also carried out some tests with the effective tax rate (t_y) as an independent variable in the ROC models. It proved to be significantly negative and took the role of GDP (or capacity utilization) as a measure of general business fluctuations. This can be interpreted to mean that the effective tax rate behaves in a countercyclical manner. This aspect was tested directly with the effective tax rate as a dependent variable. The following equation shows a downward trend in the effective tax rate:

$$t_y = \frac{1.14}{(6.90)} - \frac{0.008}{(9.27)} \text{ Trend} - \frac{0.95}{(5.60)} CU$$

$$R^2 = 0.82$$
$$DW = 1.38$$

This equation shows that the effective rate of taxation decreases as the rate of capacity utilization (CU) rises. The main reason for this behavior is that during recessions firms are unable to make full use of the accelerated depreciation and inventory undervaluation rules when determining (manipulating) their taxable income for tax purposes. By contrast, during boom periods profitability (and income) increases to such an extent that it enables firms to make more extensive use of these tax rules, thus allowing them to avoid rising tax payments. Given this background, it has often been argued in the Finnish debate on the corporate tax system that it possesses features that tend to exacerbate the cyclical fluctuations of the Finnish economy.

Conclusions

Our principal objective was to analyze the development or real profitability in the Finnish manufacturing sector in the period 1961–1980. Various measures of the real rate of return were used for this purpose. In addition, a variety of factors closely linked to the rate of return were examined, and finally we attempted to discover the basic determinants of the rate of return. We shall comment briefly here on the main results of this study:

1. Real profitability, as measured by the real rate of return on total capital at replacement cost value, has run between 7 and 10 percent (on the average), fluctuating considerably from year to year over the period 1961–1980, except for the years 1975–1977, when it ran at a much lower level.
2. The real rate of return, before taxes has averaged 8 to 9 percent and a point lower after taxes, reflecting a low effective tax rate on operating income.
3. Over the period as a whole there appears to have been no clear declining trend in profitability, but the preliminary estimates of the

rate of return for the years 1981–1982 indicate a declining trend since the latter half of the 1970s.

On average, real holding gains are of little importance for the level of real profitability, but they have quite a substantial effect on the annual fluctuations of the real rate of return measures.

4.   The real rate of return on own capital has, on average, been at a much higher level than the corresponding rate for total capital. Capital gains on own capital are the result of a decrease in real indebtedness. This effect has been important in the 1970s, in particular, and it has prevented the real rate of return from declining. The growth in capital gains enjoyed by the owners of equity capital reflects both inflation and an increase in debt ratios (debt to own capital ratio), which have increased over the period covered by this study.

5.   The average valuation ratio (Tobin's q) has reflected quite well the general cyclical fluctuations in the manufacturing sector. The variations in this ratio have, however, been smaller than those in real profitability. The estimates of the q variable are rather sensitive to the measure of market value employed.

Our estimates of the real cost of capital have, on average, been about equal to the real rate of return. The fluctuations in the real cost of capital follow closely the real rate of return. The real rate of interest has been much lower than the real cost of capital.

6.   Annual changes in the real rates of return on total capital can be explained quite satisfactorily by changes in GDP or by capacity utilization. There is also some evidence that the rate of inflation has had a positive impact on the rate of return. The inflation rate probably captures the effect of holding or capital gains on the rate of return. It should, however, be emphasized that our analysis has been of a partial equilibrium character and rather tentative in this respect. In particular, we have not taken into account the effect of decreasing price competitiveness on the manufacturing sector's exports.

7.   The ratio of corporate taxes to total return on capital (profit plus net interest), that is, the effective rate of tax on operating income, has been very low in Finland, and, if anything, has tended to fall over the last twenty years.

As an overall conclusion it can be said that the performance of Finnish manufacturing firms has been quite good in the period 1960–1980, at least in light of the development of real profitability. The average growth rate of the GDP of total Finnish economy was, over the years 1978–1981, about 4 percent, which is substantially above the average growth rate of other OECD countries. The total net foreign debt per GDP decreased from 21 percent (in 1975) to about 16 percent by the end of 1970s and the average gross tax rate (all taxes per current value of GDP) remained almost constant, at the 37 percent level. The good performance of manufacturing exports to eastern European countries (mainly the Soviet Union) through bilateral trade agreements has noticeably assisted in keeping production (and profitability) at a high level. There has, however, been some tendency of the rate of production to turn to a less favorable path since the end of the 1970s and this will be reflected in a decline in real profitability in the beginning of the 1980s.

Despite the quite good development of real profitability, annual fluctuations in the real rate of return have been very large, and this may also have exacerbated the severe cyclical problems of the Finnish economy.

Book values do not constitute a reliable basis for the analysis of the development of real profitability. Current replacement cost values of total capital and the equivalent measures of real income (profit) are necessary for this kind of analysis.

Notes

1. See W. Nordhaus (1974) in references.
2. The Bank of England has, since the mid-1970s, published various articles on corporate profitability in its *Quarterly Bulletin*. Of the Swedish studies on profitability, we can mention especially those by the IUI (Industrial Institute for Economic and Social Research), for example "Att välja 80-tal"; see references.
3. The book value of inventories has been used as the basic series and this series has been converted into the corrected value by using the undervaluation percentages shown in the study by Ylä-Anttila and Heikkilä. The series thus obtained is interpreted as the current value of inventories. It should be noted that the ratio of total sales to the corrected value of inventories has been a bit over 3 in the 1970s. This implies that the velocity of inventories has been rather high. It can hence be assumed that at the end of each year the corrected value of inventories resembles that of the current value of new products and raw materials.
4. Since the estimates of real capital are likely to include at least partially (book value) the value of land we have chosen to use the W and F symbols of total assets instead of A and O (see common glossary).
5. For the estimates of the statutory corporate income tax rate u

see table 10–3. For a methodological discussion of the concepts of own capital, see the IUI publication "Att välja 80-tal," p. 207, in references and chapter 4 in this book by Norman P. Williams.

6. During most of 1970s the state tax rate was 43 percent and the local tax rate about 16 percent. During 1960–1967 and again in 1976 manufacturing companies also paid wealth taxes on the basis of their net wealth (1.5 percent in 1976 and 1.0 percent in 1960–1967). The state income tax rate was raised temporarily after the abolition of the wealth taxes in 1967.

7. The depreciation rate for tax purposes has been on the average 25 percent, whereas the economic rate of depreciation has been estimated as 7.8 percent. But in 1976–1977 the manufacturing companies had almost a 100 percent depreciation rate (temporarily) as the government tried to stimulate investment activity in manufacturing industries.

8. Manufacturing companies have also been allowed to use some minor items to affect their taxable income, for example, reserves against losses of foreign trade credits, reserves for product guarantees, and operating reserves on the basis of paid wage costs (for small and medium-sized firms).

9. Total capital (W) as well as the other concepts of capital used in the empirical calculations of the rates of return are the averages of the beginning and end-of-year values of the corresponding capital measures.

10. p_F is here the percentage form of nominal holding gains; see table 10–4 and also equation (10.15).

11. In this case we should (strictly speaking) also consider the effect of price changes on the value of net financial assets (M), but this is not done here since we are mainly interested in the value of appreciation of fixed assets (see, however, the section entitled "Rate of Return on Own Capital").

12. There is, however, no net effect on the real rate of return on total capital by way of changes in the real value of debt capital since capital gains and losses cancel each other out.

13. In Finnish conditions it has often been argued that a good measure of the opportunity cost (discount rate) of retained earnings is the interest rate on state bonds. At the end of 1970s this interest rate after all taxes (also personal) was about 12 percent. Hence the before personal taxes interest rate ($\bar{r}$) is $0.12/(1-m)$, where m = marginal personal income tax rate (0.5) and thus $\bar{r} = 0.25$. The average increase in the CPI has been roughly 8.5 percent and hence the real interest rate on state bonds (before personal taxes) accords quite well with our

estimates of the real rate of return on own capital; see table 10–2, $REGM_W(AT)$.

14. The various series for market and nominal values of the equity capital of industrial companies quoted on the stock exchange have been provided by Kim Lindström (Union Bank of Finland). When calculating E^M we have assumed that the ratio f for companies quoted on the stock exchange approximates the behavior of all manufacturing companies. It has further been assumed that the nominal values of residual own capital $(OC-E)$ and debt (B) are equivalent to their market values. Only a very small proportion of debt is quoted on the stock market in Finland. In could be argued that the residual component of own capital and that part of the hidden reserves attributable to own capital also have market values similar to pure equity capital. This leads to our second method for calculating the market value of total own capital.

15. The general expression fo MV is

$$MV = \frac{Y}{\rho} + PVGO$$

where $PVGO$ = present value of future growth opportunities. By taking into account that $Y = ROC: W$, equation (10.25) follows (see Holland and Myers, 1978 and chapter 2 in this book).

References

Airaksinen, T. "Tutkimus kannattavuuden mittaamisesta ja komponoimisesta, sovellutuksena Suomen tehdasteollisuus vuosina 1960–1975." *Teollistamisrahasto Oy*, B:1, 1978.

Alho, K. "Pääoman tuottoaste, korko ja kansantalouden pääomanmuodostus." *Etla* B:26. Helsinki, 1980.

Clark, T.A., and Williams, N.P. "Measures of Real Profitability." *Bank of England Quarterly Bulletin* 18, no. 4 (1978).

Eliasson, A., et al. "Att välja 80-tal." *IUI*. Stockholm, 1979.

Feldstein, M., and Summers, L. "Is the Rate of Profit Falling?" *Brookings Papers on Economic Activity 1* (1977):211–77.

von Furstenberg, G.M., and Malkiel, B.G. "Financial Analysis in an Inflationary Environment." *Journal of Finance* 32, no. 1 (May 1977):575–87.

Hill, T.P. "Profits and Rates of Return." *OECD*. Paris, 1979.

Holland, D.M., and Myers, S.C. "Trends in Corporate Profitability and Capital Costs," MIT, WP 999–78, May 1978, Unpublished.

————. "Profitability and Capital Costs for Manufacturing Corporations and All Nonfinancial Corporations." *American Economic Review* 70, no. 2 (May 1980).

Koskenkylä, H. "Rate of Return, Cost of Capital and Valuation Ratio in Finnish Manufacturing 1960–1979." Bank of Finland, Research Papers, August 1981.

Nordhaus, W.D. "The Falling Share of Profits." *Brookings Papers on Economic Activity* 2 (1974):169–308.

Salo, S. "Suomen teollisuuden varastot v. 1960–1975" (Finnish industrial inventories, 1960–1975). *Etla* B:15. Helsinki, 1977.

Vihavainen-Valppu-Suokko-Björk, Pääomakanta vuosina 1965–1977, Tilastokeskus, Tutkimuksia no. 58. Helsinki, 1980.

Williams, N.P. "The Profitability of UK Industrial Sectors." *Bank of England Quarterly Bulletin* 19, no. 4 (1979).

————. "Influence on the Profitability of Twenty-two Industrial Sectors." Bank of England, Discussion Paper No. 15, March 1981.

Ylä-Anttila, P., and Heikkilä, A. "Teollisuuden kannattavuus toimialoittain" (Profitability in Finnish industry by branches). *Etla* B:24. Helsinki, 1980.

Appendix 10A
Statistical Appendix

In this appendix we tabluate the estimates of some basic variables used in the calculations of rate of return and the related figures. The series presented here are based on various data sources, national income accounts, industrial statistics, enterprise data (profit and loss and balance sheet data), financial market statistics, and capital market data. All of the series presented here are concerned with Finnish manufacturing in the period 1961–1980 (or 1960–1980).

Table 10A1
Various Estimates of Total Capital in Finnish Manufacturing 1960–80
(FIM million; series are the end of year values)

Year	$\overline{W}^a$	W^b	F^c	$\overline{W}_B{}^d$
1960	11473	9626	9624	6807
1961	12595	10708	10497	7616
1962	13809	11647	11427	8451
1963	15077	12580	12150	9419
1964	16781	14218	13459	10316
1965	18882	16110	15210	11660
1966	20461	17606	16454	12874
1967	22192	19117	17565	14491
1968	25396	21714	20184	16016
1969	28723	24576	22055	19732
1970	34240	29183	26260	23581
1971	40203	34776	30850	28774
1972	46113	40713	35204	33078
1973	57176	48999	44152	42062
1974	77527	67685	60317	53345
1975	91153	81887	71296	61875
1976	101239	90824	79496	70813
1977	111536	100565	87443	77987
1978	117584	105196	89374	84109
1979	133277	119585	101489	93014
1980	158051	140539	119355	108605

[a] $\overline{W}$ = total capital including gross financial assets.
[b] W = total capital including net financial assets.
[c] F = total fixed capital.
[d] $\overline{W}_B$ = total book value of capital.

Table 10A2
Estimates of Operating Income (Manufacturing Sector)
and Some Price Variables (Indexes) of
Finnish Economy in 1960–80

Year	p_{CP}[a]	p_I[b]	Y[c]
1960	34.48	27.75	1238
1961	35.47	28.45	1401
1962	36.96	29.96	1213
1963	38.86	31.27	1333
1964	42.03	32.83	1418
1965	43.97	34.70	1387
1966	45.49	35.91	1330
1967	48.47	37.98	1406
1968	52.82	42.11	2048
1969	54.14	44.32	3162
1970	55.75	48.38	3566
1971	59.32	53.50	2860
1972	64.41	59.53	3416
1973	72.36	69.15	4595
1974	85.88	87.18	7746
1975	100.06	100.10	5236
1976	112.99	110.38	4847
1977	126.23	123.77	4818
1978	135.86	131.64	7394
1979	146.42	143.01	11195
1980	162.14	161.43	12295

[a]p_{CP} = Consumer Price Index.
[b]p_I = investment goods price index.
[c]Y = operating income.

Table 10A3
Estimates of Market Values, Debt, and the Ratio of
Market Value to Nominal Value (Book Value) of the equity
by quoted companies (f variable)

Year	f^a	$MV_1{}^b$	$MV_2{}^b$	$D_B{}^c$
1960	2.33	13457	17379	4697
1961	2.04	14327	17617	5272
1962	2.12	15795	19502	6037
1963	2.01	17246	20582	6813
1964	2.02	19049	22796	7627
1965	1.70	20201	23407	8779
1966	1.35	21966	22897	9801
1967	1.14	23682	23143	11471
1968	1.46	27758	29055	12744
1969	1.65	31695	34747	14894
1970	1.93	38616	44096	18350
1971	2.00	45389	51965	22739
1972	2.69	55104	68228	26475
1973	3.40	70898	97192	32977
1974	2.48	89357	109166	44086
1975	2.06	103516	115274	53714
1976	1.56	111473	115120	61417
1977	1.35	121329	120896	67857
1978	1.47	129368	130742	72883
1979	1.61	146829	154350	78856
1980	1.44	169698	175338	93986

[a]f = ratio of market value to nominal value of the equity capital by quoted companies.
[b]MV_1 and MV_2 = market values; see section of chapter entitled "The Valuation Ratio and the Cost of Capital."
[c]D_B = book value of total debt.

11 Profitability in Austrian Industrial Corporations

Kurt Bayer

This chapter is concerned with a statistical analysis of the short- and long-term income performance of corporations in Austrian industry (mining and manufacturing). For this purpose time series are constructed from aggregate balance sheet statistics showing the effects of valuation practices, accounting conventions, and various tax rules on the calculation of various definitions of rates of return.

After a rather brief discussion of the concepts involved in "inflation accounting" to arrive at ex-post real rates of return for the corporate industrial sector and ten subsectors, which takes account of the historical emergence of the concepts and their applicability to the present Austrian situation, various definitions of "rates of return" are distinguished. This part then traces the construction of the Austrian data, thereby attempting to keep the various relevant concepts apart.

The methodological section is followed by empirical analysis, describing the sectoral structure of profitability and the long- and short-term behavior of various rates of return. Several hypotheses are tested as to their applicability to Austrian profitability data. By-products of these efforts are the description of capital structure (debt equity ratios) and the effective tax burden borne by the corporations, respectively the capital owners. Finally, some evidence is presented on the Austrian stock market in general and on dividend payout ratios in particular. This latter section sheds some light on the peculiarities of the Austrian capital market and its inability to play an important role as a direct provider of risk capital to firms. The section closes with a short comparison of costs and yields of capital in Austria.

The scope of the investigation is limited, insofar as it extends to industrial corporations (joint stock companies, "Aktiengesellschaften") only. These are the only enterprises required to publish balance sheets on an annual basis. These balance sheets are aggregated by sector and published by the Central Statistical Office with a time lag of approximately three years.[1] The present analysis covers the time span 1956–1980. The sector under investigation is composed of less than 200 firms and employs slightly less than 40 percent of Austrian industrial workers (see table 11–1). Since these corporations overrepresent large firms (and especially the basic industries such as mining, petroleum, and steel), an extension of the results to the total of Austrian industry is dangerous. Furthermore, there is some, if only sparse, evidence that different-sized classes of firms exhibit significantly different profitability rates, at least for individual years.[2]

The data of the published balance sheet statistics form the core of the data base. From it various estimates are carried out. This data set is supplemented by published National Income Accounting (NIA) data, especially as concerns various price indexes. Capital stock data are semiofficial estimates of the Austrian Institute of Economic Research (WIFO); stock and capital market data are published by the Austrian National Bank. The rest of the data stem from the WIFO Data Bank.

Throughout the analysis the data presented are summations over firms, that is, transactions among the firms concerned are not netted out. Thus, the sectoral or industry indebtedness ratios may be slightly overstated, since they show the weighted sum of the individual firms' indebtedness rather than that of the consolidated sector(s). On the other hand, the summing up losses of some firms are netted out against profits of other firms within one sector. In this respect the individual sector is treated like one single firm. The calculated rates of return then do not correspond to the mean of the rates of the individual firms, but rather to their weighted average.

Table 11–1
Number of Firms and Degree of Representation of Industrial Corporations (1980)

Sector	Number of Firms	Representation[a] in %
Stone-clay, glass	13	30.04
Electrical engineering	16	50.45
Machinery, vehicles	23	36.75
Chemicals	17	42.07
Food-tobacco	20	22.20
Iron, steel, metal products	24	66.09
Mining, petroleum	11	86.11
Paper	12	49.11
Wood Products	4	1.63
Leather, textiles, clothing	14	10.30
All sectors	154	36.60

[a]Number of workers in corporations within sector in relation to number of workers in sector of total industry.

Methodology of Inflation Accounting

Capital Maintenance and Income Concepts

It has been a recurring experience of the past sixty years that sustained periods of rising price levels lead to discussions on how to measure business income "correctly." The hyperinflation of the 1920s originated an extensive debate in Germany (represented in the works of Schmalenbach and Schmidt) on capital maintenance and income concepts; this debate was revived during the inflation of the 1950s, and the latest round of inflationary pressure since the early 1970s has resulted in a vast international literature on how to change accounting rules in order to take account of the effects of changing price levels ("inflation accounting"). This chapter does not intend to add to the host of proposals made in this direction, but uses an eclectic approach to adjust Austrian corporation accounts ex post, in order to obtain results on "real" profitability of these corporations. As is common in the literature on inflation accounting, the term "real" in connection with a ratio means that the distorting effects of historical cost accounting have been removed from the data, in the numerator as well as the denominator, while each component is calculated on a current price base. Thus, a "real rate of return" is the quotient of (inflation-adjusted) profits at current prices (P) and (inflation-adjusted) capital stock at current prices ($W, F,$ or such in the Common Glossary).

It should be recognized that at the core of all discussion on inflation accounting lies (at least implicitly) the debate about capital maintenance concepts. The main problem in inflation accounting is how to arrive at a profit concept such that the substance of the firms (sectors) is not endangered by too high tax payments or dividend distribution resulting from profit calculations based on accepted historical cost accounting concepts.

Basically all tax accounting and national income accounting rules agree that profit should be defined as the surplus of revenue over cost after provision has been made for maintaining the company's capital intact, that is, after deducting some definition of depreciation (UN System of National Accounts, p. 124). It should be mentioned here that the issues of inflation accounting also touch upon the question of the equity of the tax burden. It has been argued that if business is allowed to subtract from the tax base a provision for keeping its productive capacity intact, the same should apply to labor income (Welzmüller). Such a position would require two adjustments to personal income: on the one hand a "reproduction" deduction (to maintain the labor power and the wealth position of the individual), and on the other hand an indexation of the relevant deduction, in order to account for inflation.[3]

The literature on inflation accounting distinguishes among three major capital maintenance concepts (see, for example, Coenenberg-Macharzina, Schneider, Lawson, Rosenfield, etc.):

1. Nominal capital maintenance. Here the nominal (money) value of the invested capital has to be recouped before income (profit) arises. This concept forms the basis of the present (historic cost) accounting rules in most countries.

2. Real capital maintenance. The real (constant cost) value of the capital invested shall be maintained. Thus profit is the surplus after provision has been made for either (a) the loss in purchasing power of the money unit (current purchasing power accounting: CPP), or alternatively (b) for the increase in the prices of the inputs into the production process (current cost accounting: CCA).[4] According to the method chosen assets are revalued either by a single price index (GNP deflator or consumer price index—CPP method) or by asset-specific price indexes (replacement costs of assets: CCA method).

3. Economic capital maintenance. Under this concept profit arises only after provision has been made for deducting all costs that secure the reproduction of the economic value of the firm, that is, the present value of the future income streams. There is a long discussion in the literature[5] on how to make this concept, which is oriented to the future, operational. Most authors agree that from the theoretical point of view this concept is to be preferred, since economic theory defines economic profit not as the result of past activities, but as the income stream generated in the future by an investment undertaken now.

For the purpose of the present study it was decided to approximate the latter concept by applying the proposals made by Kennedy and Cripps-Godley.[6] They consider the productive potential of the firm maintained when provision has been made for the replacement of, first, machinery, equipment, and plant; second, inventories; and third, net liquid assets necessary to carry on the business (going concern assumption). This operationalization still implies a rather static, but relatively restrictive, income concept. Some authors (and business interests) would also like to include in capital maintenance provisions for necessary technological change, but no widely accepted operational version has yet been developed.

Any consistent capital maintenance concept necessitates some inflation adjustment to historic cost accounts. The application of each concept will result in a different inflation accounting method and thus in a different definition and concept of profit. There is no generally "correct" way of calculating profit. Different purposes require different concepts. The objective of this chapter leads the author to decide in favor of current cost accounting, which "guarantees" the replacement of all those assets the firms need to carry on their business. This method has the additional advantage that revenues and costs are measured at the same (= current) prices, in contrast to present historic cost calculations, where revenues are measured at current prices but costs are measured at a conglomerate of past prices of different periods.

The objective of this study, namely to estimate the past economic income performance of the Austrian corporate industrial sector, then requires the calculation of current cost (= real) profit and real rates of return, net of depreciation. Other objectives, for example, the analysis of the firms' income distribution, or a comparison with alternative money rates of interest, may not require an inflation adjustment. For such purposes book profits based on historic cost accounting are appropriate.[7] Also, different results appear depending on whether profit is calculated on total capital (entity view) or equity only (proprietary view). Both concepts are meaningful; a decision between them is not a question of faith, but depends on the objective of the investigation. In this present study the main emphasis is on total profit (entity view), since we are primarily interested in the performance of the corporate sector as such, no matter where the funds for investment come from. Equity rates of return are also discussed as a supplement. (Differences in these two concepts point to transfers between the two types of financiers; when prices rise these transfers on average benefit equity owners at the expense of creditors.)

Cash Flow Method of Profit Calculation

In several articles the present author has presented a cash flow concept for the estimation of industry profits.[8] In these previous studies no explicit attempt was made to take account of inflation problems. This extension is the topic of this chapter (table 10–2). According to this cash flow approach gross book profit is calculated as the sum of accounting profit (minus losses) plus direct taxes on corporate income and property plus net change in reserves of all kinds (excluding "re-

Table 11–2
Cash Flow Approach to Profit Calculation

+ Net Accounting Profit (adjusted for carryovers from previous year)
− Accounting Losses
+ Direct Taxes on Corporate Income and Property
+ Change in Reserves of All Kinds (net of "revaluation reserve")
+ Net Interest Payments
+ Book Depreciation
GROSS BOOK PROFIT *(HC)*[a]
− "Economic Depreciation" (calculated from book values)
NET BOOK PROFIT *(HC)*
− Fictitious Profit from Fixed Assets
− Inventory Valuation Adjustment
− Fictitious Profits (net of Losses) from Monetary Assets
NET OPERATING SURPLUS *(CC)*[b]
− (Net additions to "Social Capital")
− Net Interest Payments
+ "Geared" Proportion of Fictitious Profits
EQUITY PROFIT *(CC)*
+ Rest of Fictitious Profits
TOTAL PROPRIETARY GAIN *(HC)*

[a]HC: based on historic cost valuation (book valuation).
[b]CC: based on current cost valuation.

valuation reserve") plus net interest payable plus book depreciation. Subtraction of "economic depreciation" calculated at historic cost yields net book profit (*HC*).

When "fictitious profits," which represent the adjustments required to maintain fixed assets, inventories, and net monetary assets, are subtracted, current cost net operating surplus (*CC*) results, which corresponds to the above economic capital maintenance concept. This concept comes very close to $Y = P + I$, "income from operations," of the Common Glossary.

To arrive at current cost equity profit (proprietary profit), net additions to "social capital" and interest paid on monetary liabilities must be subtracted and the "geared" portion of fictitious profits must be added back in, since by definition fictitious profits can only be subtracted for that part of assets which is equity financed. If the remaining fictitious profits are added in, total proprietary gain (*HC*) results, which can be used for the calculation of earnings yields.

The method of calculation proposed here combines the advantages of adding in with accounting profit those elements representing revenues without cash transactions and deducting an equivalent cost concept, plus being able to accommodate the necessary inflation adjustments in order to arrive at "real" operating surplus (*CC*). These estimates have been shown to be well suited to approximate economic profit (Bayer, 1980b).

Inflation Adjustments to "Capital"

Each of the profit concepts in the previous section is related to a specific capital concept. In addition, the estimates of the inflationary elements of book profit ("fictitious profits") stem from a new estimation of the asset values at current costs. Basically, three types of adjustments to the book figures are required.

According to Austrian accounting rules fixed assets are valued at historic costs. In order to arrive at a measure of fixed assets valued at replacement cost (current costs), a new capital stock for Austrian corporate industrial enterprises $(B + E)$ was calculated on the basis of the "perpetual inventory" method (Goldsmith). The estimates and methodology are described elsewhere in detail.[9] Here a short description suffices: starting with the values of the Opening Balance 1955 ("Schillingseröffnungsbilanz 1955"), when all corporations were required to list the net replacement values of all their assets, annual capital stock figures were estimated by adding annual investment in plant and equipment (from the WIFO investment survey) and subtracting a measure of "economic depreciation." There is a long discussion in the literature on what type of depreciation formula to use in such estimates.[10] Here a degressive formula was used (in which the rate of depreciation is approximately twice the linear rate) because there is evidence that it corresponds most closely to actual firm behavior in Austria. Several authors describe the differences in profit estimates resulting from various depreciation methods.[11] These differences have to be kept in mind when the results are interpreted. For lack of additional information the sectoral capital stocks were calculated by applying the industry depreciation rate to all sectors. Real net capital stock estimates then were inflated by means of price indexes for fixed capital formation, that is, the index for machinery and equipment and the index for plant, so that current cost estimates resulted. These estimates differ from the book values in two respects:

1. They contain the "hidden reserves" resulting from the quicker write-off through accelerated depreciation schemes permitted in Austria and the effects of the shorter service lives permitted in the calculation of normal depreciation for tax purposes (cumulative difference between book depreciation allowances and economic depreciation) and

2. They contain the effect of valuation at replacement costs. The latter effect is smaller than the former, even though at times of high inflation (especially 1974, and again since 1980) the latter reaches sizable proportions.

For the purpose of revaluing stocks of inventories very rough estimates had to be carried out. For balance sheet purposes, Austrian firms are required to value their stocks by the "identity pricing method." This, however, is only possible for commodities distinguishable from each other and where the movement into and out of the stock can therefore be recorded. A vast number of commodities (fuel, raw materials, many semimanufactured goods) are indistinguishable. These commodities may be valued at various methods of average pricing, which correspond closely to those suggested by the UN National Income Accounting procedures.[12] There is no exact information in Austria as to which procedures are applied to what extent in practice. Furthermore, according to Austrian rules "synthetic" methods like LIFO or FIFO are not permitted. Thus a trial-and-error procedure had to be applied to arrive at realistic estimates of "real" inventory changes. The decision was taken to adjust the net input inventory changes (from year to year) by half the value of the increase in the price index for industry inputs, those of finished goods stocks by the industrial output price index.[13] Among several variants tested this measure yielded the most plausible inventory changes when compared with sales, production, and anticipation data. This adjustment yields "fictitious" profit elements (inventory valuation adjustment), which remain fairly stable throughout the first part of the period but rise to sizable magnitudes during the early 1970s. Nevertheless, in relation to the United Kingdom and the United States (where, according to Hill in 1974, this adjustment amounted to 48 percent respectively, 40 percent of gross operating surplus) the average-pricing procedures described above (adjustment by half the inventory price change) keep this adjustment on a smaller level (for Austria in 1974: 20 percent of gross book profits). This concept implies that actual valuation procedures of Austrian firms eliminate about half of the price effect from inventory valuation; thus only the rest enters the arguments of inflation accounting.

The third capital item requiring adjustment is net monetary assets, defined as those liquid net assets that are part of the companies' working capital. They contain liquid assets and the balance of trade debits and credits and are considered essential to the firms' ability to stay in business (Hill, p. 122). At times they can assume negative values. If these net assets are considered necessary for carrying on business, their real value must be maintained. Thus an adjustment is made to the effect that their net change between two years is split into a real component and an inflation-induced component, which is part of fictitious profits and as such is subtracted from book profit.[14] In general, this item is relatively small from the quantitative point of view, but takes on significance from the point of view of the logic of inflation accounting.

In principle there are two ways to take account of inflation adjustments in the assets estimates: either "fictitious profit" elements are calculated from book figures by means of the methods described, and these profit elements accumulated and transferred into a "revaluation reserve" or "capital maintenance fund," or each capital item is recalculated in terms of current costs. In this case no other adjustment to the capital figures, from which the profit figures are derived, is necessary.

The Austrian data situation calls for a mixture between these two methods: fixed assets are recalculated from outside sources; inventory and net monetary assets adjustments, on the other hand, are approximated from book figures and transferred to a reserve fund. Thus new series for physical capital, total capital, and also equity capital (total capital minus book debt) at current cost are developed and set in relation to the respective profit estimates, in order to arrive at real rates of return series.

Other capital items, such as financial assets, are not adjusted for inflationary bias, since they are assumed to represent nonessential (for the carrying on of the business) investments that do not warrant capital maintenance provisions. They enter the capital estimates with their book values.

Total Capital and Equity Capital

As mentioned above, the primary purpose here is to estimate rates of return on all capital invested by the corporations, that is, on equity plus debt. In this entity view of the corporations the gains accruing to the equity owners through the fall in the real value of the nominal debt in times of inflation are compensated by the equivalent loss to the creditors. When returns on equity alone are calculated, however, this income transfer from creditors to capital owners plays an important role, as the calculations show. Comparisons between rates of return on total capital and equity exhibit these transfers. The size of these transfers depends on the debt equity ratio and on the interest rate.[15]

In Austria there is a lot of discussion on whether to classify some capital components that in general go by the name of "social capital" as equity or debt. This term refers mainly to superannuation reserves, severance pay reserves, pension reserves, and other provisions of a "social" character, additions to which are (to a varying extent) tax free. Legally, in Austria some of these reserves are classed as equity, some as debt, even though they are very similar in character. Most of the social capital is earmarked for the benefit of employees. Up to 1978 additions to social capital were tax free, practically without limit; since then, tax-free net additions and the total amount of social capital have been limited. Up to that year provisions for social capital increased significantly from year to year, because they enabled firms to reduce their tax burden. If these provisions do not add to an equity owner's income in many cases, they certainly increase the firms' liquidity. Especially those parts of social capital that with high certainty are of a long-range character can be reinvested by the firms and/or represent at least an interest-free loan.

In order to take account of the increasing importance of "social capital" and also of the difficulty of classing it as equity or debt, in this chapter equity capital is defined once as including social capital, and once as excluding it. The data situation does not allow a clear definition of social capital for all years investigated, but gaps were filled by estimates.

Sectoral Structure of Rates of Return

The sectoral structure of the calculated rates of return is very sensitive to definitional differences, especially as to whether inflation accounting has been applied or not. Table 11–3 gives an overview of this structure according to various definitions. For our main result, the real rate of return on total capital, $ROC_o(BT)$, the ranking shows above-average rates (over the total period) for the stone and clay industry, machinery and vehicles, the chemical industry, electrical engineering, and food-stuffs, and below-average rates for mining and petroleum (!), iron and steel, paper and textiles and clothing. The major remarkable result in this ranking is that of the mining and petroleum sector, where the rates seem lower than expected. Several factors account for that: first, the very profitable petroleum sector is lumped together with the tradition-ally ailing coal and ore mining industries; second, inflation accounting has by far the strongest effect on this sector, because it is extremely capital intensive and also because inventory valuation adjustments (oil reserves) are very high. The Austrian oil industry does not only refine the crude oil that it extracts itself, but it imports a major share (approximately 90 percent in 1980). The problem of increasing prices of crude oil imports is not completely equivalent for this industry as that of rising inventory costs in other sectors, since the Austrian oil industry also has a major influence on adjusting the prices of its inputs.[16] In addition, part of the revenues of the (nationalized) oil industry stem

Table 11–3
Sectoral Structure of Rates of Return, Average ROR 1956–80
(*percent*)

| | Net Rates of Return on | | | | | | | |
| | Physical Capital | | Total Capital | | Equity I[a] | | Equity II[b] | |
Sector	HC[c]	CC[d]	HC	CC	HC	CC	HC	CC
Stone & clay, glass	15.9	10.7	13.2	9.3	16.6	11.2	16.4	11.0
Electrical engineering	13.0	9.4	8.7	6.8	15.8	11.3	15.6	11.0
Machinery, vehicles	13.1	9.3	9.6	8.8	18.4	13.8	18.5	13.7
Chemicals	13.0	8.3	9.9	6.8	14.1	8.7	13.6	8.6
Food, tobacco	12.5	8.0	9.3	6.3	13.4	8.7	13.0	8.3
Iron, steel, metal products	9.5	5.7	17.8	5.1	11.5	6.9	11.0	6.5
Mining, petroleum	15.1	6.3	12.7	5.9	16.3	7.1	16.0	6.8
Paper	9.7	6.1	8.3	5.5	11.4	7.1	11.2	7.0
Wood products	10.2	5.2	8.6	6.0	12.4	8.5	11.7	8.5
Leather, textiles, clothing	6.4	3.2	5.8	3.4	7.3	4.2	7.3	4.1
All sectors	11.7	7.0	9.1	6.0	13.6	8.1	13.3	7.8

[a]Equity I: inclusive "Social Capital."
[b]Equity II: exclusive "Social Capital."
[c]HC: Historic cost calculation.
[d]CC: Current cost calculation.

not from production but from trading activities, to which in the opinion of this author the rationale and concepts of inflation accounting cannot be applied in the same way as to production activities. Third, this sector has improved its ranking in the rate-of-return hierarchy significantly over time: for the eighteen years before the oil price shock (1956–1973) its rate of return ranked seventh; since then it improved to third place.

The hierarchy of rates across sectors is relatively stable over time (table 11–4): significant deviations are revealed by the iron and steel industry, which fell to the ninth rank, and the chemical industry, which fell to the eighth rank. On the other hand, the mining-petroleum sector improved its position throughout the total period (from ninth place in the late 1950s to third place 1976/80), electrical engineering has moved up from below-average rates until the late 1960s into the top ranks during the past ten years, and the paper industry also shows strong gains. The other sectors show no discernible trend, apart from the wood products industry, which because of the small sample size exhibits very unstable behavior.

All sectors show very strong cyclical fluctuations in their respective rates of return. In some sectors the sectoral cyclical movement deviates from that of total industry, and there the specific patterns deviate from the general pattern (figure 11–1). Examples are the stone and clay industry and the foodstuff industry, which for various reasons exhibit strong specific cycles.

Table 11–4
Behavior Over Time of Sectoral Real Net Rates of Return on Total Capital

Sector	1956–58	1959–63	1964–68	1969–75	1976–80
Stone & clay, glass	13.4	11.9	8.9	7.6	7.0
Electrical engineering	7.4	8.4	4.1	8.1	5.7
Machinery, vehicles	11.6	10.1	6.7	6.1	6.5
Chemicals	11.6	9.2	6.1	5.9	3.4
Food, tobacco	8.8	9.0	7.1	4.1	4.5
Iron, steel, metal products	7.5	7.7	4.3	4.8	2.5
Mining-petroleum	6.9	6.9	5.1	5.5	5.7
Paper	8.5	6.8	4.9	4.0	5.1
Wood products	9.7	11.1	6.0	2.4	3.8
Leather, textiles, clothing	5.0	4.4	2.8	3.8	1.6
All sectors	8.3	8.0	5.3	5.4	4.1

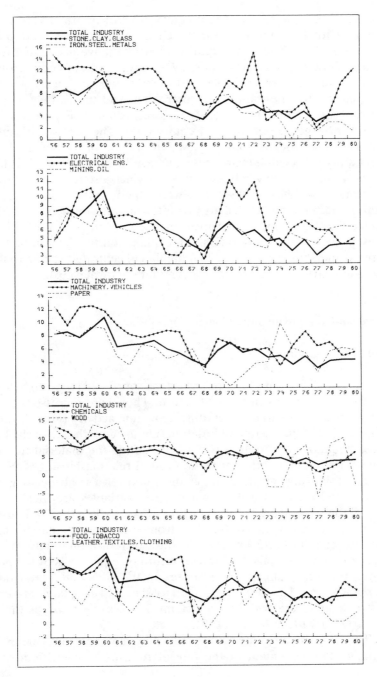

Figure 11–1. Sectoral Real Net Rates of Return

The ranking in terms of real equity rates of return is very similar to that of total capital; only for the chemical industry is there a rank difference of two places. The equity rates are on average higher for all sectors, showing the effect of positive leverage. This effect is strongest for the machinery and vehicles and the electrical engineering sectors and weakest for the mining and petroleum and the leather, textiles, and clothing sectors. The size of the leverage factor is positively correlated with the size of the debt equity ratio. The only significant exception is the foodstuff industry, which in spite of the second-lowest debt equity ratio exhibits an above-average leverage effect. It is likely that because of this low debt equity ratio (which also remained constant over time) the firms in this sector were able to obtain very favorable credit conditions, which led to low interest rates on debt. But these firms did not attempt to maximize their equity rates of return by increasing their debt equity ratios. An explanation for this can be found in the ownership structure of this highly concentrated sector (nationalized industry and traditionally strong family ownership).

Short- and Long-Run Behavior

Statistical Analysis

Tables 11–5, 11–6, and 11–7 report on the short- and long-run behavior of various definitions of rates of return. They were regressed, successively, on time, a variable denoting economic activity (growth rate of real GDP), and on the rate of inflation (annual growth rate of the CPI). These equations are more a way of presenting the material in an organized way than an attempt to find causal relationships.

The following results emerge: the trend term is always negative, when tested alone as well as when other variables are included. In general the trend term becomes slightly weaker when the GDP growth rate is added. The negative trend is stronger for before- than for after-tax rates of return and stronger for rates of return on equity than on total capital. On average, the rate of return on equity falls by 0.3 points a year, that on total capital before tax by 0.2 points, and after tax by 0.1 point a year. The rate of return on total capital calculated at historic cost (net book rate) exhibits pretty much the same trend as the real rate: $ROC(BT)$ (see figure 11–2).

The level of economic activity also plays an important role in "explaining" the movement of the rate of return: the coefficient of the

Table 11–5
Real Rates of Return on Physical and Total Capital 1956–80

		Total Capital		
Year	Physical Capital ROC_A (BT)	Before Tax ROC_O (BT)	After Tax ROC_O (AT)	Effective Tax Rate t_y
1956	10.4	8.4	5.0	40.0
1957	11.0	8.8	5.9	32.6
1958	9.3	7.8	5.4	30.7
1959	11.0	9.2	6.3	31.3
1960	14.0	11.0	7.5	31.9
1961	8.7	6.4	3.4	47.3
1962	7.9	6.8	3.9	41.7
1963	7.8	6.8	4.0	41.7
1964	8.8	7.4	4.2	43.3
1965	6.6	6.0	3.3	44.9
1966	5.9	5.4	3.0	43.8
1967	4.1	4.2	2.2	47.4
1968	3.2	3.4	1.4	60.2
1969	6.7	5.8	3.6	38.0
1970	8.3	7.1	4.4	37.3
1971	6.0	5.4	3.5	35.4
1972	7.1	6.1	4.5	25.8
1973	4.7	4.6	3.5	24.9
1974	5.4	5.0	3.3	33.3
1975	3.1	3.5	2.2	37.2
1976	5.2	4.9	3.7	23.4
1977	2.3	2.9	2.0	33.0
1978	4.0	4.2	2.9	29.4
1979	7.0	4.3	3.2	26.2
1980	10.9	4.2	3.0	29.2

GDP growth variable is always positive and highly significant: when economic activity picks up speed, in general the rate of return also increases. This variable is only a very rough approximation, since it does not measure economic activity by industrial corporations but the general economic climate in the Austrian economy, represented by GDP. In some years industrial corporations have fared quite differently from the total economy.

The inclusion of the rate of inflation added nothing to the "explanation" in nearly all cases. Only for the rate of return calculated at historic cost does the inflation variable show a significant (and positive) effect. This is to be expected, since high inflation leads to a high proportion of fictitious profits and thus to high book rates. This result holds before and after taxes. The main result of this analysis is the establishment of a falling long-term tendency in the rate of return for Austrian industrial corporations.

Table 11–6
Real Equity Rates of Return

| Year | Equity I^a ROR Before Tax REG_O (BT)I | Equity II^b ROR | | |
		Before Tax REG_O (BT) II	After Tax REG_O (AT) II	Effective Tax Rate t
1956	12.1	12.2	7.0	42.6
1957	13.6	13.8	9.4	31.9
1958	11.9	11.9	8.3	30.1
1959	11.6	11.5	7.2	36.8
1960	14.0	14.3	9.2	35.7
1961	7.9	9.2	4.8	48.2
1962	9.1	8.9	4.8	46.7
1963	8.5	8.4	4.3	49.0
1964	9.1	9.0	4.4	51.3
1965	8.0	7.8	3.9	49.5
1966	6.8	6.7	3.3	51.8
1967	5.2	5.1	2.1	58.1
1968	4.4	4.5	1.5	66.8
1969	6.6	6.2	3.0	52.5
1970	8.5	8.3	4.3	48.0
1971	7.2	7.1	4.1	41.8
1972	8.9	8.8	6.3	28.6
1973	7.4	7.1	5.3	26.3
1974	4.4	3.6	0.9	76.2
1975	4.2	4.0	1.8	55.4
1976	11.9	5.8	3.8	35.4
1977	3.7	4.7	2.9	39.2
1978	5.5	3.8	1.3	65.0
1979	7.1	6.5	4.1	37.0
1980	5.6	6.7	3.9	41.2

[a]Equity I: inclusive "social capital."
[b]Equity II: exclusive "social capital."

Testing Three Hypotheses

The statistical tests described above remain inconclusive as to the causes for the long-term fall in the rate of return. Here an attempt is made to shed some more light on this phenomenon by testing three hypotheses of so-called "crisis theory" as to their applicability to Austrian data (see Weisskopf, 1980). Each of these hypotheses posits a different reason for the initial fall in the rate of return, which in turn leads to a reduction in investment and output and thus to a recession or crisis. Each of these hypotheses can be formulated either as a long-run or a short-run theory, explaining either the trend in the rate of return or its cyclical behavior.

The theory concerned with technological change and the "rising organic composition of capital" maintains that the capitalist process of accumulation sooner or later generates an increase in the organic com-

Table 11–7
Regression Analysis of Rates of Return

Rate of Return	Constant	Time	Cyclical Variable[a]	Inflation[b]	R^2
ROC (BT)	8.82 (16.7)	-0.22 (6.5)			0.65
	7.13 (8.3)	-0.19 (5.7)	0.30 (2.4)		0.72
	7.20 (7.7)	-0.19 (4.4)	0.30 (2.3)	-0.02 (0.2)	0.72
ROC (AT)	5.38 (11.1)	-0.12 (3.9)			0.40
	4.05 (5.0)	-0.10 (3.1)	0.23 (2.0)		0.49
	4.05 (4.5)	-0.10 (2.5)	0.23 (1.9)	0.0 (0.0)	0.49
Net Book Rate ROR (HC, BT)[a,c]	11.95 (16.7)	-0.22 (4.4)			0.46
	9.46 (7.7)	-0.17 (3.6)	0.44 (2.4)		0.57
	8.56 (6.7)	-0.23 (4.1)	0.48 (2.7)	0.34 (1.8)	0.63
REQ (BT)[d]	12.4 (16.7)	-0.33 (6.5)			0.65
	9.29 (7.7)	-0.28 (5.8)	0.50 (2.7)		0.73
	9.49 (6.0)	-0.27 (4.4)	0.49 (2.6)	0.07 (0.4)	0.74

Note: t statistics are in parentheses under the coefficients.

[a] Annual percentage change in real GDP.
[b] Annual percentage change in Consumer Price Index.
[c] Calculated at historic cost.
[d] Exclusive of social capital.

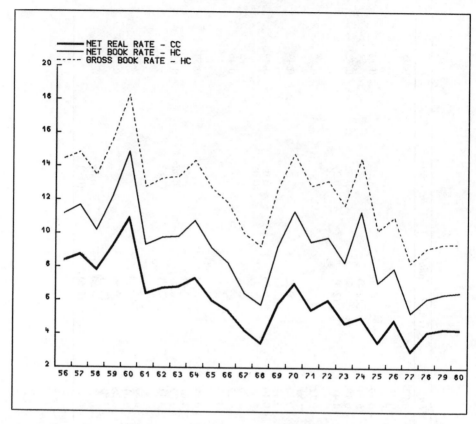

Figure 11–2. Effects of Inflation Accounting on Rates of Return

position of capital (approximated here by the capital output ratio), which is caused by changes in the relative prices of labor and capital. By means of falling capital productivity this leads to a fall in the rate of return.

A second hypothesis maintains that a major reason for the fall in the rate of return can be found in the struggle over distribution exacerbated by the rising strength of labor. According to this view the long phase of prosperity after World War II resulted (among other things) in a strengthening of the position of labor and its representatives in relation to capital, which then led to a rise in the wage share at the expense of the profit share. The short-run version of this hypothesis is based on the notion of a periodic depletion of labor market reserves that strengthens labor's bargaining position. If wages rise faster than productivity, and if this increase in unit labor costs cannot fully be passed on to prices, the wage share will increase and thus lead to a fall in the profit share and also (at constant utilization rates and capital output ratio) in the profit rate. Sometimes it is argued that the pressure of domestic and international competition additionally prevents wage increases from being passed on to output prices.

The third version tested here refers to the so-called realization problem. It maintains that in the course of accumulation imbalances arise that make it impossible to sell all the good produced at profitable prices, since there is a lack in effective demand. There are versions of "underconsumption" (Marx, Baran-Sweezy) and of "underinvestment" (Kalecki, Steindl) in the literature presented as the causes of this lack of effective demand. Reductions in production then lead to under-utilization of existing capacity and thus to a fall in profit rates.

In order to test these three hypotheses the net rate of return is broken down into three parts: the profit share, capacity utilization, and the capacity capital ratio (the inverse of the capital output ratio at full capacity).

$$r = \frac{Y}{O} = \frac{Y}{Q} \cdot \frac{Q}{H} \cdot \frac{H}{O} = a.b.c, \qquad (11.1)$$

where Y is defined as inflation-adjusted operating surplus, O as net capital stock, Q as net output (approximated by the sum of profits and wages), and H as capacity output.

The change in each of these three components can then be aligned with one of the three hypotheses mentioned above. Thus the contribution of the change of each component (hypothesis) to the change in the rate of return can be determined. For the short-run analysis the total period was divided into three complete business cycles from trough to trough (1958–1977; see figure 11–3). The boom phase of each cycle is further divided into an early (A) and a late (B) phase, in order to show the special role of the changes in the rate of return.

Over the whole period (1956–1980) this analysis shows that the rate of return falls on average by 5.4 percent per year. At the same time the profit share decreased by 3.4 percent, while the capacity capital ratio rose on average by 1.3 percent and capacity utilization by 0.04 percent per year (table 11–8).

The empirical tests show that in the short as well as in the long run, changes in the wage share exert the strongest influence on the rate of return. In the long run, about 80 percent of the fall in the rate of return is contributed by an increase in the wage share. Over the total period the long-run increase in the capital output ratio also exerts a certain negative influence on the rate of return, but this effect is only about one-third that of the wage share. Long-run changes in capacity

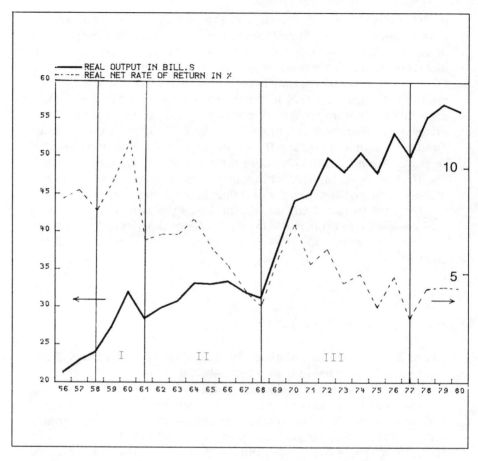

Figure 11–3. Output and Profitability

utilization (a slight long-run increase) are hardly of importance for changes in the rate of return.

The rates of return also fell among the three discernible full cycles (1958–1961, 1961–1968, 1968–1977) (table 11–8, *B*). During the 1950s and 1960s cycles only about 60 percent of the fall is accounted for by the rising wage share, while between the 1960s and 1970s this contribution was roughly 90 percent. Between the 1950s and 1960s the increasing capitalization of Austrian industry contributed around 30 percent to the fall in the rate of return, while this contribution was around 45 percent in the latter phase, in both cases about half the effect of increasing wage share. The major difference among these periods

Table 11–8
Rates of Return, Distribution, Utilization, and Technical Progress

	Cycle			Full
	I	II	III	Period
A. Values of basic variables: cycle and full period average				
Rate of return, r	8.6	5.8	4.9	6.0
Profit share, a	36.6	28.9	24.9	28.8
Utilization, b	90.6	87.0	91.9	90.0
Capital productivity, c	25.7	22.8	21.0	22.6

	I − II	II − II	Full Period
B. Average annual growth rates between cycles			
Rate of Return, r	−8.1	−2.2	−5.4
Profit share, a	−4.8	−2.0	−4.0
Utilization, b	−0.8	+0.7	+1.0
Capital productivity, c	−2.4	−1.0	−1.3

	Phase		
	A	B	C
C. Average growth rates during cyclical phases			
Rate of return, r	19.6	−7.6	−25.6
Profit share, a	13.8	−6.1	−18.4
Utilization, b	1.8	0.5	− 1.0
Capital productivity, c	3.9	−2.3	− 7.8

lies in the effect of capacity utilization, which between the 1950s and 1960s had a significant positive effect on the rate of return.

Within the business cycles the following pattern emerges: during the early boom phase (phase A), when the rate of return increases, more than two-thirds of this increase can be attributed to a rising profit share; increasing capital productivity accounts for 20 percent of the increase in the profit rate; the rest is contributed by improved capacity utilization. During late expansion (phase B) production and capacity utilization still increase, but a falling profit share and falling capital productivity (the result of continuing high rates of capital accumulation) account for a slow fall in rate of return. During the contraction phase of the cycle (phase C) the rapid fall in the rate of return is caused by a quickly rising wage share, falling capital productivity, and falling capacity utilization.

These tests show that the distribution parameter (profit share) and thus the hypothesis of the struggle over income distribution exert the strongest influence on the rate of return in Austrian industry. The theory of the rise in the organic composition of capital receives far less support. No evidence can be found for a theory based on realization failures. These tests should be considered only first steps in the causal explanation of long- and short-run changes in the rates of return and are as yet too preliminary to constitute definitive evidence.

Effective Tax Burden

It has been noted above that direct taxes paid (on income, revenue, and assets) by companies in relation to real profits (effective tax rates) vary quite significantly over time (see tables 11–5 and 11–6) and between sectors.[17] Even though statutory tax rates have not changed very much during that time, depreciation allowances have been changed and other tax-related rules varied. For industry as a whole tax rates increased as a percentage of pretax profits during the 1950s and 1960s; then fell significantly during the 1970s. For Austria, the year 1968 ("Wachtumsgesetze," "Growth Acts") marks a significant turnaround in the taxation of company income. As a result of the profit squeeze during the recession of 1967–68, which made apparent the effect of increased international competition in the face of an industry structure relying heavily on basic goods and had disadvantages in the production of final goods, the conservative government introduced a series of laws designed to facilitate structural adjustments of Austrian industry. As a result, among other effects, effective tax rates fell significantly. During the later years, a series of additional measures (especially changes in depreciation allowances) was taken to increase these effects. Recently, especially since 1980, the increase in the share of tax-deductible interest payments in net operating surplus has also contributed to the fall in the effective tax rate. Thus, as a result, the effective tax rate for industry as a whole during 1976–1980 amounted to 28 percent, in contrast to the period of 1964–1968, when it reached 48 percent (table 11–9).

Since taxes paid are not only the result of statutory tax rates and taxable profits, but also depend on capital intensity, location, and various other effects, effective tax rates differ from sector to sector and company to company. In general, above-average tax rates were levied on mining and petroleum, paper, foodstuffs, and machinery. In all sectors with the exception of stone and clay, a similar time pattern to that of total industry is apparent; since the late 1960s effective tax rates have declined significantly. This trend is even more significant when one remembers that for tax purposes inflation accounting is not permitted by Austrian law. Thus effective tax rates fall even more when applied to a book tax base (gross book profits) and not to a real base.

Table 11–9
Effective Tax Rates[a] Over Time

Sector	1956–58	1959–63	1964–68	1969–75	1976–80	1956–80
Stone & Clay, glass	37.5	36.0	32.1	34.0	40.5	35.7
Electrical engineering	28.6	28.8	56.4	25.7	27.6	33.2
Machinery, vehicles	48.9	51.8	52.2	33.6	21.8	40.4
Chemicals	35.0	34.2	51.0	27.4	30.5	35.0
Food, tobacco	33.5	47.2	28.5	74.5	52.1	64.4
Iron, steel, metal products	29.9	38.5	42.3	74.1	30.6	46.6
Mining, petroleum	32.2	39.0	63.3	44.5	28.4	42.5
Paper	31.4	35.6	43.4	79.5	16.3	45.1
Wood products	34.1	42.3	41.5	30.3	1.2	29.6
Leather, textiles, clothing	38.5	44.0	39.9	31.3	146.9	37.8
All sectors	34.4	38.8	47.9	33.1	28.2	36.4

[a]Direct taxes actually paid by companies in relation to pretax net operating surplus (CC).

Capital Costs and Returns:
There is No "q" for Austria

The Hopeless Case of the Austrian Stock Market

In most developed market economies corporations command essentially three types of financing: internal finance by way of reinvesting undistributed profits, external finance either by way of issuing stock (equity) or bonds (debt), or by way of bank loans. If a developed capital market (for stocks and bonds) exists, economic theory posits a relationship between economic performance of the firms (that is, their rate of return) and their market valuation (represented by stock and bond yields, which represent costs of capital to the firms). This whole set of arguments can be subsumed under the heading of Tobin's q and occupies a large part of literature.[18]

For Austria it is impossible to produce even halfway conclusive evidence on this relationship, since no functioning capital market exists.[19] The major difference between the United States, for example, and Austria lies not only in the nature of their stock markets, but also in the fact that in Austria the bond market is inaccessible to production firms. Historical and institutional reasons account for this: all decision-making bodies controlling access to the bond market are nearly exclusively (only exception: government representatives) manned by representatives of banking interests. As a result bonds are only issued by public bodies, semipublic utilities, and banks. The latter issue bonds and then extend credit to firms.

In a similar way the stock market has been prevented from playing its appropriate role in Austrian company finance. A brief description will make this point clear. In Austria only forty-one industrial firms (fifty-seven all together) are listed on the stock exchange. In 1978 the nominal value of all outstanding stock was 6.3 bill.S, their market value 13.6 bill.S. The relative size of the stock market can be measured by setting the market value of the stocks in relation to the value added of the respective sector: for Austrian industry this index in 1978 amounted to 7.6 percent, and for the whole economy to only 3.3 percent. Economy-wide figures for other countries are Germany, 10 percent; Italy, 8 percent; France, 11 percent; Great Britain, 21 percent; Japan, 25 percent; United States, 37 percent (Bierich). This comparison shows the limited size of the Austrian market. In addition, in Austria only a small percentage of shares is traded regularly (less than one-quarter are traded on more than 80 percent of trading days). Furthermore Austrian commercial banks make extensive use of their "right to self-entry," by which they are allowed to take shares of their customers that are to be traded into their own portfolios. This right has been estimated to comprise between 50 to 60 percent of all sales, which further limits the size of the market.[20]

Approximately 80 percent of all shares theoretically up for trade are owned by the government (nationalized industries), by nationalized banks (two of the three largest Austrian banks are nationalized), or by families, all of which are not interested in trading their shares, but rather in holding on to them. Thus only around 20 percent of the already small volume of shares are available for trading. Under these historical and institutional circumstances it is hardly surprising that no actual market for shares develops and that the financing of companies by way of the equity capital market remains on a very low level.

On the other hand, in the past the government has encouraged and subsidized savings in all kinds of bonds, which in Austria are traditionally issued by local and federal governments, the large banks, and also public utility companies, but hardly at all by production firms. Thus it has been argued that saving in stocks of industrial firms has been "discriminated against," even though in 1968 the corporate income tax rate on dividends was halved. This measure did have an effect on dividend distribution, but its effect was rather shortlived. The ratio of dividend payouts in relation to (nominal or real) equity profit shows this effect clearly for the years 1968 and 1969. The strong variation of this ratio for the period afterward (standard deviation 4.2 for 1968–

1978, versus only 1.1 for 1956–1967) combines the effect of a very constant stream of dividends (especially in relation to nominal capital) with strong movements in equity profit. It has been noted elsewhere (Bayer 1980a) that Austrian stockholders (especially those majority owners who hold on to their stocks) are more interested in a bondlike return on their stocks than in dividend payouts, which fluctuate with profitability. Thus the dividend payout decisons by management are less influenced by economic reasoning than by the wish to receive as constant a flow of dividends as possible. In this way saving in common stocks loses its specific appeal for the financial investor who would prefer a riskier, but on average higher yielding, investment to a low-yielding, practically risk-free bond. This peculiarity of the Austrian industrial stock "market" has resulted in a nearly continuous loss in implicit share values (ratio of market values to book values of quoted companies) since the boom year 1961. Since then this ratio has fallen by 62 percent (see Aiginger-Bayer, 1981, p. 73).

This description should make it clear that, for Austrian corporations, financing through the capital market is unlikely to play a major role in the near future. Very recently, the Austrian parliament passed legislation (end of 1982) giving heavy tax subsidies to investors in a series of quasi–venture-capital companies set up recently. This might mark the beginning of easier access to risk capital (direct connection between financial investor and firm) for production firms in the future, even though so far the quantitative effect is minimal. For a long time to come the financing of restructuring and expanding Austrian production will have to rely heavily on bank loans. This is where energies for reform to fulfill more flexibly the financing needs of Austrian production firms will have to be directed.

The nonexistence of a capital market for industry stocks and bonds thus makes the calculation of a q ratio impossible. The following section attempts to fill this gap in a less formalized way.

Indicators of Yields and Costs of Capital

To a large extent Austrian industrial firms are self-financed. The very substantial promotion of self-financing by means of accelerated depreciation allowances, which in Austria is more highly developed than in most other Western countries (Lehner), has led to a heavy reliance by Austrian firms on financing large parts of their investment by plowing back profits. Thus, when calculated on a current cost basis, the debt equity ratio of Austrian firms is relatively low and increased only slightly until the early 1970s (table 11–10). Since then, however, it has risen

Table 11–10
Debt Equity Ratios

	1956–58	1959–63	1964–68	1969–75	1976–80	1956–80
Historic costs						
I[a]	0.65	0.60	0.61	0.86	1.10	0.78
II[b]	0.70	0.63	0.64	0.94	1.45	0.89
Current costs						
I	0.49	0.44	0.44	0.55	0.80	0.55
II	0.52	0.46	0.47	0.59	1.01	0.62

[a]I: Equity includes social capital.
[b]II: Equity excludes social capital.

quite substantially, especially since the profit squeeze. The crisis of 1974–75 has made use of accelerated depreciation scarcer, because profits were not high enough. Thus debt financing has assumed a more prominent role. Depending on the definition (whether or not provisions for "social capital" are included) the debt equity ratio[21] between 1973 and 1980 increased from 0.64 (respectively 0.59 inclusive of social capital) to 1.21 (0.93) after it had remained practically constant (with small fluctuations) between 1956 and 1973. Also during that time the interest burden increased significantly, because, in addition to a higher debt ratio, nominal and real interest rates reached a new high. In relation to operating surplus (inclusive of interest) interest payments rose from 31 percent in 1973 to 49 percent in 1980. Since then interest rates have increased even more as a result of factors external to Austrian economic policy influences. This has resulted in a very heavy burden of the external debt.

One very rough approximation of the cost of capital to Austrian firms is given by the interest rate on long-term government, bank, and utility bonds, deflated by the CPI. This rate is significant because on the one hand it approximates the opportunity costs of potential financiers of industry (only incompletely, though, because for a number of years acquisition of such bonds was subsidized) and on the other hand movements in this rate (if not the actual level) are closely related to costs of bank loans. Again the approximation is incomplete, since for a vast array of industry loans investment premiums and interest subsidies are available, which have not been taken into account in this comparison. Other (real) capital cost indicators are reflected in the interest rates paid by the firms for loans. Unfortunately, the data published in the balance sheets do not separate interest-bearing liabilities from others. Thus two series were constructed that mark a lower and an upper limit to the actual interest burden borne by the corporate sector: the lower one defined as interest payments in relation to all liabilities, the upper limit by interest payments in relation to overdrafts and bank liabilities (table 11–11). Both series exhibit a marked upward trend, which is steeper for the latter definition.

Comparisons between costs and yields show that in the long run yields (measured by the real rate of return on total capital or by the equity rate of return) were quite significantly higher than costs (measured by the real bond rate; see figure 11–4). Only from 1966 to 1969 and in 1978 was the bond rate higher than the after-tax real rate of return on equity.

These differences between investment in productive and financial assets as shown here cannot be interpreted as representing risk premiums. This would only be true if one compared the real rate of return for an individual company, or a small group of companies, with the

Table 11–11
Indicators of Real Costs of External Capital to Austrian Firms

Year	Return to Investors[a] in Stock	Interest Burden 1[b]	Interest Burden 2[c]	Real Bond Rate[d]
		(in Percent)		
1961	22.8			
1962	−27.0			
1963	− 6.9			
1964	− 1.6			
1965	− 2.0	3.9	8.2	1.2
1966	− 2.5	4.2	9.2	5.0
1967	− 4.8	4.7	10.0	3.1
1968	3.3	4.6	10.0	4.8
1969	15.4	4.3	9.2	4.4
1970	16.3	4.6	10.2	3.3
1971	− 6.5	4.3	9.5	2.9
1972	25.2	4.2	10.9	0.9
1973	8.5	4.3	12.9	0.4
1974	0.6	5.2	15.4	−0.2
1975	8.2	5.2	16.6	1.1
1976	4.4	4.8	16.5	1.5
1977	−10.3	4.8	16.1	3.2
1978	5.4	5.0	16.8	4.6
1979	n.a.[e]	4.9	15.0	4.2
1980	n.a.	5.6	16.1	2.9

Source: adapted from Austrian National Bank (return to investors and bond rate) and Balance Sheet Statistics (all others).

[a]Return to Investors: dividends plus capital gains at current prices in relation to market value of stocks.

[b]Interest Burden 1: interest payments in relation to all liabilities.

[c]Interest Burden 2: interest payments in relation to bank liabilities.

[d]Real Bond Rate: real rate of return on government and private bonds (deflated by CPI).

[e]n.a. = not available.

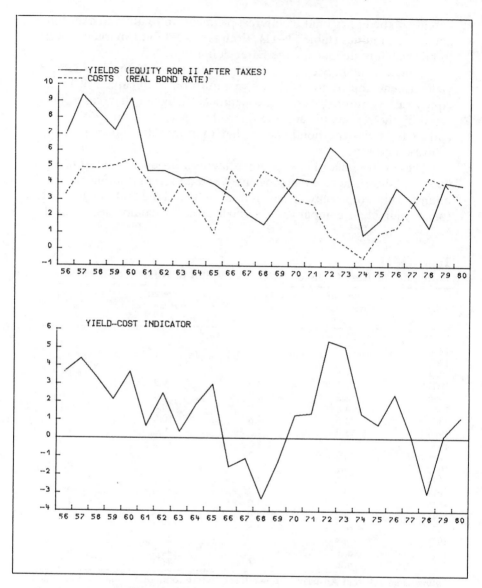

Figure 11–4. Capital Yields and Costs

bond rate. Thus the differences in the rates on financial versus productive assets can be interpreted as "real" superiority of one investment type over another. The period-to-period comparisons show that from the mid-1950s to the end of the 1960s this difference decreased substantially, recovered again to its highest value during the early 1970s, was reduced again, and then picked up during the most recent years.

The data presented here indicate strongly that capital costs relative to profits have remained quite constant throughout the 1950s, increased drastically throughout the 1960s, fell during the expansion phase of the early 1970s, rose again during the first years of the present crisis, and have been reduced again recently. A more complete discussion of capital costs and yields would have to include a thorough analysis of the role of government in influencing these magnitudes. In Austria, government plays a large role in this field, by direct intervention as well as indirectly.

Notes

1. Österreichisches Statistisches Zentralamt, *Statistik der Aktiengesellschaften,* current issues 1956–1980.
2. A recent study by the author (Aiginger-Bayer, 1980) based on a much wider firm sample by the Austrian National Bank (956 firms, 70 percent of industry workers) and applying different methodology shows some evidence that during the 1970s smaller firms were more profitable than larger ones. The same material was updated and published recently (Müllner-Richter, 1982) and shows the following size differences for (differently defined) rates of return on turnover (at book values) for 1973–1979: firms with fewer than 100 workers: 3.42 percent; 100–499 workers: 2.83 percent; more than 500 workers: 2.33 percent.
3. From an equity point of view this position makes eminent sense. Our Western societies do not share this view, however, since they allow depreciation deductions and, a fortiori, inflation accounting only for business income.
4. See on this point the discussion in the spring 1976 issue of the *Journal of Business Finance and Accounting* 3, no. 1, Oxford, for the British debate, or *Business Week,* October 15, 1979, or June 16, 1980, on the U.S. debate.
5. See, for example, D. Schneider (1968).
6. C. Kennedy (1978).
7. Ibid., p. 62, and T. Weisskopf (1979), p. 349, makes this distinction.
8. See K. Bayer (1980a), bibliography and the papers by the author quoted there.
9. Ibid., p. 46ff.
10. See, for example, R. Coen (1975) and the literature cited there.
11. Hill (1979) and Landskroner-Levy (1979), among many others, deal extensively with this point.
12. United Nations (1968), p. 111.
13. For input stock changes:

$$\Delta = G_1 - G_0 = (INV_1 - INV_0) \left(\frac{PI_1 - PI_0}{2PI_0} \right),$$

where

$$G = \text{inventories at current prices}$$
$$INV = \text{book value of inventories}$$
$$PI = \text{price index of industry inputs.}$$

The inventory valuation adjustment is then calculated as $\Delta G - \Delta INV$.

14. The "fictitious" profits component for the change in net monetary assets is then calculated as

$$(MON_1 - MON_0) \left(\frac{CP_1 - CP_0}{CP_0} \right),$$

where

$$MON = \text{book value of net monetary assets}$$
$$CP = \text{Consumer Price Index.}$$

Then

$$\Delta M = \Delta MON - \left(MON_0 \cdot \frac{CP_1 - CP_0}{CP_0} \right),$$

where

$$M = \text{net monetary assets at current prices.}$$

15. If nominal interest rates do not rise as fast as the inflation rate, equity owners gain at the expense of creditors—and vice versa. If the former occurs, there is an incentive for the equity owner, other things being equal, to increase leverage (or "capital gearing").

16. Thus valuation policies of input inventories play a very important role in determining (taxable) profit.

17. Austrian balance sheet statistics only show all direct taxes paid by companies; thus they include as major items the corporation income tax and the property tax. Using the business sector as a whole, the distribution between these taxes in 1977 was 80:20. Property tax share, even though not very significant in the long run, assumes disproportionate importance in recession years when (taxable) profits are low.

18. See J. Tobin (1969), and the references in other chapters of this volume.

19. The difference in the composition of finance between U.S. and Austrian enterprises becomes clear when the following data on sources of funds are compared:

	USA[a]	Austria[b]
Undistributed profits	23.9%	21.1%
Capital consumption allowance	39.4%	39.3%
Inventory valuation adjustment	−9.5%	—
Foreign earnings	3.3%	6.9%
Sum internal funds	56.4%	67.3%
Equity issues	1.9%	0.4%
Bonds and mortgages	15.2%	1.0%
Other debt	26.4%	31.3%
Sum external funds	43.5%	32.7%

(a) nonfinancial corporate business 1976–80; (b) production firms without public utilities 1972–77. Source: for United States: B. Friedman, "Financing Capital Formation in the 1980s: Issues for Public Policy" (NBER Working Paper No. 745, Cambridge, Mass., 1981); for Austria: P. Mooslechner. "Risikokapitalbildung in makroökonmischer Perspektive" (WIFO-Working Paper, Vienna, 1982).

20. In Germany, where a similar legal situation exists, banks have voluntarily given up this privilege in order to enhance the functioning of the stock market.

21. Here the debt equity ratio is calculated at current costs: from the total capital at market value, (nominal) debt is subtracted to obtain equity capital.

References

Aiginger, K., and Bayer, K. "Selbstfinanzierung und Betriebsüberschuß der Industrie." *Monatsberichte* 10 (Vienna, 1976).

———. "Dynamik und Selbstfinanzierungskraft industrieller Mittelbetriebe." *Quartalshefte* 2 (Vienna, 1980).

———. *Ausmaß, Funktion und Verzinsung des Eigenkapitals in der österreichischen Industrie.* Vienna: Bundesministerium für Finanzen, 1981.

Baran, P., and Sweezy, P. *Monopoly Capital.* New York: Monthly Review Press, 1966.

Bayer, K. "Die Struktur der Kapitalrenditen in der österreichischen Industrie." *Monatsberichte* 11 (Vienna, 1977).

———. "Inflation Accounting für Österreich." *Empirica* 1 (Vienna 1980a).

————. "Scheingewinn und Realgewinn." *Monatsberichte* 7 (Vienna, 1980b).

————. "Erklärungshypothesen für den Verlauf der Kapitalrendite in den österreichischen Industrieaktiengesellschaften." *Quartalshefte* 2 (Vienna 1982).

Bierich, M. "Probleme der Kapitalausstattung—Möglichkeiten zur Förderung des Aktiensparens." *List-Forum* 5 (1980).

Coen, R. "Investment Behavior, the Measurement of Depreciation and Tax Policy." *American Economic Review* 65, no. 1 (1975).

Coenenberg, A.G., and Macharzina, K. "Accounting for Price Changes: An Analysis of Current Developments in Germany." *JBFA* 3, no. 1 (Spring 1976).

Cripps, R., and Godley, W. "Profits and Stock Appreciation." *The Times,* October 1, 1976.

Glyn, A., and Sutcliffe, B. *British Capitalism, Workers and the Profits Squeeze.* London: Pantheon Books, 1972.

Friedman, B. "Financing Capital Formation in the 1980s: Issues for Public Policy." NBER Working Paper No. 745, September 1981.

Goldsmith, R.W. *A Perpetual Inventory of National Wealth, Studies in Income and Wealth,* vol. 14. New York: NBER, 1951.

Hill, T.P. *Profits and Rates of Return,* Paris: OECD, 1979.

Holland, D., and Myers, S. "Profitability and Capital Costs for Manufacturing Corporations and All Nonfinancial Corporations." *American Economic Review,* May 1980.

Journal of Business Finance and Accounting (JBFA) 3, no. 1 (Oxford, 1976).

Kalecki, M. *Theory of Economic Dynamics.* London: Allen and Unwin, 1954.

Kennedy, C. "Comment to Lawson." *JBFA,* Spring 1976.

————. "Inflation Accounting: Retrospect and Prospect." *Economic Policy Review,* no. 4 (Cambridge, 1978).

King, M. "The United Kingdom Profits Crisis: Myth or Reality?" *Economic Journal,* March 1975.

Landskroner, Y., and Levy, H. "Inflation, Depreciation and Optimal Production." *European Economic Review* 12, no. 4 (October 1979).

Lawson, G.H. "Sandilands: Holding Gains, Debt-financing, Working Capital and Current Corporation Accounting." *JBFA* 3, no. 1 (1976).

Lehner, G. *Die steuerlichen Investitionsförderungssysteme und die Unternehmensbesteuerung in der BRD, in Schweden, der Schweiz und Österreich.* Vienna: Österreichisches Institut für Wirtschaftsforschung, 1979.

Marx, K. *Das Kapital,* vols I and II. Berlin: Marx-Engels-Werke, 1974.

Österreichisches Statistisches Zentralamt. *Statistik der Aktiengesellschaften*, current issues, Vienna, 1956–1980.

Rosenfeld, P. "The Confusion between General Price-Level Restatement and Current Value Accounting." *Journal of Accountancy*, October 1982.

Schenk, W., and Fink, G. "Das Brutto-Sachanlagevermögen der österreichischen Industrie 1955 bis 1973." *Monatsberichte* 10 (Vienna, 1976).

Schmalenbach, E. *Dynamische Bilanz*. 6th ed. Leipzig: Gloechner, 1933.

Schmidt, F. *Die organische Bilanz im Rahmen der Wirtschaft*. Leipzig: Gloeckner, 1921.

Schneider, D. "Ausschüttungsfähiger Gewinn und das Minimum an Selbstfinanzierung." *Zeitschrift für betriebswirtschaftliche Forschung* 20, no. 1 (1968).

Shoven, J.B., and Bulow, J.I. "Inflation Accounting and Nonfinancial Corporate Profits." *Brookings Papers* 3 (1975) and 1 (1976).

Steindl, J. *Maturity and Stagnation in American Capitalism*. New York: Monthly Review Press, 1952/1976.

Sweezy, P. *The Theory of Capitalist Development*. New York: Monthly Review Press, 1942.

Tobin, J. "A General Equilibrium Approach to Monetary Theory." *Journal of Money, Credit and Banking*, February 1967.

United Nations. *A System of National Accounts*. New York: United Nations, 1968.

Weisskopf, T. "Marxian Crisis Theory and the Rate of Profit in the Postwar U.S. Economy." *Cambridge Journal of Economics* 3 (1979).

Welzmüller, R. "Unternehmensgewinne in den Volkswirtschaftlichen Gesamterchnungen—Entwicklung seit 1970." *WSI Mitteilungen* 11 (Cologne, 1979).

Appendix 11A
Data Appendix

The following ten tables contain the data from which the various definitions of rates of return for Austrian manufacturing corporations were calculated. The definitions used are the same as in the text. The symbols correspond to those of the Common Glossary.

Table 11A1
Total Profit Estimates
(in millions of Schillings)

| | | Historic Costs | | Current Costs | | |
| | | Net Book Profit | | Net Operating Surplus | | |
Year	Gross Book Profit on Total Capital	on Total Capital	on Physical Capital	on Total Capital Y	on Physical Capital	on Total Capital after Tax Y − T
1956	5 950	4 608	4 461	3 931	3 784	2 358
1957	6 636	5 236	5 091	4 569	4 424	3 078
1958	6 455	4 885	4 576	4 419	4 110	3 064
1959	8 131	6 378	5 934	5 716	5 272	3 927
1960	10 509	8 557	8 423	7 595	7 461	5 175
1961	8 160	5 947	6 236	4 915	5 204	2 590
1962	9 151	6 729	6 260	5 668	5 199	3 305
1963	9 721	7 131	6 568	6 029	5 466	3 516
1964	11 040	8 292	7 829	6 984	6 521	3 962
1965	10 388	7 482	6 698	6 055	5 271	3 338
1966	10 333	7 221	6 360	5 823	4 962	3 270
1967	9 243	5 943	4 791	4 687	3 535	2 467
1968	8 736	5 406	4 325	3 933	2 852	1 567
1969	12 535	9 091	8 290	7 213	6 412	4 470
1970	16 119	12 399	11 339	9 802	8 742	6 145
1971	15 679	11 605	10 312	8 527	7 234	5 505
1972	17 904	13 307	12 096	10 562	9 351	7 837
1973	17 911	12 691	10 483	9 057	6 849	6 806
1974	25 209	19 684	17 504	11 577	9 397	7 726
1975	19 840	13 751	10 778	8 850	5 877	5 555
1976	23 671	17 088	14 190	13 198	10 349	10 115
1977	19 332	12 295	8 538	8 349	4 592	5 592
1978	22 883	15 316	11 282	12 341	8 307	8 712
1979	25 202	17 171	19 061	13 463	15 353	9 934
1980	27 227	18 763	20 965	13 949	16 151	9 874

Table 11A2
Equity Profits
(in millions of Schillings)

| Year | Historic Costs Total Proprietary Gain | | Current Costs Equity Profit without Gearing | Current Costs Equity Profit with Gearing | |
	I^a	II^b		I	II
1956	4 198	4 148	3 583	3 731	3 691
1957	5 155	5 119	4 174	4 698	4 671
1958	4 954	4 825	4 000	4 625	4 502
1959	5 491	5 324	5 306	5 012	4 856
1960	7 513	7 465	7 185	6 818	6 784
1961	4 943	5 548	4 423	4 209	4 820
1962	5 963	5 792	5 140	5 226	5 063
1963	6 026	5 909	5 464	5 240	5 132
1964	6 982	6 861	6 457	5 995	5 886
1965	6 836	6 626	5 537	5 684	5 491
1966	6 088	5 922	5 196	5 083	4 933
1967	4 931	4 772	3 988	3 963	3 822
1968	4 649	4 660	3 361	3 511	3 541
1969	7 035	6 602	6 665	5 629	5 225
1970	9 857	9 493	9 060	7 938	7 616
1971	9 741	9 355	7 548	7 557	7 222
1972	11 879	11 436	9 508	9 919	9 528
1973	11 789	11 127	7 557	9 165	8 575
1974	11 640	10 148	9 266	6 370	5 056
1975	9 521	8 910	6 443	6 439	5 943
1976	21 539	10 985	10 914	19 002	8 699
1977	8 670	9 285	5 992	6 189	7 039
1978	10 720	7 088	9 440	9 017	5 585
1979	13 927	11 360	10 829	11 832	9 535
1980	12 216	12 218	10 313	9 553	9 896

^{a}I: inclusive "social capital."
^{b}II: Exclusive "social capital."

Table 11A3
Capital Assets at Historic Costs
(in millions of Schillings)

Year	Fixed Assets	Fixed Assets Including Hidden Reserves	Inventories	Other Circulating Capital	Financial Assets	Total Capital
1956	18 955	20 639	11 687	9 571	1 422	43 319
1957	18 351	21 542	12 411	10 644	1 577	46 174
1958	18 364	24 161	12 371	11 443	1 733	49 708
1959	18 566	26 970	12 528	12 599	2 347	54 444
1960	19 146	30 033	13 915	13 812	2 800	60 560
1961	20 490	34 046	15 042	14 778	3 137	67 003
1962	21 041	37 256	15 111	15 348	2 907	70 622
1963	21 109	39 850	15 358	16 455	2 858	74 521
1964	21 185	42 271	16 005	17 880	3 041	79 197
1965	21 633	44 707	17 200	18 756	3 383	84 046
1966	22 778	47 877	18 226	20 536	3 608	90 247
1967	23 713	50 765	17 546	21 682	3 956	93 949
1968	22 306	51 224	17 327	21 572	4 435	94 558
1969	22 479	52 991	19 017	25 148	5 438	102 594
1970	24 909	57 236	23 719	27 968	6 613	115 536
1971	27 954	62 674	26 671	31 599	7 372	128 316
1972	32 943	70 725	26 262	38 252	8 197	143 436
1973	38 461	80 301	30 588	41 430	10 313	162 532
1974	40 220	85 002	40 148	47 583	11 718	184 451
1975	43 642	93 675	44 242	53 658	13 040	204 615
1976	47 839	101 272	48 069	61 120	14 146	224 607
1977	51 291	108 858	53 167	64 601	15 835	242 461
1978	56 031	116 414	54 260	67 990	18 433	257 097
1979	60 033	123 556	60 313	74 040	20 485	278 394
1980	63 654	130 217	66 115	79 899	21 677	297 908

Table 11A4
Capital Assets at Current Costs
(in millions of Schillings)

Year	Net Fixed Assets B & E	Inventories G	Net Monetary Assets M	Financial Assets and Other Circulating Capital (at Historic Costs)	Total Capital O
1956	26 397	11 990	637	10 389	49 413
1957	29 804	12 541	415	11 819	54 579
1958	33 401	12 236	1 245	11 940	58 822
1959	37 551	12 502	1 871	13 095	65 019
1960	42 681	14 055	1 734	14 905	73 375
1961	47 691	15 187	227	17 742	80 847
1962	53 349	15 126	1 089	17 174	86 738
1963	56 215	15 396	2 459	16 885	90 955
1964	61 324	16 075	4 148	16 866	98 413
1965	64 571	17 336	4 063	18 292	104 262
1966	67 948	18 319	4 351	19 865	110 483
1967	69 276	17 599	5 683	20 125	112 683
1968	74 279	17 302	5 877	20 283	117 741
1969	79 545	19 169	6 466	24 296	129 476
1970	88 519	24 282	5 831	29 025	147 657
1971	101 470	27 227	6 355	32 877	167 929
1972	107 125	26 641	7 392	39 444	180 602
1973	128 937	31 061	5 293	46 977	212 268
1974	145 098	44 349	4 235	55 518	249 200
1975	149 856	45 491	5 950	61 068	262 365
1976	152 480	48 582	7 979	67 699	276 740
1977	156 553	53 974	4 183	76 669	291 379
1978	160 095	54 396	6 284	80 273	301 048
1979	162 858	61 466	7 183	87 568	319 075
1980	167 580	68 500	11 205	90 811	338 096

Table 11A5
Equity Capital
(in millions of Schillings)

Year	Historic Costs		Current Costs	
	Equity I[a]	Equity II[b]	Equity I	Equity II
1956	24 470	23 817	30 870	30 217
1957	26 922	26 225	34 586	33 889
1958	29 689	28 909	38 744	37 964
1959	33 253	32 326	43 233	42 306
1960	36 699	35 664	48 628	47 593
1961	39 565	38 808	53 113	52 356
1962	42 227	41 687	57 212	56 672
1963	45 226	44 542	61 445	60 761
1964	48 389	47 586	66 224	65 421
1965	50 896	49 927	71 228	70 259
1966	53 577	52 420	74 332	73 175
1967	56 854	55 535	76 005	74 686

Table 11A5 *(continued)*
(in millions of Schillings)

	Historic Costs		Current Costs	
Year	Equity I[a]	Equity II[b]	Equity I	Equity II
1968	58 916	57 523	79 438	78 045
1969	60 628	59 023	85 513	83 908
1970	63 815	61 811	93 641	91 637
1971	67 929	65 550	104 254	101 875
1972	72 776	69 982	111 438	108 644
1973	80 161	76 815	123 450	120 104
1974	86 525	82 102	143 640	139 217
1975	92 629	87 154	154 146	148 671
1976	104 573	93 515	159 981	148 923
1977	113 938	97 910	165 418	149 391
1978	119 084	101 548	165 309	147 773
1979	126 845	106 210	167 383	146 749
1980	132 555	110 637	170 622	148 704

[a]Equity I: inclusive "social capital."
[b]Equity II: exclusive "social capital."

Table 11A6
"Fictitious Profit" Elements
(in millions of Schillings)

Year	Fixed Assets	Inventories	Net Monetary Assets	Sum
1955	342	200	18	560
1956	374	303	33	710
1957	537	130	13	680
1958	601	− 135	9	475
1959	688	− 26	20	682
1960	822	140	27	989
1961	887	145	54	1 086
1962	1 046	15	8	1 069
1963	1 064	38	31	1 133
1964	1 238	70	93	1 401
1965	1 291	136	216	1 643
1966	1 305	93	72	1 470
1967	1 203	53	170	1 426
1968	1 498	− 25	153	1 626
1969	1 726	152	176	2 054
1970	2 034	563	275	2 872
1971	2 522	556	261	3 339
1972	2 366	379	387	3 132
1973	3 161	473	527	4 161
1974	3 906	4 201	452	8 559
1975	3 652	1 249	320	5 221
1976	3 328	513	412	4 253
1977	3 139	807	416	4 362
1978	2 839	136	134	3 109
1979	2 555	1 153	226	3 934
1980	2 429	2 385	440	5 254

Table 11A7
Direct Taxes Paid by Industry Corporations
(in millions of Schillings)

Year	
1956	1 573
1957	1 491
1958	1 355
1959	1 789
1960	2 420
1961	2 325
1962	2 363
1963	2 513
1964	3 022
1965	2 717
1966	2 553
1967	2 220
1968	2 366
1969	2 743
1970	3 657
1971	3 022
1972	2 725
1973	2 251
1974	3 851
1975	3 295
1976	3 083
1977	2 757
1978	3 629
1979	3 530
1980	4 075

Table 11A8
Dividend Payout Ratios in Austrian Industry

Year	Dividends in Millions of Schillings	Dividends in Relation to			
		Equity II[a]		Equity II Profits	
		Nominal[b]	Real[c]	Nominal	Real
1956	381	1.60	1.26	9.19	10.33
1957	409	1.56	1.21	7.99	8.76
1958	378	1.31	1.00	7.84	8.40
1959	411	1.27	0.97	7.72	8.46
1960	574	1.61	1.21	7.69	8.46
1961	537	1.38	1.03	9.67	11.14
1962	469	1.12	0.83	8.09	9.26
1963	542	1.22	0.89	9.17	10.56
1964	573	1.20	0.88	8.35	9.73
1965	538	1.08	0.77	8.12	9.79
1966	513	0.98	0.70	8.66	10.40
1967	453	0.82	0.61	9.48	11.84
1968	693	1.21	0.89	14.88	19.58
1969	849	1.44	1.01	12.86	16.25
1970	926	1.50	1.01	9.76	12.16
1971	989	1.51	0.97	10.58	13.70
1972	988	1.41	0.91	8.64	10.37
1973	732	0.95	0.61	6.58	8.54
1974	1 186	1.44	0.85	11.68	23.45
1975	850	0.97	0.57	9.54	14.30
1976	984	1.05	0.66	8.96	11.31
1977	841	0.86	0.56	9.06	11.95
1978	1 047	1.03	0.71	14.77	18.75
1979	1 337	1.26	0.91	11.77	14.02
1980	1 131	1.02	0.76	9.26	11.43

Source: *Statistik der Aktiengesellschaften,* Austrian Central Statistical Office.
[a]Equity II: equity capital exclusive of social capital.
[b]Nominal: without inflation accounting.
[c]Real: after inflation accounting.

Table 11A9
Rates of Return on Total and Physical Capital
(percent)

	Historic Costs			Current Costs		
		Net Book Rate		Net Real Rate on Total Capital	Net Real Rate after Tax	Net Real Rate on Physical Capital
Year	Gross Book Rate on Total Capital	on Total Capital	on Physical Capital	ROC_O (BT)	ROC_O (AT)	ROC_A (BT)
1956	14.5	11.2	14.6	8.4	5.0	10.4
1957	14.8	11.7	15.4	8.8	5.9	11.0
1958	13.5	10.2	13.0	7.8	5.4	9.3
1959	15.6	12.2	15.6	9.2	6.3	11.0
1960	18.3	14.9	20.2	11.0	7.5	14.0
1961	12.8	9.3	13.4	6.4	3.4	8.7
1962	13.3	9.8	12.3	6.8	3.9	7.9
1963	13.4	9.8	12.2	6.8	4.0	7.8
1964	14.4	10.8	13.8	7.4	4.2	8.8
1965	12.7	9.2	11.1	6.0	3.3	6.6
1966	11.9	8.3	9.9	5.4	3.0	5.9
1967	10.0	6.5	7.1	4.2	2.2	4.1
1968	9.3	5.7	6.3	3.4	1.4	3.2
1969	12.7	9.2	11.8	5.8	3.6	6.7
1970	14.8	11.4	14.8	7.1	4.4	8.3
1971	12.9	9.5	12.1	5.4	3.5	6.0
1972	13.2	9.8	13.0	6.1	4.5	7.1
1973	11.7	8.3	10.1	4.6	3.5	4.7
1974	14.5	11.3	14.8	5.0	3.3	5.4
1975	10.2	7.1	8.2	3.5	2.2	3.1
1976	11.0	8.0	9.9	4.9	3.7	5.2
1977	8.3	5.3	5.5	2.9	2.0	2.3
1978	9.2	6.1	6.8	4.2	2.9	4.0
1979	9.4	6.4	10.8	4.3	3.2	7.0
1980	9.4	6.5	15.8	4.2	3.0	10.9

Table 11A10
Equity Rates of Return
(percent)

	Historic Costs		*Current Costs*			
			Equity I without Gearing	*Equity I with Gearing*	*Equity II*	*Equity II after Tax*
Year	*Equity I[a]*	*Equity II[b]*	$REQ_o(BT)I$	$REG_o(BT)I$	$REG_o (BT)II$	$REG_o(AT) II$
1956	17.2	17.4	11.6	12.1	12.2	7.0
1957	19.1	19.5	12.1	13.6	13.8	9.4
1958	16.7	16.7	10.3	11.9	11.9	8.3
1959	16.5	16.5	12.3	11.6	11.5	7.2
1960	20.5	20.9	14.8	14.0	14.3	9.2
1961	12.5	14.3	8.3	7.9	9.2	4.8
1962	14.1	13.9	9.0	9.1	8.9	4.8
1963	13.3	13.3	8.9	8.5	8.4	4.3
1964	14.4	14.4	9.8	9.1	9.0	4.4
1965	13.4	13.3	7.8	8.0	7.8	3.9
1966	11.4	11.3	7.0	6.8	6.7	3.3
1967	8.7	8.6	5.2	5.2	5.1	2.1
1968	7.9	8.1	4.2	4.4	4.5	1.5
1969	11.6	11.2	7.8	6.6	6.2	3.0
1970	15.4	15.4	9.7	8.5	8.3	4.3
1971	14.3	14.3	7.2	7.2	7.1	4.1
1972	16.3	16.3	8.5	8.9	8.8	6.3
1973	14.7	14.5	6.1	7.4	7.1	5.3
1974	13.5	12.4	6.5	4.4	3.6	.9
1975	10.3	10.2	4.2	4.2	4.0	1.8
1976	20.6	11.7	6.8	11.9	5.8	3.8
1977	7.6	9.5	3.6	3.7	4.7	2.9
1978	9.0	7.0	5.7	5.5	3.8	1.3
1979	11.0	10.7	6.5	7.1	6.5	4.1
1980	9.2	11.0	6.0	5.6	6.7	3.9

[a]Equity I: inclusive "social capital."
[b]Equity II: exclusive "social capital."

12 Rate of Profit and Return on Financial Assets in Italian Industry 1951–1981

Paolo Onofri and *Anna Stagni*

The aim of this chapter is to obtain an empirical estimate of the rate of return on fixed capital (that is, equipment and the buildings in which the equipment is located) of Italian industry as well as on the portfolio of securities associated with it.

We shall start from the problems involved in the definition of the concept of income to be used, stressing the opportunity to refer to income valued at constant productive capacity when measuring the rate of profit on fixed capital, and the need to specify income at constant purchasing power of wealth when measuring the rate of return on financial assets.

In every stage of this work we shall stick to an ex-post definition of both of these concepts of returns since this is the most immediate information that can be obtained from empirical observation. As a consequence, the definition of cost of capital we shall derive will be closer to a concept of real cost of financing than to a measure of opportunity cost of capital.

Measurement of Income and Profitability

The total income (R_v) earned by holding an asset in a unit of time is given by the yield (E) and by the change in the market value of the asset between the beginning and the end of the period (ΔV):

$$R_{vt} = E_t + \Delta V_t$$

In so doing, we are assuming a definition of an individual's weekly income as "the maximum value which he can consume during the course of a week, and still expect to be as well off at the end as he was at the beginning" (Hicks, 1939). We are also implicitly assuming that the initial conditions taken as a reference correspond to the market value of the asset at the beginning of the period.

If, however, by "initial conditions" we mean the purchasing power

465

of the asset at the beginning of the period, our definition of income must take into account the change in the prices of the goods purchased. If purchasing power is expressed in terms of a basket of consumption goods the price of which is P, then the change in the value of the asset, which actually can be reckoned as income, is given by:

$$\Delta V_t = V_t - \left(1 + \frac{\Delta P}{P_{t-1}}\right) V_{t-1},$$

where V_t and V_{t-1} denote end of period values and $\Delta P_t/P_{t-1}$ the proportional rate of growth of the prices of the consumption goods. Under these assumptions the rate of return on the asset will be

$$r_{vt} = \frac{E_t}{V_{t-1}} + \frac{V_t}{V_{t-1}} - \left(1 + \frac{\Delta P}{P_{t-1}}\right).$$

Since, for the single asset

$$\frac{V_{t-1}}{V_t} = \left(1 + \frac{\Delta P_v}{P_{vt-1}}\right),$$

where $\Delta P_v/P_{vt-1}$ is the rate of proportional change of the price of the asset, we can also write

$$r_{vt} = \frac{E_t}{V_{t-1}} + \frac{\Delta P_v}{P_{vt-1}} - \frac{\Delta P}{P_{t-1}}.$$

If we compare income and profitability derived from holding an asset in various periods with different rates of inflation, it is conceptually possible to distinguish between the nominal and the real value of such a flow of income and hence to define a real rate of return (r_v^*), which will be

$$r_{vt}^* = \frac{E_t}{1 + \dfrac{\Delta P}{P_{t-1}} V_{t-1}} + \frac{\dfrac{\Delta P_v}{P_{vt-1}} - \dfrac{\Delta P}{P_{t-1}}}{1 + \dfrac{\Delta P}{P_{t-1}}}.$$

The definition of the initial conditions as the purchasing power of the asset on a basket of consumption goods fits specifically the holder of financial wealth. As regards the total income earned by holding real assets, the preceding definition may imply a different concept of "initial conditions."

Assuming that E_t' is the flow of earnings already net of the current costs of production and of depreciation at the costs of the preceding periods, total income will be given by:

$$R_{ct} = E_t' - \frac{\Delta P_c}{P_{ct-1}} C_{t-1}\delta,$$

where by $\Delta P_c/P_{ct-1}$ we mean the proportional change between the beginning and the end of the production period in the price of the real asset (whose value was C_{t-1} at the beginning of the period), while δ denotes the proportional decay per unit of time in the asset's productive capacity.

As can be observed, in the case of physical capital and under the assumption of a continuous process of production, the increase in the value of the asset does not represent part of income, but an imputed cost to restore the productive capacity at the beginning of period level. Such a definition of total income corresponds to the measurement of the firm's income at replacement costs.

Let us now proceed to determine, as before, the rate of return:

$$r_{oct} = \frac{E_i'}{C_{t-1}} - \frac{\Delta P_c}{P_{ct-1}}\delta.$$

As we have noted, when total income is calculated on the basis of the purchasing power of wealth, the rate of return depends on the evolution of the price ratio of assets to consumption goods. In this case, when total income is calculated on the basis of intact productive capacity, the relative price effect might be neglected if we assume that the purchasing power is exercised on capital goods. Hence the above rate of return can also be considered as a real rate of return.

The Return on Real Assets:
Italian Industry 1951–1981

In order to measure the returns on fixed capital in postwar Italian industry, we shall attempt to express the concepts of income and profitability discussed above in quantitative terms.

Using the data from sectoral national income accounts, we can separate employed labor income from other types of income for industry in the narrow sense. These items are, however, composed of elements that, in certain respects, may prove to be heterogeneous. From the item "other income," we have isolated that part which, although not representing employed labor income, is still imputable to labor services.

Regarding capital income, after having deducted from "other income" labor income imputed to self-employed workers, we obtain the figure for profit by also deducting depreciation allowances at replacement cost.

The unavailability of data on inventories makes it possible to deal with fixed capital only. When prices increase, however, this gives rise both to an underestimate of replacement costs of total productive capacity, and hence to an overestimate of profits, and, at the same time, to an underestimate of them because of the failure to take account of the gains deriving from the sale of undesired inventories, which are not going to be reproduced.

The ratio of income earned in the period to the current value of reproducible fixed capital at the beginning of the period (in this case, too, we have an underestimate of total capital not only because of the absence of information on working capital but also of data on the value of land and buildings other than those containing equipment) measures the rate of return r_{oc}. Since we are working with annual data, the income flow of the year is earned not only from the capital existing at the beginning of the year but also from the capital goods acquired during the year. This phenomenon can be captured by dividing income by the current value of the capital stock at the middle of the year.

In figure 12–1 we show the evolution of this ratio. Owing to the fact that available data on corporate taxes refer to the overall aggregate, it was impossible to separate taxes paid by manufacturing firms. Therefore we could not compute an after-tax profit rate.

The Rate of Return of Financial Assets Associated with Industry's Fixed Capital

To obtain an empirical measure of the return on financial assets associated with industry's physical capital, we must allow for the fact that the assets representing capital take different forms: equities and debt securities. Let us imagine, then, that the rate of return we are looking for consists of the income accruing every year to the holder of a portfolio containing the combination of debt and equity securities historically observed. We shall therefore assume that the market value of industrial corporations is represented by the market value of their shares and by their long-term debt.

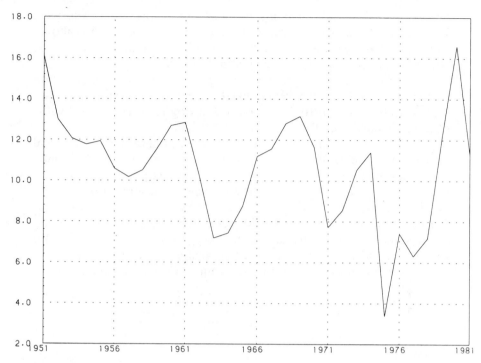

Figure 12–1. Rate of Profit (before Taxes) in the Italian Industry

In calculating the long-term debt of industrial corporations, it appears necessary to take account of the existence of particular financial institutions whose specific activity is to collect funds to finance firms. A better approximation of long-term debt will therefore be given by the sum of the bonds issued by firms and of those issued by these institutions, rather than by corporate bonds only.[1]

As already noted in the preceding sections we must recall that the measurement of the return on financial assets implies a definition of income different from the one adopted for the measurement of the rate of profit on physical capital. In particular, the measure of income from financial assets, instead of keeping intact productive capacity, guarantees the constant purchasing power of the assets. We already expressed this return in the following way:

$$r_v = \frac{E_t}{V_{t-1}} + \frac{\Delta P_v}{P_{vt-1}} - \frac{\Delta P}{P_{t-1}}.$$

In our specification the flow of earnings (E) is given by the sum of interest and dividend payments received during the year.[2] The term V represents the sum of the value of shares and bonds defined as above, while $\Delta P_v/P_v$ is the weighted average of the change in their market value and $\Delta P/P$ is the proportional change in the CPI.

The time series thus obtained (see figure 12–2) shows the evolution of the purchasing power remaining to the holders of the securities representative of industrial capital after having restored the real value of their financial wealth.

The return we have described is frequently indicated as the real return, since the whole flow of income from financial assets is defined as the nominal return, and the flow of purchasing power in real terms is obtained by deducting from it the change in consumer prices.[3]

Accordingly, the distinction between nominal and real return does not lie so much in measuring a flow of purchasing power in monetary or constant terms as in measuring that flow allowing or disallowing for the change in the purchasing power of wealth. If, on the contrary, we follow our definition of income, according to which income is always

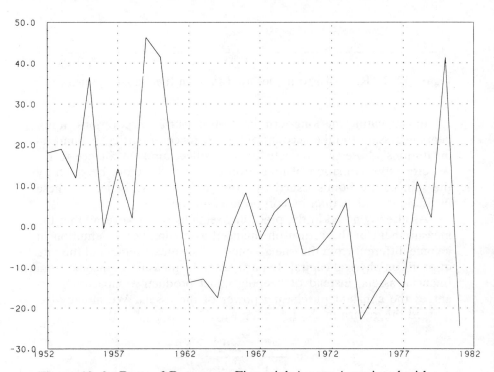

Figure 12–2. Rate of Return on Financial Assets Associated with Industrial Fixed Capital

net of what is necessary to restore the real value of wealth up to its initial level, such a distinction has no basis.

It has already been pointed out that the return of financial assets measured at constant purchasing power is specified as the return from holding the assets in a single unit of time. As a result, the real rate of return ought to be expressed as

$$r_v^* = \frac{r_v}{1 + \dfrac{\Delta P}{P_{t-1}}}$$

or even as

$$r_v^* = \frac{r_v/P_t}{V_{t-1}/P_{t-1}},$$

where

$$r_v = \frac{R_v}{V_{t-1}}.$$

In this way, the series obtained relates a flow of real income to the real value of the stock of wealth.

The time series obtained is reported in appendix 12A and, as already anticipated, it differs from the rate r_v to a decidedly negligible extent.

The Cost of Capital

Since the returns on financial assets discussed in the preceding section represent an *ex-post* measure of the income perceived by a representative holder of a portfolio of securities, they cannot be considered an estimate, not even approximate, of the opportunity cost of capital.

As is well known, the opportunity cost of capital is the market capitalization rate of a stream of expected future earnings, thus involving the concept of ex-ante income obtainable from the new capital goods. It is commonly accepted that the true cost of capital (ρ) could be defined as

$$\rho = \frac{\overline{X}}{P_A A + P_B B} G,$$

where $P_A A$ is the market value of shares, $P_B B$ is the market value of firm's debt, $\overline{X}$ is the expected return from current assets, and G is an adjustment factor for special growth opportunities incorporated in the market valuation of equity.[4] Denoting by r_b the average rate of interest on bonds, and by Y the expected profits net of interest payments, we could write: $\overline{X} = Y + r_b P_B B$.

In order to infer from market data some information on the true cost of capital it is necessary to make some strong assumptions. First' of all one has to assume (a) either that there is no retention of profits or that dividend payments are proportional to expected profits and the proportion is stable over time, and (b) that G is also stable over time. Once these assumptions are accepted, we can proceed to define the cost of capital in terms both of the dividend rate (r_A) and of the interest rate on bonds. That is to say,

$$\rho = w_A r_A + w_B r_B,$$

where

$$w_A = \frac{p_A A}{p_A A + p_B B}$$

and

$$w_B = \frac{p_B B}{p_A A + p_B B}.$$

The value of ρ obtained in this way is plotted in figure 12–3. For the period from 1951 to 1961, the cost of capital is continuously declining as market interest rates were also slowly but steadily decreasing and, contemporarily, future growth opportunities were capitalized in the market value of equities, thus reducing recorded dividend rates.

In the subsequent years, the cost of capital evolution reflects the 1962–1965 downward business cycle and the deterioration in prospective corporate profitability.

In the 1970s the cost of capital has steadily increased because of (1) the increase in interest rates induced by inflation, (2) the growing weight of debt, and (3) the more substantial reversal of expectations on future profits, which was reflected in a fall of equity prices.

After 1977 the cost of capital declines in spite of the further increase (at the end of the sample) of the interest rate on debt securities. This result can be imputed, on the one side, to the recovery of share prices and correspondingly to the fall of the dividend rates and, on the other side, to the reduced market value of the outstanding debt.

Comparing r_{oc} and ρ, we observe that in the first twenty years of the sample both rates have fluctuated around fairly flat trends with much wider oscillations for the rate of profit. During that period, however, the rate of profit remains always above the cost of capital. After 1974, the cost of capital becomes higher than the rate of profit; as such this observation does not allow us to deduce that a true modification

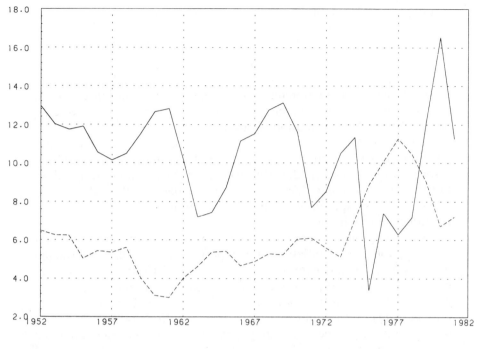

LEGEND

—————— Rate of Profit (r_{oc})

-------- Cost of Capital (ρ)

Figure 12–3. Rate of Profit and Cost of Capital

in the relative profitability of real and financial assets occurred. Actually, this measure of the cost of capital is distorted by the presence of inflation, which occurred at two-digit rates since 1973.

Since, as we shall argue further on, we cannot assume that inflation was completely anticipated and embodied neutrally in the rates of return, in interpreting the behavior of our variables we must analyze carefully the effect of inflation on these magnitudes. In particular, the problems are caused not so much by the reliability of the declining values of r_{oc} as by the sharp increase in ρ and hence by the fact that ρ embodies ex-post different rates of inflation.

Let us compare the expressions of ρ thus obtained with the rate of return on financial assets defined by us as

$$r_v = \left(r_A + \frac{\Delta P_A}{P_{At-1}} - \frac{\Delta P}{\cdot P_{t-1}} \right) \frac{P_A A}{V} + \left(r_B + \frac{\Delta P_B}{P_{Bt-1}} - \frac{\Delta P}{P_{t-1}} \right) \frac{P_B B}{V};$$

r_v and ρ will coincide if

$$\frac{\Delta P_A}{P_{At-1}} \cdot \frac{P_A A}{V} + \frac{\Delta P_B}{P_{Bt-1}} \cdot \frac{P_B B}{V} = \frac{\Delta P}{P_{t-1}}.$$

If the monetary policy remains unchanged and in the absence both of inflation and of changes in the growth prospects of firms (otherwise P_A would change), this condition is fulfilled.

If there is inflation but no changes in growth prospects, the previous condition is still satisfied if the price of shares increases not only in response to the change in the price of capital goods induced by inflation, but also because the reduced burden of the debt on the value of the firms' assets is capitalized. In both cases the measure of ρ would not be influenced by inflation.

Since empirical observations reflect a variety of effects that are not solely attributable to inflation, it is impossible to establish beforehand whether inflation has been neutral on the rates of return. There is no doubt, however, that ρ and r_v behave completely differently during the period in question. It is difficult, however, to justify this difference only in terms of a fall in the firms' future growth prospects. A deterioration of these prospects certainly took place in the 1970s; nonetheless, the evolution of r_{oc} (if we assume it is an aproximation of the marginal efficiency of capital) would not appear to justify the collapse of stock exchange quotations. Therefore we may assume that the effect just mentioned has been reinforced by a nonneutral effect of inflation. In this way, therefore, ρ and r_v are conceptually distinct: r_v denotes the return obtained by the holders of financial assets, while ρ appears to be an indicator of the cost of financing for firms. In this respect, however, precisely because we have assumed nonneutral effects of inflation, it is necessary to express such a cost in real terms.

Cost of Capital and Inflation

Let us compare a situation where there is no inflation with one where there is. Let us also suppose that inflation affects all goods uniformly. The a posteriori effect on the rate of profit r_{oc} ought to be regarded as nil, since money profits and current values of physical capital change at the same proportional rate. Assuming r_B as constant, the first impact of inflation on the cost of capital shows up through changes in the money flow of profits. This will reduce the weight of interest payments on money profits, and, in the case that the market value of shares does not change, it will also be reflected in an increase in r_A.

In this situation, when the price of capital goods is higher than the price of financial assets representing them, the preference for these assets will increase, such a preference being also strengthened by expectations of an increase in r_A. In fact, if interest payments remain unchanged, dividends will increase proportionally more than total profits, so that, even if the price of shares increases at the same rate as the price of capital goods, r_A will remain above its previous level. But, assuming that this previous level also corresponded to the desired value r_A, the price P_A can rise even more than the price of capital goods until r_A drops back to its desired level. In this case, the declining weight of bonds resulting from inflation will lead to an increase or a reduction in the cost of capital depending on whether $r_A \gtreqless r_B$.

In other words, higher inflation raises the weight of the value of shares. If the return on shares is higher than the return on debt, the cost of capital increases; and it diminishes in the opposite case, where the return on shares is lower than the return on debt.

The above considerations of the effects of inflation on the cost of capital observed in a given unit of time presuppose the constancy of certain variables that, in an inflationary situation, are, on the contrary, likely to change. The most evident case is represented by the rate of interest on outstanding debt of the firms—both the interventions of monetary authorities and the increased preference for shares are likely to push this rate upward. Inflation affects not only the flow, however, but also the firms' assets account as well.

If we still assume that shareholders are capitalizing correctly the effects of inflation on share values, it follows that r_B will be swollen by inflation, unlike what happens to r_A.

In order to take into account the effects of inflation on the purchasing power both of interest flows and the stock of debt, it is necessary to define the cost of capital as

$$\rho^* = r_A \frac{P_A A}{V} + \frac{\left(r_B - \dfrac{\Delta P}{P_{t-1}} \right)}{1 + \dfrac{\Delta P}{P_{t-1}}} \cdot \frac{P_B B}{V}.$$

The cost of capital as thus defined excludes the fact that shareholders perceive the change—favorable to them—inflation causes in firms' asset accounts. In principle the fall in the purchasing power of the outstanding debt securities should be counterbalanced by the capitalization by the shareholders of the resulting reduction in future debt burden. As we have already pointed out, no definitive test can be used to prove such a hypothesis. What is in any case indisputable is that in the 1970s there was a deterioration in the prospects of the firms' growth that has certainly more than balanced the real financial leverage effect. In these circumstances, there are no a priori reasons why the expression of the cost of capital should coincide with that of the rate of return on financial assets. The time series denoted by ρ^* cannot therefore be used as a proxy for the opportunity cost of capital, but merely the cost of financing in real terms.

From figure 12–4, where ρ^* is plotted, we can therefore observe that the effects of inflation on the total value of firms' debt are such to give rise to negative capital costs for the years 1974 and 1975 and almost nil for 1976 and 1977. As a result, the gap between rate of profit and cost of capital is brought back to positive values. In other words, even if the rate of profit dropped from 1970 to 1978, so did the real cost of financing.

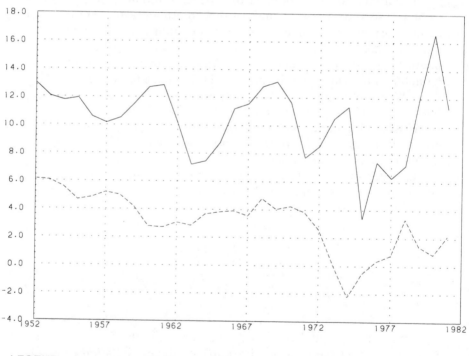

LEGEND

⎯⎯⎯   Rate of Profit (r_{oc})

------   Real Cost of Capital (ρ^*)

Figure 12–4. Rate of Profit and Real Cost of Capital

Conclusions

In the thirty years under investigation the rate of return to capital does not show any detectable decreasing trend. It shows, however, fluctuations following the overall business cycle of the economy. Its fall after the first oil shock expresses the reaction of industrial activity and income distribution to an unprecedented event. Actually, as such the rate of profit is not affected by the rate of inflation, as is shown by its upsurge after the second oil crisis.

The cost of capital in nominal terms shows an upward trend since the 1970s; values of this indicator higher than the rate of profit for the years 1975–1977 are the result of the distortion of high inflation rates. Once such distortion is corrected, the real cost of capital comes back to more consistent levels.

After 1977, however, more efficient mechanisms of protection against inflation have been built in the system, and once the absorption of the first oil shock effects has opened new prospects for profit growth, the nominal cost of capital also starts declining.

In more general terms, insofar as inflation is not neutral, the real cost of financing (ρ^*) and the rate of return of financial assets (r_v) constitute two distinct concepts that tend to be associated with two different economic agents—firms and households.

The comparison between r_v and ρ^* brings out how the rate of return for holders of financial assets has fallen to a greater extent than the cost of financing for firms during the double-digit inflation period. All this merely stresses the separation between decisions on the uses of savings (portfolio allocation) and investment decisions. In other words, financial and real assets become imperfect substitutes.

Notes

1. It is clear, however, that this procedure will imply an overestimate of the debt, since these credit institutions finance all corporate and noncorporate firms, but we assume that the error is smaller than it would be if the bonds issued by these credit institutes were ignored.

2. We must point out that the monetary flows accruing to the bondholders, being calculated on the basis of actual returns on bonds, include the virtual payment of the present value of the difference between the nominal value of the securities and their current average value during the present year.

3. In fact, what is measured is not so much a flow of purchasing

power in real terms as the change in real purchasing power of the whole stock of wealth.

   4. See Modigliani and Miller (1958) and Modigliani, Ando, Rasche, and Turnovsky (1974).

References

Hicks, J.R. *Value and Capital.* Oxford: Oxford University Press, 1939.

Modigliani, F., and Miller, M.H. "The Cost of Capital, Corporation Finance and the Theory of Investment." *American Economic Review* 48 (1958).

Modigliani, F.; Ando, A.; Rasche, R.; and Turnovsky, S.J. "On the Role of Expectations of Price and Technological Change in an Investment Function." *International Economic Review* 15 (1974).

Appendix 12A
Statistical Appendix

Legend

r_{oc} rate of profit
r_v^* rate of return on financial assets
r_A rate of dividend on industrial shares
P_A average price of industrial shares (index)
P_B average price of industrial bonds (index)
r_B rate of interest on bonds
ρ cost of capital
ρ^* real cost of capital

Table 12A1
Statistical Appendix

Year	r_{oc}	r_v^*	r_A	P_A	r_B	P_B	ρ	ρ^*
1951	16.12	—	—	—	—	—	—	—
1952	13.01	18.04	6.40	85.2	6.98	92.38	6.50	6.13
1953	12.06	18.95	6.10	100.0	6.97	92.76	6.28	6.06
1954	11.77	11.86	6.08	111.3	6.92	93.17	6.26	5.59
1955	11.94	36.64	4.72	157.5	6.83	93.98	5.06	4.65
1956	10.59	−0.60	5.12	152.4	6.93	93.25	5.44	4.84
1957	10.17	14.20	5.00	170.8	7.08	92.71	5.37	5.20
1958	10.52	1.93	5.34	168.1	6.72	95.17	5.63	5.00
1959	11.55	46.37	3.77	250.9	5.50	101.13	4.08	4.16
1960	12.70	41.47	2.77	373.2	5.13	101.91	3.12	2.76
1961	12.86	11.05	2.61	418.7	5.21	101.18	3.01	2.70
1962	10.19	−13.71	3.57	351.0	5.87	98.06	4.02	3.07
1963	7.20	−12.85	4.13	302.6	6.20	95.90	4.63	2.85
1964	7.45	−17.46	4.60	235.4	7.36	88.83	5.39	3.67
1965	8.76	−0.03	4.66	227.4	6.89	92.11	5.43	3.84
1966	11.19	8.33	3.86	244.0	6.51	95.43	4.68	3.93
1967	11.56	−3.23	4.16	227.1	6.27	95.38	4.90	3.56
1968	12.80	3.47	4.44	225.7	6.70	94.99	5.31	4.80
1969	13.16	7.03	4.14	245.9	7.06	93.67	5.26	4.06
1970	11.64	−6.67	4.25	229.0	9.10	83.44	6.07	4.25
1971	7.72	−5.47	4.34	187.5	8.21	88.33	6.13	3.84
1972	8.56	−1.20	3.66	172.3	7.45	93.09	5.62	2.60
1973	10.53	5.83	2.89	212.7	7.53	93.18	5.14	0.05
1974	11.39	−22.81	3.48	172.1	10.35	82.41	7.09	−2.22
1975	3.38	−16.61	5.97	133.5	10.99	79.44	8.92	−0.53
1976	7.43	−11.14	5.11	119.1	13.42	76.60	10.13	0.34
1977	6.31	−14.97	5.79	86.8	14.57	74.47	11.32	0.79
1978	7.19	11.12	6.21	107.2	13.51	79.80	10.49	3.38
1979	12.19	2.15	4.02	123.4	13.78	81.40	9.05	1.43
1980	16.60	41.52	3.07	237.9	15.64	78.80	6.73	0.84
1981	11.30	−24.36	2.38	186.9	19.77	71.30	7.23	2.18

Statistical Sources

The data for the rates of profit are our own elaborations on the basis of the Istat National Income Accounts (Istat, *Annuario di contabilità nazionale,* Rome, yearly issues). The data for the financial variables are our own aggregations and elaborations of the basic data published in the monthly bulletins of the Bank of Italy from 1950 on (Banca d'Italia, *Bollettino,* Rome, monthly issues).

Index

About the Contributors

Horst Albach is professor of business economics at Bonn University. He received a master's degree in business administration from Cologne University in 1956 and a master's degree in economics from Cologne University in 1957. He holds a Ph.D. degree in economics (summa cum laude) from Cologne University. He is a consultant on business taxes, on taxation policy, and in antitrust cases. He has served on various government commissions, including the Board of Economic Advisers. His academic research has centered on questions of business investment policy and capital budgeting. He has published also on the theory of the growth of firms.

Kurt Bayer was born and raised in Graz, Austria. His studies include law (University of Graz, Dr.jur., 1966), international relations (Johns Hopkins Bologna Center, Italy, 1967), and economics (University of Maryland, Ph.D., 1971). Since 1971 he has worked as an economist in the Industry Department of the Austrian Institute of Economic Research at Vienna and published extensively in the fields of company finance, structural change, income distribution, and energy problems.

Lars Bertmar is associate professor in accounting and finance at the Stockholm School of Economics, where he also received his Ph.D. He has served as consultant on taxes, mergers, and acquisitions to companies and as an advisor to Committées appointed by the Swedish government. His scholarly research has mainly focused on the growth, capital structure, and rate of return of companies but has also included issues on investment policy and company taxation. He has written several books, the main one being *Capital Growth, Capital Structure and Rates of Return*. His articles have appeared in *Skandinaviska Enskilda Banken Quarterly Review* and in many Swedish journals. During 1980– 1981 he was a visiting associate professor at the University of California, Berkeley. He is presently senior vice-president of the Svenska Handelsbanken.

Mervyn King is Esmée Fairbairn Professor of Investment at the University of Birmingham in England and a research associate of the National Bureau of Economic Research. He was a member of the Meade Committee on the Structure of the British Tax System and a former editor of the *Review of Economic Studies*. He is the author of *Public Policy and the Corporation, The British Tax System* (with John Kay), and *The Taxation of Income from Capital* (with Don Fullerton). During 1983–84 Mervyn King is Visiting Professor of Economics at MIT.

Fumiko Kon-ya is an economist in the Econometrics Division of the Japan Securities Research Institute, which is a center for economic and econometric research into the Japanese capital markets. Her main area of interest is in the test of efficiency of Japanese securities markets. She is also engaged in measurement of rates of return on various kinds of securities. One of her recent studies appeared in the *Journal of Portfolio Management,* Fall 1982, "The Japanese Market and the Economic Environment," written with Yasuhiro Yonezawa.

Heikki Koskenkylä is head of the research department at the Bank of Finland (Central Bank). He received a B.Sc. from the University of Helsinki in 1968 and a Lic.Econ.Sc. from the same university in 1973. He has served as an economist at the Bank of Finland since 1968. His scholarly research has focused on two areas: the investment behavior of firms and the long-term (structural) problems of the Finnish economy. His articles have appeared mainly in Bank of Finland publications and in the *Economic Journal* published in Finland.

Jacques Mairesse is Administrateur de l'Institut National de la Statistique et des Etudes Economiques (INSEE—Paris, France), and professor at Ecole des Hautes Etudes en Sciences Sociales. He has graduated from the Ecole Polytechnique and the Ecole Nationale de la Statistique et de l'Administration Economique (ENSAE) in 1965. His scholarly research has focused on the measurement of capital and the econometrics of production and technological change. He has been engaged in various comparative studies and is currently working on comparisons of industrial productivity, investment, and research and development, using panel data of firms.

Stewart C. Myers is professor of finance at the Massachusetts Institute of Technology's Sloan School of Management, past president and director of the American Finance Association, and a research associate of the National Bureau of Economic Research. His research is primarily concerned with valuation of real and financial assets, corporate financial policy, and financial aspects of government regulation of business. He is active as a financial consultant to corporations and government.

Kazuhiko Nishina is associate professor of finance at Yokohama City University. He received a Master of Economics degree from Tokyo University in 1972. His scholarly research has focused on the theory of finance, especially capital market theory. His articles have appeared in the *Economics Studies Quarterly, Contemporary Economics,* and other journals. He has been a visting scholar at the Alfred P. Sloan School of Management at the Massachusetts Institute of Technology from 1979 to 1981.

Paolo Onofri is professor of economics at the University of Bologna and coordinator of the Italian forecasting group Prometeia Associates. He has studied economics at Oxford University. In 1979–1980 he was delegate for the Italian government with Working Parties no. 2 and 4 of the Economic Policy Committee of OECD. In 1980–82 he served the Treasury Minister as economic consultant.

Anna Stagni graduated in economics at the University of Bologna in 1971 and was visiting fellow of the Economics Department of Princeton University in 1973–74. She is associate professor of economics at the University of Bologna and member of the scientific committee of the Italian forecasting group Prometeia Associates. Presently she is also coordinator of the Italian group working on the construction of a multicountry macrosectoral econometric model for the EEC Commission.

Abraham Tarasofsky has been a senior economist with the Economic Council of Canada since 1979. He received a B.Comm. from Concordia University in 1958 (winning the Sun Life Prize in Economics) and an M.A. and Ph.D. from McGill University in 1962 and 1968, respectively. He also became a chartered accountant in 1956. He was a member of the Department of Economics at Concordia University, first as assistant professor and then as associate professor, from 1962 to 1975. He served as research officer on the Royal Commission on Taxation during 1963 and 1964. He received a Canada Council Leave Fellowship to spend the 1969–70 academic year as honorary research fellow at Harvard University. Between 1975 and 1978, he was chief of Health and Hospital Economics, Department of National Health and Welfare. Although most of his research has concerned issues in public sector economics and in public finance, his recent research has also focused on inflation accounting and the economics of technological change.

Moriaki Tsuchiya is professor of business administration at Tokyo University. He received a B.A. from Tokyo University in 1957. His recent scholarly research has focused on two areas: the development of Japanese business and corporate strategy and technical innovation. He has published several books on business management in Japanese.

Takaaki Wakasugi is associate professor of finance on the Faculty of Economics, University of Tokyo. He received the Bachelor of Economics degree in 1966 and a Master of Economics degree in 1968 from the University of Tokyo. His academic interest is in business economics and focuses especially on business finance and recent capital market theory. His articles may be found in the *Annals of the Association of Business Finance Study of Japan* and other journals.

Norman P. Williams (B.A., M.A.) has been an economist with the Bank of England since 1976, working in the areas of company profitability and finance, followed by capital flows, the money supply, and the exchange rate. His previous research into profitability in the United Kingdom has been published in the Bank of England's *Quarterly Bulletin* and in its Discussion Paper series.

About the Editor

Daniel M. Holland has been a professor of finance in the Alfred P. Sloan School of Management, Massachusetts Institute of Technology, since 1958. Prior to that he taught at New York University and Columbia University, and was on the research staff of the National Bureau of Economic Research. Professor Holland has had a special interest in public finance, and has been editor of the *National Tax Journal* since 1966. His publications include four books—*The Income Tax Burden on Stockholders, Dividends Under the Income Tax, Private Pension Funds: Projected Growth,* and *The Assessment of Land Value*—and numerous articles in scholarly journals. Professor Holland has served as a consultant to a number of business firms and government agencies, including the United States Treasury, the Department of Housing and Urban Development, and the City of Boston. He had also been on several government commissions, and participated in tax studies in Jamaica, Bolivia, the Philippines, Puerto Rico and other countries.